OXFORD THEOLOGICAL MONOGRAPHS

OXFORD THEOLOGICAL MONOGRAPHS

REVELATORY POSITIVISM?

BARTH'S EARLIEST THEOLOGY
AND THE
MARBURG SCHOOL

SIMON FISHER

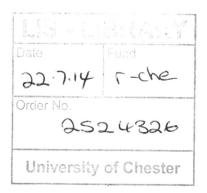
OXFORD UNIVERSITY PRESS

*This book has been printed digitally and produced in a standard specification
in order to ensure its continuing availability*

OXFORD
UNIVERSITY PRESS

Great Clarendon Street, Oxford OX2 6DP

Oxford University Press is a department of the University of Oxford.
It furthers the University's objective of excellence in research, scholarship,
and education by publishing worldwide in

Oxford New York

Auckland Bangkok Buenos Aires Cape Town Chennai
Dar es Salaam Delhi Hong Kong Istanbul Karachi Kolkata
Kuala Lumpur Madrid Melbourne Mexico City Mumbai Nairobi
São Paulo Shanghai Singapore Taipei Tokyo Toronto

with an associated company in Berlin

Oxford is a registered trade mark of Oxford University Press
in the UK and in certain other countries

Published in the United States
by Oxford University Press Inc., New York

© Simon Fisher 1988

ISBN 0-19-826725-8

For
Ulrich Simon

We cannot form any real conception of the highest being; but philosophy properly consists in the perception that this inexpressible reality of the highest being underlies all our thinking and all our feeling; and the development of this knowledge is, according to my conviction, what Plato meant by dialectics. But further than this, I believe, we cannot get.

Schleiermacher to Jacobi

it is not necessary that everything
that is possible should exist in actuality;
it is possible for that which has a potency
not to realize it

Aristotle, *Metaphysics*, 1003^{a}2
1071^{b}13

ACKNOWLEDGEMENTS

I T used to be said with little justification that modern theology originates in Germany, gets corrupted in America, and is put right in England. Whatever Englishmen may have thought about their Continental and American colleagues in the past, it must be said firmly that this work is considerably indebted to the scholarship and fellowship of many Americans. This book would never have seen the light of day without encouragement and criticism from Merlyn Satrom, from whose considerable insights into German theology I benefited enormously. He read early drafts and offered invaluable assistance in ways too numerous to mention. Special thanks are due to Professor Albert Outler of Perkins School of Theology. During a year's studentship at SMU his graduate seminar on nineteenth-century theology proved a great stimulus. I am indebted to him for teaching me how to read the *Critique of Pure Reason*, which I was encouraged to read at least twice before daring to offer a paper to his seminar. I likewise benefited from attending seminars with Charles Wood and from discussions with my friends, Ken and Carol Robertson.

A more specific debt must be acknowledged to two scholars who discussed the theological and philosophical issues about which this book is particularly concerned with great clarity and much insight. Roger A. Johnson's *The Origins of Demythologizing* was an immense stimulus, because he unravelled, with much clarity and precision, the complex of philosophical influences, including that of the long-forgotten Marburg School of Cohen and Natorp, which helped to shape the thought of Bultmann. When research was already at an advanced stage, much rethinking was prompted by Hans Frei's dissertation *The Doctrine of Revelation in the thought of Karl Barth 1909–1922: The Nature of Barth's Break with Liberalism*. Therein I found a discussion of Barth's early theology unparalleled for its clarity, rigour, and sensitivity. The influence of this magisterial study turned out to be pervasive.

My debts to Continental scholars are likewise considerable. Since several of Barth's earliest writings were never published, gratitude must be expressed to the staff of the Barth Archives who made texts available for consultation and to Dr Stoevesandt for his advice and interest in this project. I thank the Cohen Archives in Zurich for making available a copy of Cohen's *Der Begriff der*

viii   ACKNOWLEDGEMENTS

Religion im System der Philosophie and also Eleonore von La Chevallerie for information about Troeltsch's lectures on *Religions-philosophie*. Information, encouragement, and much needed criticism was generously given by Professor Gerhard Sauter of Bonn, to whom I am greatly indebted. Turning to England, special thanks must be given to Ruth Dipple, librarian of Lady Margaret Hall, for her willing and most generous assistance, and also to Ernest Wilkinson. Colleagues in Oxford who were liberal with their criticism include John Macquarrie, Barrie White, and Trevor Williams. I am exceedingly grateful to the staff of the University Press for their advice and also to the staff of the Bodleian Library for their assistance. For the manifold imperfections and shortcomings which this work doubtless contains, I alone am responsible.

When research for this book began, Cohen's voluminous writings were consulted in their original editions which Cohen frequently revised. As work was progressing, however, Olms Verlag were publishing their own edition of Cohen's *Werke* which at the time of writing (1986) is still incomplete. Wherever possible my notes refer readers to the Olms edition and I am grateful to Olms Verlag for permitting this. I am grateful to the B'nai B'rith International Commission on Continuing Jewish Education for permission to quote from Eva Jospe's admirable translation of essays by Cohen in *Reason and Hope: Selections from the Jewish Writings of Hermann Cohen*; to the University Press for permission to cite Kolakowski's *Main Currents of Marxisim*: i, *The Founders*; and to Fortress Press for passages from Hefner's translations of Ritschl in *Albrecht Ritschl: Three Essays*. When dealing with Barth, I preferred to make my own translations and I am grateful to the Theologischer Verlag Zurich and Kaiser Verlag for permitting me to cite in translation several passages from *Das Wort Gottes und die Theologie* and *Die Theologie und Kirche* as well as from Peter Fischer-Appelt's edition of Wilhelm Herrmann's *Schriften zur Grundlegung der Theologie*. Finally I would like to thank Professor Frei for allowing me to quote from his study of Barth.

This book is offered to my former teacher at King's College London as a small thank-you for everything I received.

                                                        M.S.F.
Oxford,
Feast of the Stigmatization of Francis, 1986

REFERENCES
AND NOTE ON ABBREVIATIONS

KARL BARTH

Anslem
Fides Quaerens Intellectum, Gesamtausgabe ii/13, Theologischer Verlag Zürich, 1981.

Antwort
'Antwort an D. Achelis und D. Drews', *Zeitschrift für Theologie und Kirche*, 19 (1909), 479–86.

BPG
Der Glaube an den persönlichen Gott', *Zeitschrift für Theologie und Kirche*, 24 (1914), 21–32, 65–95.

CD
Church Dogmatics, T. & T. Clark, 1936–69.

Gotteswort
Das Wort Gottes und die Theologie, Kaiser Verlag, 1924.

GUG
'Der christliche Glaube und die Geschichte', *Schweizerische Theologische Zeitschrift* (1912), 1–18, 49–72.

Jesus
'Ob Jesus gelebt hat?', *Gemeinde-Blatt für die Deutsche reformierte Gemeinde Genf* Nr. 36 (1910).

Metaphysics
'*La Réapparition de la métaphysique dans la théologie*', lecture delivered to the Société pastorale Suisse de Genève, 1911 (unpublished).

Prinzipienlehre
'Die dogmatische Prinzipienlehre bei Wilhelm Herrmann', *Die Theologie und die Kirche*, Kaiser Verlag, 1928, 240–80.

Reichsgottesarbeit
'Moderne Theologie und Reichsgottesarbeit', *Zeitschrift für Theologie und Kirche*, 19 (1909), 317–21.

Religionsphilosophie
Ideen und Einfälle zur Religionsphilosophie (unpublished fragment n.d.).

Romans II
Der Römerbrief (Zwölfter, unveränderter Abdruch der neuen Bearbeitung von 1922), TVZ reprint, 1978.

Schleiermacher I
'Schleiermachers *Weihnachtsfeier*', *Die Theologie und die Kirche*, 106–35.

Schleiermacher II
'Schleiermacher', *Die Theologie und die Kirche*, 136–89.

Schleiermacher III
Die Theologie Schleiermachers (Göttingen lectures 1923–4), *Gesamtausgabe* ii/11, TVZ, 1978.

Schleiermacher IV   Chapter 11 of *Die Protestantische Theologie im
                        19 Jahrhundert*, Evangelischer Verlag, 1947.

HERMANN COHEN

Das Prinzip   *Das Prinzip der Infinitesimal-Methode und seine
                        Geschichte: Ein Kapital zur Grundlegung der
                        Erkenntniskritik* (1883), *Werke V*, Olms Verlag,
                        1984.

ERW   *Ethik des reinen Willens, Werke VII*, Olms Verlag,
                        1981.

KBE   *Kants Begründung der Ethik*, Dümmler, 1877.

LRE   *Logik der reinen Erkenntnis, Werke VI*, Olms Verlag,
                        1977.

Reason and Hope   *Reason and Hope: Selections from the Jewish Writings of
                        Hermann Cohen* (E. Jospe, trans.), W. W. Norton,
                        1971.

Religion I   'Religion und Sittlichkeit', *Jüdische Schriften*,
                        Akademie für die Wissenschaft des Judentums,
                        1924, i. 98–168.

Religion II   *Der Begriff der Religion im System der Philosophie*,
                        Töpelmann, 1915.

Religion III   *Religion der Vernunft aus den Quellen des Judentums*,
                        Kauffmann Verlag, 1929.

WILHELM HERRMANN

Schriften   *Schriften zur Grundlegung der Theologie*, edited in two
                        volumes by Peter Fischer-Appelt, Kaiser Verlag,
                        1966–7.

IMMANUEL KANT

(Texts are cited from Kant's *Gesammelte Schriften* in the edition
sponsored by the Imperial Prussian Academy of Sciences 1902–)

KDPV   *Kritik der praktischen Vernunft*, v.

KDRV A   *Kritik der reinen Vernunft* (1st edn.), iv.

KDRV B   Ibid (2nd edn.), iii.

KU   *Kritik der Urtheilskraft*, v.

PAUL NATORP

PPP   *Philosophie: Ihr Problem und Ihre Probleme*,
                        Vandenhoeck & Ruprecht, 1911.

Psychologie   *Allgemeine Psychologie nach kritischer Methode*, 2nd
                        edn., J. C. B. Mohr, 1912.

Religion innerhalb   *Religion innerhalb der Grenzen der Humanität*, 2nd
edn., J. C. B. Mohr, 1908.

FRIEDRICH SCHLEIERMACHER

(Texts are cited from *Friedrich Schleiermachers Sämmtliche Werke*, Berlin,
1834–64, unless stated otherwise)

Dialektik   *Dialektik aus Schleiermachers handschriftlichem
Nachlasse*, iv/2.

Glaubenslehre   *Der christliche Glaube nach den Grundsätzen der
evangelischen Kirche im Zusammenhange dargestellt*,
iii–iv.

Kurze Darstellung   *Kurze Darstellung des theologischen Studiums zum Behuf
einleitender Vorlesungen entworfen*, i.

Reden   *Über die Religion: Reden an die Gebildeten unter ihren
Verächtern*, cited from the edition prepared by
Rudolf Otto, 5th impression, Vandenhoeck &
Ruprecht, 1926.

ERNST TROELTSCH

Writings   *Ernst Troeltsch: Writings on Theology and Religion*,
(R. Morgan and M. Pye, eds.), Duckworth, 1977.

Unless otherwise stated, the emphases in translated texts are those of
the authors. Since many of Cohen's emphases represent obscure plays
on German, Greek, and Latin words, it was decided to omit most of
them.

CONTENTS

INTRODUCTION
OBJECTIVES AND METHOD

RICHARD Niebuhr encapsulated the conclusion to which this study of one theologian leads. When Christianity deals with revelation and reason, he suggested, what is ultimately in question is the relation of the revelation in Christ to the reason which prevails in culture.[1]

Although it is not surprising that an influential theologian like Barth, who had such rich and diverse sources, should attract much scholarly attention, the reader is nevertheless due some explanation for why yet another book on Barth merits publication. Many have recognized that Barth's theology is no mere patchwork of biblical images or metaphors. Some, indeed, find structural similarities between Barth and Heidegger or Husserl; others detect Hegelianism, Platonism, or simply idealism, and suggest that some such particular philosophy gave coherence and structure to his thought. Whatever the virtues and vices of such publications, they draw attention to the symphony of extra-theological considerations that helped to shape Barth's thought. Indeed the master of the *Dogmatics* himself admitted: 'A free theologian does not deny, nor is he ashamed of, his indebtedness to a particular *philosophy* or ontology, to ways of thought or speech. These may be traditional or a bit original, old or new, coherent or incoherent. No one speaks exclusively in Biblical terms . . .'.[2]

This book intends to be nothing more than a marginal footnote to the theology of Karl Barth in its attempt to trace the influence of one 'particular *philosophy* or ontology' upon a theologian who must surely rank as one of the Fathers of the Church. It is marginal in the sense that interest focuses upon Barth's earliest theological attempts which pre-date his break with liberalism and which, moreover, he later dismissed as containing little of lasting value. It is a footnote in the sense that it hopes to supply one small piece to the Barthian jigsaw that has been missing from much English-speaking scholarship.

Throughout his years as a student and during his period as an assistant minister in Geneva, Barth was a 'convinced Marburger'.[3] Marburg, a name which now evokes the hermeneutics of

Heidegger and the exegesis of Bultmann, was the home of a very different theology and philosophy before the First World War. It was a Marburg where the idealism of the Jewish philosopher, Hermann Cohen, reigned, and the city from which the theology of Wilhelm Herrmann exercised a powerful hold over the countless students who flocked from Germany, Switzerland, America, and Britain to hear him lecture. There can be little doubt that Barth was decisively influenced by the theology and philosophy of pre-war Marburg. His debt to Herrmann has often been noted, but that he received something from the neo-Kantian philosophers of Marburg is a detail which is often overlooked. Busch, Barth's biographer, notes how Barth read Cohen 'copiously' and even sought to introduce the Workers' Association of Safenwil to Cohen's philosophy, though with little success.[4] It is likely that Barth attended some of Cohen's lectures whilst a student at Marburg and, moreover, that his private library contained a number of books by Cohen and the other leading philosopher at Marburg, Paul Natorp.[5]

In recent years one urgent voice calling for a radical reassessment of Barth's earliest writings has come from Marquardt. This writer notes that Barth, upon completing his studies and after working on the editorial staff of the Marburg-based journal, *Christliche Welt* continued to be theologically active whilst he was an assistant pastor in Geneva. It was there, to quote Marquardt, that Barth created 'a scientific-theoretical, religious-philosophical, framework which overcame the old Kantian-Schleiermacherian opposition between "religion" and "science"' and, he adds significantly, 'this framework was to govern his entire theological work to come'.[6] Although Marquardt perhaps claims a little too much for Barth's earliest theological endeavours, it is certain that the details of this 'framework' were not original creations. They owe much to the neo-Kantian philosophy of Cohen, to Herrmann's systematics, as well as to the interdisciplinary debates on *Religionsphilosophie* which were rife in pre-war Marburg. That Barth was indebted to the philosophy of Marburg is a fact commented upon by only a handful of writers; though one even went so far as to suggest that his theology resembled an inverted neo-Kantianism.[7] Even Barth himself was aware of this influence, for in the 1926 preface to his famous commentary on Romans he wondered whether his readers were presented with 'what is no more than a rehash, resurrected out of Nietzsche and Kierkegaard and Cohen'.[8]

Although a case could be made in favour of the Marburg philosophy exercising an enduring influence over Barth, this book has the more modest objective of examining his earliest writings against the background of the Marburg School. Though Wilhelm Herrmann gained international repute through translations of his celebrated *The Communion of the Christian with God*, the works of the Marburg philosophers were not widely read in Britain and America. As far as I have been able to ascertain there are no English translations of Natorp and the only complete book by Cohen translated into English was his very last, a philosophy of religion based upon Judaism. The result has been that few English-speaking theologians have been aware of the precise nature of the Marburg philosophy, let alone of the ways in which it influenced Barth.

It should be obvious by now that much of this book will be concerned with theological method. When I first began the research for it, I was strongly influenced by debates and studies on methodology and hermeneutics. During the following years I became increasingly aware of the dangers that arise from treating method in isolation from concrete doctrinal and philosophical issues. From the outset, therefore, there are three perceptions of methodological research from which I seek to distance myself. The first could be termed the 'prospective' approach to studies in theological method. Here the pursuit of method is analogous to the prospector's relentless explorations. The quest is not for precious minerals, but for the philosopher's—or better—the systematic theologian's stone. The expectation is that studies in hermeneutic and method will result in some sort of blueprint, which, it is hoped, might supply systematic theologians with a framework for their constructive efforts. Studies in theological method have, by and large, been unable to fulfil this expectation. They have shown themselves to be subject to Parkinson's Law. Methodological questions have a distasteful habit of unearthing further methodological questions; so whilst the systematic theologian is patiently waiting for some creative synthesis to emerge, those dealing with method have to offer only a few important clarifications plus a whole host of additional meta-questions.

A second approach to method in theology has often been based upon a concept of method allegedly employed in natural science. This is to be seen, for example, in Lonergan's preliminary notion of method as a 'normative pattern of recurrent and repeated operations yielding cumulative and progressive results'.[9] But this and associated approaches to theological method can be naïve. The work of Kuhn, Koyre, and others suggests that the methods of natural science are exceedingly more complex, diverse, and less straightforwardly progressive than was previously supposed. The conviction, secondly, that the integrity of theology depends upon its possessing a method analogous to that which natural science supposedly has, is a metaphysical and epistemological premiss which is by no means self-evident and beyond question. In addition, it is legitimate to enquire how far the great theologians of the past first wrought a method and then applied it to produce a theology. Some, for example Ritschl, may have spoken in ways suggesting that this is how they set about doing theology;[10] for most, however, the relation between doctrine and method appears to have been more of a correlative relationship that can only be executed *en route*.

A third, and perhaps distressing, role reserved for methodological analysis is negative or reductive. It may be suggested, for example, that a particular theologian operated with an unsound method and, for that reason, his work is to be discounted. It is often argued that Barth's theology is wedded to a form of idealism and anti-realism which adversely affects the entirety of his work. Because such a stance is methodologically deficient, it is urged that the whole is a swamp of conceptual quagmires. It must be remembered, however, that it is one thing to criticize someone's method, but something else to write theology. The debates following Tillich's *Systematic Theology*, Barth's *Dogmatik*, Bultmann's exegesis, or Rahner's *Theological Investigations* arose from and depended upon the work of creative theologians. This relationship between theology and enquiry into method is not necessarily reversible. Where there is no vision the people perish.

In the following pages I attempt to do justice to the vision of the earliest Barth and to examine the philosophical and cultural influences which no doubt helped to inspire it and offered the conceptual means for its expression. Though a later Barth might welcome a view of theological method as an imperfect means to an imperative end, these researches have convinced me that in relation to method a simple dichotomy between means and ends will not do.[11] This applies as much to Arius and his logic, Augustine and neo-Platonism, and Thomas's Aristotelianism, as to Barth and neo-Kantianism. To reformulate Niebuhr's words, when we examine the method of a particular theologian, what is ultimately in question is the relation of his understanding of theology to the patterns of religion, philosophy, and social ethos which prevail in his culture. Should this introduce a heavy dose of relativity into theology, then so be it. It is something we will have to learn to live with.

The famous words of 1 Corinthians 13: 9 ff. suggested to Aquinas that no one in this present life is capable of perceiving the essence of God. There is indeed the prospect of contemplation for those who seek God and virtue for those who serve him, but both these joys are imperfect. Studies in theological method tend to underline the imperfect, enigmatic, and partial character of our theology; yet in the face of much contemporary theological scepticism it needs to be affirmed that we do see, however imperfectly.

That there is a definite vision animating the earliest theology of Barth is something which cannot be doubted. It will also become evident that it is very different from the one normally associated with the name of Barth; that it achieves only a fleeting expression is something which few will regret. By 1914, however, chariots of wrath and horsemen long forgotten announced their presence. Last year's vision seemed to vaporize in the presence of the apocalyptic revelation. Theology, said Barth, is always *theologia viatorum*. The Greek word *Methodos*, explained Coleridge, 'is literally a *way* or *path of Transit*. . . . The term Method, cannot therefore, otherwise than by abuse, be applied to a mere dead arrangement, containing in itself no principle of progression.'[12]

NOTES

1. R. H. Niebuhr, *Christ and Culture* (Faber, 1952), 26.
2. K. Barth, 'The Gift of Freedom', in *The Humanity of God* (Fontana, 1967), 90.
3. E. Busch, *Karl Barth: His Life from Autobiographical Texts and Letters* (SCM, 1976), 44 ff.
4. Ibid. 56, 59.

5. See Appendix I.
6. F.-W. Marquardt, 'Socialism in the Theology of Karl Barth', in G. Hunsinger (ed.), *Karl Barth and Radical Politics* (Westminster Press, 1976), 70. See also *Der Christ in der Gesellschaft 1919–1979* (Kaiser Verlag, 1980).
7. O. Noordmanns cited in N. T. Bakker, *In der Krisis der Offenbarung: Karl Barths Hermeneutik dargestellt an seiner Römerbrief—Auslegung* (Neukirchener Verlag, 1974), 174. See also M. Strauch, *Die Theologie Karl Barths* (Kaiser Verlag, 1924); H. W. van der Vaart Smit, 'Die Schule Karl Barths und die Marburger Theologie', *Kantstudien*, 34 (1929), 333–50; H. F. Ulrich, *Das Transzendenzproblem bei Karl Barth* (Diss. Tübingen, 1936); D. Bonhoeffer, *Gesammelte Schriften* (Kaiser Verlag, 1958–), iii. 118–19, v. 221, etc.; W. Pannenberg 'Dialektische Theologie', in *Die Religion in Geschichte und Gegenwart*, 3rd edn. (O. C. B. Mohr, 1958), ii. 168–74.
8. *Romans II*, p. xxv.
9. B. J. F. Lonergan, *Method in Theology*, 2nd edn. (Darton, Longman, & Todd, 1975), 4.
10. See e.g. Ritschl's remarks in ch. 2 n. 3.
11. In the address already quoted Barth also had this to say about the free theologian and his method: 'he is a philosopher "as though he were not" and he has his ontology "as though he had it not". . . . His ontology will be subject to criticism and control by his theology, and not conversely.'
12. *Collected Works*, iv/1 (Routledge & Kegan Paul, 1969) 457.

1
MARBURG NEO-KANTIANISM

I. THE NEO-KANTIAN MOVEMENT

VLADIMIR Illich Lenin was no lover of the neo-Kantian movement which he ridiculed as thinly veiled priestcraft disguised only by an academic veneer of agnosticism. He was particularly vitriolic about the achievement of two Marburg professors of philosophy, Friedrich Albert Lange and his successor, Hermann Cohen. The former, according to Lenin, falsified the history of materialism whilst the latter perfected this fraud by mystifying modern science. With merciless mockery he parodied Marburg philosophy:

Electricity is proclaimed a collaborator of idealism, because it has destroyed the old theory of the structure of matter, shattered the atom and discovered new forms of material motion ... so unusual and 'miraculous' that it permits nature to be presented as *non-material* (spiritual, mental, psychical) motion. Yesterday's limit to our knowledge of the infinitesimal particles of matter has disappeared, hence— concludes the idealist philosopher—matter has disappeared (but thought remains).[1]

Lenin was critical of Marburg philosophy not only because it became associated with revisionism. The tidal wave of idealism which swept through Europe during the last decades of the nineteenth century and the first decade of the twentieth represented a retreat from the dialectical insights of Marx orchestrated by the bourgeois forces of reaction.

Though Lenin's reconstruction of the history of German philosophy is not without flaw, his protest has some justification. It is impossible to begin any study of neo-Kantianism without mentioning the fracture which Absolute Idealism suffered after the death of Hegel. The story of the split into left- and right-wing Hegelianism is often told;[2] less well-known is its sequel. The tremors of this rift were felt by German philosophers throughout the rest of the century. The disappointment to liberal hopes after 1848, moreover, discredited Absolute Idealism even further. Faced with authoritarian reaction and political repression, history no

longer seemed a progressive march of rationality in time. Even
when the aged Schelling was called to Berlin to counteract the
influence of Hegel's more radical disciples, he already represented
an age that had become grey. Kant was out of favour by this time
and as a reaction to idealism in all its forms there arose a popular,
non-dialectical, supposedly scientific materialism. Reviewing the
state of philosophy at this time, Heidegger lamented:

The total collapse of the Hegelian School precipitated a general decay in
philosophy. . . . Philosophy completely lost its prestige in an environment where the positive sciences (history and natural science) were in the
ascendancy. Where philosophy was carried on, it was done so in a
manner which disregarded and betrayed its own nature. In the face of
the scientific consciousness then holding sway, philosophy aimed at
procuring respect by a self-negating adaptation to the positive sciences as
a natural-scientific 'philosophy' (psychology) or as philosophy of history.[3]

Such anti-idealist philosophies of the mid-century were often
extremely crude. Büchner, who in 1855 published *Kraft und Stoff*,
the so-called 'materialists' Bible', became an infamous figure in
scientific and philosophical circles with his polemical slogan 'no
phosphorus, no thought'. Figures like Moleschott, who suggested
that the brain secretes thought just as the liver secretes bile,
Büchner, Vogt, and later, Haeckel, were deemed prophets of a
brave new scientific *Weltanschauung*. Militant materialists fought
their battles in public, welcomed and sought controversy, and
exploited every possible opportunity to aid their cause. When, for
example, Darwin's *Origin of Species* appeared in translation, it
was hailed as a weighty confirmation of materialist philosophy and
many members of the German intelligentsia were won over. Even
before Darwin appeared on the German scene, an extremely
acrimonious debate involving philosophers, scientists, and theologians was conducted in journals, at congresses, and in the public
press.[4] By the end of the 1850s triumphant materialism spoke and
acted as victor in a battle of *Weltanschauungen*.

Given these circumstances, had anyone in the 1850s predicted
or counselled a return to Kant, they would have been laughed out
of court. This, however, is precisely what did occur in the 1860s.
Many historians trace the beginnings of the neo-Kantian movement to the work of a Jewish philosopher, Otto Liebmann, who
published *Kant und die Epigonen* in 1865. This widely read work,

distinguished not so much for its profundity, as by its recurring refrain, attracted the attention of a new generation of philosophers. Liebmann's 'Also muss auf Kant zurückgegangen werden' served as a battle-cry. Philosophers who felt that philosophy should once again be established on a firm critical footing rallied to the defence of the a priori.

This general desire for a critical philosophy was the sole common feature of the earliest neo-Kantian movement. Originally more of a trend than a concerted restoration, neo-Kantianism never was a homogeneous movement; there were at least seven distinct types by the end of the century. Despite the diversity, there emerged a general pattern distinguishing this particular philosophical style. First, it must be stressed emphatically that no neo-Kantian wished to restore Kantian philosophy as its originator left it. It was generally agreed that a proper critical philosophy involved going beyond Kant and many did so in a surprisingly un-Kantian manner. Secondly, neo-Kantians availed themselves of what they called 'the transcendental method' in conscious opposition to psychological or empirical methods. Knowledge, in order to be truly objective, must rest upon secure foundations that are necessary, universal, and apodictically true, and not upon a series of contingent propositions or *ad hoc* suppositions derived from some piece of natural science. Thirdly, neo-Kantians often minimized the importance of empirical intuition as a source of knowledge, so much so that in certain forms of neo-Kantianism it almost vanished. Reason, on the other hand, was actively dynamic, responsible for giving experience form and coherence; being capable of constructing a coherent whole from random parts, it was regarded as the supreme organ of synthesis. Finally, neo-Kantian epistemologies were emphatically idealist: acquiring knowledge was akin more to construction than to discovery.[5]

The two most influential schools of neo-Kantianism were those of Baden and Marburg. The Baden School originated with Wilhelm Windelband (1848–1915) who commenced his philosophical career as a pupil of Lotze. Windelband gained repute both in Britain and America through his influential work on the history of philosophy which, along with other works, appeared in translation. Leadership of this school passed into the capable hands of Heinrich Rickert (1863–1936), author of the influential *Der Gegenstand der Erkenntnis*, which first appeared in 1892. The other leading school, that of Marburg, first achieved fame when F. A. Lange, author of the famous *History of Materialism* which Lenin hated so much, accepted a chair at Marburg. Lange, an attractive figure, was no narrowly academic philosopher; he was also a journalist, founder of a popular newspaper, an active politician in both Germany and Switzerland, and an educational reformer. Though in no way sympathetic to the dialectics of Marx and Engels, his polemical work, *Die Arbeiterfrage*, of 1865, marked Lange's transition to a radical form of social democracy which advocated democratic reforms, trade union rights, industrial cooperation, and social welfare. It was he who cajoled the University of Marburg into the unprecedented step of appointing a Jew, Hermann Cohen, to an academic post, thereby paving the way for his own successor.[6] Though Cohen is the philosopher who gave Marburg Kantianism its distinctive style, the impression left by Lange's mixture of idealism and socialism was never effaced. The third professor in the Marburg triumvirate was Paul Natorp (1854–1924). Natorp, along with Cohen, developed the 'Marburg System', though it must be said that he followed the Logos in novel directions after the First World War. Cohen hoped to be succeeded by his most promising pupil, Ernst Cassirer, but since Cohen's relations with the university became strained, principally on account of his alleged socialist sympathies though he himself suspected active anti-semitism, academic politics resulted in the appointment of an obscure experimental psychologist. Cassirer became the most famous Marburg Kantian outside Germany. He gained a wide academic hearing after leaving Germany for exile in 1933, finding refuge first in Oxford and then in Sweden. He finally became a professor in Yale where he continued to teach and write until his death in 1945. Many of Cassirer's works, including his early *Kants Leben und Lehre* and the magisterial *Philosophie der symbolischen Formen*, were translated, and in this respect he was more fortunate than either Cohen or Natorp.

The schools at Baden and Marburg reached the peak of their influence in the years immediately before the First World War. From 1918 onwards their importance rapidly diminished. The sudden and swift disappearance of neo-Kantianism from the German philosophical forum is a remarkable phenomenon: in the space of a decade the impressive systems were almost forgotten. A number of factors contributed towards this sudden demise. First, many of the neo-Kantian philosophers and their pupils, especially those attracted to the Marburg School, were either Jewish, socialistically inclined, or, more often, a mixture of the two. For these men academic preferment was not easy. Secondly, the leading neo-Kantian philosophers witnessed the defection of their most promising pupils to the philosophy of Husserl. Heidegger, for example, who began his doctorate under Rickert, and Jaspers, who was also influenced by Rickert, both became phenomenologists, as did Ortega y Gasset, who studied under Cohen in 1907 and again in 1911.[7] When Heidegger arrived at Marburg as Natorp's successor in 1923, he was a phenomenologist and not a neo-Kantian. Consequently a new generation of Marburg graduates was inducted into 'phenemonological seeing' and not into the 'transcendental method' of Cohen. A further example of this transition from neo-Kantianism to phenomenology and existentialism is afforded by the philosophy of Heinrich Barth, the brother of Karl. Heinrich, though never actually a student at Marburg, regarded himself as a disciple of Natorp, so much so that his doctoral thesis attempted to depict Descartes's philosophy as a precursor of the Marburg System. Heinrich's adoption of existentialism was slow and reluctant, but this stance clearly distinguishes his *Erkenntnis der Existenz*, which was posthumously published in 1965.[8]

There is, thirdly, the overwhelming effect of war and defeat upon German culture. After the war German philosophy was in a state of shock. As intellectuals took to heart-searching and questing for a new understanding of the order of things, neo-Kantianism, which like many pre-war institutions tended to be optimistic about historical development and confident in its proclamation of moral evolution, seemed no longer to offer a secure answer to those moral questions raised by war and defeat. Angst, nothingness, and finitude were more in tune with the times than an ideal, optimistic, and rationalist philosophy.[9] Paul Natorp, the veteran and bulwark of neo-Kantian orthodoxy, questioned his previous endeavours. As well as turning to social philosophy he began to formulate a new, more mystical, philosophy.[10]

Before considering in detail some of the problems addressed by the neo-Kantian thinkers, it is important to note how theology responded to changing trends in philosophy during the latter

half of the nineteenth century. Claude Welch once remarked
that the collapse of idealism between 1835 and 1870 was experienced in Germany as the collapse of Christianity itself.[11] Not
only was the alliance between philosophy and Protestant
Christianity threatened, but the increasingly popular philosophies of matter were avowedly anti-Christian and atheistic.
Attempts at refuting materialism by early neo-Kantians and
thinkers such as Lotze were not unnoticed by theologians; the
significance of Ritschl and his followers lies precisely here. But
though Ritschl's determination to address philosophical and
epistemological issues was certainly inspired by contemporary
non-materialist philosophy, he cannot himself be called a 'neo-
Kantian'.[12] Quite apart from his contributions to doctrine,
Ritschl attempted to avert a head-on collision between theology
and natural science through his critique of metaphysics. His
main criticism of metaphysics was that it overlooked a fundamental distinction between *Natur* and *Geist*; a distinction
ignored by Absolute Idealists and advocates of materialism
alike.[13] The realm of *Geist*, he argued, could not adequately be
explored by those laws of mechanism and matter that are
essential for comprehending *Natur*, thereby advocating a separation of methods and perspectives between theology and natural
science. Ritschl's concern for the integrity of religion in the face
of materialist criticism and various forms of reductionism was
shared by Wilhelm Herrmann, who taught at Marburg from
1879 until 1917. It was he who was responsible for a dialogue
between theology and the contemporary philosophy of Marburg.
Herrmann regarded his own work as complementary to that of
Cohen and Natorp and aimed to mediate between the knowledge of the world presented by Marburg philosophy and the
Protestant tradition. From the publication of *Die Religion im
Verhältnis zum Welterkennen und zur Sittlichkeit* (1879) onwards,
Hermann was a valiant fighter for the autonomy (*Selbständigkeit*)
of religion. He argued that religion could not simply be reduced
to being some ancilliary support to other dimensions of culture
such as ethics or aesthetics, but was itself a necessary and
irreducible feature within the total life of *Kultur*. Any philosophical account of reality, such as the one being advocated by
his colleagues at Marburg, should afford to religion a unique
and positive role if that philosophy is to be complete. In a similar

way the other major school of neo-Kantianism also witnessed a dialogue between philosophy and theology with Ernst Troeltsch gaining much from Wildeband and Rickert.[14]

This remarkable era of theological and philosophical debate proved extremely fertile and was to have profound influence upon German theology during the following decades. Both Barth and Bultmann were keen students of Herrmann. During this period Paul Tillich wrote his two dissertations on Schelling's philosophy and his books were reviewed in *Kant-Studien*, the official journal of the *Kant Gesellschaft*. Later he contributed articles to that august periodical. Gogarten was certainly influenced by Natorp and even after the latter's retirement continued an interesting correspondence with him. Thus many theologians, whose work was to be fruitful and influential later in the century, were initially influenced at a time when neo-Kantian philosophy was in the ascendancy and inherited a dialogue between theology and philosophy which began during the last decades of the previous century.

From these introductory remarks about the origins of neo-Kantian philosophy it should be evident that its roots were deeply implanted in the nineteenth century. Before Cohen became a professor at Marburg, philosophers such as Liebmann, Lange, Zeller, and Lotze were sympathetic to Kant's critical epistemology and resolute in their opposition to materialism. They sought an alternative epistemological account of modern science which precluded the metaphysics of matter. None of these thinkers, nor any of the later neo-Kantians, was hostile to natural science: it was the materialist philosophies which appealed to contemporary science that they objected to. Indeed, many prestigious scientists were deeply sympathetic towards a renewed critical idealism. Figures such as Helmholtz, author of *Über das Sehen des Menschen* (1855), and Hertz, who wrote his famous *Die Prinzipien der Mechanik* in 1894, were keen to lend their prestige and support. Cohen, like most of his colleagues, had great reverence for what he called 'the facts of science'. Being deeply impressed by what seemed a progressive teleological accumulation of scientific knowledge, Cohen followed with fascination developments in mathematics, electro-magnetism, dynamics, and non-Euclidean geometry. As the Newtonian world, based upon mechanism and force, gave way to the strange new world of field theories and quanta, neo-Kantian philosophers keenly observed the demise of the one and the rise of the other. Later Natorp and Cassirer were to assess Einsteinian relativity from a neo-Kantian perspective.

Something of the animus of early neo-Kantianism may be imbibed from the writings of Lange. His masterly *Geschichte des Materialismus* suggested that materialism was a weak philosophical doctrine in that it was fraught with internal contradictions, barbaric in its neglect of culture and ethics, and fraudulent in its account of scientific method. Though disrespectful of scientific achievement and culture, Lange nevertheless detected some grain of truth in materialism, believing it to be pragmatically useful as a maxim or method for the empirical investigation of nature. On the other hand he insisted that the sensible world arose from interactions between the human organism and some unknowable reality. Unlike Kantian *Dinge-an-sich*, Lange's unknown realities were phenomenal, not noumenal entities. He concluded that his own brand of 'phenomenal materialism' was probably the truth about reality as far as it could be known. There are, however, other dimensions of reality, which could not be ignored by philosophy; and it is here that the humanism so characteristic of neo-Kantian philosophy makes it appearance. Humanity, whatever scientific heights it scales, cannot live by science alone. The human spirit has other needs—moral, religious, aesthetic—which achieve fulfilment by fashioning an artificial secondary environment. The 'work of culture' was regarded by Lange not as a luxurious hobby for the refined nor as a dispensable pastime for the privileged, but as a labour upon which the nobility of civilization depended.

He deemed it imperative that mankind supplement the reality of phenomenal materialism with an ideal order of its own creation. Such an ideal order was, in Lange's words, 'a world of value against which neither logic nor touch of hand nor sleight of eye can prevail'. Metaphysical systems, religious dogma and myth, works of art, moral codes, literature, and drama were, to use a phrase of Jasper's, ciphers of transcendence. The adornment afforded by Lange's ideal order, like the script of ciphers, was purely aesthetic, though under certain circumstances it had profound importance for the moral well-being of humanity. This dimension of humane values was created by poetic fancy (*Dichtung*) and its imaginative canopies posed no threat to, but rather enhanced, what natural science can discover about reality:

No thought is calculated so much to reconcile poesy [*Dichtung*] and science [*Wissenschaft*] as the thought that all our 'reality' [*Wirklichkeit*] . . . is only appearance [*Erscheinung*]. Yet this truth still remains for science, that the 'thing-in-itself' is merely a limitative concept [*Grenzbegriff*]. Every attempt to turn this concept into a positive one leads us undeniably into the sphere of poesy; and only what endures when measured by the standard of poetical purity and nobility can claim to serve a generation as instruction in the ideal.[15]

Though it is inevitable that we know an austere world of matter, mechanism, and force; for consolation, moral enlightenment, vision, and nobility of spirit, humankind must turn to the poetical world of Goethe, Schiller, religion, and metaphysics, discovering therein deep resources that will nurture civilization in its quest for enduring values.

A scientist, whose work affords further insight into the idealist epistemologies of neo-Kantianism, is Heinrich Hertz. The introductory epistemological comments to his work on mechanics were greeted by many neo-Kantians and exercised considerable influence, particularly upon the pupils of Cohen. Hertz believed that 'mathematical physics' arose from a symbolic representation of experience. The most important epistemological feature of natural science lies, according to Hertz, in its ability to predict future events. The method by which natural science derives the future from past experience consists in the formation of inner symbols or fictions of outward objects:

We fashion for ourselves images or symbols of external objects; and the form we give them is such that the necessary consequents of the images in thought are always images of the necessary consequents in nature of the things pictured. . . . The images of which we are speaking are our own ideas of things. They have one essential agreement with things, namely that the images fulfill the requirement of producing future predictions or consequents, but further agreement with things is not necessary to their purposes. Actually we do not know, and have no means of discovering, whether our ideas of things accord with things in any other respect than in this one fundamental relation.[16]

Though surprisingly modern, these words date from the end of the nineteenth century and Hertz anticipated possible objections. Realizing that not all symbols or non-iconic models are equally valuable in achieving the desired end of prediction, he suggested two criteria for assessing their validity. The first was a criterion of correctness which affirmed the validity of symbols only if they serve as good simulators of experience. Secondly, he appealed to a criterion of permissibility, so reducing the multiplicity and relativity of symbolic fictions by requiring coherence. Here a symbol is affirmed valid only when it coheres with other scientific symbols.

A particularly emphatic feature of Hertz's epistemology was its stress upon the indispensable contribution of thought and symbolic ideas to natural science. Symbolic thinking was responsible for organizing experience scientifically and for making knowledge possible. This was something for which the materialist hypotheses were unable to account, and Hertz was quite firm with those who ridiculed his epistemology as meaningless metaphysic: 'No consideration which makes any impression on our mind can be disposed of by labelling it as "metaphysical"; every thinking mind has needs which the natural scientist is wont to call "metaphysical".'[17]

It is worth pondering the distinctive characteristics of Hertz's epistemology since they afford some indication of how neo-Kantians addressed natural science. First, the patterns of rationality employed by scientists are completely different from those advocated, for example, by Mill's Canons. Here the scientist is not so much investigating facts or collecting 'data' from which general laws arise, as creating theoretical symbols to be tested against past experience which has itself previously been organized by other symbols. What is crucial here is not only the rejection of inductivism, but rather an explicit appreciation of the fecundity of symbolic thought and ideas for knowledge. The attractiveness of renewed idealist epistemology, for both philosophers and scientists, was partially due to the manner in which thought was presented as a dynamically productive agency. Thought, in the guise of ideas, symbols, or models, bestowed upon experience its form, coherence, regularity, and predictability; so much so that without this creative agency experience would recede to nought. It is at this point, thirdly, that idealist ontology begins. Lange, it will be recalled, advocated a 'phenomenal materialism' in which the ultimate substance of the universe consisted of unknowable phenomenal entities. Hertz likewise was agnostic as to whether finite beings could attain complete knowledge about the nature of things, but going beyond Lange, he said that it did not matter.

Thought and its symbols possess the strongest accent of reality, against which any other 'reality' palls to the point of attenuation. It is almost as if thought was itself creating a cosmos, a universe of order, and one, moreover, which could be controlled by its creator. A final point about Hertz's epistemology, and others like it yet to be encountered, is the recognition that not just any old sort of thought attains a cosmos, only one that is ordered, coherent, and systematic. Only thought possessing *Gesetzlichkeit* can fashion and control an ordered universe. Lange, along with the earliest neo-Kantians, who were deeply impressed by the omnipotence of human thought exhibited in the astonishing scientific advances of the nineteenth century and who enjoyed a Victorian optimism regarding the perfectibility of this thought-laden universe and its rational agents, suggested that the 'legality' of such thought arose from and depended upon the human organism.[18] Later, however, when Cohen wrote his *Logik der reinen Erkenntnis* and Rickert his *Der Gegenstand der Erkenntnis*, the new quest was to exhibit, codify, and demonstrate the *Gesetzlichkeit* of thought and its cognitive structures as universal, a priori, necessary, and as possessing a juridical claim which rested not upon some contingent connection with the psycho-physical constitution of the human organism, but upon a *de facto* right arising from the very nature of thought itself. Additionally, since thought creatively produced knowledge in areas other than natural science, there arose an attempt to find *gesetzlich* patterns of cognition in ethics, aesthetics, history, jurisprudence, and sociology.

A final feature of Hertz's work, and one shared with Lange's, was its humanism. Lange attached considerable importance to the creations of *Dichtung*, whilst Hertz recognized what Schopenhauer called 'man's need for metaphysics'. It was not merely a passion for architectonic that impelled neo-Kantian thinkers to fashion systems that amounted to intricate philosophies of culture, but a humanist vision. With no culture humankind forfeits moral dignity and labours without purpose. Likewise the individual, dependent for orientation and goals upon a system of values, without *Kultur* would lose all sense of direction. Leading an aimless life, he or she sinks to a subhuman level of existence. The criticism that neo-Kantianism, being an essentializing philosophy, affords little consideration to the dynamics of particular existence, is therefore misplaced. Though it has been said that the individual appears in such systems only inasmuch as he or she is subsumed under an intricate system of culture and consequently lacks any independent ontological status, the neo-Kantian revival arose from debates about the existence and nature of the human soul which were part and parcel of the mid-century *Materialismusstreit*. Marburg neo-Kantianism indeed placed much emphasis upon the moral autonomy and freedom of each individual; but whether the individual of neo-Kantian systems was alive in Germany after 1918 is another question.

Concern about the soul was expressed at two levels in neo-Kantianism; one relating to the discipline of psychology, the other arising from more 'existential' questions. At the beginning of the nineteenth century psychology was chiefly a speculative discipline and even at the end of the century philosophers and psychologists alike were unsure about its aims and methods. Much confusion arose from this uncertainty. It was in the middle of the century that Fechner began to pioneer what was to become experimental psychology. His famous *Elemente der Psychophysik* of 1860 sought to establish psychology as an 'exact science of the functional relations or relations of dependency between body and mind'.[19] Fechner was in many ways typical of those philospher-scientists who figured prominently in the mid-century debates. Originally a physicist, Fechner's interests ranged far and wide until he arrived at his own unique and somewhat eccentric synthesis. Believing Hegelianism to be totally irreconcilable with contemporary science and the philosophies of matter to offer unsatisfactory accounts of the human mind, Fechner embraced a metaphysics in which matter and consciousness were two manifestations of one substance. Plants, animals, the heavenly bodies, as well as people, were varied forms of that all-embracing psychic substance. Materialism studied consciousness from a 'night viewpoint' and this, said Fechner, should be supplemented by a 'day viewpoint' which beholds matter from the perspective of consciousness. Given these metaphysical beliefs to which Fechner was deeply committed, it seemed logical that an experimental science could discover the laws of interconnection between the two elements of the one universal substance. From these speculations there arose the cardinal principle of experimental psychology that psychic life may be studied through its material or somatic media. Early neo-Kantians, though critical of Fechner's pan-psychism, were keen supporters of psycho-physics, hoping that it would offer solutions to the major questions of philosophy. The prospect of a new scientific psychology that did not reduce human agents to material entities devoid of spirituality was deeply attractive to thinkers who sought to combine humane values with a critical epistemology for the new sciences. When later in the century the attractiveness of psycho-physics began to pall, neo-Kantian thinkers remained keenly interested in the theoretical foundations of psychology, whilst simultaneously developing what might be called a neo-Kantian existentialism that was to be particularly important for their philosophies of religion.

That psycho-physics could offer firm empirical support to such features of Kantian philosophy as the a priori character of forms and categories proved quickly to be an empty mirage. Hermann Cohen was as keen as anyone for an alliance between science and a renewed critical idealism, but not at the price of investing so much capital in one branch of experimental science, however promising. He argued, and in doing so convinced his senior colleague Lange, that no amount of experimental findings could secure the validity of those principles, forms, and categories upon which science itself rested. What was needed was rather a totally different approach which, being both scientific and critical, would demonstrate the absolute validity of the foundations from which all knowledge derives. Cohen and Natorp challenged the world with a radically new transcendental philosophy: 'Whoever is bound to us stands with us on the foundation of the transcendental method . . . Philosophy, to us, is bound to the fact of science as this elaborates itself. Philosophy, therefore, to us is the theory of the principles of science and therewith of all human culture.'[20]

II. COHEN'S NEO-KANTIAN PHILOSOPHY

Hermann Cohen, born on 4 July 1842 in Koswig, was the son of Gerson Cohen, teacher of the local synagogue school. After attending gymnasium in Dessau, Hermann entered the Jewish Theological Seminary of Breslau which had adopted the moderate reform Judaism of Zacharias Frankel.[21] These rabbinic studies and Cohen's religious upbringing were responsible for nurturing an enduring vision of Israel's mission amongst the nations which proved to be a spring that enriched his thought and lent moral passion to his understanding of the tasks facing philosophy. In 1861 Cohen registered at the University of Breslau and within three years decided to put aside a vocation to the rabbinate in favour of studying philosophy at Berlin. The first period of Cohen's philosophical activity seems to have been occupied in the study of classical philosophy and comparative philology. His turn to Kant was largely due to the controversy over the subjectivity of space and time between Trendelenberg, the senior philosopher at Berlin, and Kuno Fischer.[22] A study of Kant resulted in a series of commentaries on the three *Critiques*. The first, *Kants Theorie der Erfahrung* of 1871, was widely read and earned Cohen a reputation as an important Kantian thinker. These early works are distinguished by their attacks upon the psychologism of the earliest neo-Kantians such as Lange and also by the beginnings of a radical revision of Kantian philosophy. On the strength of his first commentary Cohen went to Marburg, shortly succeeding Lange in 1876.

A third phase of philosophical development began with the publication of *Das Prinzip der Infinitesimal-Methode und seine Geschichte* (1883). This phase was one of systematization and resulted in the publication of Cohen's own system of philosophy. The first part of the system, the *Logik der reinen Erkenntnis*, appeared in 1902 and was soon followed by his *Ethik des reinen Willens* and the *Ästhetik des reinen Gefühls*. The fourth part of Cohen's system was to be entitled *Psychologie als Enzyklopädie der Philosophie*, but its author did not live to complete this work. The three published parts of the system were each indebted to that strange sounding work on the infinitesimal method, for in it there began a love affair with the mathematics of calculus that led Cohen to conceive an unusual and novel theory of knowledge. Upon reaching the age of seventy Cohen resigned his professorial chair and settled into retirement as a founder member of the Jewish Academy in Berlin, pursuing his Talmudic studies and researches into the history of Jewish thought.

Though Cohen published a number of articles on religious topics throughout his career,[23] his later years witnessed his most important contributions to the philosophy of religion. A book which was widely read, and which the young Karl Barth had in his library, was *Der Begriff der Religion im System der Philosophie* (1915). Containing references not only to Jewish thinkers, but also to

Christian theologians such as Luther, Schleiermacher, Troeltsch, and Herrmann, this book is a testimony to the interdisciplinary debates at Marburg and essential reading for anyone wishing to understand the philosophical theology of the Marburgers. Cohen's *Die Religion der Vernunft aus den Quellen des Judentums*, a philosophical theory of Judaism, was published posthumously. This amazing work, the only one of Cohen's books to be translated into English, was based partly upon the system for which Cohen was famous, but also upon the biblical writings, the Talmudic tradition, and Jewish philosophical thought from Maimonides to Mendelssohn. The specifically Jewish dimension of Cohen's work is once more beginning to receive recognition, though contemporary seminal figures such as Rosenzweig and Buber acknowledged their debt to him.[24]

The sequel to Cohen's life makes tragic reading. Many of his pupils, Germans and foreigners alike, were either killed or forced into exile during the three decades following his death. Cohen's young wife, Martha, the daughter of one of the leading synagogue musicians of the nineteenth century, survived his death until 1942. In the September of that year she shared the fate which befell many of her people. She was incarcerated in the concentration camp of Theresienstadt, only to die within ten days. Her ashes were cast into the Eger River. More touching is the fact that the inscription on Cohen's tomb in Marburg, which during the period of National Socialist ascendency had been partially defaced, was recently restored. Cohen's prophecy on the eve of the twentieth century, 'Unfortunately one must admit that we had overestimated the maturity of the times. We are unfortunately not on the eve of the Messianic Age', proved tragically apt.

Cohen's critical philosophy aspired to develop a universal mathesis, a sort of logic, as the foundation upon which all knowledge rests. When Marburgers talked of *Logik* they did not mean formal, modal, or, indeed, any recognized system of logic, but a transcendental logic of their own devising. Being a follower of Kant, Cohen believed that the chief task of philosophy was to offer a systematic presentation of knowledge in the form of a critique of thought; yet in executing what he called 'the transcendental method' Cohen departed so radically from Kant that, in the judgement of Fritz Kaufmann, Marburg neo-Kantianism bordered on anti-Kantianism.[25]

A. THE TRANSCENDENTAL METHOD

1. *The Nature of Thought*

Cohen, like Heidegger after him, believed that his own philosophy rested upon the insight of Parmenides' cryptic saying, 'to gar auto noein estin te kai einai', and that the 'Eleatic signpost', the identity of being and thinking, was the corner-stone of his system.[26] Not content with this, Cohen argued that 'to be' not only meant 'to be thought', but 'to be known' as well, claiming thereby to have reconciled that ancient *Gigantomachia* between being and becoming through his own understanding of the nature of thought. Being, he suggested, achieves existence by becoming thought, and the two are held together by a dynamic, never-ending, process of knowing. In order to appreciate this process fully, a critique of thought is essential and this would be undertaken by logic. The logic, however, had to be a specialized form of logic. Since its concern is to draw up an inventory of those deep structures of mind upon which all cognitive experience rests—whether it be of the natural world, of persons as moral agents, or of aesthetic experience—the logic in question could not be dependent upon such experience. The appropriate stance is rather 'transcendental', enquiring what structural cognitive patterns enable us to enjoy any cognitive experience whatsoever. Not being a relativist, Cohen was only interested in those transcendental structures of thought, which being responsible for indubitable knowledge, had to be universally, necessarily, and apodictically true. An important task of logic was the complete demonstration of this truth.

For Cohen, as for many other late nineteenth-century idealists, thought was essentially judgement. Invoking Aristotle, he said, 'The basic elements of thinking, as the basic elements of being, according to him are not properly designated concepts, but rather judgements', and in judging the mind is spontaneously active, not passively intuiting some extra-mental phenomena nor even copying facts or data.[27] It is important from the outset to distinguish between particular judgements and the activity of judging. Kant, who often formed the departure for Cohen's philosophy, explicated two types of particular judgements. The first was based upon a modified version of Leibniz's analytical theory of judgement which followed from his combinatorial theory of concepts.[28] Kant's analytic judgement, however, is, first, one whose predicate is 'contained' in its subject and, secondly, one which can be proven by the principle of contradiction.[29] Yet another particular judgement was the one in which the *Critique of Pure Reason* was most interested. With synthetic judgements the predicate is not contained in the subject and they cannot be proven by the principle of contradiction alone. Synthetic judgements 'expand' knowledge, and it is these judgements that characterize cognition in natural science. Kant argued that mathematical judgements were synthetic and that physics used a priori synthetic judgements as principles. Accordingly his first *Critique* attempted to demonstrate the possibility of synthetic a priori judgements and also to show how they provide the foundational principles for valid knowledge of appearances.[30]

When one considers the act of judging, rather than particular judgements, it emerges from the Kantian critique that synthetic a priori judgements are only possible to a spontaneously active mind which possesses a definite character and a special sort of unity. Judging is itself a unifying act, so that when human beings judge they create a unity. Before any successful cognition can occur it is essential that there be a systematic unity—a sort of epistemological grid—to give experience coherence, order, and structure. Kant termed this unity the 'transcendental unity of apperception'. Under the influence of Newtonian physics, and writing before either non-Euclidean geometry or relativity, Kant argued that the knowledge acquired by physics depended upon certain a priori formal assumptions. First, in order to gain knowledge of any object, that object must be located in space and capable of being distinguished from other objects in time. As well as a spatio-temporal continuum, Newtonian science required the additional assumption that the world it was to investigate be an ordered one, and ordered in such a way that the mathematician-scientist can explore, explain, and discover this regularity by formulating laws to which any empirical experience would conform. Kant argued that these three unities—space, time, and the physical world—depended ultimately upon a fourth, namely the cognitive apparatus or 'consciousness' of the rational agents who make such assumptions. It is not the case, suggested Kant, that such rational assumptions are inferred or derived from exploration or experimentation of phenomena. On the contrary, these assumptions make possible any experimentation and scientific knowledge whatsoever. The scientific mind credits the physical world with a discoverable regularity, asks questions, and formulates laws:

> Hitherto it has been assumed that all our knowledge must conform to objects. But all attempts to extend our knowledge of objects by establishing something in regard to them a priori by means of concepts, have ended in failure on this assumption. We must therefore make trial whether we may not have more success in the tasks of metaphysics, if we suppose that objects must conform to our knowledge.[31]

The most essential prerequisite for Kant's Copernican Revolution in epistemology is thus a cognitive agent that can think in terms of unity, project order, and synthesize diverse experience, not in a random or poetic manner, but in one which is governed by logical rules, laws, and mathematics. Only this sort of consciousness can attain scientific knowledge and it is precisely this synthesizing–unifying activity which constitutes judging.

An important correlate of this view of cognition concerns criteria for truth. Whereas a common-sense approach might regard a judgement as true when it corresponds to an independent reality and false when it does not, Kantian Idealism laid foundations for a coherence theory of knowledge. The account of cognition as an activity involving synthesis and systematization, encouraged the view that one essential criterion of truth in cognition is the systematic coherence of knowledge. Knowledge is distinguished from supposition by its being coherent, ordered by definite principles, capable of systematic expression and, in natural science at least, by its ability to make reliable predictions about future events. Kant's weaker form of coherence as a criterion of truth must be distinguished from later idealism, in which coherence also provides a definition of truth and furnishes an account of reality. Hegel, followed by later idealists, agreed that truth must be 'the whole' and, accordingly, system. Truth here requires that knowledge be articulated in the complete systematic coherence of judgements, concepts, and assertions, not in an *ad hoc* fashion, but absolutely so. Moreover, coherence could not serve as the criterion of truth if reality itself lacked coherence and this, it was urged, must be the primordial assumption for any rational account of the nature of things. Kant, it should be stressed, did not embrace these later developments towards an absolutist theory of coherence, since an accent of realism in epistemology and a certain agnosticism in ontology prescribed limits to his idealism.

The theory of judgement developed by Cohen lies somewhere between Kant and Hegel. Cohen accepted that coherence was not only the criterion of truth, but also an account of the nature of truth, and that philosophy's task was to give an account of this truth in the form of a system. The 'whole', however, is not given all at once, but must be progressively unfolded by the dynamism of thought. Since thought and cognition ceaselessly work at ever-new challenges, Cohen argued that the outcome could never be the attainment of absolute knowledge: there will always be new challenges for cognitive thought to solve and master. When knowledge advances, more new dimensions of reality come to light, but since these dimensions are unknown until thought sets to work on a particular problem, no system could make pretensions to an absolute knowledge of reality. Thought, then, for Cohen, is the orderly progressive development of logical judgements and categories which procures knowledge.

Cohen insisted that a critique of pure thought must begin with thought as an a priori synthesis to provide the skeletal bounds of coherence for valid cognitive activity. Arguing that such a synthesis must be transcendental because this structural coherence alone makes cognition possible in the first place, he could not allow his synthesis to be derived from random empirical conjectures about the nature of things. Since Cohen, like Kant, stressed that judgement was an activity, he viewed thought as dynamic and active. The initial synthetic unity was not regarded as undifferentiated, but rather as a unifying network that contained a plurality. Thought accordingly unifies or 'integrates' into a unity and divides or 'particularizes' a plurality. The two processes of *Vereinigung* and *Sonderung*, generated by thought alone, formed the first necessary synthesis in Cohen's epistemology.[32] Next he argued that this transcendental synthesis was no haphazard expansion and contraction of thought, but an activity (*Tätigkeit*) governed by discoverable logical elements. These logical elements were the particular judgements of Cohen's system and in his *Logik* there are twelve such judgements.[33] These judgements supposedly supplied the *Grundform* of both thinking and being; simultaneously they were the foundational elements of knowledge. Thought, the dynamic movement of integration and differentiation, 'functions' with these judgements. When judging, however, thought does not engage in a chaotic process of forming arbitrary connections, but follows discernible regular patterns, called by Cohen 'categories'; his system has twelve categories corresponding to his twelvefold inventory of judgements. The categories supply the basic directions (*Grundrichtungen*) in which thought moves when judging: 'The direction between category and judgement is reciprocal. The category is the goal of judgement and judgement follows the path of the category.'[34]

Once Cohen secured his thesis that thought is a process of unification and differentiation which employs judgements and categories, he drew attention to a further activity of thought called conservation (*Erhaltung*). Differentiation and unification could not simply be regarded as two separate compartments of thought, one relating to a plurality, the other to a unity; both are much more functions of one operational totality. Cohen's concern here, it should be emphasized, was with 'pure' thought; with the ideal forms and functions of thought, and not with psychological processes or thought in relation to extra-mental empirical phenomena. Thought thus became the content of thinking and the two movements facets of one reality. Thought itself conserves the unity in plurality and plurality in unity.

Cohen's theory of judgement could well be termed a generative theory of judgement. Not only does thought generate itself as a plurality in unity but, working with judgements and categories, becomes synthetic in the Kantian sense. When thought judges it produces knowledge and being.

2. *A Mathematical Model*

Words like paradigm and model have enjoyed popularity in the philosophy of science since Kuhn's book about the nature of scientific revolutions. Though critics detect certain inconsistencies in the way words like model or paradigm are sometimes used, there can be no doubt that scientists do employ various devices— some theoretical, others experimental—to simulate processes or phenomena under investigation and to aid the formation of fruitfully elegant theories.

Numerous models appear to be employed in science ranging from more abstract and mathematical models, through experimental ones, to those which have been called 'theoretical models'. These, according to Ian Barbour, are 'imaginative mental constructs invented to account for observed phenomena. Such a model is usually an imagined mechanism or process, which is postulated by analogy with familiar mechanisms or processes'.[35] Such models are used to devise a theory which in turn will correlate a series of observations, Barbour's instructive example of the 'billiard-ball' model of gas being a particularly compelling instance of theoretical models. Three noteworthy features characterizing these and similar devices should help to explain the particular theoretical model which lies at the heart of Marburg Kantianism. First, there is the presence of analogy, whereby an analogical relation is postulated between the familiar and something to be explicated. Secondly, there emerges an intricate relation between the model adopted and the theory used to account for processes or phenomena simulated by the model. Finally, theoretical models aid discovery and also become pedagogically useful by providing a unitary mental picture more easily understood than some abstract series of equations.

In the following pages it will be suggested that model-building was essential to the philosophy developed at Marburg by Cohen, Natorp, and Cassirer. These philosophers, like Barbour's scientists, were concerned to explicate a process, committed to a definite theory, and, not surprisingly, they used a model analogous to an operation well known outside philosophy. First, then, is the process or phenomenon which Marburg philosophy hoped to explicate. Unlike natural science, which often focuses upon a series of problems arising from observation of the natural world, the task of Marburg Kantianism was primarily epistemological— to explain or 'justify' scientific knowledge in its entirety. Secondly, the theory adopted arose form Kant's transcendental approach to the problems of epistemology. Finally, this theory became modified in singular ways through the adoption of a definite model which imaginatively pictured how the human mind (in Marburg terminology the 'scientific consciousness') acquires knowledge.

The previous section introduced the doctrine of judgement that was a cardinal feature of the Marburg understanding of thought.

When Cohen and his colleagues said that thought postulates a series of relations, integrates a unity, particularizes or differentiates a plurality, or that thought functions with judgements and categories, it is not too difficult to perceive that terminology drawn from mathematics was being used. To be more precise, the vocabulary of calculus is evidently pressed into service, and it is this that distinguishes the model employed by the philosophers of Marburg.

Their model was intended to explicate those ideal forms of thought the Marburgers held to be responsible for the existence of scientific knowledge. Now it is manifestly difficult to arrive at a naturalist account of how the cognitive mind works transcendentally, since by definition no amount of observation and experimentation could possibly investigate a phenomenon which is held to be essentially non-empirical. To remedy this lacuna and to make their theory about the transcendental functioning of consciousness more accessible and comprehensible, the Marburgers postulated an analogy between the operations involved in solving a problem with the aid of calculus and the ideal workings of the cognitive mind. Those who want to search for an exact correspondence between some example of problem-solving with calculus and the transcendental operations of the ideal cognitive subject will do so in vain. Like all forms of analogical reasoning, the relation between the two terms involves dissimilarity as well as similarity, but hardly anywhere in Marburg philosophy is there a detailed comparison between the two. Effort was rather expended upon constructing their model and then attempting to make it work in the realm of epistemology. Indeed so imprecise and attenuated does the relationship between calculus and transcendental logic become, that it might be more appropriate to call the relation metaphorical rather than analogical in the strict sense.

It should be evident, therefore, that much imprecision lies in the mathematical model developed at Marburg. The attractiveness it held for these idealists must have been first and foremost aesthetic and, next, pragmatic, when it appeared successfully to illuminate their idealist theory of knowledge. In either case a veritable imaginative leap was demanded by the practitioners of this philosophy in order to accept their model of consciousness, even if on rational grounds alone one was persuaded of the validity of the transcendental approach to epistemology.

Detailed examples of the logical calculus developed at Marburg appear in the cumulative historical argument advanced in its favour over several chapters of Cassirer's *Substanzbegriff und Funktionsbegriff* of 1910;[36] but a more general introduction to the Marburg model may be given. When one wishes to solve certain problems, such as rates of velocity or acceleration, the first step is to mathematize the problem. Using Cohen's terminology, there is a problem or task (*Aufgabe*) which calls one's cognitive powers into operation (*Ursprung*). The problem is then tackled by investigating relations between various mathematically expressed values and, for reasons which will become evident, the Marburgers called this step the 'positing of laws'. Finally, through a series of mathematically controlled steps, a solution is worked out. In Marburg philosophy this stage was called *Erzeugung* (generation or production). Should, however, integral or differential calculus be used in one's *Rechnung*, it was firmly believed that the postulation of infinitesimally small units was essential and these too were regarded as 'generations' of thought.

The important thing about all these steps is their productive character. From a given (*gegeben*) problem one 'generates' a solution through a series of controlled mental operations. From the supposition that one is able to leap from mathematics to transcendental logic, the followers of Cohen deduced that knowledge is produced in response to a challenge or task. It is created, first, by pure thought positing certain mathematical-type relations (or laws) for the problem being addressed and, secondly, by logically 'generating' a solution from these posited foundations. Since, however, thought alone is active here, Cohen stressed there was no need to suppose it worked on some extra-mental 'stuff', such as sense-data or material intuited through sensuous perception. In other words, thought, as well as generating knowledge, simultaneously generates the reality to be known: being is a function of thinking. The resultant ontological style was fittingly characterized by Natorp as a 'monism of experience' or, better, as a 'methodological monism'.[37]

3. *System and Symmetry*

The unitary character of theoretical models was emphasized by Barbour in his previously quoted work. A model, he suggests, is grasped as a whole and, by giving a summary of complex relations in a vivid form, if offers 'epistemological immediacy' or 'direct presentation of meaning'.[38] It is likewise stressed that models contribute towards the unity of knowledge and, quoting Nagel, Barbour argues that the presence of analogies in the structure of theories encourages systematic integration of widely divergent domains:

Models also contribute to the achievement of inclusive systems of explanation. A theory that is articulated in the light of a familiar model resembles in important ways the laws or theories which are assumed to hold for the model itself; and in consequence the new theory is not only assimilated to what is already familiar, but can often be viewed as an extension and generalization of an older theory which had a more limited scope.[39]

This applies as much to the model of Marburg philosophy as it does to natural science. The Marburg conception of how we come to know, along with its account about the nature of known objects, offered an ontology and an inclusive system of explanation which would in principle be valid for any domain of knowledge whatsoever. What excited these philosophers about their model was the belief that it presented a system which could gather the varied knowledge-producing categories, judgements, and concepts, into one harmonious whole. To this extent, despite some divergency between the various philosophers, it is legitimate to speak of the Marburg System. The model, being exceedingly malleable, was stretched to address epistemological problems beyond those of natural science and mathematics. The resultant system embodied the Marburg vision of the essential unity of all knowledge and to its creators represented 'the triumph of pure thinking'.

This quest for a unified and uniform epistemology has deep roots in the Western philosophical tradition and figures prominently in German Idealism. Kant, for example, attached considerable importance to architectonic,[40] and Hegel proclaimed that truth was system. As well as being indebted to this tradition and impressed by the architectonic character of contemporary natural science, the neo-Kantian philosophers were keen aesthetes. A system possessing unity, wholeness, and symmetry held a deeply aesthetic attractiveness, though it soon began to pall for the post-war generation. An additional factor impelled Cohen's pursuit of system. His appreciation of the essential unity and harmony of our knowable world was almost certainly inspired by a profoundly religious vision to which he was deeply committed.

Cohen and his followers, being consistent monists, said not only that thinking is being, but also that being is 'being known'. The three principal divisions of philosophical study (ontology, epistemology, and logic) were accordingly approached symmetrically.[41] Using their model based upon infinitesimal calculus, the Marburg Kantians devised a symmetrical system of philosophy. Logical thought became a dynamic and productive method of relating and calculating (*Rechnung*). Acquiring knowledge was a 'reckoning' of objects according to the laws supplied by logic and, because something new achieved determination and definite existence through this process of thinking and knowing, ontology took care of itself. A consequence of this philosophical style was that no positive philosophical significance could be afforded to anything that threatened the symmetry of the system. Anything outside the symmetrical ordering of logic, epistemology, and ontology, would thus lie beyond the methodological limits of the transcendental method as *Grenzbegriffe* (concepts at the limits of knowledge). Marburgers encountered such limitative concepts in religion, psychology, in Kant's things-in-themselves, as well as in mythical thought and the problem of individuality.

The requirement of symmetry had yet further implications. The continuing validity of the system depended upon an absolute and systematic coherence of logic, epistemology, and ontology. Were it suggested that a different relation obtained between epistemology and ontology (*Denken und Sein*) other than that prescribed by Cohen's logico-mathematical model, an asymmetry would upset the entire system. The symmetry of the Marburg System was in fact constantly threatened by its inability to deal adequately with what Kant called *Empfindung*. Later the battle-cry 'to the things themselves' sounded a death toll for the transcendental method. With Husserl and the pupils he captured from neo-Kantianism, the relation between thought and things was no longer that of ideal generation. Between thought and reality, now regarded as a field already organized prior to thought, there existed a consciousness which intended objects and did not create them.[42]

4. Departures from Kant

Nagel's contention that a new theory arising from a different model may, in certain circumstances, be viewed as an extension and generalization of an older theory which had a more limited scope, certainly holds good for the relation between Marburg neo-Kantianism and the philosophical theories of Kant. Though even informed scholars, including Paul Tillich, often speak of neo-Kantianism as an ill-fated attempt to rehabilitate practical reason and its God as an indispensable postulate of ethics, most neo-Kantians sought to understand Kant better than he understood himself.[43] Since the prefix 'neo' is apt to mislead people into supposing that neo-Kantianism was merely an anachronistic Kantian revival, it is important to note from the outset some of the more radical innovations which distinguish the philosophy developed in pre-war Marburg from the philosophical bequest of Kant himself.[44]

Cohen, like Kant, believed that natural science presented philosophy with the task of inquiring into the epistemological foundations and also of justifying them. The system of natural science which most impressed Kant was, of course, Newtonianism, whilst Cohen, living in a later epoch, was fascinated by developments in electricity, geometry, physics, and mathematics. The epistemological inquiry inaugurated by Kant was termed transcendental because its goal was to exhibit the a priori, necessary, and universal logical conditions which make scientific knowledge of nature possible and apodictically valid. Cohen believed that Kant tackled this task imperfectly, for at times he seemed to have abandoned purely logical considerations by developing a psychology of the knowing subject. Instead Cohen demanded that critical philosophy should concern itself with pure forms of thought alone and leave questions about psychology to the natural sciences. Accordingly Cohen sought to purify Kantian methodology by formalizing Kant even more and by introducing his new form of transcendental logic based upon the calculus model.

A second innovation that led Cohen to deny a central tenet of Kant's philosophy was indebted to his persistent obsession with the purity of thought. Kant argued that there were two indispensable presuppositions of knowledge, the first of which was thought, since any knowledge worthy of the name needed forms, categories, and concepts, such as space, time, cause, and substance. Furthermore, and especially after his Humean awakening, Kant stressed that sensible intuition was the second prerequisite of knowledge. In order to produce a coherent body of experience, that is, scientific knowledge of appearances, the conceptual machinery of thought needs data supplied through the senses on which to work. The importance of these two requirements for Kant's epistemology is evident from the oft-quoted statement, 'Thoughts without content are empty, intuitions without concepts are blind.'[45] In Cohen's mature system sensible intuition is firmly rejected as a condition of knowledge. Arguing that nothing exists outside thought and that all knowledge has its origin (*Ursprung*) in thought alone, he accounted the presence of sensible intuition in epistemology as absurd and irrational.

A third departure from Kant concerns Cohen's treatment of *Dinge-an-sich*. According to Kant's first *Critique*, things-in-themselves were entities which have to be thought but, paradoxically, he denied it was possible to gain any knowledge about them. Any attempt to acquire knowledge of a *Ding-an-sich* would inevitably involve using the categories of thought in an illicit manner. Categories like cause and effect or *substantia et accidens* produce knowledge of phenomena, not of noumena, and are validly used with reference to appearances alone. This paradoxical position may have been adopted by Kant for ethical reasons. The idea of a noumenal realm, like the ideas of God, freedom, and immortality, had importance for practical reason. If phenomena alone exist, the kingdom of ends could not be postulated as an ideal reality having practical significance for human concerns. Obviously Cohen could not accept such an asymmetrical relation between *Denken* and *Sein*. There was no place in his system for a problematic realm of reality above, beyond, or even alongside, that which thought produced. The only reality he reckoned with was that generated by thought.[46]

The expulsion of *Dinge-an-sich* from Marburg philosophy therefore implied there was no ontological distinction between apearances and noumenal reality: everything that is, is known and produced by thought; yet the notion of *Dinge-an-sich* was nevertheless retained and given a new significance. Things-in-themselves became *Grenzbegriffe*, meaning thereby signposts or tasks for further research. At any given time the sum total of knowledge is limited, but not absolutely. The limits of today's knowledge will always recede as research advances, but even tomorrow there will remain tasks for scientific thought to surmount. Such, then, was the new positive significance attributed by Cohen to Kant's thing-in-itself. Simultaneously, however, he also developed a negative meaning for the term and this had particularly decisive influence upon the Marburg approach to myth which, thanks to the good offices of Rudolf Bultmann, persisted well into the twentieth century. Negatively the thing-in-itself became an ontological quirk and an epistemological monstrosity produced by mythical thought. These 'pseudo thing concepts' issued from insufficiently logicized forms of thought that lacked the *gesetzlich* character of valid knowledge. A mythical object for Cohen and Natorp was one which had not been rendered knowable by the mathematics and laws of thought perfected in contemporary natural science. Mythical objects and mythological presentations of reality were therefore remnants of a pre-scientific understanding of the world and for that reason they possessed little epistemological value for science, philosophy, ethics, or religion.[47]

It is no overestimation to say of Marburg Kantianism that it owed as much to Cohen as it did to the historical Kant. In Cohen's own words, 'Der historische Kant war nur der Eckstein, in dessen Richtung das Weiterbauen erfolgen müsse.'[48]

B. THE LOGIC OF PURE KNOWLEDGE

The following pages offer a summary of the leading technical terms of Marburg philosophy and, in order to explain them adequately, it will be necessary to refer to some of the complicated terminology used by Kant in his *Critique of Pure Reason*. To make things even more difficult for the non-philosopher, Marburg philosophy, though systematic, is exceedingly intricate and highly complex. This intricacy is due to the very character of the System itself. Since Marburg philosophy regarded thought as an organ of synthesis which acts as a network for interrelating various posited relations, it should be no surprise to discover that its various technical terms turn out themselves to be related to each other in a fascinating variety of ways. A further difficulty is linguistic. Much of the force of Marburg philosophy depended upon subtle word-plays, inversions, and neologisms, for which the German language has a genius. The language of Cohen, moreover, is particularly challenging. Even sympathetic contemporaries, who felt Cohen had something worth while to say, invariably found his grammar and syntax somewhat taxing. One reviewer, for example, commenting upon his book about the infinitesimal method, said: 'Cohen's book is generally accounted the most difficult book of German philosophy and one can even hear discreet people saying that the only thing they had understood in the entire work were quotations from foreign authors.'[49]

But some appreciation of Marburg *Logik* is essential for an understanding of the *religionsphilosophisch* debates at Marburg. While a further point of historical and exegetical importance lies in the fact that Barth availed himself of this technical vocabulary not only in his earliest writings, but in his book on Anselm and also in the *Church Dogmatics*.

It is with Cohen's work, *Das Prinzip der Infinitesimal-Methode und seine Geschichte*, that an account of Marburg logic must begin. Ostensibly a work on the history of calculus, the real aim of the book was twofold.[50] First, as the subtitle, *Ein Kapital zur Grundlegung der Erkenntniskritik*, would lead one to suppose, Cohen begins to develop his project of a transcendental method based upon calculus. That a special form of logic might demonstrate and 'justify' the epistemological foundations of modern science becomes particularly evident by the way *transzendentale Logik* and *Erkenntniskritik* are treated as equivalents throughout. The second major theme of the work is ontological. With relentless determination Cohen pursues the question of the nature of reality and gradually, but clearly, his own singular answer begins to emerge. This work on the history of calculus with its new concept of reality marks a transition in Cohen's philosophical development. Whereas previously he had devoted much energy to commenting upon Kant, from 1883 onwards Cohen set about building his own system which resulted in the *Logik der reinen Erkenntnis* of 1902.

Whitehead, in an introductory work on mathematics, noted how

the general effect of the success of the Differential Calculus was to generate a large amount of bad philosophy, centring round the idea of the infinitesimal calculus ... Leibniz held that, mysterious as it may sound, there were actually existing such things as infinitesimally small qualities and, of course, infinitesimally small numbers corresponding to them.[51]

Though Leibniz's actual position was more complex, it is correct to say that Newton came closer to providing an adequate account of calculus by basing it upon the doctrine of limits. The dx and dy of a differential are nothing in themselves and dy/dx is not a fraction. A satisfactory definition of the differential, moreover, requires no reference to actual infinitesimals, but Cohen was ignorant of Whitehead's advice and believed there were infinitesimally small qualities and infinitely small numbers corresponding to them.[52]

The logical doctrine of the work argued that an operative transcendental synthesis of thought supplied the first necessary conditions for any scientific knowledge. As was previously explained, Cohen's logic was a logic of operative thought concerned with the cognitive 'movements' (*Bewegungen*) of thought in judging. Judgements, along with categories and principles, give coherence and bring unification to experience. This unity is the unity of thought itself which integrates and differentiates in the process of judging.

The ontological position of Cohen's book arose from his quest for a pure logic, one, that is, which is radically independent of sensation. The highly original part of *Das Prinzip* is Cohen's definition of reality which occurs in a radical interpretation of Kant's 'Anticipations of Perception'. The *Critique of Pure Reason* contrasted the manifold of sensible impressions and the plurality of the categories. Since knowledge was regarded as resulting from an ordered application of categories and concepts to sense experience, Kant postulated a connecting link between the two called 'schemata'. A schema, in the words of one commentator, is 'a rule or procedure for the production of images which schematize or delimit, so to speak, a category so as to permit its application to appearances'.[53] Without schemata supplied by the imagination, categories would remain empty 'thought things' and the manifold a chaotic mess of unorganized impressions. The schemata, by supplying rules for connecting categories with sense perceptions, make knowledge possible. Cohen, however, chose to apply his logical categories without the aid of a schematism which, in his opinion, introduced extraneous elements (that is, the manifold of sensuous intuition) into transcendental logic.

Having dispensed with schemata, Cohen leaped from his logical categories to Kant's anticipations of perception. In the section of his *Critique* entitled 'Analytic of Principles', Kant argued that the understanding produces certain principles a priori which supply rules for using the categories objectively. They state conditions for the possibility of objective experience (meaning thereby, know-ledge of objects) and Kant derived his principles from the table of schematized categories. Now the principles or *Grundsätze* corres-ponding to the schematized categories of quality were called 'anticipations of perception' and the principle which anticipates all perception reads as follows: 'In all appearances sensation [*Empfindung*], and the real [*das Reale*] which corresponds to it in the object [*realitas phaenomenon*], has an *intensive magnitude* [*intensive Grösse*], that is, a degree.'[54] With the aid of this *Grundsatz* Kant demonstrated to his own satisfaction that all sensuous perception must be capable of measurement. Cohen's book completely reformulated Kant's principle so that prior to any experience there existed a union (*Verbindung*) between intuition and thought. An anticipation of something to be determined, of an '*x*' given through sensuous perception, was bound to the category of reality (*Realität*) so as to produce an '*x*' now determined by thought. This 'making the given real' (*Realisierung der Gegebenheit*) constituted the intensive magnitude capable of being mathematized or calculated by the infinitesimal method.[55] What Cohen understood by reality will require further consideration, but in *Das Prinzip* reality is, first, what occurs when thought makes a series of judgements in accordance with logical laws and, secondly, consists of infini-tesimal points which in the first instance form 'intensive magni-tude' and then the 'extensive magnitude' that permits measurement of what some might regard as objects of sensation.

This book about the history of mathematics, epistemology, and the nature of reality won admiration from some, scorn from others. At least one critic claimed it was 'eine der monströsesten Geburten in der Geschichte der Philosophie'.[56] Cohen, un-deterred by criticism, pressed on with his great work and made it even more internally consistent. When the *Logik* appeared in 1902 'the given' was completely expelled from epistemology. This radical thesis clearly marks his mature philosophy. Any 'given' outside and apart from thought had neither epistemological value nor ontological reality: 'The merely empirical, that is, the unphilosophical and unscientific element, is only a temporary question-mark for science to dispose of.'[57] Before continuing to examine the intricacies of Cohen's logic, it is important to recall the enthusiasm which Marburg neo-Kantianism inspired in some quarters. Barth, for example, could not help being impressed by the fervour and almost priestly devotion with which philosophy was pursued at Marburg. Boris Pasternak was perhaps typical of many Russians and foreigners who made the pilgrimage to hear Cohen lecture. Two years before his journey to Germany the word 'Marburg' was constantly upon his lips. As a student of philosophy in Russia he soon found that 'the place of Kant and Hegel was taken by Cohen, Natorp, and Plato'. The Marburg philosophy being 'entirely original, breaking fundamentally with everything else' promised a 'rejuvenation of philosophy'. Pasternak was particularly attracted to Marburg Kantianism by its sound 'historical sense', for 'the Marburg School turned to prime sources, that is, to those genuine inventors of ideas which human thought has accumulated in the history of science'. Ortega y Gasset likewise lavished praise on Cohen, who 'renovated the impulse towards system, which is the essence of philosophical inspiration' and acknowledged his indebtedness to his teacher for 'at least half my hopes and almost all of my discipline'.[58]

1. *Generation*

As the importance of the given receded in Cohen's mature system, the idea that thought produces its own objects became increasingly prominent. This is particularly evident in Cohen's use of the word *Erzeugung*, around which was built an intricate philosophy of thought.

Judging, it will be recalled, involved thought, first generating an initial logical synthesis or epistemological grid and, next, actively conserving this plurality in unity. In *The Logic of Pure Knowledge* Cohen was eager to insist that nothing external impinges upon such transcendental activity: 'Thinking itself is the goal and object [*Gegenstand*] of its activity. This activity does not switch gear and attach itself to a thing, it does not come from anything external to itself.'[59] Because there is nothing outside thought and because thought requires nothing at all to be given to it for the creation of knowledge, Cohen's judgements become productive as they 'move' in the categories. It is during this dynamic process of judging that thinking 'generates' being, since 'Only thinking itself can generate [*erzeugen*] what validly counts as being'.[60]

Some interpreters of Cohen suggest all this should be understood axiomatically and formally, implying thereby that Cohen did not teach that thought produces objects. It is manifestly true that Cohen is laying down axioms and formal rules of methodology, yet it cannot be denied that the exclusion of sense intuition as a source of knowledge has obvious ontological implications. In one section, for example, Cohen insists that the *Stoff* of thought does not come form *Empfindung*; it is, rather, a generated content (*Inhalt*) produced by thought: 'The activity of thought generates the content. The complete indivisible content of thought must be the generated result [*Erzeugnis*] of thinking. It is the total indivisible activity of thinking that constructs the content.'[61] This demand for the purity of thought, together with the absence of any reality other than thought, allows the ontological aspect of the theory of logical generation to achieve clear expression: '. . . das Denken seinen Stoff sich selbst erzeugen soll'.[62] In judging thought not only supplies the logical a priori structures which make knowledge possible, it also generates the reality to be known.

2. Origin

Cohen's belief that sensible intuition possesses no epistemological value and is deficient in reality is central to another term in the Marburg philosophical vocabulary, that of origin. Philosophy, said Cohen, must begin with thinking and recognize that thought needs no 'origin' outside itself.[63] Cognition, therefore, could not be the process of re-presenting some external reality, despite the fact that Kant availed himself of the vocabulary of *Vorstellung*. Cassirer, perhaps more clearly than Cohen, elucidated this feature of Marburg philosophy: 'Thought does not reproduce an outward reality; it is the foundation and very core of reality . . . there is no being, no objectivity, no "nature of things" *that does not originate in thought*. A reality outside the sphere of thought and exempt from its principles and conditions is a meaningless concept.'[64] The firm commitment to thought's self-sufficiency amongst Marburg philosophers arose from what was taken to be scientific method. Scientific knowledge, they believed, begins with basic mathematical-type principles which need to be posited before any research can commence. These basic elements supposedly govern the whole course of investigation and, when applied to specific problems or tasks, produce scientific knowledge.

Cohen's conviction that knowledge and being alike originate in thought led him to develop a principle of origin which features prominently in the *Logik*. His formulation of the principle of origin depends upon three meanings of the word *Ursprung*. In the first place the origin is a point of commencement. Just as scientific method depends upon a number of elementary principles, so pure thought, the thinking of knowledge and being, depends upon principles, presuppositions, or hypotheses, which it posits at the beginning of its cognitive labours. All valid knowledge is the result of an ordered 'unfolding' or 'development' (*Entfaltung, Entwicklung*) of such logical elements. Although the totality of these elements forms a plurality in unity which is the transcendental *Grund* of knowledge, each element remains a product of thought. Cohen, having something of a weakness for mathematical symbols, compared a single logical element to an x sign: 'This sign signifies not indeterminateness, but determinateness. Consequently it is equivalent to the true meaning of the given. For in the x there is the question from whence it might have come, from whence its source. Thus x can be used in logic as the correct symbol for an element of pure thought.'[65]

The origin of being and knowledge in thought is obviously not a question of spatial or temporal origin, it is, rather, a question of logical origin. An origin, a point of commencement, is the beginning of cognition, and from this start an origin combines with generative thinking to produce knowledge and being. Thought thus begins with a self-posited element and then proceeds to develop or unfold it. Confirmation of this view was forthcoming through an appeal to antiquity. According to Cohen the central discovery of ancient philosophy is that thought effects a transition from a relative nothing (*me on*) to being, and this amazing insight was claimed to have received the most definitive formulation possible in his own *Logik*.[66] It takes no mathematician, however, to perceive that behind x and the *me on* of

Cohen's Greeks there lies the infinitesimally small numbers which he felt to be at the heart of calculus.

This note of movement, transition, or development, leads to a second meaning of *Ursprung* in Cohen's system. An origin actively governs the course of cognition by performing, as it were, the function of a signpost indicating the path generative thinking must follow in order to attain knowledge and being. The *Ursprung*, being a law for thought (*Denkgesetz*), stipulates the trajectory for pure thinking to traverse in pursuit of its cognitive and ontological goals. Once again this notion is rooted in Cohen's understanding of calculus and his estimation of its importance for logic:

> The judgement and *Denkgesetz* of origin, which has to control all the cycles of pure thought, stakes its claim on this new orientation. Mathematical thinking must above all fulfill the demand of origin, without which there would be no legitimate beginning. The demand is valid for each advancing step taken in the process of mathematical thinking. If mathematics, as the mathematics of natural science, should determine this cognitive movement which advances in ceaseless development, it must establish its own origin for this movement. The origin is valid not only at the commencement of the movement, but its every advancement must continually originate anew in the same origin.[67]

It is interesting to note how the logical foundation of cognition becomes fecund: from the *Ursprung* there arises a continuous developmental process which is governed by that very same origin. Just as a curve might be 'generated' from a mathematical equation so, Cohen argued, the ordered '*gesetzlich*' process of generative thinking is determined by and produced from an origin.

It is at this point that a third meaning of origin becomes evident. *Ursprung*, as an active principle, could in this context be translated as either 'originary' or 'originative'. This aspect of Cohen's origin stresses the potency of thought, since pure thinking autonomously generates knowledge and being from its own inner resources. Thought needs nothing in the way of fuel for its dynamism, nor does it require any pre-existing matter as raw material for its creations. Perhaps it is easier to grasp this nuance of potency in Cohen's understanding of origin by recalling Kant's hypothetical Archetypal Knower (the Divinity). In several writings Kant contrasted human cognition with the sort of intellectual cognition which, according to the rationalist schools, characterizes the mind of the maker. The former was called by Kant *intuitus derivativus*, since human knowledge depends upon there being something in existence for it to discover and, by implication, upon empirical intuition. Divine intuition, being *intuitus originarius*, is not so dependent. It is *originarius* because it creates the objects of its knowledge either *ex nihilo* or from its own thought. With Cohen's philosophy human thought becomes *originarius* in that it is creative and productive.[68]

That a principle of origin is eminently fecund, is evident from the following two quotations. In the first Cohen suggests that a 'principle' (that is, a logical principle or some mathematical hypothesis of natural science) would remain unproductive without the potency of an origin: 'Without origin the principle can neither be exact nor productive. The general significance of the principle as foundation must gain depth by the foundation of the origin.'[69] The second passage testifies to the belief that originative thought marks the supremely productive methods of natural science, which of course are themselves indebted to the 'thought-produced' hypothesis of the infinitesimal:

Physics . . . followed the path of mathematics which led to the hypothesis of the infinitesimally small. Whatever exists, substance, and force, gain definition and determination from motion [*Bewegung*]. Thus to the concept of the infinitesimal there fell the task of developing being. This discovery is true scientific generation. Infinitesimal analysis is the legitimate instrument of mathematical natural science. In its certainty rests the certainty of science. . . . The mathematical generation of motion [*Bewegung*] and through that the generation of nature is the triumph of pure thinking.[70]

These three meanings of *Ursprung* in Cohen's logic were summarized by a contemporary as follows:

The demand of origin is the demand for an unending methodical justification of thought. Every justification of a beginning (or of a principle) from its methodological origin makes this origin into a beginning. This can only be expressed by the *Denkgesetz* of origin (i.e. that thought generates its own content and has its justification in an unlimited methodological unity) which continually raises itself anew and is further developed to infinity.[71]

3. Givenness and Task

To emphasize the radical self-sufficiency of cognitive thought and its complete independence from sense intuition, Cohen coined the slogan that nothing is externally given (*gegeben*) to thought, everything is rather a problematic task (*aufgegeben*) for thought to master. The contrast between givenness (*Gegebenheit*) and task (*Aufgabe*) is a direct consequence of the principle of origin. Knowledge and being both originate in thought and the two are developed by generative thinking. Thought lays down a mental task for itself and works at it by logically generating both knowledge and being: in other words, thought receives the given from itself.

Sensation, for example, does not give thought any data, it is rather a question mark inviting further research. Cohen and his colleagues regarded sensation as an 'unknown' comparable with a mathematical factor, such as an x, that requires determination. *Empfindung* could not therefore supply data for scientific cognition: it was 'a mere blob', an 'undetermined x', which in due course would be determined by the methods of what Cohen called 'mathematical natural science'.

One contemporary sought to illustrate this contrast between givenness and task with the following example. We are accustomed to treat colours like red and green as sensations. As soon as the two are distinguished, a cognitive process is initiated; therefore in order to determine properly what red and green are, these problem-provoking concepts must be submitted to the logico-mathematical methods of natural science. The so-called given of sensation consequently turns out to be a task for logical thought.[72]

According to the principle of origin then, the only given with which thinking 'reckons' is a given postulated by itself: '. . . thought may regard as given only that which it may discover from itself'.[73]

4. Law

One feature of Cohen's understanding of origin, it will be recalled, was that of directionality. The notion that thought generates knowledge and being by following a law-governed trajectory received more precise formulation in the Marburg teaching about law. An outstanding feature of Kant's first *Critique* is the conviction that cognition is governed by detectable rules and laws. These laws, arising from the understanding, result in objective knowledge when validly applied to appearances:

We may now characterize the understanding as *the faculty of rules.* . . . Sensibility [*Sinnlichkeit*] gives us forms of intuition, but understanding gives us rules. The understanding is always busy with investigating appearances in order to discover some rule in them. Rules, so far as they are objective, and therefore necessarily depend upon knowledge of the object [*des Gegenstandes*], are called laws. . . . Thus the understanding is something more than a capacity for formulating rules by a comparison of appearances; it is itself the law-giver of nature.[74]

Cohen agreed with Kant's estimation of the importance of laws for cognition, though with one obvious difference. Since the Marburgers denied that sensation had any positive role to play in the generation of knowledge and being, laws could no longer combine with sense perception to produce objective knowledge (that is, knowledge of objects).

An inevitable consequence of this 'purified' Kantian epistemology is that laws become the sole distinguishing feature of known objects: 'Things are appearances, but are they phantasms? Not at all! Appearances are, insomuch as there are laws, in which the reality of appearances is grounded and in which the reality of appearances subsists.'[75] This quotation is from a writing published before the *Logik* in which Cohen was still operating with the thesis that thought 'realizes' the given.[76] Even in this earlier writing, however, the given is so thought laden that reality is almost entirely associated with law: 'Law is reality [*die Realität*], which means reality is to be conceived of as an abstract thought, as a sign of value for valid knowledge, and nothing more.'[77] Law here is no longer an organizing rule that orders material supplied by empirical intuition to produce objective knowledge of appearances; the reality of 'things' becomes constituted through their being determined by a law of thought! 'The so-called things have their reality in the aggregate of the laws of appearances; they (the laws) are appearances. . . . Appearances are truly objects [*Objekte*]; they alone are the real things which, through the laws of pure thought, become definite objects [*Gegenstände*] of intuition.'[78]

With the publication of the *Logik der reinen Erkenntnis*, in which the radical thesis about the given is articulated, the object itself becomes nothing but a generated nexus of laws.

5. *The Object*

Given the nature of Marburg philosophy, particularly its conviction that nothing apart from thought exists and that thought needs
no extra-mental givens, it should not be surprising that the object
of thought received detailed scrutiny so that it could be incorporated into the system without producing asymmetries. One of the
most important ways of achieving this end was by devising a new
definition of the object. Cohen therefore made a distinction
between two German words for object— *Gegenstand* and *Objekt*,
with *Gegenstand* being the preferred term. To use Cohen's own
words, it should not be supposed that the object, like sensation, is
a starting-point for cognition; it is rather the ultimate aim of cognition. The *Objekt* is a *Vorwurf* in the literal sense of 'something cast
before', that is, cast before thought during the process of
generative thinking. At any given time cognition enjoys knowledge
of *Gegenstände* determined by the law-governed patterns of
thought. The *Objekt*, by contrast, is an unending and alluring
theme for research.

The need to arrive at a new understanding of the object was
frequently stressed by Cohen with an almost missionary enthusiasm: 'The word which presents the new meaning of object
[*Objekt*] is *der Gegenstand*. ... The distortions which had been
present in *Objekt* are now removed. Any subjectifying activity is
rejected. The object is set upon its own feet and held over and
against the understanding as a *Gegenstand*.'[79] On the negative side
a new interpretation of the object of cognition demanded the
removal of distortions, which might lead one to suppose that
knowledge is partly dependent upon empirical intuition, as well as
the rejection of 'psycho-physical' theories that suggest cognition is
due to an associational procedure arising from interaction
between external phenomena and the human organism. From
Cohen's logical point of view it seemed irrational to believe that a
chaotic bombardment of sense impressions could give rise to
knowledge or that pure thought was anything other than a
sequence of logical laws. Being content to leave questions about
perception to natural science, Cohen reserved his energies for
concentrating upon the legitimate epistemological question
concerning the object, which was, of course, a matter for pure
Logik.

Positively Cohen traced the genesis of an object to its origin in pure thought: just as an equation might contain a formula for constructing a curve, so the origin itself contains or posits laws for generating an object. The object, in short, is generated according to a law as thought follows its path (*Richtung*) to knowledge and executes its task (*Aufgabe*). Such logical generation of an object by pure thought was termed objectification: 'Objects depend upon the methodology of law; thus the object [*Gegenstand*] is the sum total of laws, but the peculiar problematic the object presents is precisely the objectification [*Objektivierung*] of laws.'[80] Thought provides a systematic transcendental foundation for knowledge which, being a plurality in unity of basic principles, judgements, and categories, contains various *gesetzlich* trajectories that direct the course of generative thinking. The *Gegenstand* is generated from this *Grund-Einheit*, not arbitrarily, but logically according to laws of thought. It is these that become objectified in the process of cognitive generation.

An excellent summary of the Marburg understanding of object is provided by Werkmeister in an essay devoted to Cassirer's neo-Kantian background: There he writes:

the 'object' of cognition becomes an anticipation, a 'projection', and ceases to be an unapproachable 'thing-in-itself', a something which literally and in the absolute sense transcends all cognition. There is no longer any need for the assumption that 'objects' exist in and by themselves. All we need to accept now is the possibility of an orderly progress of cognition, the possibility of establishing an all-comprehensive context according to law, the method of securing scientific cognition. The 'object' becomes the ultimate goal of that process, the ultimate determination of the x in our initial question.[81]

Strange though it may seem, the object of cognition for this philosophy is not something discovered, but rather created by thought in response to a cognitive challenge. This epistemology, in which the object is a generated nexus of laws constructed in the operation of objectification, exercised considerable influence not only in philosophy, but also in sociology, psychology, and related disciplines. One of the strange features of twentieth-century theology is that such formative theologians as Barth and Bultmann understood and continued to utilize the Marburg conception of object long after it had ceased being popular in philosophical circles.[82]

6. *Content*

If the Marburg account of how objects are known centred on the process of objectification, the more metaphysical question regarding the nature of known objects was answered in terms of content (*Inhalt*). The ontological status of an object is that of its being a content of thought: 'The content of thought is no mere thing, but the *Gegenstand*.'[83] The object, generated from principles by the logical activity (*Tätigkeit*) of thought, becomes an objectified content of thought for 'consciousness':

The *Stoff* of thought is not the primal matter of consciousness . . . the substance of thought can only be content, that is, unity. . . . Cognitive thinking demands thought as unity and only as unity. The meaning and value of this can be expressed in the following statement: the activity of thought is itself the content. The product of generation [*Erzeugnis*] is itself generated [*Erzeugung*]. Unification is unity.[84]

Since the consistent monism of the Marburg philosophers demanded a reformulation of any 'common-sense' understanding of consciousness, when it was suggested that an object is a content of thought for consciousness, what they meant by consciousness was neither self-consciousness nor awareness of objects supposedly external to thought, but the pure consciousness of an ideal epistemological subject.

Cassirer, in his famous work about symbolic forms, gives a remarkably clear account of how a content of thought becomes objective for consciousness:

Just as the differential equation of a moving body expresses the trajectory and general law of its motion, we must think of the general structural laws of consciousness as given in each of its elements, in any of its cross sections—not however in the sense of independent contents, but of tendencies and directions which are already projected in the sensory particular. This, precisely, is the nature of a content of consciousness; it exists only in so far as it immediately goes beyond itself in various directions of synthesis. . . . The 'integral' of consciousness is constructed not from the sum of its sensuous elements (a, b, c, d . . .), but from the totality, as it were, of its differentials of relation and form (dr_1, dr_2, dr_3 . . .). The full actuality of consciousness is merely the unfolding of what was present as 'potency' and general possibility in each of its separate factors.[85]

The content of consciousness is thus the result of a complex synthesizing activity by which objects are generated from a transcendental unity of posited laws.

In order to distinguish his logical concept of consciousness from any employed by contemporary psychology or philosophy that might be incompatible with his system, Cohen contrasted *Bewusstsein* (an active being conscious of thought's contents) with *Bewusstheit*: '*Bewusstheit* is myth: *Bewusstsein* is science [*Wissenschaft*].'[86] *Bewusstheit*, which may be translated as 'knowness' or 'mere awareness', was, in Cohen's estimation, a feature of the animal kingdom. Animals possess no logically ordered *wissenschaftliche Welt*; they bump into their environment in a manner which totally lacks any logos. *Bewusstheit* was also held by Cohen to mark the way in which primitive mentality encountered its world before the advent of science. Not surprisingly, 'Mythical *Bewusstheit* is surmounted through scientific consciousness'[87] and is destined to become obsolete.

Yet another example of confusion between the two occurs when it is suggested that sensible intuition has some positive role to play in cognition. Such 'sensualism' is a veritable relapse into a pre-scientific mode of thinking, since it was a dogma of the system that knowledge could not be attained by confounding *Bewusstheit* with the true neo-Kantian understanding of consciousness. Cohen encountered this serious error when philosophers and psychologists portrayed cognitive thought as a psycho-physical phenomenon or when speculations arose about the origins of *Bewusstheit* and how it may have been transmuted into consciousness during evolution. The nature of consciousness and its contents could be addressed only from a logical analysis of the ideal scientific consciousness in which resided all the possibilities of knowledge: 'All pure consciousness is consciousness of the object. The object is the content which pure generation effects.'[88]

7. *Possibility*

One of the most important and fascinating judgements of Marburg logic was that of possibility. Kant, as usual, was the starting-point, who, towards the end of a section in his first *Critique* entitled the 'Analytic of Principles', offered an account of the postulates of empirical thought. These have a unique feature in that, 'in determining an object they in no way enlarge the concept to which they are attached as predicates'.[89] The principles of modality are only an 'explanation' of modal concepts (possibility, actuality, and necessity) in their 'empirical employment':

. . . they restrict all categories to their merely empirical employment, and do not approve or allow their transcendental employment. For if they are not to have a purely logical significance, analytically expressing the form of *thought*, but are to refer to the possibility, actuality, or necessity of *things*, they must relate to possible experience and its synthetic unity, in which alone the objects of knowledge can be given.[90]

Kant argued that though certain alleged phenomena, such as telepathy and precognition, were logically possible, he denied that such events could ever occur because they were 'concepts, the possibility of which is completely groundless, as they cannot be based upon experience and its known laws'.[91] That is, although the concepts of telepathy and precognition are without contradiction and therefore both analytically true and logically possible, Kant's point was that such concepts could never claim objective reality because they fall outside the empirical conditions of knowledge. In opposition to contemporary metaphysics Kant thereby restored the venerable Aristotelian principle which stated that everything possible need not of necessity become actual.

Whereas Kant allowed the conditions of empirical knowledge to prescribe limits to possibility, Cohen's philosophy, with its advocacy of the radical independence of cognition from empirical intuition, could not limit possibility in this manner. Instead Cohen equated the possible with whatever could be thought logically (*das Denkbare*).[92] Possibility was now found to originate in consciousness—the pure scientific consciousness of the ideal epistemological subject: 'In ancient ontology possibility is indeed the foundation for the determination of being: but in its place here enters consciousness. Possibility depends upon consciousness; possibility is contained [*enthalten*] in consciousness and the modes of consciousness unfold [*entfalten*] the modes of possibility.'[93] Consciousness is here depicted as an operative synthetic plurality in unity. In it reside the possibilities of being and knowledge of objects; it is these possibilities that generative thought develops into actual knowledge and being.

Cohen's new definition of consciousness, which precluded both self-awareness and awareness of extra-mental sensations or perceptions, is paramount to the following quotation. Here consciousness obviously means either an objectified content of thought (that is, an object) or the possibility of constructing such an object:

All pure consciousness is consciousness of the object. The *Gegenstand* is the content which pure generation effects. The problem cast before consciousness is accordingly that which the object presents. The rational quest for the object is the rational quest for the possibility of the object. Thus one again sees how consciousness and possibility belong together. Moreover one thereby sees that the possibility of consciousness signifies the possibility of the object.[94]

The way in which consciousness 'unfolds' its possibilities for generating knowledge was given a very precise term in Cohen's logic, namely, 'correlation'. Correlation 'is a basic scientific form of thinking used in our technical terminology of judgement. The general name for correlation is purpose [*Zweck*]. Where a logical system is set in motion [*angestellt wird*], a teleological development [*eine Zwecksetzung*] is also established [*wird aufgestellt*].'[95] In this correlative relationship the two relata (consciousness and possibility) are not static, but combine with each other to become implicated in a purposeful development which is logically determined. Accordingly the possibilities contained in consciousness combine with consciousness (now an active transcendental ground of generative thinking) to produce being and knowledge.

Cohen, it must be stressed, postulated three principal modes of consciousness: logical or scientific, ethical, and aesthetic, with each mode possessing a number of foundational logical principles as presuppositions. Natural science, for instance, has certain logico-mathematical hypotheses as its foundational principles and it is these possibilities that are unfolded when thought pursues tasks of a scientific nature. Ethics and aesthetics were approached in a similar manner, yet Cohen insisted these two modes depend ultimately upon the first—the logical, transcendental, and fecund ground from which being and cognition of being originate:

If possibility, as a category, has to guarantee each one of these meanings of consciousness, they must all have a common methodical significance which can only be established from the first mode of consciousness (—i.e. the logical or scientific mode—), since that alone has the sufficient and original capability of raising the concept of presupposition or foundation to the value of pure knowledge.[96]

The foundation (*Grundlegung*) for any branch of cognition is, of course, supplied by the logic of origin: 'If one asks, "Why foundation and only foundation?", the reply is to be made, "Because only foundation is pure generation and because only pure generation creates these true foundations".'[97] Cohen, abiding by his logical monism, suggests that the foundational possibilities of all valid cognition are themselves generated by thought.

To summarize, it can be said that for Marburg philosophy consciousness is a 'logical ideal of the all-comprehensive context of experience in and through which each "posited" element leads to all other elements of that context. It is the ideal of "systematic" thinking, the idea that all thinking ultimately strives towards a systematic unity.'[98]

Before leaving consciousness and its possibilities it should be noted how Cohen's system, having first dissected the three principal modes of consciousness and shown their interrelations, put them back together. Consciousness and its contents, viewed as a whole, was called either *Kulturbewusstsein* or, less frequently, *Geist*, by the philosophers of Marburg. It was their aim to depict the three main dimensions of cognition, one concerned with truth, the others with goodness and beauty, as the ultimate cultural system that alone claimed universal validity. The system was in fact a microcosmic copy of the prevailing cultural macrocosmos, yet it was powerless to survive, once the culture it strove so valiantly to protect and perfect itself disintegrated. That the system might become culturally anachronistic and therefore relative to its times, was a thought Cohen never entertained.

8. *Reality and Actuality*

Though the two German words *Realität* and *Wirklichkeit* may be translated by the one English word 'reality', Cohen's philosophy drove a logical wedge between the two. They are clearly distinguished even in Cohen's earliest works, but the distinction became increasingly precise as his philosophy developed. Take, for example, an early commentary on Kantian ethics, where reality is almost synonymous with law: 'Law is reality [*die Realität*], that is to say, reality is to be conceived as an abstract thought, as a sign for valid knowledge.'[99] The book about the infinitesimal method likewise associated reality with law and also contrasted reality with actuality: 'Reality lies neither in crude sensation nor in pure sensible intuition; it must rather be accepted as a unique presupposition of thought . . . reality signifies a unique category entirely distinct from actuality.'[100]

One of the things that sorely bothered Cohen about *Wirklichkeit* was its connection with sensation. Since sensation was nothing more than a mathematical x, a question mark, or a mere blob lacking determination, it was obviously less than real. The real, by contrast, was associated in Cohen's mind with pure thought, generation, law, and science, all of which lacked the logical deficiencies of random sense impressions. However contradictory it may sound, the writing of 1883 advocated an 'ideal correlation' between thought and sensation which was achieved with aid from the *Denk-Mittel* (logical tool) supplied by the category of reality:

Reality, as a logical tool, must be able to overcome any collision with sensation . . . reality takes an active part in generation and in the characteristic of critical idealism: it not only shows how a particular configuration of thought constitutes nature, but also that sensibility may only be assessed according to the original contribution which (the category of) reality makes to the existence of knowledge.[101]

This tortuous passage suggests, first, that the logical category of reality produces unambiguous knowledge of nature and, secondly, that it is the criterion of what some might be tempted to call sensation.

Cohen, it will be recalled, operated in this writing with the assumption that thought realizes, that is, makes real, the given.[102] This realization of the given, produced by the category of reality, is the first element of knowledge and being. It creates the primary building-block of ontology which, for reasons that should become evident, was called intensive magnitude. Such a minute element of reality was compared with an infinitesimally small number in calculus. Generative thought, by integrating and differentiating its logico-mathematical principles, incorporates or separates infinitesimal components of reality into (or from) a larger whole.

By 1902 Cohen abandoned his thesis about thought realizing the given and propounded in its stead the logic of origin which recognized no givens apart from self-posited pure forms of thought. Intensive magnitude still, however, appears as the basic unit of reality and the contrast between reality and actuality is, if anything, sharpened: 'Actuality may not be equated with reality because actuality appeals to sensation. The substitution of sensation is presupposed by the reality of the infinitesimally small.'[103]

The first step towards explaining the presence of infinitesimals in Cohen's appraisal of reality lies in the fact that the *Logik* classifies the judgement of reality as a mathematical judgement and Cohen regarded it as legitimate to speak of an infinitesimal element of reality as of an infinitesimally small number. It is from such infinitesimally small units, whether they be regarded as numbers or qualitative attributes of thought, that the reality of 'finite' objects is constructed: 'The finite, every finite, inasmuch as it falls within the realm of mathematics, should find its sufficient reason in this new number. This ground of the finite is the infinitesimally small.'[104] So wedded was Cohen to his mathematical model that the infinitesimal, which he deemed essential to calculus, became the metaphysical building-block of his ontology. Just as Whitehead's later philosophy argued that reality consisted of minute psychic events called 'actual occasions', so Hermann Cohen believed that reality is constructed from infinitesimal units of thought. The calculus model, offering a key to epistemology and scientific methodology, exercised such a powerful attraction for Cohen that we even hear of the 'infinitesimal as reality' or of reality as a judgement based upon calculus.[105] The autonomy, purity, and productivity of calculus were yet other examples of the triumph of pure logic and generative thought: 'it is founded upon pure thought alone and by virtue of this it is able to construct the basis of the finite. ... To this autonomy of the infinitesimal method (i.e. especially its independence from sensation) there must correspond a proper mode of judgement and this we designate the judgement of reality.'[106] For the *Logik der reinen Erkenntnis*, an element of reality is nothing more than a logical point produced by generative thinking through the judgement of reality. The work seems to suggest that such an infinitesimal point is to be equated with 'intensive reality' (his earlier intensive magnitude) as the basic unit of scientific knowledge. Being not only units of measurement, but also infinitesimal elements of reality, these points, when co-ordinated by laws, must presumably form the *Gegenstand*. The infinitesimal is thus the monad of Cohen's System, albeit one created by human, not divine, thought. Its existence depends upon there being a thought-posited system of logical archetypes in the 'consciousness' or 'spirit' of the ideal epistemological subject: 'The question about the reality of the infinitesimal is now integrated into the general problem of the reality of ideal scientific principles [*Grundbegriffe*] . . . The being of the infinitesimal does not lie in an external given, but rather can be established as a free and pure generation of the spirit itself.'[107] The judgement of reality simply pays ontological compliments to the thought-produced entities generated from an origin by the logical laws of thought.

Turning now to *Wirklichkeit*, the other twin of this pair, it is an obvious question to ask why Cohen associated it so much with sensation. The answer, like that to many other problems in Cohen's philosophy, is to be found in Kant's first *Critique*, in which actuality appears as a postulate of empirical thought. Kant formulated this postulate as follows: 'That which is bound up with the material conditions of experience, that is, with sensation [*Empfindung*], is actual [*wirklich*].'[108] This recommendation, that sensation should be the condition of ascribing actuality to some event or phenomenon, did not please Cohen for the obvious reason that his radically anti-intuitionalist stance precluded sensation from being a criterion of actuality. Not surprisingly, 'Actuality presents the most difficult impediment to pure thought because one is tempted to believe that actuality is concealed in sensation and is given only in sensation.'[109] Cohen, faced with this difficulty arising from Kant's philosophy, was in something of a dilemma. He wished to retain actuality as a 'methodological judgement', but was simultaneously forced to deny that *Empfindung* could contribute anything to knowledge, since such an admission would create a disastrous asymmetry for the entire system.[110]

In order to find some way out of the dilemma Cohen offered two approaches. First he appealed to the distinction between *Bewusstheit* and *Bewusstsein*. Any admissible account of sensation must approach it from the logical perspective of consciousness and not from that of primitive pre-scientific *Bewusstheit*—the implication being that viewing sensation as empirically given involves a relapse into unscientific and mythical speculation! Secondly, Cohen attempted to reassess sensation in terms of pure thought. Once actuality is recognized as the problem of the particular, this new perspective allows the particular to be understood as a measurable magnitude: 'So much does thought relate itself to sensation that upon further examination there occurs a self-relating of pure thought in the judgement of actuality. The contents of sensation become mathematical magnitudes.'[111] It is thereby proposed that sensation should not be regarded as awareness of some empirical reality transcending thought, but rather as thought's awareness or, better, measurement, of its own generated contents. Throughout a series of intriguing passages Cohen depicts a process whereby a generated reality develops logically from 'possibility' to reach the 'pinnacle' of consciousness as possibilities become 'actualized' by pure generation. In the judgement of actuality, thought as it were refracts and takes stock of its constructed reality. The goal of Cohen's approach to the problems presented by actuality was therefore to 'characterize sensation as a magnitude so it can only be symbolized by infinitesimal reality. The thought that sensation arises from the infinitesimally small and so develops until it enters consciousness, makes sensation into an integral and thereby into something finite.'[112] *Wirklichkeit*, as an ideal index or measurement, was, according to Cohen's estimation, used in all forms of scientific activity. Historical science, for example, involves chronology which is an obvious form of measurement; methodologically, therefore, the criterion for historical actuality is measurement and to that extent historical science depends upon the logic of the infinitesimal method.

Despite these ingenious arguments for dealing with judgements of actuality and possibility from a radical idealist perspective, sensation did create a manifest asymmetry in Cohen's philosophy. Although it is a mere blob, a question mark, or an undetermined x, it is nevertheless still there and the common-sense connotations of the word sensation proved difficult to define away. Furthermore, the distinction between consciousness and *Bewusstheit* was nothing less than a subterfuge designed to prohibit any non-idealist account of sensation and empirical intuition.

A final outrageous consequence arising from Cohen's approach to possibility and actuality was that the process of actualizing the possibilities of consciousness had a certain inevitability about it. Once the possible was equated with *das Denkbare* and correlated with the generative operations of consciousness, possibilities necessarily became actualized. The result was that the prevailing

Kultur, its science, ethics, and religion, was depicted as arising from and developing towards an ideal order by logical necessity. Cohen's enthusiasm for pure thought and for a truly scientific philosophy led him to ignore Aristotle's distinction between logical possibility and actuality, according to which necessity need not always intervene betwixt the two! 'It is not necessary that everything which is possible should exist in actuality. ... It is possible for that which has potency not to realize it.'[113]

III. EXTENDING THE SYSTEM

The philosophers of Marburg, having passionate confidence in the system they were constructing, proclaimed it to be the culmination of all previous philosophy. It was, moreover, a unitary system which in principle would not only justify valid cognition in all dimensions of culture, but also educate humanity how to pursue the ideal order of things. Cohen was entirely serious when he said: 'the Idea of society creates true unity for a nation founded upon culture of spirit. This highest goal, the ethical and political realization of the *Volksidee*, is the sum-total of tasks facing idealism.'[114] Absolutely nothing then could escape the systematic web woven by Cohen and his colleagues.

It would be a mistake, however, to regard Cohen's system as simply descriptive of the prevailing culture. From the outset it sought to sanction only valid patterns of cognitive thought, the bounds of validity, of course, being prescribed by the canons of the system. To this extent the Marburg System became a sort of meta-science, dictating what knowledge was cognitively and culturally acceptable and what was not.[115] Patterns of cognition which failed to fit into the uniform epistemological grid prescribed by the system had either to be redefined, so they could be incorporated without creating asymmetries, or abandoned as being mythical and pre-scientific. There were only three valid patterns of cognition recognized at Marburg.

A. THE DIRECTIONS OF KNOWLEDGE

The three published parts of Cohen's system dealt successively with logic, the foundation of valid knowledge, ethics, and aesthetics. Though such a division of knowledge was traditional since the three Kantian *Critiques*, a novel feature was Cohen's deduction of these three branches of knowledge from three attributes of consciousness: thinking, willing, and feeling. These activities, when combined with innate hypotheses, ideas, or foundations, generated knowledge of mathematics and natural science, ethics, and aesthetics. These three directions (*Richtungen*) of knowledge thus had a common root in consciousness or *Geist*. An unpublished part of Cohen's system, a philosophical psychology, was to investigate these three as a complex unity.

It has already been seen how the demarcation of three valid directions of knowledge conspired to deny cognitive value to 'mythical consciousness', *Bewusstheit*, and sensation. Two particularly difficult and persistent challenges were presented by psychology and religion. Was, for example, the cognition claimed by religion logical, ethical, purely aesthetic, or was it simply a product of mythical speculation? Similarly with psychology it had to be asked whether knowledge of the soul could be attained and, if so, how. The way in which religion was approached by Cohen and Natorp will be addressed in the following chapter, but the closely related problem of the nature of the soul demands immediate attention.

B. THE NATURE OF PSYCHOLOGY

Confusion abounded when Marburgers talked about psychology. This, however, was by no means unique to the philosophers of Marburg. At this time, long before psychoanalysis made its dramatic public appearance, there were a variety of psychologies ranging from experimental psychology, *Völkerpsychologie*, clinical psychology, psychologies amounting to nothing more than anthropological speculation, to religious and metaphysical accounts of the soul. These various disciplines seemed to be talking at cross purposes with the inevitable result that hardly anyone was quite sure what psychology was meant to study, let alone what methods it should use. A certain amount of clarification arose after William James became influential in Germany, but by and large it is often difficult for readers of the late twentieth century to fathom what the various references to psychology were meant to convey. An example of this, familiar to theologians, arises in the writings of Ernst Troeltsch who, in one particularly important essay, suggested that the historical figure of Jesus was not so much a dogmatic necessity, as a psychological necessity for the Christian community.[116] What he meant by this is far from clear.

Cohen and Natorp found this confusion both intolerable and challenging, so with the aid of their scientific philosophy they set about clarifying the situation. Their principal clarification proposed a methodological distinction between a purely philosophical psychology, something which today would be recognized as philosophical anthropology, and experimental psychology, which they considered to be a legitimate branch of natural science. Unfortunately however, the two methods were constantly confused, principally because the finished article had to be incorporated into their system without creating asymmetries of a logical or ontological nature, and the entire undertaking ended in failure.

1. *Objectification and Subjectification*

Natorp perceived that if the methodological monism of the Marburg System was to be maintained, there could be no ontological duality between subjective and objective. Augmenting and clarifying Cohen's epistemology, Natorp called the formal epistemological subject of pure knowledge 'pure subjectivity'. Subject and object were accordingly not two different ontological and epistemological realities, but two unending processes which generate cognition and being. One commentator sought to explain Natorp's complicated theories on this issue along the following lines: 'An unending consciousness contains nothing other than the totality of being. Now it is evident that the totality of objects to be determined is an unending task for finite human consciousness and that a similar unending task is meant by the idea of pure subjectivity.'[117]

These two infinite tasks, understood as operative processes, were called by Natorp 'objectification' and 'subjectification'. He arrived at this strange notion of subjectification through a literal interpretation of the word *Gegenstand* as 'something standing against' and that against which it stood as *das Subjekt*: 'Only from the standpoint of the objective is there a subjective, but, furthermore, objectivity signifies a proper character of being [*Seinscharakter*] only in opposition to the former ...'[118] A feature of subjectification is that like its elder twin, objectification, it was an unending task: 'As the goal of the entire series of objectification is pure objectivity, so the goal of the series of subjectification is pure subjectivity. But ultimately the goal cannot be spoken of as arriving at an end point ...'[119] Subjectification was thus an *Umkehrung*, a mirror image, of objectification. When thought objectifies its contents according to laws, a corresponding move of subjectification was postulated to correlate with the primary movement. Any actual subject thus disappears in a series of intricate operations, by becoming enveloped in a monism of pure thought. Natorp conceded that this understanding of *das Subjekt* implied there could not possibly be a science of the soul, only a scientific logic of thinking. If, however, there can be no logos of psyche because there are no souls, but only thoughts and thinking, what then does psychology study?[120]

2. *Two Kinds of Psychology*

Natorp argued it was indeed consistent to have a scientific psychology without postulating the existence of souls and believed that this type of psychology was practised by what today is called experimental psychology. Like all other natural sciences it proceeds by way of objectification and produces knowledge based upon laws (*Gesetzerkenntnis*). The laws of such a psychology, suggested Natorp, would be statements about neurological processes analogous to the laws of chemistry or physics.

Natorp, almost instinctively, felt something was missing from this future discipline which was already developing in Germany. It was sadly incapable of describing inner experience (*Erlebnis*) from the perspective of the individual, precisely because its methods depended upon objectifying the tasks it encountered. This difference between scientific psychology and individual awareness of the world, its culture, textures, and beauties, was therefore to be remedied by a new philosophical discipline called reconstructive psychology.

A 'mighty and central' province of this study would be a

description of the foundations of consciousness ... which must not be restricted to the pure forms of knowledge, volition, and art, and further-more to the pure foundations of religious consciousness, but may be extended to the ... imperfect objectifications of opinion, belief, and imagination—regardless of and unlimited by, their inner relations to truth and the realm of laws. ... Even the most irresponsible opinion, the darkest superstition, the most boundless imagination, utilize the categories of objective knowledge; they are still ways of objectification, however poor the means and impure the performance of this process may prove to be.[121]

Reconstructive psychology returns to the subject that rich polyform texture of awareness (*Erlebnis*) which the Marburg System had reduced to a vast series of logical processes co-ordinated by laws. Yet even reconstructive psychology, according to Natorp, could not attain knowledge of the psyche. It examines imperfect objectifications maybe, but the *Ich* of immediate awareness eludes the grasp of any discipline concerned with objectifications: 'The immediacy of one's own consciousness, not to mention that of others, cannot be grasped . . . immediately, in itself, but only in its expression which, as expression, is indeed always alienation, a stepping out of one's own sphere into the sphere of objectivity.'[122]

3. *Individuality*

The attempt to clarify psychology and its aims unexpectedly strained Natorp's monism of experience to breaking-point. The passage quoted above, with its contrast between 'one's own sphere' and the 'sphere of objectivity', almost enjoins a dualism between inner and outer. Although logically Natorp could not accept the hypothesis of human souls, his philosophy increasingly spoke of inner experience as an ontological realm completely different from the methodological sphere of logical objectivity.

When writing about psychology or *Erlebnis* Natorp seemed to veer towards what might be called a neo-Kantian existentialism. It sought to describe the *Ich* as immediate consciousness, conscious-ness, that is, with a direct awareness of its personal environment which enjoys a direct perception of inner experience totally different from that objective knowledge of reality presented in Marburg logic. Yet, despite all this, Natorp felt inner experience to be something altogether inscrutable.

Paradoxically Natorp deemed it most important to preserve the integrity of the *Ich* and its experience, since it was something intimately human. Indeed, any form of objectification actually distorts the inner experience of subjectivity: 'We do not demand of ourselves or of others that one should renounce this objectification of the I. One must realize however that it is no longer the I that one has before one's eyes, but its image, reflection, representation in another form . . .'[123] In even stronger language: 'It is axiomatic that we must not objectify the I. The I and its relation to the object should in no way be made into a *Gegenstand*.'[124] The Marburg System appears to have omitted something essential from its account of culture and even Cohen seemed aware of this: 'The problem of life [*Leben*] requires a new kind of *Gegenstand*, a new category which appears to create a contradiction, an antithesis, to the structure of the whole System. This new category is to be designated as the category of the individual.'[125] Whilst Cohen set about resolving the problem of *das Individuum* with teleological and ethical categories in his *Ethik des reinen Willens*, Natorp chose to characterize the inner side of the first-person experience as a unique form of feeling (*Gefühl*). Feeling, he thought, was the 'complete, pregnant, immediate experience of selfhood' which affords the *Ich* immediate awareness of its own rich inner life (*Erlebnis*). Since Natorp was inspired by Schleiermacher here, a more detailed discussion of his theory of feeling must await the next chapter.

Before leaving this introductory account of Marburg logic a theological point of great importance cannot be left unnoted. It arises from one of the more sinister purifications of Kantian philosophy. The *Logic of Pure Knowledge* discussed at one point 'neo-Platonic ontological arguments' and Cohen interpreted these arguments not as proofs of divine existence, but as logics of divine thought:

God as essence should signify absolute perfection. It is an old saying that his thought is his word and his word is his act. Possibility in him ceases to be potentiality, it becomes potency. But should reality be thought in him alone? . . . It is thought in and also from him; furthermore the reality of beings is grounded in him, for whatever God thinks is done.[126]

Cohen continues to note that after scepticism reality was still thought 'in' God, but no longer 'from him'. It is rather 'from' human thought.

The logic of origin looks surprisingly like a parody of the knowledge which characterized the mind of the Archetypal Knower in rationalist metaphysics: the deity knows all because his intuitive thought creates all. With Cohen's system this kind of generative thought becomes attributed to pure thought generally, so that when humans think and calculate, a world is created and known.

It is perhaps no coincidence that when Natorp wished to convey something of the spirit of the Marburg System he often chose a significant quotation from Goethe's *Faust*:

> In the beginning was the act, the creative act of the formation of the object, in which alone man built up himself, his human nature, and as he objectified himself in this, the stamp of his spirit was fundamentally and in a completely unified manner impressed upon his world. . . . The creative ground of such a deed as the formation of the object is the law: that fundamental law which one still designates as *Logos*, *Ratio*, *Vernunft*.[127]

If, however, through some strange and unforeseen theological pressures, originary thought was once more attributed to the divine mind, the neo-Kantian philosophy would start to resemble neo-Platonism. This move, analogous to that ancient intellectual movement which began to turn Platonic Ideas into divine thoughts, increasingly challenged the methodological monism of Cohen and Natorp. Should there next emerge a latter-day Augustine, who believed the most important divine ideas to be revealed in the Christian religion, he, like Barth, would doubtless say:

> Above and beyond the apparently infinite series of possibilities and visibilities in this world, there breaks forth, like a flash of lightning, impossibility and invisibility, not as some separate, second, other thing, but as the truth which is now hidden, as the origin [*Ursprung*] to which all things are related, as the dissolution of all relativity, and therefore as the reality of all relative realities.[128]

NOTES

1. From 'Materialism and Empirio-Criticism: Critical Comments on a Reactionary Philosophy', in V. I. Lenin, *Selected Works* (Lawrence & Wishart, 1939), xi. 335.
2. See further L. Kolakowski, *Main Currents of Marxism* (Clarendon Press, 1978), i; K. Löwith, *From Hegel to Nietzsche: The Revolution in Nineteenth Century Thought* (Constable, 1965); W. Lütgert, *Die Religion des Deutschen Idealismus und Ihr Ende* (Olms Verlag Reprint, 1967); H. Marcuse, *Reason and Revolution: Hegel and the Rise of Social Theory* (Beacon Press, 1960); T. E. Willey, *Back to Kant: The Revival*

of Kantianism in German Social and Historical Thought, 1860–1914 (Wayne State University Press, 1978); W. Windelband, *Die Philosophie im deutschen Geistesleben des 19. Jahrhunderts*, 3rd edn. (J. C. B. Mohr, 1927).

3. 'Zur Geschichte des philosophischen Lehrstuhles seit 1866', in H. Hermelink and S. A. Kähler (eds.), *Die Philipps-Universität zu Marburg 1527–1927* (N. G. Elwertsche Verlagsbuchhandlung, 1927), 681.

4. The debates about materialism achieved the status of public controversy when Rudolf Wagner read a paper entitled 'Über Menschenschöpfung und Seelensubstanz' to a congress of scientists at Göttingen in 1854. The materialist controversy and consequent 'struggle for the soul' lasted well into the 1860s and served to keep materialism in the public eye. Ritschl, who arrived at Göttingen in 1864, was well aware of the materialist threat to religion. His criticism of metaphysics was directed as much to this foe as to Absolute Idealism. For further information about this convulsion of the *Zeitgeist* see O. Chadwick, *The Secularization of the European Mind in the Nineteenth Century* (Cambridge University Press, 1975); Lütgert, *Die Religion*, iii. 249ff.; and H.-M. Sass, 'Daseinsbedeutende Funktionen von Wissen und Glauben im Jahrzehnt 1860–1870', *Zeitschrift für Religions- und Geistesgeschichte*, 20 (1968), 113–38. The tastelessly triumphalist *A History of Freethought in the Nineteenth Century* by J. M. Robertson (Rationalist Press Association, 1929) gives information about the heroes of freethought and the German materialists.

5. That construction is a hallmark of idealist epistemologies was stressed by A. C. Ewing in *Idealism: A Critical Survey* (Methuen, 1934).

6. For further information about Lange see Willey, *Back to Kant*, and B. Russell's introductory remarks to the English translation of Lange's *History of Materialism*. P. Gay's *Freud, Jews, and Other Germans: Masters of Victims in Modernist Culture* (Oxford University Press, 1978) and G. L. Mosse, *Germans and Jews* (Orbach & Chambers, 1971), both offer interesting observations about the position of Jewish scholars in academic life and discuss Cohen from this perspective.

7. See M. Heidegger, *On Time and Being* (Harper & Row, 1972), 74 ff. and K. Jaspers, 'Philosophical Autobiography', in P. A. Schlipp (ed.), *The Philosophy of Karl Jaspers* (Library of Living Philosophers, 1957), 30 ff. G. Ramming studies Jaspers's neo-Kantian background in *Karl Jaspers und Heinrich Richert: Existentialismus und Wertphilosophie* (A. Francke Verlag, 1948).

8. See H. Barth, *Descartes Begründung der Erkenntnis* (Max Drechsel, 1913), and 'Hermann Cohens Religionsphilosophische Schriften', in the *Blätter für Deutsche Philosophie*, 5 (1931), 110ff.; and P. Guertler's study *Der philosophische Weg Heinrich Barths* (Schwabe, 1976).

9. For reminiscences about philosophy at this time see H. Arendt, 'Martin Heidegger at Eighty', in the *New York Review of Books* (Oct. 1971) and H.-G. Gadamer's two essays, 'The Philosophical Foundations of the Twentieth Century' and 'The Phenomenological Movement', in *Philosophical Hermeneutics* (University of California Press, 1976).

10. These changes in Natorp's thought were to have some impact on the later 'dialectical theologians', particularly upon the two Barths and Gogarten. See especially 'Logos, Psyche, Eros' published as an appendix to the second edition of P. Natorp's *Platons Ideenlehre* (Felix Meiner, 1920); H. Barth, *Das Problem des Ursprungs in der Platonischen Philosophie* (Kaiser, 1921), and his lecture 'Gotteserkenntnis', in J. Moltmann (ed.), *Die Anfänge der dialektischen Theologie* (Kaiser, 1963), i. For Gogarten and Natorp see P. Natorp's *Philosophische Systematik* (Felix Meiner, 1958). According to Busch, Karl Barth visited Natorp when he returned to Marburg in Feb. 1922 and presented him with a copy of the second edition of the Romans commentary (E. Busch, *Karl Barth* (SCM, 1976), 136).

11. *Protestant Thought in the Nineteenth Century: 1799–1870* (Yale University Press, 1972), 3.

12. The endless debates about Ritschl's philosophical background if anything confirm the opinion of J. Richmond who quite correctly says that Ritschl was no systematic philosopher and that his philosophical views lack coherence; see *Ritschl: A Reappraisal* (Collins, 1978). Ritschl's approach was eclectic. He adopted existing philosophies and epistemological theories only in so far as they suited his theological purposes. Although many scholars, such as O. Pfleiderer in *Philosophy of Religion on the Basis of its History* (Williams & Norgate, 1887), i, classify Ritschl as being a neo-Kantian theologian, this is misleading.

13. Ritschl's critique of metaphysics is most fully worked out in his *Theologie und Metaphysik* of 1881. His emphasis upon the differences between nature and spirit is reflected in his famous theory of value judgements, in which there develops an epistemological distinction between theoretical and religious knowledge. The mind deals with given impressions in one of two ways. By focusing upon them as objectively given, it seeks to connect them according to definite laws

as a system of nature. This form of theoretical knowledge is very different from religious knowledge which 'moves in the sphere of independent judgements of value', when the mind judges impressions according to their value for the 'spiritual' subject. One of the best exegeses of Ritschl's value judgements is still Principal Orr's *The Ritschlian Theology and the Evangelical Faith* (Hodder & Stoughton, 1898). Though Ritschl's epistemology helped to neutralize a collision between religion and natural science, it had less wholesome effects in the years following his death. As the century progressed, and as Herrmann adapted this theory in response to Marburg neo-Kantianism, Ritschl's distinction developed into an epistemological dualism which was to have great influence on Barth and Bultmann.

14. See further R. Morgan's excellent essay in Troeltsch's *Writings*, 12 ff.

15. *Geschichte des Materialismus und Kritik seiner Bedeutung in der Gegenwart*, 3rd edn. (Bädeker, 1876), ii. 63.

16. 'Die Prinzipien der Mechanik', in *Sammelte Werke* (J. A. Barth, 1894), iii. 1–2.

17. Quoted in F. Kaufmann's essay 'Cassirer's Theory of Scientific Knowledge', in P. A. Schlipp (ed.), *The Philosophy of Ernst Cassirer* (Library of Living Philosophers, 1949), 206–7.

18. Later neo-Kantians and historians often refer to Lange and the earliest figures of the Kant revival as adopting a 'psycho-physical method' in contrast to the later 'transcendental method' of Cohen and his followers. Cohen's own critical appreciation of Hertz and Lange is to be found in his 'Einleitung mit kritschem Nachtrag' to Lange's *History* which is published in H. J. Sankuehler and R. de la Vega (eds.), *Marxismus und Ethik: Texte zum neukantischen Sozialismus* (Suhrkamp, 1974), and in Cohen's *Werke V*.

19. Quoted in J. C. Flugel, *A Hundred Years of Psychology*, 2nd end. (Duckworth, 1959), 99. For further discussions of A. Fechner's philosophy and psychology see Pfleiderer, *Philosophy of Religion*; F. Ueberweg, *A History of Philosophy* (Hodder & Stoughton, 1872), ii. 321 f.; W. Windelband, *A History of Philosophy* (Macmillan, 1901), 644 ff.

20. Cohen and Natorp quoted in L. W. Beck, 'Neo Kantianism', in *The Encyclopedia of Philosophy* (Macmillan and the Free Press, 1967), v. 470.

21. Since H. L. Ollig's fine monograph, *Religion und Freiheitsglaube: Zur Problematik von Hermann Cohens später Religionsphilosophie* (Forum Akademicum, 1979), gives a good Cohen bibliography that requires only a minimal amount of supplementation to bring it up to date;

for the benefit of English readers these bibliographical notes are confined to some of the principal works about Cohen which have appeared in their own language: J. B. Agus, 'Hermann Cohen', in *Modern Philosophies of Judaism* (Berham House, 1941); A. Altmann, 'Theology in Twentieth Century German Jewry', *Yearbook*, 1, of the Leo Baeck Institute (East & West Library, 1956); S. H. Bergman, 'Hermann Cohen: The Religion of Reason from the Sources of Judaism', in A. Jospe (ed.), *Faith and Reason: An Introduction to Modern Jewish Thought* (Schocken, 1963): —— 'Herman Cohen', in A. Altmann (ed.), *Between East and West: Essays Dedicated to the Memory of Bela Horovitz* (East & West Library, 1958); E. Fackenheim, *Hermann Cohen—After Fifty Years* (Leo Baeck Institute, 1969); E. Fischoff, 'Hermann Cohen', in S. Novek (ed.), *Great Jewish Thinkers in the Twentieth Century* (B'nai B'rith, 1963); J. Guttmann, 'Hermann Cohen', in *Philosophies of Judaism* (Routledge & Kegan Paul, 1964); W. Jacob, 'Hermann Cohen on Christianity', in *The Central Conference of American Rabbis Journal*, 68 (Jan. 1970); E. Jospe, 'Introduction' to *Reason and Hope: Selections from the Jewish Writings of Hermann Cohen* (B'nai B'rith, 1971); M. M. Kaplan, *The Purpose and Meaning of Jewish Existence* (Jewish Publication Society, 1964); S. Kaplan, 'Introductory Essay' to Cohen's *Religion of Reason* (Ungar, 1972); H. Liebeschutz, 'Jewish Thought and its German Background' in *Yearbook*, 1, of the Leo Baeck Institute; J. Melber, *Hermann Cohen's Philosophy of Judaism* (Jonathan David, 1968); N. Rotenstreich, 'From the Ethical Idea to the True Being', in *Philosophies of Judaism in Modern Times: From Mendelssohn to Rosenzweig* (Holt, Reinhart & Winston, 1968); S. S. Schwarzschild, 'Franz Rosenzweig's Anecdotes about Hermann Cohen', in H. A. Strauss and K. R. Grossmann (eds.), *Gegenwart in Rückblick* (Lother Stein Verlag, 1970); —— 'The Tenability of Cohen's Construction of the Self', in *Journal of the History of Philosophy*, 13 (1975); —— 'Germanism and Judaism—Hermann Cohen's Normative Paradigm of the German-Jewish Symbiosis', in D. Bronsen (ed.), *Jews and Germans from 1860–1933: The Problematic Symbiosis* (Carl Winter, 1979); —— 'Introduction' to Cohen's *Werke VII* (Olms, 1981); H. Slonimsky, 'Hermann Cohen' in *Essays* (Hebrew Union College Press, 1968); L. Strauss, 'Introductory Essay' to Cohen's *Religion of Reason*; U. Tal, *Christians and Jews in Germany* (Cornell University Press, 1975); T. Weiss-Rosmarin, *Religion of Reason: Hermann Cohen's System of Religious Philosophy* (Bloch Publishing Co., 1936).

22. For Cohen's account of the controversy see 'Zur Kontroversie zwischen Trendelenburg und Kuno Fischer', *Zeitschrift für Völkerpsychologie und Sprachwissenschaft*, 7 (1871), 249–71.

23. Cohen's religious articles were collected in 3 volumes and published as *Jüdische Schriften* after his death with an appreciation by F. Rosenzweig (Academie für die Wissenschaft des Judentums, 1924).
24. As well as Rosenzweig's essay referred to above, see also M. Buber's 'The History of the Dialogical Principle', in *Between Man and Man*, 8th imp. (Macmillan, 1972), which pays tribute to Cohen's contribution to the development of the dialogical principle.
25. 'Cassirer, Neo-Kantianism, and Phenomenology', in Schlipp (ed.), *Ernst Cassirer*, 812.
26. *LRE*, 15 ff., 188, 588.
27. Ibid. 47.
28. For Leibniz's doctrine of concepts, judgement, and inference see G. Martin, *Leibniz: Logic and Metaphysics* (Manchester University Press, 1964), and E. Cassirer's *Leibniz' System in seinen wissenschaftlichen Grundlagen* (N. G. Elwertsche Verlagsbuchhandlung, 1902).
29. *KDRV*, A6 ff./B10 ff.
30. Ibid. B14–18.
31. Ibid. B, xvi.
32. *LRE*, 60 ff.
33. These judgements are classified as follows:

1. Judgements of the law of thought (*Denkgesetz*)	2. Mathematical Judgements
(a) Origin	(a) Reality
(b) Identity	(b) Plurality
(c) Contradiction	(c) Totality
3. Judgements of Mathematical Natural Science	4. Methodical Judgements
(a) Substance	(a) Possibility
(b) Law	(b) Actuality
(c) Concept	(c) Necessity

34. *LRE*, 52.
35. I. G. Barbour, *Myths, Models and Paradigms* (SCM, 1974), 30.
36. Translated as *Substance and Function* (Open Court, 1923).
37. The phrases 'being is a function of thinking', 'monism of experience', and 'methodological monism' hail from Natorp; see *PPP*, 39, 161.
38. Barbour, *Myths, Models and Paradigms*, 33.
39. Nagel, quoted in ibid. 41.
40. *KDRV*, A832/B860; 'By architectonic I understand the art of constructing systems. As systematic unity is what first raises ordinary knowledge to the rank of science, that is, makes a system

out of a mere aggregate of knowledge, architectonic is the doctrine of scientific knowledge.'

41. In the following pages logic, when not referring specifically to Marburg *Logik*, is used to mean ideal forms of thought, epistemology, a theory of how we come to know, and ontology, an account of the nature of known objects.

42. For Husserl's intentional consciousness see M. Natonson, *Edmund Husserl: Philosopher of Infinite Tasks* (Northwestern University Press, 1973).

43. P. Tillich, *Perspectives on Nineteenth and Twentieth Century Protestant Theology* (SCM, 1967), 215 ff.

44. Following T. K. Oesterreich (ed.), *Die deutsche Philosophie des 19 Jahrhunderts*, in *Überwegs Grundriss der Geschichte der Philosphie* (Schwabe, 1951), iv. 436.

45. *KDRV*, A51/B75.

46. For Cohen's understanding of reality see pp. 51 ff.

47. See further A. Jospe, *Die Unterscheidung von Mythus und Religion bei Hermann Cohen und Ernst Cassirer* (Diss., Breslau, 1932).

48. Quoted in Oesterreich, *Die deutsche Philosophie*, 436.

49. Quoted in P. Schulthess's introduction to *Das Prinzip* in Cohen's *Werke V* (Olms, 1984), 37.

50. Though condemned by the mathematician A. A. Robinson as 'deservedly unknown' in his *Selected Papers: Non Standard Analysis and Philosophy* (Yale, 1979), ii. 560, one English philosopher who commented upon the book was Bertrand Russell. He found the historical part of the work 'admirable', but its constructive theory vitiated 'by an undue mysticism'; *The Principles of Mathematics*, 2nd edn. (George Allen & Unwin, 1937), 326. Russell, it should be noted, was one of the few English philosophers familiar with the work of the Marburg School. He certain read Lange's History and Cohen's *Das Prinzip*, but, perhaps finding both wanting, he seems to have had little interest in later writings of the Marburg School.

51. A. N. Whitehead, *Introduction to Mathematics*, 2nd reprint (Williams & Norgate, 1924), 226–7.

52. It is thus a little perverse to defend Cohen's procedure here on the grounds that he offered an 'anti-fictive' account of number as certain of Cohen's supporters do.

53. F. Copleston, *A History of Philosophy* (Image Books, 1964), vi/2. 51.

54. *KDRV*, A166.

55. *Das Prinzip*, 27–9. For Cohen's interpretation of the 'Anticipations' see E. Cassirer, 'Hermann Cohen und die Erneuerung der Kantischen Philosophie', *Kantstudien*, 17 (1912), 260 ff. For reality and number see Russell's *Principles*, 342 ff., and V. Zeman,

'Leibniz's Influence on the Marburg School, in particular on Hermann Cohen's Concept of Reality and of the "Infinitesimal-Methode"', in *Studia Leibnitiana Supplementa*, 21 (Franz Steiner Verlag, 1980), iii.

56. Quoted by Schulthess, 'Introduction', 41.
57. Cohen quoted by Holzhey in his introduction to the *LRE*, *Werke VI* (Olms, 1977), p. xiii.
58. Busch, *Karl Barth*, 44; B. Pasternak, *Safe Conduct* (Elek Books, 1959), 191–3; Ortega y Gasset, 'Meditación del Escorial' and 'Prólogo para alemanes', in *Obras completas*, ii; viii. The case of Pasternak shows that Lenin's worries about neo-Kantianism were justified, for Cohen had a following in Russia especially amongst the Jewish intelligentsia and was much acclaimed when he visited there in 1914.
59. *LRE*, 29.
60. Ibid. 81.
61. Ibid. 59.
62. Ibid.
63. Ibid. 13.
64. E. Cassirer, 'Hermann Cohen 1848–1918', *Social Research*, 10 (1943), 226.
65. *LRE*, 83. The given, now reformulated, refers not to data supplied through sensuous intuition, but to the generated principles of thought.
66. Ibid. 84 ff.
67. *LRE*, 123. In order to understand the mathematical metaphor informing this passage, it should be noted that the word translated as 'cycle' (*Periode*) when used mathematically means 'repetend' (that part of a repeating decimal which keeps recurring). In Cohen's philosophy the word *Bewegung* has at least 3 meanings: motion, as postulated by laws of motion; the process of solving a mathematical problem; and thinking, as that logical movement of thought which unfolds knowledge and being.
68. See *KDRV*, b71–2, and *KU*, §77 and §78. For further exegesis see E. Cassirer's *Kant's Life and Thought* (Yale University Press, 1981), 349 ff. and M. Heidegger's *Kant and the Problems of Metaphysics* (Indiana University Press, 1962), 29 ff.
69. *LRE*, 36.
70. Ibid. 33. *Bewegung* has here the various meanings noted above.
71. A. Görland, 'Hermann Cohens systematische Arbeit im Dienste des kritschen Idealismus', *Kantstudien*, 17 (1912), 231.
72. W. Kinkel, 'Das Urteil des Ursprungs', *Kantstudien*, 17 (1912), 280–1.

73. *LRE*, 82.
74. *KDRV*, A126.
75. *KBE*, 20.
76. See pp. 37 ff.
77. *KBE*, 21.
78. Ibid., 23.
79. *LRE*, 318. In this passage Cohen, typically mingling his own philosophy with that of his predecessors, presents his interpretation of the object in the thought of the Enlightenment which he proceeds to develop. The word translated 'distortions' (*das Werfen*) is an obvious German word-play upon the Latin *objectare–objectum*.
80. Ibid.
81. W. H. Werkmeister, 'Cassirer's Advance beyond Neo-Kantianism', in Schlipp (ed.), *Ernst Cassirer*, 765.
82. For the influence of Marburg epistemology on Bultmann see the excellent study by R. A. Johnson, *The Origins of Demythologizing: Philosophy and Historiography in the Theology of Rudolf Bultmann* (E. J. Brill, 1974).
83. *LRE*, 69.
84. Ibid. 59–60.
85. Ernst Cassirer, *The Philosophy of Symbolic Forms*, 10th imp. (Yale University Press, 1973), i. 104–5.
86. *LRE*, 424.
87. Ibid. 423.
88. Ibid. 426.
89. *KDRV*, A219/B266.
90. Ibid. A219/B266–7.
91. Ibid. A223/B270.
92. Cohen thus effectively confounds the Kantian distinction between analytic and synthetic judgements.
93. *LRE*, 420.
94. Ibid. 426.
95. *Religion II*, 47.
96. *LRE*, 428.
97. Ibid. 428–9.
98. Werkmeister, 'Cassirer's Advance beyond Neo-Kantianism', 763.
99. *KBE*, 21.
100. *Das Prinzip*, 14.
101. Ibid. 128.
102. See pp. 37 ff.
103. *LRE*, 128.
104. Ibid. 125. By 'finite' Cohen means definite objects.

105. Ibid. 126ff.
106. Ibid. 126, 128.
107. Cassirer, *Leibniz' System*, 201.
108. *KDRV*, A218/B266.
109. *LRE*, 592.
110. i.e. between cognition (*Denken*) and ontology (*Sein*).
111. *LRE*, 491.
112. Ibid. 493.
113. *Metaphysics* ii. 1003ª2; xi. 1071ᵇ13.
114. See Cohen's introduction to Lange's *History of Materialism*, in *Werke V*.
115. For the use of this term with references to philosophies of Idealism see G. Sauter, *Theologie als Wissenschaft* (Kaiser, 1971), 24 ff.
116. See 'The Significance of the Historical Existence of Jesus for Faith', in *Writings*, 182ff.
117. 'Die Philosophische Bedeutung Karl Natorps', in P. Natorp's *Philosophische Systematik* (Felix Meiner, 1958), p. xiii.
118. *PPP*, 151.
119. Ibid.
120. Ibid. 153.
121. *Psychologie*, 241f.
122. Ibid. 99.
123. Ibid. 30.
124. Ibid. 29.
125. *LRE*, 347–8.
126. Ibid. 410–11. Compare Philo, *De Sacrificiis Abelis et Caini*, xviii, 65, 'God spake and it was done—no interval between the two—or it might be a truer view to suggest that His Word was deed'; *De Vita Mosis*, i. li, 283, 'He will utter nothing at all which shall not certainly be performed, for His Word is His deed'; and *De Decalogo*, xi, 47, 'Whatever God says is not words but deeds.'
127. Quoted in Johnson, *The Origins of Demythologizing*, 48. Natorp's favourite quotation, 'Im Anfang war die Tat', was particularly provocative to people like Kutter who knew the original biblical quotation 'Im Anfang war das Wort'.
128. *Romans II*, 315–16.

2

THE PLACE OF RELIGION

It may seem strange that a philosophical school, concerned primarily with the philosophy of natural science, should turn its attention to religion.[1] The increasing involvement of Marburg philosophy with religion was due to a combination of several factors, the first of which was the personalities of its leading figures. Cohen was a liberal, yet devout Jew, who believed that the religion and piety of his forefathers possessed great moral significance for humanity. Nurtured in a deeply religious environment, Cohen's formative experience was completely different from that of Natorp. He, by contrast, espoused a very liberal Protestantism with mystical overtones. Though never friendly towards dogmatic theology and churchy piety, Natorp was instinctively drawn to the affective aspects of religious experience where he expected to find 'rest in the eternal'.[2] This interest, coupled with subtle changes in his philosophical stance, prompted a radical revision of his earlier philosophical views at the very end of his career.

A second factor was the architectonic nature of the Marburg System which, as a 'meta-science', had to concern itself with the totality of human culture and therefore had to adjudicate every claim to knowledge. Religion, being a cultural and historical fact, could not for one moment escape the systematic cognitive web being woven by Cohen and his colleagues. An additional factor encouraging involvement with religion was the problem which Marburg philosophy had with the *Ich*. Both Cohen and Natorp became aware that the formal epistemological subject of their *Logik*, *Ethik*, and *Ästhetik*, somehow failed to do justice to the experience of self-awareness. Since the *Individuum* could manifestly not be constituted through the three unending cognitive *Richtungen* alone, there arose a quest for some unity, some principles of individuation, to account for *Selbsterlebnis*. Natorp turned to religious feeling, Cohen to the religion of Judaism.

The increasing involvement of theologians in contemporary philosophical debates more than anything else encouraged Marburg philosophy to clarify its position on religion. Ritschl, of course, encouraged his followers to believe that an essential prerequisite to any systematic theology was a sound epistemological basis, which would not confound the distinction between *Natur* and *Geist* nor embrace a mysticism that boasted immediate knowledge of the divine.[3] Ritschl himself drew upon the epistemologies of Kant and Lotzte, combining them in a somewhat eclectic manner with his own theological insights gained from studies of Luther and Melanchthon.[4] In Wilhelm Herrmann, who taught at Marburg from 1879 until 1917, Ritschl had an able successor. Herrmann was determined to furnish theology with a sound epistemological foundation by augmenting Ritschl's work and by drawing upon the epistemology of Marburg neo-Kantianism. Thus when Cohen and Natorp turned their attention to religion there was already a considerable body of theological literature which addressed the relations between theology and philosophy. Luther, Ritschl, Schleiermacher, Herrmann, and Troeltsch, to name but a few, quickly fell under the critical scrutiny of Natorp and Cohen.

Once it was decided that there were three, and only three, valid spheres of knowledge (logico-scientific, ethical, and aesthetic), there arose the problem as to which of these, if any, religion belonged. This chapter describes the various solutions to the inevitable problem of what place religion could have within the Marburg System. The first, and perhaps most straightforward, answer was offered by Cohen, whose earliest writings on *Religionsphilosophie* reduced religion to ethics, and then, later, sought to reserve a place for the special character of religion (*Eigenart*) within the system. In his last writing on religion a more subtle approach was adopted that advocated a religion of reason, with revelation becoming a revelation of reason. Natorp's solution was quite sophisticated. Rather than reducing religion to either ethics or aesthetics, he embraced a theory of feeling in which *Gefühl* was the hidden psychic dynamo of all cognitive striving and the inaccessible source of everything that makes personal experience authentically human. The following chapter will consider another approach to this problem which was advocated by Herrmann. He, like Cohen, insisted upon an intimate relation between religion and ethics, but additionally maintained that religion was an independent, authentic, and morally necessary dimension of life, which could not simply be reduced to ethics, or to any other cognitive *Richtung*, without leaving a remainder. Faced with much philosophical criticism, Herrmann did not dispute the right of Marburg philosophers to develop a universal system of knowledge, but fighting resolutely for the integrity and irreducibility of religion, he insisted that reason had limits. Once *Wissenschaft* respected its own proper limits and perceived its inability to address fundamental problems of human life without religion, Herrmann found a place for religion as a personal experience of revelation and redemption.

I. RELIGION WITHIN THE LIMITS OF HUMANITY

Although Natorp wrote a short critical review of Herrmann's *Die Religion im Verhältniss zum Welterkennen und zur Sittlichkeit* in 1881, his *Religion innerhalb der Grenzen der Humanität* (1894) dealt systematically with *Religionsphilosophie* in its attempt to fit religion into the Marburg account of cognition and culture without creating asymmetries. Its title, an obvious parody of Kant's *Die Religion innerhalb der Grenzen der blossen Vernunft*, immediately betrays an approach which Rudolf Otto thought wrong-headed from the outset: 'this proceeding of constructing a "humanity" prior to and apart from the most central and potent capacities is like nothing so much as the attempt to frame a standard idea of the human body after previously cutting off the head.'[5]

Natorp's understanding of humanity is outlined at the beginning of his work where the *Begriff der Humanität* represents

the full vigour of what is human in mankind. Human culture I understand not as the one-sided development of the intellectual, moral, or aesthetic capacity, nor yet as the merely physical energies of work and pleasure. It is rather the unfolding of all these aspects of human nature in their healthy, normal, and correct relation to each other.[6]

Importantly, and following the socialist tradition inaugurated by Lange, Natorp insisted that an authentically human life is to be had only in so far as the individual participates fully in the cultural tradition of a moral *Gemeinschaft*, for life would merely be a repetitive series of physical and biological rhythms without community. To this extent even religion, if it is to represent anything of worth, needs to be seen as a communal factor which, as his French contemporary Durkheim was busy showing, invades, inspires, and invigorates the entire system of cultural values in any society.[7] Those who believe that 'religion stands in no necessary internal relation with humanity' but may, at most, 'exist alongside humanity' patently misrepresent religion. Such falsifiers of religion were first of all Marxist theoreticians who proclaimed religion to be a purely private affair, devoid of any significance for life in society. On the other hand, certain supporters of religion made the same fatal error by emphasizing the supernatural, other-worldly, aspects of religion. These, with their conviction that mankind has tasks of a 'higher order' which transcend the mundane workaday world and its human occupants, who seek to relate humanity to a supra-sensible divine order, likewise turn religion into something totally a-social.

Religion is thus for Natorp a factor immanent in human culture and not some *Privatsache* relating the individual to some heavenly culture:

... the humane, the moral, stands at the centre of religion. Without being identical with morality, religion grows directly from the kernel of moral consciousness and preserves a connection with it in each of its phases. Religion acquires for itself here a human, indeed a super-human character, becoming so much of a communal entity that the name 'God' is almost the only suitable expression for this, the highest pinnacle of human consciousness, from which alone a unity evolves for the human race.[8]

A religion such as this does indeed stand in a necessary, internal, and systematic connection with the ideal concept of humanity. Far from relating to extra-terrestrial transactions between *Diesseits* and *Jenseits*, it is an inner-worldly force animating culture and stimulating *Bildung*. Such social religion marked not only the writings of Kant, but also, according to Natorp, the 'pure monotheism' of second Isaiah, where faith in God is faith in the unconditional reality and invincible efficacy of the moral ideal. The sublime moral law, the humane ideal for society, and the quest for enduring values do not, however, exhaust the depths of religion, which finds its strength in human consciousness. Natorp believed Schleiermacher had portrayed this *Grund* of religion more adequately than anyone else.

In appropriating Schleiermacher's philosophy of affectiveness,

Natorp perceived that asymmetries would arise in his system were *Gefühl* given a positive cognitive status alongside logic, ethics, and aesthetics. He consequently denied that religion was a *selbständig* region of cognition, possessing a special *Richtung* of consciousness from which it could generate objects and valid knowledge. Instead Natorp regarded religious feeling as a fundamental attribute of human consciousness *an sich* signifying 'the complete *inwardness* of the soul's life, the authentic self-being of the soul. Knowledge, will, and aesthetic sentiment are only *external expressions* in comparison with it. Feeling envelops or, as it were, embraces them all in itself as their ultimate root.'[9] This remarkable passage shamelessly distinguishes between the cognitive functions of the Marburg *Kulturbewusstsein* and feeling. They are merely *Äusserungen* of an inner, almost private, experience called *Innerlichkeit*. The objective world, generated by the process of objectifying laws, is invariably presented as a form of reality that is alien, external, and impersonal, whenever Natorp compares it to the immediacy of *Gefühl*.[10] Though never completely severed from those cognitive dimensions of culture which it engenders, feeling takes pre-eminent place in the inner life of the mind according to Natorp's philosophy.

Gefühl, this inner side of consciousness, being the modality in which consciousness is present to itself, is immediately aware of its powers, capacities, and energies. It is the *Untergrund* of all psychic life, 'a limitless and formless stirring and moving, which precedes all formation of objects and is at their foundation. In consciousness the object is something firm and fixed, but in feeling nothing is firm and fixed; all is in the flux of becoming, all is united in an uninterrupted continuum.'[11] It is obvious here that Natorp is attempting to combine two fundamentally contrary conceptions of *Bewusstsein*: one of which is an abstract epistemological category and another which refers to a subject's active awareness of meaningful and vivid experience. In his writings on *Religionsphilosophie* the latter gains explicit priority over the former as its objectless, non-cognitive, but fecund *Grund*. These two characteristics of feeling—its non-cognitive intuitive aspect and its role as the foundational energy of *Kulturbewusstsein*—encouraged Natorp to disagree most strongly with certain misleading emphases he detected in Schleiermacher's concept of *Gefühl*. In the first place he was keen to stress that feeling was something dynamic, active, or spontaneous, and could not therefore call it a receptive *Zustand* (using Schleiermacher's own word) in which one is patient, rather than agent, in awareness of an Other. Secondly, because Natorp was adamant that feeling was not a *Richtung* of knowledge, but a potent power accompanying all forms of mental life, he denied it could have an object as its goal. The first implied that feeling could never be a feeling of being dependent, the second that it had no transitive reference, whether to something natural or divine.[12]

It therefore seemed highly illogical to suggest that the infinite could be known. *Unendlichkeit*, even in Natorp's earliest writing on *Religionsphilosophie*, is no genuine object of cognition, but only an infinite striving for knowledge, a sort of passionate yearning at the heart of things.[13] Furthermore when religion posits the infinite as an object of cognitive knowledge, Natorp warned that it threatened the ever-advancing *Entfaltung* of reality by displaying 'an objectional tendency to falsify the true knowledge of science'.[14] It even obstructs moral endeavour because 'it is patently impossible to act uprightly towards the Infinite, but only in relation to the finite, since none other than finite powers are available to moral volition'.[15] To prevent such antagonism, Natorp preferred to speak, not of a feeling of the Infinite, but of *die Unendlichkeit des Gefühls*. Although it is the foundation of consciousness and expresses consciousness's own awareness of its magnitude, powers, and potentialities, feeling was not here made into some alien, external *Gegenstand* of knowledge.

Natorp, being eager to retain what he felt to be the humane significance of religion, could offer it philosophical accommodation only inasmuch as it remained 'within the limits of humanity' or, that is, within the limits of his system. The price religion had to pay for this haven was a renunciation of its claims to enjoy knowledge of the divine. From the perspective of Marburg philosophy therefore, 'religion, or what previously covered this term, is only to be retained in so far as it remains enclosed *within the limits of humanity*'.[16] Just as Natorp affirmed the possibility of psychology without a soul, so now he advocated a religion without God. What then remains of such traditional religious 'objects' as God, providence, or grace in this form of religion? Natorp was uncompromising in his response: 'what was believed to be immediate reality is *either filtered into a pure idea or reduced to a mere symbol*'.[17] Religion, not only on account of philosophical considerations, but even for its own good, should be 'purified' of anything that might be termed objective. Only this will pave the way to realizing the ideal concept of humanity:

Dogma as such is abandoned in order to make room for a pure conception of the moral ideal—a concept which, in the strictest and most satisfying sense, fulfills the deepest requirement of truth. On the other hand the religious portrayal of reality remains, though only as representation [*Vorstellung*], retaining its naïve symbolic power.[18]

This understanding of religion, said Natorp, originated with the great enlighteners of humanity such as Kant and Lessing; he claimed it was now time to put it into practice! Far from devaluing religion, Natorp was convinced that his plea for a pure spirituality would in fact satisfy the most profound religious aspirations of mankind as well as uncompromisingly promote intellectual integrity in any worthwhile philosophical quest for truth. It was furthermore alleged to offer a more adequate account of that inner core experience which is the hallmark of authentic human existence than anything encountered in doctrinal religion.

Psychologically, *Gefühl*, having no existence independent of the entirety of psychic life, opposes all particularity and separation, since it is concerned with, 'the totality, the originary concretion of immediate experience'.[19] As the *Urleben* of the soul, 'religion takes into account all sides of human spiritual life . . . it also sets in motion the powers of thought and volition'.[20] Religious feeling can thus express itself through imaginative fancy, seemingly logical concepts, as well as in moral effort. These dynamic expressions of feeling, unlike truly valid *Gesetzerkenntnis*, possess no cognitive value. They witness, albeit with varying degrees of eloquence, to something deeply human and moving which, ironically, is epistemologically weak in comparison to the *gesetzlich* objectifications of science, art, and ethics; though these very cognitive powers of *Denken*, *Wollen*, and *Fühlen* owe their potency, dynamism, and infinite potentiality for development to the inexhaustible energies of *Gefühl*.[21]

This brief presentation of Natorp's *Religionsphilosophie* should be sufficient to show how his philosophical critique of religion resulted not in an abstract deism, but in a religious humanism which binds the totality of human culture into a unity. The creative force of religious sentiment therefore informs and directs all striving in science, ethics, and art. A more critical Barth only presented one side of this theory when he said that for Natorp religion was nothing more than an objectless emotion which accompanies moral effort.[22]

Natorp, like many fellow philosophers and theologians, was anxious to affirm the formative influence of religion upon culture. Perhaps the closest parallel to his theory of religion is to be found in the writings of the young Paul Tillich. Tillich was equally concerned with the problem of how religion related to the three primordial branches of cognition. Like Natorp he chose not to reduce religion to any one particular *Richtung*, but preferred to see it as an animating force in every dimension of cognition, a religious potency, which 'is actualized in all spheres of spiritual or cultural life'.[23] Whatever is true, good, and beautiful in culture thus arises from and depends upon religious resources. An unforeseen consequence of *Religionsphilosophien* like these, however, was that when faith in cultural supremacy and moral development is shaken, such as occurred in Germany after 1918, the theories of religion expressing and confirming such beliefs become severely attenuated.

It is impossible to ignore the extreme scepticism concerning the cognitive value of religion in Natorp's philosophy. His strange amalgam of prescription and description resulted in a religion without a God and a pure spirituality purged of any *Transzendenz-ansprüche*. Systems such as that of Natorp, in which everything develops logically from a seamless immutable nexus of posited laws, could have no room for an interventionist understanding of divine activity nor for doctrines of providence. Such scepticism, which of course was nothing new to the nineteenth century, though attractive to certain mentalities, seemed fundamentally incompatible with any religious response to reality; yet Natorp, like Durkheim, claimed that religion had a certain inevitability about it, however weak its cognitive claims for modern man.

Yet one more theme in Natorp's account of religion was also shared by contemporaries and that is its emphasis upon affective and dispositional aspects of religion. Natorp was of course writing before the vocabulary of existentialism became available to German philosophers, but it is not difficult to see how easy it was for many of his students to embrace this later conceptuality. About the same time as the Marburg School was devoting its energies to religion, contemporary *Lebensphilosophie* sought to maintain the integrity and irreducibility of *Stimmungen* and *Erlebnisse* which supposedly supplied the individual of culture with a certain uniqueness, value, and human authenticity. It was perhaps no accident that Kierkegaard's writings began to make their German debut about this time.[24]

Before leaving Natorp's *Religionsphilosophie* it is essential to note one aspect which was to have profound significance for theology and philosophy after 1918. Although he adopted and modified Schleiermacher's theory of feeling in a typically Natorpian manner, he also absorbed something from it that introduced a major asymmetry into his critical idealism. Schleiermacher, influenced by Romanticism and *Naturphilosophie*, suggested that theoretical thought destroys, shatters, and irredeemably disintegrates an original perception. This is clearly encountered in the first edition of the *Reden* whenever the word *Reflexion* appears.[25] That such a dedicated pan-logicist as Natorp should adopt this separation of pre-theoretical experience from theoretical thought and, in one special case (religious feeling), magnify the former to the detriment of the latter, is quite remarkable. Nobody reading Natorp's work carefully can fail to ignore the asymmetrical relation that obtains between feeling which, paradoxically, is immediately experienced but incapable of objectification, and knowledge of being, which is generated *gesetzlich* by cognitive thought. Consequently the iron law of Marburg monism, the identity between *Denken* and *Sein*, was irreparably fractured. It is perhaps not surprising that by 1920 Natorp was no longer speaking of 'religion within the limits of humanity', but of 'religion *in* the limit of mankind'.[26]

II. THE ETHICAL IDEAL AND THE GOD OF ABRAHAM

According to the *Genesis Rabbah*, when God decided to create the world, it was to the law (*Torah*) that he first turned. Indeed, 'the world and the fullness thereof were created only for the sake of the Torah'.[27] Though the last chapter, which presented Cohen's logic, epistemology, and ontology, might easily lead one to suppose that this formal and rational system had nothing to do with religion, it is important to understand how even Cohen's most intricate and formal piece of methodology was not unrelated to his religious beliefs. His devotion to the law, for example, was far more than reverence to the 'facts of science' or loyalty to Kantian criticism, it grew from his faith. The ancient belief about the pre-existence of the Torah, for example, parallels Cohen's appreciation of the ideality and the apriority of cognitive and moral structures. His enthusiasm for the purity of thought, moreover, is almost levitical; as though purging thought and will from contamination with 'heterogeneous elements' was one way of fulfilling Israel's eternal call to sanctification. His entire system, and not only his writings on *Religionsphilosophie*, confirms Troeltsch's judgement about Cohen being a modern Philo. Throughout his life he remained existentially committed to the devotion of Judaism. Speaking of his faith Rosenzweig said, 'Cohen was basically a straightforward person. He was a pious man' and believed such piety lay at the heart of everything Cohen stood for.[28] Indeed Cohen seems to have become increasingly involved with the philosophy of religion as he neared retirement and thus failed to complete his system with the promised volume of psychology.[29] Yet being committed passionately to reason, as well as to the piety of his fathers, Cohen's understanding of the relations between religion and philosophy was far from simple. Barth once suggested that were philosophers really to understand what dogmaticians say, they would perceive that the end of philosophy was at hand; Cohen took the opposite view.[30] True religion, he said, is based upon the truth of systematic philosophy, religion must become thoroughly rational, and, consequently, 'Ein ehemaliger Theologe ist immer ein Philosoph.'[31]

Cohen faced problems similar to those encountered by Natorp when accommodating the concept of God or, in his own terminology, *die Gottesidee*, to his system. The 'idea of God' could 'enter' philosophy only as long as it remained within the limits prescribed by Marburg logic, ontology, and epistemology. Like Natorp, Cohen refused to allow religion and its God any *Selbständkigkeit*. Religion represented no independent sphere of reality or cognition and its truth claims were dependent upon those of ethics.[32] This conviction is particularly evident in Cohen's *Ethik* which, like his *Logik*, was no mere restatement of Kant's moral philosophy. The second part of his system, *Die Ethik des reinen Willens*, sought to understand will in a manner analogous to the functioning of

Denken in his *Logik*,[33] and postulated another *Richtung* of consciousness which was the province of pure will. Here the 'purity' of will consisted of its being purged from all contamination by psychological pressures, external constraints, and 'sensual hedonism'. Since, however, logical thought is what makes knowledge possible and actual, Cohen argued that the will must be credited with *gesetzmässig* structures similar to those of truly scientific thought. Thus ethics was regarded as a form of scientific knowledge and it was even suggested that as logic grounded the foundations of natural science, so a fully scientific ethics would ground the science of jurisprudence.[34]

Though Cohen argued for methodological correlation between *Denken* and *Willen*, he acknowledged a major difference between them, for each had its own particular concept of reality. If logic is to be regarded as the science of being (*Sein*), ethics, by contrast, must be accounted the science of what should be (*Sollen*). Just as *Denken* generated being, the task of willing was to realize the ideal Good. Importantly, and once again showing his indebtedness to the tradition of neo-Kantian socialism started by Lange, Cohen argued that pure will and ethical action could not exist in a solipsistic vacuum of interiority or moral sentiment. Ethics, being primarily concerned with the just ordering of relations between individuals, communities, and nations, had to subsume these relations under an ideal totality. This ideal ordering of human and communal relations, which Cohen believed to be true socialism, and the progressive realization of the moral good, could be seen in a moral teleology that informed the whole course of history. In his ethics, the community and ideal state are logically prior to smaller social units and individuals. The individual can only achieve moral identity in and through human institutions, communities, and associations.[35]

As well as insisting upon this communal dimension to ethics, Cohen demanded not only freedom, but radical autonomy, for the will. Here is yet another instance of Cohen's departure from the *Critique of Practical Reason* where freedom was a postulate. For Cohen, freedom, like the self, is not posited (*Satz* or *Gesetztes*) as a postulate, but is rather a project (*Vorsatz*) or task. In order to become a truly free moral subject, the will must function without any internal or external constraints and Cohen found there were four characteristics that mark the truly autonomous 'moral self-consciousness': *Selbstgesetzgebung*, *Selbstbestimmung*, *Selbstverant-wortung*, and *Selbsterhaltung*.[36] The first acknowledged that the moral self does not exist before any moral acts and acquires moral character only through acting and willing according to the moral law. The second emphasized self-selection of a particular action and this implied the third, complete responsibility. The fourth was the *conditio sine qua non* of all ethics: the integrity of the self should be preserved in all cultural and social activity. All this conspired to lend a radicality to Cohen's understanding of persons which brought him into conflict with the theologians. Acquiring and maintaining one's humanity is a ceaseless moral struggle. The soul, self, or *das Ich*, is not simply bestowed by God from the outset or created in a religious experience of revelation. It is no more a given datum than is, say, sensation for scientific thought. The self is a moral character which is only gradually acquired through a lifetime of nurture in, and observance of, the moral law. Like the challenges facing scientific thought, it is an *Aufgabe* to be pursued with diligence and earnestness.[37]

The intimate relation between *Zweck* and *Gesetz* in Cohen's ethics meant that the operative character of *Denken* was attributed to the will. Since, however, ethics is the science of what ought and should be, the laws followed by the will have a special relation to the future:

The future is the momentum of the law and self-consciousness is the content of this law. Law here means the moral law and self-consciousness the moral self, which is only *Ich* in so far as it is *Wir*. By relating self-consciousness to the future, the entire course of morality is directed towards the future ... From the perspective of the system of philosophy, therefore, not only the law or norm but morality in general is distinguished methodologically and systematically from the law of nature, and from nature too, through the concept of the future.[38]

The laws of ethics are thus distinguished from the laws of nature by this future emphasis and Cohen laid great stress upon 'the eternity of the ethical process'. What ought to be, such as goodness and justice, has ideal existence, and in willing or doing the ideal order of things becomes progressively real; but like the knowledge of natural science it would never reach an end. It remains an infinite task because the ideal moral order could never be fully incarnate at any one time. In the words of one perceptive critic, 'here, as in other parts of Cohen's system, we plainly see the shift from truth in *reality* to truth in *progress*, from the goal to the pursuit, from victory, to the struggle'.[39]

On purely philosophical grounds Cohen suggested that ethics remained incomplete without the idea of God. This idea, however, was believed to enter the system only upon the completion of ethics; it was not required for the scientific grounding of ethics. Within the entire system Cohen's *Gottesidee* functioned in a variety of ways. First it solved one particular problem, namely the relation between ethics and scientific logic. Since ethics was concerned with *das Sollen* and logic with *Sein*, the architectonic nature of the system demanded that the two be interrelated. At a more mundane level, furthermore, Cohen insisted that moral action cannot remain a contemplation of ethical ideas, but demands realization within the sphere of nature. Since these two dimensions of reality are not static—nature unfolds when thought executes its infinite tasks and morality develops teleologically in history when moral agents apply their wills or actions to the ethical ideal—both require each other for their continuous progress and for the development of culture. It is the idea of God that guarantees there will always be a world for the realization of morality: 'In the idea of the conservation of the world, God therefore becomes the author of its ceaseless actuality. The idea of God means the guarantee that there will always be existence [*Dasein*] for the infinite continuation of morality.' Cohen believed that this function attributed to God was not without scriptural basis, for the covenant between God and humanity in the person of Noah signified that the order of nature would evermore remain the forum in which moral agents could work out their own salvation.[40] Not only did the *Gottesidee* guarantee the constancy of nature, but secondly, from a teleological perspective, its very ideality guaranteed the triumph of the Good: 'The triumph of the Good means securing the Good against all doubts, misgivings, and experience consequent upon the natural and historical incompleteness of human existence.'[41]

This leads to a third role for the idea of God in Cohen's system. Each part, concerned in turn with logic, ethics, and aesthetics, naturally recalls Plato's three ideas, truth, goodness, and beauty, but Cohen suggested that everything he had written in the *Logic of Pure Knowledge* was concerned with validity, not truth. The weighty demands of architectonic, however, required that each part of the system had to be internally related to the others and to ward off any logical or ontological asymmetry between the various parts of the system. Cohen felt, first, that an idea was needed to secure its systematic coherence and, secondly, that this complete systematic coherence could alone be regarded as the criterion of truth. God, then, as truth, was given important methodological functions to perform:

If it is now established that the concept of God achieves the necessary connection between eternity and nature and, consequently, between ethics and logic, the methodological character of the concept of God is thereby proven. . . . This bond between logic and ethics corresponds to the fundamental law of truth. It is in this precisely defined sense that the concept of God becomes the concept of truth.[42]

The *Gottesidee*, functioning as a methodological principle of truth, regulates the principal parts of the system and ensures their ultimate coherence. It binds nature with morality and beauty in a teleological whole because truth is system and the truth of the whole.[43] It might now be understood why Cohen insisted that the idea of God could begin to receive systematic attention only upon the completion of the first two parts of the system. It belongs logically to the completion of ethics, not at the commencement:

Truth alone is the law of the necessary connection of the knowledge of nature with the knowledge of morality. This truth is more than exactness or validity, more even than finality. Truth is the accord of theoretical causality with ethical teleology. This accord of both kinds of lawfulness had been from old the philosopher's stone. . . . Through this concept of truth we mark out the concept of God. God means that peculiar lawfulness which demands, as well as brings to completion, the harmony between the two kinds of knowledge. . . . Truth is God's being [*Wesen*].[44]

The idea of God performs one final role in Cohen's religious and moral writings, it acts as a pattern for moral action: 'God does not mean the power from which mankind can create its morality, but solely the paragon or pattern according to which it has to organize its actions.'[45] Max Scheler argued against Cohen that it is difficult to understand how the idea of God could serve as a pattern for finite moral action. Cohen could nevertheless reply that if the being of God is the moral law, then that indeed is the *Urbild* and *Vorbild* of all morality. Moreover it must be said that here too he was influenced by traditional Jewish thought. Whenever God appears to perform apparently lowly actions, Philo, the Rabbis, and later writers of religious philosophy, suggest that he was teaching humanity lessons. When, for example, God provided clothes for the primal couple, he was teaching both modesty and the skill of tailoring.[46]

Having indicated the leading positive offices performed by the idea of God, it is as important to note some of the qualities which were denied this ideal, logical God. First Cohen insisted that personality could not be attributed to God, because in the system God is an idea having only ideal reality. To predicate personality to such an idea involved not only anthropomorphism, but an unpardonable lapse into mythology. Scientific ethics could have nothing to do with myth which was a pre-scientific form of cognition.[47] Cohen's methodological monism, secondly, led to difficulties about the nature of divine existence. His earliest writings on *Religionsphilosophie* invariably refer to God as *die Gottesidee* so presumably it would enjoy the same mode of ideal existence afforded to other ideas and principles. In order to emphasize that God is an idea representing methodological truth, it was denied that existence (*Dasein*) could be attributed to God. Any talk of divine *Dasein* would, according to Cohen, lead ultimately to pantheism and confuse God with nature.[48] In terms of his own system this meant that the careful distinction between *Sein* and *Sollen* would be overturned. The idea of God, moreover, was calculated to perform the methodological function of ensuring that the various parts of the system would achieve synthetic coherence but not at the cost of identifying the being of God with either nature, feeling, or will. Cohen's religious writings, in agreement with traditional rabbinic teaching, preferred therefore to speak of the uniqueness, rather than of the existence or unity of God. When he sought to clarify the relation between God and the world, or the relation between the deity and nature, he chose his logical term origin. God consequently becomes the *Ursprung* of *Dasein*.[49]

In the third place, Cohen offered a unique interpretation of divine transcendence which was indebted to his own under-standing of God as a sign for truth. From the perspective of each single part of the system, *die Gottesidee* did indeed transcend each *Richtung* of logic, ethics, and aesthetics, since it was the transcendent function of this idea to ensure their coherence in one operative totality. When the system was viewed in its entirety, however, the idea of God is immanent everywhere, because it creates the ultimate harmony which binds all together. Being a modest person, Cohen did not claim originality for his interpretation of divine transcendence and immanence, for he believed it was anticipated by the way in which Augustine and later philosophical theologies expounded the doctrine of the Trinity.[50]

It must finally be noted how Cohen's *Gottesidee* was severely limited by the system it was designed to regulate. Not only in the *Richtung* of nature and scientific knowledge, but also in that of ethics, the deity could not intervene in any way contrary to the laws governing the development of cognition and morality. Therefore not only were miracles denied this deity, but the notion of God's involvement in human morality was unthinkable because it contradicted the most fundamental laws of Cohen's ethics: radical autonomy and freedom, the necessary conditions for the advent of a moral subject. This God did not supply grace in the Christian fashion, since the realization of the moral ideal was a task solely for human volition, striving, and work. In the most radical meaning of the words, human beings had to work out their own salvation, though admittedly with the guidance of the moral law. Though seemingly stoic in both its estimation of human capacities and its refusal to allow God any direct involvement in human affairs, Cohen's rationalist system, even at this point, was indebted to Judaism. The path to salvation for individuals and the nation lies in observance of the Torah, with its ordinances, statutes, or 'ideals', located not in some superhuman order, but in the human heart.[51]

Depending upon one's perspective it may be viewed as either extreme *hubris* or a mark of reverence that the idea of God, as the idea of truth, should become the crowning glory of Cohen's system. This idea bestows a teleological dynamism upon the entire system and receives thereby the highest possible philosophical accolade. Though some may prefer to see this as an idolatrous deification of the system, it certainly compares favourably with the ideals of another Jewish systematic philosopher, who beheld philosophy as expressing an intellectual love of God. At the very least one must admire Cohen for his courage in drawing the inevitable consequence from his rational principles: 'die Religion in Ethik sich auflösen müsse'.[52] This statement, like the injunctions of Natorp, was a practical manifesto which Cohen hoped would be heeded by philosophers, theologians, state authorities, and believers of both the Christian and Jewish faiths.

Cohen's programme consequently demanded a radical reappraisal of both Judiasm and Christianity. Traditional Christian doctrine, and Christology in particular, appeared, from the perspective of the system, to be nothing less than unsuccessful attempts at clothing myth in philosophical dress. A truly religious and scientific way forward would involve purging doctrine of its pre-scientific mythical roots and providing it with a systematic justification by incorporating its teachings into the Marburg System. This was not a matter of *Entmythologisierung* and of existential reinterpretation of religious concepts such as was later advocated by Bultmann. Cohen's hermeneutics was governed by his ethics and circumscribed by the circle of his own system. He therefore urged that religious beliefs, dogmas, doctrines, and sacred writings should submit to *Idealisierung* (idealization).

There are two particularly interesting examples which wonderfully illustrate this hermeneutics of idealization. Cohen was critical of doctrines of incarnation not only because they owed more to myth than to systematic thought about religion, but also because they confused the distinction between *Sein* and *Sollen*. Such confusion between the natural and the ethical in Christological doctrine had the unsavoury consequence of pantheism. When idealized, however, Cohen found such Christologies entirely compatible with *Ethiko-Theologie*:

For the history of ethics the incarnation of God certainly finds its deepest and most fruitful basis in the foundational rationale of ethics: morality must be the work of man. In so far as now both God and morality are conceived as identical, God precisely must become man . . . the incarnation of God signifies the deification of one man . . . Deification permits a natural idealization which signifies both purification and an elevation to the sublimest ideal of morality.[53]

Neither was Judaism exempt from this procedure, for its beliefs about a Messiah and a Messianic Age were as much indebted to myth as Christian doctrine. Once these ancient beliefs are idealized, however, they no longer refer to an expected redeemer nor even to a restored theocracy in the land of Palestine. All emphasis should rather fall upon the messianic future of mankind, upon the never-ending task of realizing the moral ideal in this world. Eschatology consequently becomes subordinate to that ever-distant kingdom of ideal ends which even in principle could never be fully realized. This idealized concept of a Messianic Age certainly falls within the *Grenzen* of scientific philosophy.[54]

III. ECSTATIC REASON AND THE AMBIGUITIES OF RELIGIOUS EXPERIENCE

Religion thus appears to possess no *Selbständigkeit* within Cohen's system. In later life, however, he seems to have become increasingly aware that this project of idealizing faith offered only a lifeless account of religion. The religious life apparently refused to be reduced to ethics and ideal concepts. Devotion, piety, dispositional states, and specifically theological virtues were indelible 'peculiar marks' of religion. Could these, therefore, be incorporated into scientific philosophy without contradicting its fundamental principles? Could this 'particular problem' of religious life be made into an *Aufgabe* without implying that such experience is *gegeben*? If philosophy were to recognize the validity of all these authentically religious traits, could it speak of a specifically religious God, without suggesting that it is a *Gottesidee* generated by human thought?

These problems, addressed in Cohen's last attempts at *Religionsphilosophie*, illustrate one central difficulty encountered in all strictly deductive and a priori accounts of religion, its rituals, myths, and social ideals. Theorizing about religion is obviously indebted to either some existential experience, corporate involvement, or empirical study of its cultural and historical actuality, yet systems like Cohen's deny they are based upon any specific given experiences. They tend to be resolute in their opposition to induction and a posteriori argument, but in the end they must offer some assessment of religious experience.[55]

This difficulty marks all the *religionsphilosophisch* writings of Cohen. Devoted equally to the philosophical logos and the devotion of his ancestors, religious experience presented itself to this deeply religious man and thoroughgoing rationalist as problematical and ambiguous. A pathos, a philosophical perplexity, informs an inner dialogue between reason and piety, which, in the opinion of one authority, 'seems to remain an uncompleted dialogue through all Cohen's Jewish writings'.[56] An intimate letter to a friend likewise clearly testifies to this restless dialogue between head and heart.

If there be those who counsel *sacrificio dell'intelleto*, I would accuse: *del sentimento*. You know how much I am bound to the inner life of our religion with the deepest stirrings of my heart . . . Yet here, too, abstraction is my fate and only what is philosophically legitimate am I able to understand and tolerate.[57]

Piety, reverence to God, *Vertrauen*, and prayer, seem incompatible with a deity which is an Ideal lacking personality. On the other hand, was devotion to a personal God consistent with the *Grundgesetz* of ethics—radical human autonomy? In the writings of this late German idealist there is profound awareness of a lacuna in Kantian-type *Ethiko-Theologie* which certainly had a counterpart in the early history of German Idealism. Schelling too became increasingly aware of, and irritable over, the seemingly lifeless character of Kant's ethical deity. Far from placing religion on a firmer footing, this abstract moral God, posited only in the interests of ethics, contradicted, falsified, and betrayed religion which, in Schelling's opinion, had far more to offer philosophy than anything Kant ever dreamt of: 'The longing for the real God and for redemption through him is, as you see, nothing else but the expression of the need of *religion*. . . . without an active God . . . there can be no religion, for religion presupposes an actual, real relationship of man to God'.[58] Unlike Schelling, who turned to a positive philosophy of mythology and revelation, Cohen did not want to abandon his system in favour of a new philosophy. He sought instead to give greater prominence to the peculiarly dispositional and experiential aspects of devotion by permitting religion to express what he called its *Eigenart* within his existing system. Nevertheless as Cohen sought to allow for the 'special marks of religion', the position of the deity *innerhalb* the system became increasingly ambiguous: 'Theoretically God may not in any way be regarded as a legitimate object of knowledge. Accordingly in a suspension between knowledge and morality, intellect and will, metaphysics and ethics . . .' there is a place within the system for the God of religion.[59] This suspension, however, does not bestow any *Selbständigkeit* upon religion over and against knowledge and morality; it simply reserves a place for the special character (*Eigenart*) of religion in relation to cognition and will. The task, then, faced by Cohen's later *Religionsphilosophie* was to show how the *Eigenart* of religion could be incorporated into the system without creating asymmetries.

Cohen's *Eigenart* doctrine is easy to grasp. In relation to ethics, for example, the special character of religion shows itself through a modification of the content (*Inhalt*) of ethics. Although the radical autonomy of the individual was stressed in Cohen's ethics, it was no less emphasized that the individual may only acquire moral character in the forum of society. The formalism of Cohen's ethics, however, appeared to subsume individuals under an intricate complex mesh of legal, moral, and political structures to such a degree that the *Ich* or *Selbst* almost completely disappeared. *Der Begriff der Religion im System der Philosophie* still argued that scientific *Ethik* only required *die Gottesidee* for its completion, but the specifically religious awareness of guilt, sin, and forgiveness merited further consideration. In less religious terms Cohen acknowledged that individuals often fail to 'realize' the Good and consequently feel that the relationship between themselves and the Ideal is fractured. Being burdened with guilt and sin, the individual experiences estrangement from the ideal moral order. It is here that the religious God enters and speaks to the individual in his solitude, finitude, and estrangement. At this point ethics perceives that it is the task of the authentically religious God to effect the redemption of the individual. Although the autonomy of the moral subject still remains an unassailable presupposition of any moral action, and though even the God of religion does not lift from the individual the responsibility for his actions or participate in his moral striving, this very individual is incapable of freeing himself from awareness of guilt. God alone can do this:

Man continues in moral work, but God, who does not himself participate in this labour, is conceived as the token [*Wahrzeichen*] which effects this deliverance from sin ... As God in ethics guarantees the realization of the Good for humankind, in religion he accomplishes this realization in *the individual*. In ethics God radiates humanity with the confidence of morality upon earth; in religion he radiates *the individual* with confidence of his personal deliverance from sin and of his restoration to the task of moral freedom. ... As such the God of forgiveness, redemption, and reconciliation is not something mythic, but forming a necessary

completion to the God of ethics, he also enables the reconciling work of
the individual, without which the goal of grace would lose all sense of its
way.[60]

The God of *Ethik* is a God afar off, but the God of religion is close
at hand to free *the individual* from self-imputed guilt. The way in
which Cohen often contrasts the God of ethics and the individual's
religious God is at first sight most perplexing. What he was
attempting to illustrate by this contrast was simply how the
Eigenart of religion can be recognized by the system. In the
instance quoted above the *Inhalt* of ethics indeed undergoes
modification, but not, Cohen urged, at the price of sacrificing
moral autonomy. On the contrary ethics is enriched and brought
to completion.

It is at this point that a particularly difficult feature of Cohen's
Eigenart doctrine comes to light. In recognizing its special
characteristics, not only was religion idealized, but Cohen
explicitly admitted that a modification to the content of ethics and
logic had also occurred. Just how great this modification was, is
something that has continued to provoke controversy. On the one
hand Cohen wholeheartedly believed that the recognition of
religion's *Eigenart* in no way introduced asymmetries into the
system or precipitated a new philosophy. On the other hand the
new modified content of ethics and logic certainly altered
the tenor of his philosophy. With the increased emphasis upon
traditional religious virtues, practices, and beliefs, Cohen begins to
use language which is at once both dispositional and theoretical.
We hear of prayer that effects atonement, man's yearning for God,
the nearness of God to man, religious love and humility, and the
empathy in which the *Ich* of the individual discovers itself in the
Du of the fellow man.[61] Whether this suggests that Cohen had
forsaken a purely methodological God lacking personality for a
more traditional personal and living God, has often been debated.
Whatever the outcome of this continuing debate, the previous
quotation encapsulates the tension. God, it would appear, does
not actively participate in the moral struggle: following good
Jewish precedent Cohen recognizes that reparation and atonement are to be wrought by man. Yet also, and here is the paradox,
he clearly and firmly speaks of God's 'contribution' to the work of
atonement, namely forgiveness—something which human beings

cannot effect. It is here, however, that Schwarzschild's most recent account of Cohen's philosophy must be mentioned. He is resolutely opposed to those who detect in Cohen's last religious writings an ontologizing of what were supposedly merely formal or methodological principles and entirely correct to counsel caution when dealing with the 'retro-effect' of the God of ethics upon either logic or ethics; yet it is surely the case that this perplexing medley of logical, ethical, and dispositional terms testifies to something fundamental about the character of these later writings.[62] The answer which this present writing offers to the discussion will become evident as more attention is given to the later works in which the *Eigenart* of religion makes its presence felt.

In *Der Begriff der Religion im System der Philosophie* Cohen begins to explore the consequences of the special character of religion for logic. Following traditional philosophical theology the God of Jewish monotheism is now Being, for Cohen took the divine name Yahweh to mean 'Being as such' or 'true Being'. Being, however, according to the *Logic of Pure Knowledge* stood in an operative relationship to thought: 'Nur das Denken selbst kann erzeugen, was als Sein gelten darf.'[63] So, how, it may be asked, does the biblical revelation of God as Being participate in the ideal principles and laws of thought? Just as Cohen's logic made a distinction between *Sein* and *Wirklichkeit*, so now the God of religion demanded a distinction betwen *Sein* and *Dasein*. This God, the God of religion, could be nothing less than the author of everything existent and accordingly Cohen chose one of is logical terms to illustrate this relationship. God, here, perhaps not unexpectedly, becomes the *Ursprung* of *Dasein*.[64] Yet another logical term, *Korrelation*, was also pressed into service when Cohen sought to give greater prominence to the special character of religion.[65]

According to another writer of philosophical theology, Paul Tillich, the term correlation may be used in three ways: 'It can designate the correspondence of different series of data . . . it can designate the logical interdependence of concepts . . . and it can designate the real interdependence of things or events in structural wholes.'[66] Though Tillich certainly knew of Cohen's work and though the article on *Korrelation* in the *Historisches Wörterbuch der Philosophie* cites thinkers who were strongly influenced by Cohen (Buber, Rosenzweig, and Löwith) as the only other users of this term in modern times, nobody seems to have enquired whether Tillich may have been indebted to Cohen for the term.[67] Correlation in Cohen's writings certainly designates the logical interdependence of concepts, as well as the interdependence of particular concepts or ideas in the structural whole of his system, but his use of the term was reserved for relationships that involve purpose, though sometimes he did speak of correlation as a term implying reciprocal relations.[68] A correlative relationship is thus a teleological relation 'which we set between God and man and also between God and nature. When I wish to construct the concept of God, I must accordingly establish a teleological development [*eine Zwecksetzung*] between God and man and so gain the concept of man from the structure informing the very content of the concept of God, and vice versa.'[69] On Cohen's authentic admission, the teleological relation between God and the world in *Logik* and a similar relation between God and man in *Ethik* complete the system of philosophy.

Elsewhere Cohen could express the correlation between the religious God and nature on the one hand and morality on the other, in more biblical terms:

It is no dispensable mythical residue whereby the true God enters a covenant with Abraham and before that with Noah for the conservation of nature. God comes to exist [*entsteht*], he generates himself [*erzeugt sich*] in this covenant with man, his origin is the covenant with man. This covenant is God's work, not man's.[70]

This strange, unusual, and, at first sight, problematical use of philosophical and biblical language, is a feature characterizing all the religious writings of Cohen, especially his later ones. Here correlation gives way to covenant, but terminology from the *Logik* is also present. God thus 'generates' himself in the covenant (that is, the teleological relation or correlation) with man and, from the perspective of the system, this religious God has his logical *Ursprung* in that same covenant. This passage, and many others like that could have been cited, illustrates how Cohen rearranged the terms of his system in order to give a more prominent place to the *Eigenart* of religion.

The correlation between man, world, and God has significance for both morality and the purpose of the created order. It lends an ultimate teleology to Cohen's entire system:

THE PLACE OF RELIGION

What purpose does God have for the existence [*Dasein*] of nature or, also, what purpose does the existence of nature have for God? In both cases purpose performs the function of an idea: the idea of God, the idea of man; or, more precisely, purpose effects itself in an idea. The identity between purpose and idea consists in logical activity.[71]

With the language of purpose homage is paid to what Heidegger called 'the ontological difference', but with Cohen the difference is not between *Sein* (how things are) and *Dasein* (the specifically human modality of being there in time); it is much more the contrast between the ideal and actual worlds, since for Cohen only the ideal could qualify as being. Nevertheless the two are not eternally opposed, for they ultimately serve the same final purpose. God is thus the origin of *Dasein* because 'without him there would be no *Dasein*. Here there appears a spiritual kinship with the foundational thoughts of the *Logic of Pure Knowledge*.'[72]

A singular feature of Cohen's *Religion of Reason* is God's increasing resemblance to a principle of origin: 'But purpose, the correlation of God and world, arises beyond creation; it raises creation to conservation. Conservation is a new creation. And thus basically creation means nothing other than the renewal of conservation.'[73] God becomes guarantor of the 'ceaseless actuality' of nature and, having posited a teleological 'correlation' between God and world, the whole course of reality may be dynamically 'unfolded' as a purposeful system:

The share of reason in religion has to discover the logical meaning of the principle of origin for the problem of creation . . . the idea of creation is thus taken into the concept of God. The riddle of creation is accordingly resolved through the definition of God. For now creation rather means God's Being, which is the being of the originative principle . . . God is not inert: this implies he is the originative principle of activity. In this way Maimonides explains the original name of God . . . He is sufficient to produce things besides himself. . . . Creation is God's primary attribute. It is not only the consequence of God's Being, creation is simply identical with it. If the Unique God were not creator, being and becoming would be the same. Nature would be God. This however, would mean: God is not, for nature is the becoming that needs being as its foundation. Being is a first principle which is not contained in becoming, it rather has to be the foundation of becoming.[74]

It is not difficult to perceive what has happened here. The recognition of religion's *Eigenart* has brought a modification to the content of logic through teleological concepts of purpose. Simultaneously, however, the logical principles upon which the system rests undergo an ontological transformation. Whereas in the *Logic of Pure Knowledge* principles were something posited by and for thought, God, now endowed with the attributes of a principle of origin, is identified with that ideal reality in which the being of logical ideas subsists. Taking unto himself the supremely productive properties of a principle of origin, God becomes action itself, a sort of *intellectus agens*, purposively directing the entire process of being and thinking. God does not merely receive logical compliments, rather he exemplifies them and actively establishes the harmony of the system:

There must be a concept whose task it is to deal with all other concepts and not only to control each one separately, but to examine its harmony with all others. This harmony of the great species of knowledge, which also must be extended to the third part of the system, aesthetics, is the proper content of the concept of God, the proper content of the concept of truth.[75]

An even more subtle aspect of Cohen's ontology arises from the fact that the word *Korrelation* is not only a technical term of logic, but also a form of personal relationship between God and the individual. It is at once cognitive and dispositional. There is a correlation between man and man in ethics, God and the individual in redemption and prayer, God and the world in logic, and, ultimately, between God and the entire system of philosophy. It is from this perspective that Cohen criticized Natorp. Religion, said Cohen, could not be 'grounded' in *Gefühl*, whether it be Natorp's 'infinitude of feeling' or Schleiermacher's 'feeling of absolute dependence'. First because *Gefühl* is just one dimension of cognition (aesthetics) and, secondly, because the feeling about which these philosophers wrote is really a feeling of finitude. The God of the system must establish a teleological harmony for all branches of cognition and the God of religion must correlate purposely with the individual in forgiveness, reconciliation, and atonement.[76]

Some form of symmetry still holds between thinking and being, but the identification of God's essence and activity with the being and function of logical and moral principles, means this symmetry is ontologized, if not deified. Here, surely methodological formal-

ism has indeed been transcended, though ambiguities nevertheless remain. Being, which is now identified with God, whose
essence (*Wesen*) is the fecund being of logical principles, appears
as the *Voraussetzung* of becoming. Is Cohen saying that all
becoming, including the sort of logical thought through which
humans generate cognition, is dependent upon the Archetypal
Knower and his Ideas, or is it his thesis that the whole system of
logic, ethics, and aesthetics, posits and generates a God for the
completion of its tasks? Does being, especially the ideas of God's
essence, now become the a priori condition of the becoming
generated by human thought? Cohen was not clear on these
points, perhaps intentionally so, but whatever the answers may be,
Tillich's observation seems an appropriate comment upon what
occurs in the idealist tradition when pure thought discovers an
a priori, original, God:

The theological concepts of both idealists and naturalists are rooted in a
'mystical *a priori*,' an awareness of something which transcends the
cleavage between subject and object. And if in the course of a 'scientific
procedure' this *a priori* is discovered, its discovery is possible only
because it was present from the very beginning.[77]

IV. THE HEART'S DESIRE

The ancient *shema*' of Israel proclaimed, 'The Lord our God is one
Lord and thou shalt love the Lord thy God with all thine heart,
and with all thy soul, and with all thy might', and this confession
of faith was central to Cohen's own philosophical religion. His
passion for system, unity, and unification which was central to this
thought was as much indebted to Judaism as to Greek teachings
about the sameness of thinking and being.

The uncompromising operationalism which marks Cohen's
approach to reason was explicitly connected by him to belief in the
Unique God of Israel, the True Being. Though he was not so naïve
as to equate monotheism with monism, Cohen did argue that the
teleological efficacy of True Being had implications for philosophical method, epistemology, and religion. The value and
nobility of reason was held to lie in its operationalism because it
incessantly sought to unify seemingly diverse tasks into a
harmoniously developing wholeness. Unification, rather than

unity, was the origin and goal of thought. Even prayer in Cohen's religious writings becomes a passionate yearning, a longing for wholeness and unification. The apparent 'dualism' or 'spirit' nature of the *Ich*—its biological, natural aspect and its spiritual and mental capacities—begins to achieve unification through the prayer of yearning (*Sehnsucht*), from which alone arises an authentically personal existence:

Longing becomes the thread which unites both natures of the I, and prayer consolidates these threads into concern and hope for the rights of the individual. When, at last, heaven and earth are connected, then there creeps into the prayer, even more openly, the divining rod of the personal.[78]

In one writing, devoted to a consideration of divine uniqueness, Cohen clearly reveals the religious dimensions of his theorizing. It begins with a succinct presentation of the nature of thought:

Unity serves as the most fundamental and universal implement of thought. Thinking as such is a unifying process that pulls together the diverse elements of which any thought-material is composed. In fact, any such material, offered to the mind by perception and all forms of representation, is transformed into thought-substance only by this unifying mental process. Unity, therefore, is a constitutive characteristic of the mind.[79]

A decisive moment in the history of philosophy was when Xenophanes, the first partisan of the One, denied the existence of anthropomorphic gods and instead regarded the cosmos as being permeated by a divine principle of oneness. This, according to Cohen, was but a preliminary step towards monotheism, for Xenophanes and his followers fused cosmos and God into a unified whole, thus identifying the two. The Hebrew scriptures, though in less philosophical language, likewise betray some idea of unity which had to emerge 'in order to reveal the God of spirituality as the God of truth, over and against the multiplicity of gods and sensate existence'.

Biblical thought nevertheless uncompromisingly rejected the concept of unity and in its place envisaged a 'new God', the God who is uniquely One, because the position held by thinkers like Xenophanes led ultimately to pantheism, which would be a complete defeat for monotheism. With this 'new God', the God who is Unique Being, biblical thinkers, albeit in rudimentary form, begin to wrestle with the problem of thinking and being. They

do not speculate about the nature of thinking. But their attempt to go beyond sense perception and to grasp the nature of conceptual thinking by trying to discern its authentic content and substance becomes evident in their idea of being—a notion no less basic than unity and identity.[80]

This massive step in religious thought had a counterpart in Greek philosophy:

Then came Parmenides, who, though maintaining the principle of cosmic unity, did not transmute it into the idea of God. Instead, he transposed it into that other basic concept of thinking: being. From here on, the problem of philosophy is no longer the cosmos but being. Being and thinking become correlative concepts of philosophic speculation.[81]

Once more the monotheistic thinking of the Bible and the conceptual thought of Greek philosophy display surprising accord:

When God first reveals Himself out of the midst of the burning bush, Moses asks Him what he should reply when the children of Israel question him about the God who has sent him and about His name. Whereupon God answers: '*I am that I am.* . . . Thus shalt thou say unto the children of Israel: *I am* hath sent me unto you'. Truly, there is probably no greater miracle in intellectual history than that disclosed by this sentence. Here, a primeval language, emerging without any philosophical concepts, stammers the most profound word of any philosophy. . . . God is the I that signifies being as such.[82]

The ancient Jewish confession of faith, it will be recalled, demanded that this Unique God should be loved with heart, mind, and will. Concerning this unification of the entire personality in the service of God, Jewish thinkers, from Saadyah to Maimonides,

invoke the Torah, which repeatedly speaks of knowledge as fundamental to all matters of the human heart, mind, and volition. 'Know this day, and lay it to thy heart . . .' (Deut. 4: 39). . . . More telling than any quotes, though, is that basic tenet of faith, the unity of God, whose corollaries are 'unity of heart' and 'unity of action'. . . . 'Unify our hearts so that we may love and venerate Your name'—had Bahya's *Duties of the Heart* disclosed to us no other concept than that of a unity of heart, action, and veneration of God, this alone would suffice to make it a work of considerable value.[83]

This ardent desire or passionate longing for unification is particularly evident in Cohen's religious anthropology. Whenever he writes about *Sehnsucht*, which was regarded as an aesthetical concept, an almost Platonic *eros* for unification breaks through. The longing in question, however, is something uniquely religious and personal:

> If we now enquire about the origin of longing, we consequently recognize that this in no way originates morally, but that it has an utterly religious origin. The correlation between man and God would not achieve its goal without longing; it would not attain its living and true completion. . . . Religion is the history of the individual and the God of the individual is the God of religion. . . . When the psalmist, in contrast to the prophets, considers the messianic idea and directs the yearning of his soul towards it, it is not so much the fulfillment of time, the end of war, peace amongst nations and people of earth that he longs for. It is much more the anguish and agony of his own soul that he lays before his God. When he is pervaded by this yearning he does not concern himself with politics—for him heaven and earth are no longer pressing realities; the soul alone, his own selfhood, is his unique concern. This concern wells up as longing, in which alone he perceives the power and strength to redeem him from his anguish. The God of yearning is the God of redemption. What the idea of the messiah signifies for mankind, the idea of redemption signifies for the individual.[84]

Such yearning desires not mystical union with God, but redemption, unification, and the nearness of God. Though a uniquely religious aspiration, this *Sehnsucht* inevitably pervades every direction of consciousness. Viewed from a logical perspective, it is a teleological power which 'effects' and 'actualizes' the correlation between God and the individual. Having an ethical and psychological dimension, longing is a power which establishes the individual as an authentically moral person in the sight of God. It effects a unification of all directions of consciousness:

> The unity of consciousness is the highest problem of systematic philosophy. Religion in its own way adopted this problem; for all the struggles and contradictions of the heart, prayer seeks unity and pleads for it as the highest grace. Sin is only the religious expression for cleavage of heart, and reconciliation, therefore, is the religious expression of this unification which the heart attains again in itself. Thus the God of

redemption becomes also the redeemer of the individual in the psychological sense, the saviour of his self-consciousness. Prayer, which
pervades the effort of redemption and concludes it as its song of triumph,
becomes the linguistic medium that continuously secures and establishes anew the unity of consciousness, the unity of heart, which is always
threatened and always at stake.[85]

The biblical heart accordingly becomes the hallmark of human
integrity and unification; yet *Sehnsucht* no less pervades the
aesthetical direction of consciousness and the ardent desire of pure
passion achieves its most eloquent form in the 'lyric poetry' of the
psalter. The psalms give voice to the psalmist's desire for redemption, unification, and purity in their entreaties for a clean heart,
renewal of God's spirit within, and nearness to God. As well as
expressing love and yearning, this form of lyrical poetry has a
peculiar healing power. It expresses not some finite and transitory
moment of human experience, but the sum total of one's life
before God. What is finite and transitory is portrayed as infinite
and eternal in the religious poetry of the psalter. The therapeutic
agency of this aesthetic lyricism is its power to anticipate the future
and make it effective in the present. It consolidates and renews the
impetus and longing for the ideal. Using analogies based upon
eros, it idealizes this longing as the highest end of life, that is,
redemption from sin and nearness to God. Existentially, therefore,
longing originates in dread, the fear of self-loss and the temptation
to flee from one's finitude and moral tasks. The positive existential
intention of longing corresponds to the natural urge of not
despairing of oneself, of clasping the anchorage of self-assurance in
order not to be ruined by despair and self-abandonment. The
prayerful longing of the psalms thus wrests itself away from the
struggle for repentance and turns into the hope of redemption. It
grasps this hope through which the I is renewed and, abiding in
this hope, the power of anticipation, celebrates the triumph in
liturgical prayer, personal devotion, song, and poetry.

Though tragedy is transcended through religious longing,
Cohen was adamant in his insistence that even here, human
beings are not severed from their humanity. The authentically
religious yearning of the psalter and synagogue prayers is directed
not towards union with God which carried, for Cohen, antitheistic
overtones of pantheism, but rather towards approaching God. His
own translation of Psalm 73: 28 reads, 'The nearness of God is my

Good', and this pure passion of longing, unlike mythical love, does not desire God himself, only his forgiveness and nearness. Speaking of *Yom Kippur*, Cohen says:

While reconciliation with God means man's redemption from the sinfulness which is his alleged nature, it does not mean a redemption from his finiteness nor from his human fate. Such an interpretation would reflect the errors of pantheism. The monotheistic concept of redemption neither belittles nor euphemizes man's this-worldly, sensate existence. It does not catapult man into a beyond that is expected to provide him with some consolation for his otherwise unalleviated suffering; nor does it relieve him from the routine of his everyday existence. In short, it does not exempt him from the here-and-now of life with its duties and hopes; it merely saves him from the allegation that he is in the unbreakable grip of evil. Or, to put it differently: man's redemption from sin in no way signifies a redemption from or suspension of his human condition; it signifies his reconciliation with God. ... neither reconciliation nor redemption means that man will be released from his this-worldly, finite existence. Rather than create illusions and phantasmagoria, these concepts set up ideals for the moral work of moral beings. Redemption has nothing to do with death or the beyond: man is not redeemed from life on earth with all its pain and sufferings, but merely from his errors and mistakes.[86]

Was not the divine promise to Moses simply, 'Behold, there is a place by me'?

Before leaving Cohen's thoughts on *Sehnsucht*, two points must be made. First, it was held by him to characterize the purest passion of love. Though somewhat unhappy with sensualistic notions of human love for God, Cohen sought to idealize the yearning of love. Even in the case of sexual love, it is the idealized person, the idea of the beloved, that is loved. To those who asked him whether it is possible to love an idea—and whatever God may or may not be in Cohen's thought, he certainly is an idea—Cohen replied, 'How is it possible to love anything but an idea?' Pure love, including pre-eminently religious love, is directed towards archetypes, towards models upon which pure moral action should be patterned. One strives not to imitate the divine archetype, but only to emulate it. The emulation in question, however, must have its origin in the entire unity of consciousness. Intellect and will alone are insufficient bases for this emulation; spirit and feeling must also become involved. This merging of all powers alone enables a worthy aesthetic feeling of love to arise.[87] Here it is interesting to observe how in many writings the systematic philosopher insisted that knowledge, rather than love, was the goal of religion, meaning thereby, ethical knowledge, the knowledge of right action. In Cohen's later writings, however, love appears alongside knowledge as specially distinguishing the cognitive style of religion. Once more there is evidence of that never-ending dialogue between head and heart that characterizes Cohen's religious writings: 'Love is not knowledge. And yet Scripture demands knowledge as well as love. Although it demands love on the basis of knowledge . . . it does not hold them to be identical with each other.'[88] Yet higher than either love and knowledge or even holiness and unity is truth which, according to the Talmudic tractate, *Shabbat*, is the seal of God:

Truth and holiness would be identical if holiness did not limit itself to morality. Truth, however, unites theory with ethics and consequently becomes the ideal of reason even more than holiness. Truth is, therefore, what binds science, including ethics, with religion. If one is to ask for his highest good, he must ask for truth . . .[89]

The God of religion is truth, as is also the God of systematic philosophy.

A second tension also characterizes Cohen's portrayal of religious yearning. Like the cognitive striving upon which it is modelled, it never arrives at a conclusion. Just as the knowledge of pure thought never attains absolute knowledge, but remains for ever in pursuit of its infinite tasks, so with *Sehnsucht*; the individual never possesses his God as an actuality. In a very real sense the quest is the goal:

The desire for God expressed in prayer is a quest for God and always wants to be nothing other than a quest. The finding cannot be actual, but can have as its goal only 'the nearness to God', only the drawing close to God. This drawing near, however, is always love, always longing, always a moral passion, and never an intellectual attitude alone. . . . God can never become actuality for human love. The quest is the end in itself of the religious soul. The longing signifies and fills the entire inner life of the soul inasmuch as it is centred upon the correlation with God for the purpose of engendering religion.[90]

Yet, despite this, Cohen seemed aware that love, even religious love, desires more than pursuit, more than the distant goal, and more than ceaseless activity. Perhaps it should not long for actuality, but at the very least it longs for *essence*:

Longing is the idealist element of moral passion. Although longing desires the actual presence of the beloved, it is based upon the substitution of presence by the distant image, which it paints with the glow of its heart. Longing, therefore, holds fast to its distant goals without which it cannot accomplish the activity of approaching the beloved . . . Love is the longing for the essence, which is not present in perceptible actuality, and should not be, in so far as it is being longed for.[91]

In Cohen's philosophy essences are almost displaced by their functional attributes, yet there are those essential ideas which, being supremely active in thought, generate valid knowledge of being. Is there, one wonders, some special essence, a particular idea which, though producing those dynamic effects common to all ideals, hypotheses, and laws, is not actually present to either love or knowledge? Is there some idea which is not posited by thought and one, perhaps, upon which the very dynamism of thought is itself dependent?

V. THE REVELATION AT SINAI

When, on their desert journeyings, the children of Israel were sore pressed, languishing for lack of nourishment, and close to revolt, they were, as Philo knew well, sustained by a providential gift. Though the biblical accounts offered various descriptions of this gift, Philo also knew that the people reacted to this divine grace by asking themselves the question *man hu'*, meaning in Greek, *to esti touto* ('what is this?'). Later exegetical traditions elaborated the manna stories considerably, the gift in question becoming, for example, the delights of paradise, a promise to deliver Israel in times of economic need, something which Elijah will restore. With Philo, however, manna, being a gift received without toil or trouble, became a symbol of wisdom and virtue, for which no encyclical education is required. It was heavenly wisdom bestowed upon souls who desire to know God and his ways. A detail upon which Philo seizes is the question 'what is this?', which he took to have ontological implications. The question about manna remains a question and the gift is not named. To Philo this suggested that manna is the 'most generic' of all things, the interrogative and indefinite pronouns implying that the 'something' in question belongs to no class. In the same way, God transcends the categories of genus and species, for as with manna, one says of him 'what is this?', implying thereby that finite beings do not know the divine essence.[92]

Another exegetical tradition, which is of some importance for appreciating Cohen's approach to revelation, likewise concerns the legends about manna. From early times the gift of manna was associated with the gift of the *Torah* and when later Jewish religious philosophy turned its attention to revelation, the giving of the law on Mount Sinai became the paradigm of what serves as revelation.[93] As one might expect with Cohen, he praises the rationality of Jewish theology 'in the circumscriptive definition of revelation' as revelation at Sinai:

The bible refers to the revelation at Sinai by a term that would seem to reject, with naive determination, any semblance between this event and a mysterious disclosure or unveiling: the 'Giving of the Torah' [*Mattan Torah*]. That means that the Jewish genius for language emphasizes here not the object given, the gift, but exclusively the act of giving, that is, communication. And this communication signifies God's giving of Himself, as indeed He gives Himself in everything that issues from Him.[94]

This passage appears in a writing dating from 1917, so it certainly represents the last thoughts of Cohen on this particular topic. By contrast the work of 1915, *Der Begriff der Religion im System der Philosophie*, a book which Karl Barth possessed, has only fleeting references to revelation. There, regarding the a priori conditions (*Ursprung*) of religious knowledge, it is stated that: 'without aiming at truth, no connection between religion and philosophy could be established. The a priori of religion must also conform to the foundation of this philosophic methodology. Through this a priori religion is bound with knowledge.'[95] Such accord between religion and philosophic methodology not surprisingly has implications for the methods of dogmatics:

The dogmatics of religion has to submit to this unitary method. . . . Just as religion has only to strive for recognition of its special character [*Eigenart*], so must theology. As theology is dependent upon the methods of philosophy and history when dealing with literary and historical sources, so *Glaubenslehre* is no less dependent upon philosophy and ethics in particular.[96]

Revelation cannot therefore 'engender' an independent dimension of knowledge nor, for that matter, have its own special kind of *Logik*:

The foundations of religion can consequently be nothing other than foundations. The idea of the Good is an idea and remains an idea. Revelation must accordingly accept its idealist interpretation in being compared with and posited in a manner analogous to the a priori of knowledge. Removed from the changes of chance it is then understood as the eternal which lies at the base of all development.[97]

Religious knowledge and revelation must consequently receive justification from within the unity of Cohen's system. On the negative side this implied that religious knowledge could not be secured by induction. Concepts, principles, and foundations, that have their source in pure thought, form the basis of religion. Secondly, there is no way in which Cohen could allow religion and its revelation to be derived from feeling or experience. Neither, thirdly, could religious knowledge be gained from historical experience, for

reason is meant to make religion independent of the descriptions supplied by the history of religion. We do not shrink from the argument that reason must rule everywhere in history. However, history in itself does not determine the concept of reason. The concept of reason has to engender [*erzeugen*] the concept of religion. The concept is always a separate problem which must serve as a presupposition for the problem of development.[98]

In the *Religion of Reason* Cohen offered a lengthy discussion of revelation. Revelation signifies that God forms a relation with human beings; it is not revelation in, but always revelation to, it is always a relational term. Cohen affirmed that the 'whereunto?' of revelation is addressed specifically to human reason. Revelation is thus a revelation of reason, 'reason' here being simultaneously an objective and subjective genitive. It is reason (the rationality of being) that is revealed and, moreover, reason also executes the revelation.[99] Revelation, therefore, is not a miraculous event. Just as rationality is immanent in all culture, so it is immanent in religion where it is called revelation. It is the eternal rationality which precedes all development of knowledge in science, morals, and art. On the one hand revelation may be viewed as something which creates reason. On the other hand, reason becomes the 'discoverer of God':

It is as if God's being were actual [*aktuell*] in man's knowledge only, so tremendous is the effect of the correlation. Man is no longer merely God's creature, but his reason, by virtue of his knowledge and also for the sake of it, makes him at least subjectively, as it were, the discoverer of God.[100]

Since all the concepts used by Cohen have a special function to perform within the system, it should not be surprising to discover that this is so for revelation. The particular problem it solves is the relationship between being and the becoming of human rationality, particularly of moral reason. Since Cohen's doctrine of creation already posited being or, in religious terms, the Unique Being of God, as the foundation (*Ursprung*) of everything that is to be (*Dasein*), he argued that it must likewise form the foundational presupposition of human reason. Revelation means simply the creation of human rationality:

Revelation ... differs only in this respect from creation: the latter is concerned with the general metaphysical problem of becoming which, however, borders on the special problem of morality. This problem is taken up by revelation. It is therefore possible to say that revelation is the continuation of creation in so far as it sets as its problem the creation of man as a rational being.[101]

Perhaps the clearest illustration of this teaching about revelation is to be found in Cohen's exegesis of Genesis. The Fall is not, as much traditional exegesis might suggest, a fall from innocence to sin that had the consequence of spreading sin and guilt to all subsequent generations. The Fall is much more a dynamic transition whereby Unique Being becomes the logical (not, it must be stressed, the temporal) foundation for the development of cognition and morality. In a very real sense the Fall is a *felix culpa* for Adam and his posterity (that is, for human rationality). The idealized exegesis is worth quoting in full:

Creation is the logical consequence of God's Unique Being, which would be devoid of meaning if it were not the presupposition for becoming. In all becoming, however, man is the focal point, not, that is, in so far as he is living creature, but inasmuch as the tree of knowledge blooms for him. Mythical language expresses it in this way: knowledge brings death or, as

the serpent interprets it, 'And ye shall be as God, knowing good and evil.'
Thus the question of creation in regard to man now concerns knowledge
and, with knowledge, the question concerns the relation of man to God.
The serpent calls it identity, but our philosophical vocabulary uses the
word *Korrelation*, which is the term for all concepts of reciprocal relation.
A reciprocal relation exists between man and God. . . . In the case of
man, God's Being must be the presupposition for knowledge. And
knowledge is concerned not only with the knowledge of nature, but also
with 'the knowledge of good and evil'. The essence of man is dependent
upon the knowledge of morality. Reason is not ony theoretical, but also
practical and ethical. The creation of man must mean the creation of his
reason.[102]

The dignity of humanity consequently lies in its correlation
between the Unique Being and reason. Since, however, correlation is a term for reciprocal relations, the two relata must effect
each other teleologically. Human rationality is thus active and not
passively receptive in a revelatory situation. Immediately before
his words about reason being the discoverer of God, Cohen says:

Reason is the concept through which the correlation between God and
man is accomplished and therefore must be common to God and man.
Creation and revelation take effect only through reason. Both of these
concepts turn out to be expressions of the correlation, and therefore both
of them are based on the concept of reason that is achieved in the creation
of the man of reason and also in the revelation of God to man. Already
the creation as the creation of reason does not leave man in passivity, for
this would contradict the concept of correlation. Revelation even more so
cannot make man passive, for this would contradict not only the concept
of correlation, but even more so the concept of reason, which is what
revelation has to reveal.[103]

This section began with Philo's exegesis of the manna legends
and it was noted how manna could symbolize the gift of the *Torah*.
For Cohen too, revelation, the creation of human rationality, has a
Gesetzlichkeit without which neither knowledge of nature nor
morals would arise. Without the laws which govern pure thought
and nurture the realization of ethical ideals in willing and doing,
there would be no human beings, only 'living creatures' devoid of
logos. This 'idealized' account of revelation, it will be appreciated,
is concerned so much with the rationality of revelation that love
and longing receive hardly any mention. Furthermore, despite
later protests about God never being actual to either love or

knowledge, Cohen affirms that the correlation between the rationality of Unique Being and human reason is so great that it is 'as if' God were *aktuell* in man's knowledge.

There is, however, another most interesting dimension to Cohen's religious philosophy which also has links with traditional Jewish thought. Philo took manna, which literally meant 'what is this?', as symbolic of God who, being beyond both species and genus, must be incomprehensible. One may only know of God that he exists and that he performs certain providential actions; what God is, is incapable of definition. Even 'direct' knowledge of God, gained through revelation and prophetic inspiration, is a knowledge of God's existence, not of his essence.[104] God remains surrounded by thick darkness. With Philo there is striking accord between epistemology and ontology. Knowledge of God's existence and creative attributes is certainly attained by reason as it considers the created order and is also acquired through the revelation in which God himself is teacher. Neither, however, gives information about the essence of God. It is in Cohen's treatment of the divine essence that the tension between philosophy and religion, or ontology and theology, is at its most acute. On the one hand, his writings affirm the divine nature to be truth, morality or moral archetypes, and a concept to be determined through correlation.[105] On the other hand, however, the section devoted to revelation in the *Religion of Reason* surprisingly affirms the incomprehensibility of divine being.

Alongside the giving of the Law, the revelation to Moses at the bush, and the promises to Noah and the Patriarchs, the passage of scripture that held much importance for Jewish religious philosophy was the account of the theophany to Moses at Mount Sinai. When Cohen considered the legends in Exodus 33: 12 ff., he was at pains to show that the people (human rationality), not Moses alone, received revelation. Following traditional exegesis, Cohen detected two accounts here, one of which is fraught with myth and anthropomorphism, the other more ideal and eminently compatible with pure monotheism and morality. Moses, representing the entire people, makes two requests of God, one is granted, the other refused. Moses's request, 'Let me see your glory' in verse 18 is, according to Cohen, dangerously materialistic. Not only is it a request for a theophany, it is an entreaty for knowledge of God's essence. This verse is contrasted to the prayer in verse 13, 'Show me your ways that I may know you', which is a request to know God's action in the world, not his essence. Cohen then turns his attention to the verses: 'And the Lord said, "Look, there is a place beside me. Station yourself on the rock, and, as my glory passes by, I will put you in a crevice of the rock and shield you with my hand until I have passed by. Then I will remove my hand and you will see my back, but my face shall not be seen".'[106] Despite his horror at materialistic presentations of God, Cohen is able to rescue this passage through the hermeneutics of idealization. Particularly interesting is Cohen's treatment of one of the most daring anthropomorphisms of the scriptures. Being indebted to traditional exegesis, he translates the word *'aḥōrāy* in verse 23 as 'my effects'. On the grounds that this word appears more often in the singular form (as in Isaiah 41: 23, 'Declare the things that are to come hereafter', with a sense of futurity, 'Jewish exegetics has always tried to eliminate the offensive meaning of the sentence. According to this intepretation, the sentence would mean that only by his works, only by that which follows from his essence, can God be known, not, however, by this essence itself.'[107]

Despite the traditional idealizing exegesis of this passage, Cohen finds that verse 19 offers a more acceptable alternative answer to Moses's petition. This verse, in Cohen's own translation, reads, 'And he said: "I will make all my good pass before thee; and will proclaim the name of the Eternal before thee; and I will be gracious unto whom I will be gracious, and will show mercy on whom I will show mercy."' The Hebrew word *tōv* is not taken to mean beauty or anything signifying glory, that is, God's essence, but rather 'what proceeds from goodness: the good'. Yet even in this verse there is the offensive phrase 'I will make pass by'. Here, however, the 'passing by' of God refers to a revelation of divine effects, not, that is, to a theophany of glory and essence:

The opposition to Moses's entreaty for the show of glory, hence of essence, becomes clear here and as a consequence it is removed: 'My effects you shall see, then I shall call, the Eternal is before you. These effects are my good, grace, and mercy.' Thus Jewish exegetes were correct in understanding the word, which occurs in this grammatical form only once, not as a bodily backside, but as the effects of the action of God's essence.[108]

These 'after effects' or 'consequences' of the Unique Being, which turn out to be God's attributes, are taken by Cohen to be teleological archetypes, that become productive when they correlate with human rationality. God is thus known through his effects, that is, through the unfolding revelation or rationality which produces knowledge of the world, ethical reality, and art. Correlatively, as this 'ontic' rationality develops and unfolds, human agents become aware of the 'ontological' *ratio*, the *ratio Dei*, the Eternal Idea or Unique Being which logically 'is before you'. It is this great Originative Principle which must be the eternal foundation of all rationality. Being sheer activity, it works in and through the human rationality which 'proceeds' from it and 'discovers' it when pursuing infinite moral and cognitive tasks. Yet despite this rationalism, the nature or essence of the Unique Being is neither known nor revealed.

There is, then, a reverent reserve in Cohen's approach to the revelation of reason. Though he was not at all happy at patterning revelation after models of hiddenness and disclosure, God's Being remains something entirely unique; so unique, in fact, that only negations express it adequately. All analogies based upon biological concepts are inadequate to express the Being of God and likewise God cannot be spoken of as a person, for this too would compromise his uniqueness. Despite this Uniqueness of Divine Being, there is a real 'connecting link' between the Unique Being and humanity, in that God has established his reason in the hearts of human beings. The entire unity of *Bewusstsein*, which aspires to teleological unification and complete sanctification, testifies to the fact that God has established his holy spirit (that is, cognitive and moral reason) in the heart of humanity. The 'Thou shalt be Holy' is an imperative injunction of practical reason and through accomplishing this task of self-sanctification the human *Geist* shows it proceeds from God and aspires to emulate him. In the correlation between God and man, this holy spirit is constantly renewed and strengthened:

Man should be able to become a saint in the sense that he should surpass human limitation and actually be allowed to draw near God. At the same time it is to be understood that this drawing near is rather an eternal task, only his eternal aim of carrying out the correlation with God. The holiness of man consists in self-sanctification, which, however, can have no termination and therefore cannot be permanent rest, but only infinite striving and becoming.[109]

Cohen's last book, *The Religion of Reason*, was given the important words *Out of the Sources of Judaism* as its subtitle. This, perhaps more than anything else, succinctly illustrates his approach to the relations between the scriptural revelation of God as Unique Being and philosophy. Jewish religious philosophy from the times of Philo has entertained three views concerning the relation between philosophical reasoning and the revelation of God to which scripture testifies. First there has been a double faith theory, according to which faith is either assent to scriptural revelation without the aid of philosophy or assent to scripture with the services of philosophy. Secondly, there has been the single faith theory of rationalism, whereby faith is assent to scriptural revelation with the aid of philosophy. Finally, there is the single faith theory, in which faith is assent to the scriptural revelation of God without any assistance from philosophy.[110] Cohen's own philosophical religion certainly accords with the second type, according to which faith is intellectual and moral assent to the God revealed in scripture with the aid of philosophy. This philosopher, moreover, could not regard any other form of assent as qualifying for faith, because the other theories refused to give sufficient emphasis to the gift of rationality which God has established in the human heart and mind. The alternative approaches seemed to forget that the relation between God and man is correlative and therefore rendered humanity inactive at its most important level.

Before leaving Cohen's *Religionsphilosophie*, it is interesting to note how his exegesis of Genesis proffers the view that human beings were made finite from the start. God created death in the Garden and finitude is natural for human beings. Even the share of God's Holy Spirit does not entitle humankind to participate in the eternity which is proper to God's Unique Being:

The human spirit is by no means transfigured into a divine spirit after death . . . it remains the spirit of man. Nor does it become one with God; rather it becomes once more what it has always been: God's creation. God constitutes its home. He has 'formed the spirit of man within him' (Zech. 12: 1); but the Creator of man's spirit has put it into man's body. Now that the body returns to the earth to which as dust it belongs, the spirit returns to God, from whom it has come.[111]

Whatever else may be said of Cohen's theism, it is certainly not a bad faith which offers celestial bliss to compensate for the tribulations of mundane life. Life on this earth, in which morality is to be realized, remains the messianic goal for finite creatures and, if there be any legitimate consolation, it is to be offered only by finite beings to other finite beings. Evils are to be protested against and remedied through social welfare and humane responses to suffering, distress, and poverty. Only moral praxis of this kind will contribute towards the coming Messianic Age. When Moses asked to see God's glory, the request was not granted. Instead Moses witnessed the divine attributes of action, those moral ways according to which God interacts with the world and humanity. Cohen's own confession of faith was 'the nearness of God is my good' and, having drawn close to his God, he trusted those words which were spoken to Moses, 'Behold, there is a place beside me'.

NOTES

1. During the early part of this century philosophies of religion inspired by neo-Kantianism proliferated. For a general survey see J. Hessen's *Die Religionsphilosophie des Neukantianismus* (Herder, 1924). A. Görland's *Religionsphilosophie* (de Gruyter, 1922) was inspired by the Marburg School, and those stemming from the Baden School include J. Cohn, *Religion und Kulturwerte, Philosophische Vorträge der Kant-Gesellschaft*, 6 (Reutler & Reinhard, 1914); W. Windelband, *Das Heilige: Skizze zur Religionsphilosophie* (J. C. B. Mohr, 1916); G. Mehlis, *Einführung in ein System der Religionsphilosophie* (J. C. B. Mohr, 1917). Troeltsch's numerous reviews of contemporary philosophy are useful, as is P. Tillich's *Über die Idee einer Theologie der Kultur* (Reutler & Reinhard, 1920). Finally it should be noted that Rudolf Otto, who was a professor at Marburg from 1917–29, did not exercise influence until after the First World War.

2. See further S. S. Schwarzschild's 'Introduction' to Cohen's *Werke VII* (Olms, 1981), pp. xxviiff.

3. '. . . every theologian, as a scientific worker, is under the necessity or obligation to proceed according to a certain epistemology of which he is himself aware and whose correctness he must demonstrate.' *Theologie und Metaphysik* from P. Hefner's translation in *Albrecht Ritschl: Three Essays* (Fortress Press, 1972), 187.

4. For detailed consideration of Ritschl's philosophical background see P. Wrzecionko, *Die philosophischen Wurzeln der Theologie Albrecht Ritschls* (Töpelmann, 1964). Such recent reappraisals as that by

Richmond have done much to correct the misunderstanding that
Ritschl was one who reduced Christian theology to an arid Kantian
moralism, and stress his indebtedness to the theology of the
Reformation. See also P. Hefner, *Faith and the Vitalities of History: A
Theological Study based on the work of Albrecht Ritschl* (Harper & Row,
1966), and D. W. Lotz, *Ritschl and Luther: A Fresh Perspective on
Albrecht Ritschl in the Light of his Luther Study* (Abingdon Press, 1974).

5. Quoted in M. Scheler's *On the Eternal in Man* (SCM, 1960), 174. For
Natorp's review of Herrmann's early work see 'Über das Verhältniss des theoretischen und praktischen Erkennens zur Begründung
einer nichtempirischen Realität', in *Zeitschrift für Philosophie*, 79
(1881), 242–59.

6. *Religion innerhalb*, 1.

7. Though he could not tolerate any rigid separation between the
sacred and profane, it is perhaps no coincidence that Natorp's
understanding of religion shares similarities with that advocated by
Durkheim, for Durkheim did visit Germany where he approved of
the Kantian revival. Steven Lukes mentions how Durkheim was
certainly influenced by French neo-Kantian philosophy. See *Emile
Durkheim: His Life and Work* (Penguin Press, 1973), 54–6, 87.

8. *Religion innerhalb*, 15.

9. Ibid. 27.

10. This idea, that the external or objective world, though generated by
human thought, is nevertheless something alien when contrasted
with immediate experience, was to have great influence upon the
understanding of the relations between subject and object in
modern German theology in general and upon Bultmann in
particular. See A. R. A. Johnson, *The Origins of Demythologizing*
(E. J. Brill, 1974), 65 ff.

11. *Religion innerhalb*, 33.

12. One wonders how much this interpretation of feeling adversely
prejudiced contemporary assessments of Schleiermacher.
Herrmann, though friendly towards the Schleiermacher of the
Reden, reacted strongly to Natorp's massive reduction and expelled
Gefühl from his theological vocabulary, using instead the word
Erlebnis to characterize the affective mode of religious awareness.
His apologetic misgivings about feeling certainly influenced Barth's
estimation of Schleiermacher. See *Prinzipienlehre*, 249 ff.

13. Natorp, 'Über das Verhältnis', 257: 'That the eternal is utterly
nothing to be sought for in a world of things and minds, but is alone
found in the theoretical, as well as practical, consciousness we have
of ourselves and things, means that the world is no longer torn apart
into this side and the other side and that the eternal is not severed

from the temporal. Eternity ought not to mean anything more to us than the standpoint from which we view the temporal.'

14. *Religion innerhalb*, 40.
15. Ibid. 40–1.
16. Ibid. 49.
17. Ibid. 57.
18. Ibid. 61.
19. Ibid. 86.
20. Ibid. 91.
21. No doubt confusions about psychology inform Natorp's account of feeling. He oscillates between psychology as an experimental science and a new form of psychology which he and his fellow Marburgers hoped to construct. Here, in a psychological description of religion, psychology is concerned with consciousness's own immediate awareness of itself. It is accomplished by an act of reflection in which consciousness refracts and turns towards itself in order to become aware of its own life.
22. *Prinzipienlehre*, 249.
23. Tillich, *Über die Idee einer Theologie der Kultur*, 34.
24. For an account of such philosophies see W. T. Jones, *Contemporary Thought of Germany* (Williams & Norgate, 1930–1), ii. 127 ff.
25. See e.g. the famous passage on p. 46 of Otto's edition of the *Reden*: 'Aber eine notwendige Reflexion trennt beide [Anschauung und Gefühl], und wer kann über irgend etwas, das zum Bewusstsein gehört, reden, ohne erst durch dieses Medium hindurch zu gehen? Nicht nur wenn wir eine innere Handlung des Gemütes mitteilen, auch wenn wir sie nur in uns zum Stoff der Betrachtung machen und zum deutlichen Bewusstsein erhöhen wollen, geht gleich die unvermeidliche Scheidung vor sich . . .'.
26. The revised edition of *Platons Ideenlehre* (Felix Meiner, 1920), 512. At this juncture a comparison between Natorp's 'infinitude of feeling' and Bradley's 'immediate experience' is instructive.
27. Jacob Neusner, *Torah: From Scroll to Symbol in Formative Judaism* (Fortress, 1985), 118–19. It must be stressed that law for Cohen means not only the laws for the cognition of nature, but pre-eminently the moral law. In Judiasm, moreover, 'the One god would become a useless machine were He not the eternal source of moral law. Judaism simply denies any possible conflict between the concepts of God and of moral reason. Moral law must and can be both: the law of God and the law of reason' (*Reason and Hope*, 81). Cohen's interpretation of the pre-existence 'myth' is most interesting. It signifies to him that the created realm is a forum for teleology: nature exists for the realization of moral ideals.

28, Quoted by K. Löwith in *Philosophie der Vernunft und Religion der Offenbarung in H. Cohens Religionsphilosophie* (Carl Winter, 1968), 7. Concerning purity, the following words merit quotation: 'Through his purity of soul, man becomes the image of God. . . . how could the idea of God be formulated if not by a mode of thinking distinct from all sense perception?' (*Reason and Hope*, 90–1).

29. See H. L. Ollig, *Religion und Freiheitsglaube* (Forum Akademicum, 1979), 204.

30. 'Philosophie und Theologie', in G. Huber (ed.), *Philosophie und christliche Existenz: Festschrift für Heinrich Barth* (Helbing & Lichtenhahn, 1960), 104.

31. Quoted in Löwith, *Philosophie der Vernunft*, 9.

32. Cohen's thought is thus closer to Kant's understanding of religion in *Die Religion innerhalb der Grenzen der blossen Vernunft* than is that of Natorp.

33. For a discussion of Cohen's ethics see Ollig, *Religion und Freiheitsglaube*, 142 ff.; Schwarzschild's 'Introduction' to Cohen's *Werke VII* and his article 'The Tenability of Cohen's Construction of the Self' in the *Journal of the History of Philosophy*, 13 (1975).

34. *ERW*, 66 ff.

35. *ERW*, 29 ff. The recent revival of Cohen research in Germany and Switzerland has shown great interest in the political dimensions of neo-Kantian thought; see particularly H. J. Sandkühler and R. de la Vega (eds.), *Marxismus und Ethik* (Suhrkamp, 1974). This is important to the history of theology, for the much-debated 'socialism' of Karl Barth seems to have been more indebted to Cohen than to either Marx or Lenin. F.-W. Marquardt's *Der Christ in der Gesellschaft 1919–1979* (Kaiser, 1980), 51 ff. carries forward his earlier thesis by suggesting that Cohen's emphasis upon the *Allheit* of moral and communal relations influenced Barth. It is perhaps important to note that Cohen regarded Kant as the founder of socialism and that though neo-Kantian socialism was not a politically strong force in Germany, many did believe that Marxism needed to be supplemented by the ethics of Kant. See K. Vörlander, *Kant und Marx: Ein Beitrag zur Philosophie des Sozialismus* (J. C. B. Mohr, 1911).

36. *ERW*, ch. 7

37. See *Reason and Hope*, 218: 'Selfhood is the result of an unending relation of the I and Thou as well as its abiding ideal. True, the ideal remains the ideal, as the task of ethical action remains the task. But an ideal is an ideal only because and insofar as it asks to be emulated so that I may approximate it. And a task is a task only because I am charged with it, because it is incumbent upon me. By

working at this task, I work on myself, toward my selfhood. In short, selfhood ensues from the interaction between I and Thou.'

38. *ERW*, 282–3.

39. N. Rotenstreich, *Jewish Philosophy in Modern Times: From Mendelssohn to Rosenzweig* (Holt, Reinhart & Winston, 1968), 54.

40. *Religion II*, 51. It should be noted that Cohen's exegesis of the Genesis story in many ways reflects that of Philo. As well as being aware of the moral dimension to the Noachine commandments and covenant, Philo also believed that the covenant with Noah signified the indestructibility of the world and the rainbow sign the immutability of the laws of nature. See H. A. Wolfson, *Philo: Foundations of Religious Philosophy in Judaism, Christianity, and Islam* (Harvard University Press, 1948), i. 295 ff., 347 ff.

41. *ERW*, 452.

42. Ibid. 441.

43. See further J. Guttmann, *Philosophies of Judaism* (Routledge & Kegan Paul, 1964), 354 ff. Schwarzschild, moreover, in his introduction to Cohen's *Ethik*, p. ix, calls attention to the rabbinic saying which Cohen himself sometimes quoted, 'the seal of God is truth', and suggests that 'Cohen's entire identification of "God" with "truth" is one extended philosophical commentary on that famous Talmudic dictum'.

44. *Religion III*, 476, 480.

45. *Religion I*, 135.

46. Ibid. 135. For Scheler's criticism see *Formalism in Ethics and Non-Formal Ethics of Values* (Northwestern University Press, 1973), 588: 'It should be clear that the idea of God, unlike the ideal types of the person . . . does not function as an *exemplary* model [*Vorbild*]. For it is senseless to say that a finite person takes the infinite person as a model.' Perhaps once more a comparison with Philo is in order, for he too suggested that both the logos and ideas serve as paradigms of the natural and moral order.

47. *ERW*, 453.

48. Ibid. 16, 458 ff.

49. Tillich too, it should be recalled, denied existence of God, albeit in order to emphasize God as being-itself. Throughout his writings Cohen insists upon fundamental differences between his idealist monism and Spinozistic 'substantial pantheism'. Cohen's many criticisms of Spinoza rely on one main insight, namely that his obsession with the necessity of laws of nature makes any teleology impossible. Cohen quotes Spinoza's saying that teleology is 'the asylum of ignorance' and comments, 'His concern is exclusively with the necessity of the laws of nature, that is, with causality. And

because of the existence of these laws, he recognizes no mode of being other than that of nature' (*Reason and Hope*, 97).

50. *ERW*, 464 ff., 447.
51. Deut. 30: 11–14, a favourite quotation of Cohen, reads, 'For this commandment which I command thee this day, it is not hidden from thee, neither is it far off. It is not in heaven, that thou shouldest say, Who shall go up for us to heaven, and bring it unto us, that we may hear it, and do it? Neither is it beyond the sea, that thou shouldest say, Who shall go over the sea for us, and bring it unto us, that we may hear it, and do it? But the word is very nigh unto thee, in thy mouth, and in thy heart, that thou mayest do it.' Cohen's almost rabbinic commentary on these verses reads, 'This removes the last shadow of doubt one may have harbored with regard to the pure spirituality of revelation. The teaching is not in heaven but in man's mouth, in his faculty of speech and in his heart, and therefore also in his mind. It did not come to man from without; it originated within him. It is rooted in his spirit which God, the uniquely One, has put into man as the holy spirit, the spirit of holiness. And that is the spirit of morality' (*Reason and Hope*, 101).
52. *Religion II*, 42.
53. *Religion I*, 136.
54. Ibid. 142 ff. It should be noted that Cohen's interpretation of traditional messianic beliefs not only suited his own system, but was very much related to contemporary theological reconstruction. In Jewish theology, particularly that influenced by the Reform Movement, emphasis was likewise placed not upon the Messiah as an expected future deliverer, but upon the Messianic Age. This, in turn, was often interpreted in terms of moral and ethical progress. Theologians and believers of this persuasion likewise often 'denationalized' the Messianic Age, so that it became a hope for all humanity on this earth and not the hope for a new State of Israel. The task of Israel was to abide in its dispersion, seek the good of the nations, and help civilize them. These beliefs were eloquently expressed in the Pittsburg Platform of 1885 by the liberal leaders of American Jewry, who always retained close contacts with their kindred in Europe. 'We recognize in the modern era of universal culture of heart and intellect the approaching of the realization of Israel's great Messianic hope for the establishment of a kingdom of truth, justice, and peace among all men. We consider ourselves no longer a nation, but a religious community, and therefore expect neither a return to Palestine, nor a sacrificial worship under the sons of Aaron, nor a restoration of any of the laws concerning the Jewish State.' Beliefs such as these, to which Cohen was extremely

sympathetic, brought him into conflict with the emerging Zionist movement in Germany. A heated exchange of letters between Cohen and the young Buber on this very issue may be consulted in vol. ii of Cohen's *Jewish Writings*.

55. See the remarks of P. L. Berger in *The Heretical Imperative: Contemporary Possibilities of Religious Affirmation* (Collins, 1980), 60 ff. etc.

56. S. Kaplan's introduction to the English translation of Cohen's *Religion of Reason* (Ungar, 1972), p. xxii.

57. Quoted by Löwith, *Philosophie der Vernunft*, 10.

58. *Sämmtliche Werke* (Stuttgart & Augsburg, 1856), xi. 568.

59. *Religion II*, 106.

60. Ibid. 64 f. (emphases added).

61. Cohen, not Buber, rescued the I–Thou relationship from Feuerbach and endowed it with a positive moral and religious significance. From these two writers it passed into Christian theology. See, for example, *CD*, iii/2. 222 ff.

62. See Schwarzschild's introduction to Cohen's *ERW*, pp. xviii ff., where it is stated that the entire project of Cohen's *Ethik* involved 'ethical de-ontologization' and that its terms are to be understood functionally, not ontologically. On pp. xxii–xxiii he castigates both Jewish and Christian scholars who 're-ontologize' Cohen and exploit his philosophy for theological purposes.

63. *LRE*, 81.

64. In *Religion II*, 47 ff., Cohen speaks of a spiritual *Gemeinschaft* between the *Grundgedanken* of pure knowledge and religion.

65. For Cohen's use of *Korrelation* in logic see pp. 49 f. where a teleological relation is posited between thought and the possibilities of consciousness.

66. *Systematic Theology* (Nisbet, 1968), i. 68.

67. See vol. iv, cols. 139–41. J. P. Clayton's excellent work, *The Concept of Correlation: Paul Tillich and the Possibility of a Mediating Theology* (De Gruyter, 1980) makes no reference to Cohen's thoughts about this concept.

68. For correlation as involving reciprocal relations see *Religion III*, 101, and for Cohen's equation of this with teleology see the important quotation on p. 50. Cohen believes that this form of teleology had already been anticipated in Old Testament texts which show clear traces of 'idealizing' primal narratives and myths. 'Mythical man is interested only in the question of the world's "where-from?". With the development of religion, this question recedes into the background, dislodged by a new one: "where-to?". . . . Yet the mythical mode of cognition, still characteristic of much

theological thinking, persists in its logical inquiry, the question of the world's "where-from?". There, creation remains an act of divine omnipotence. But with the emerging notion of the world's day-by-day renewal through which the concept of creation is transformed into that of providence, theology turns into teleology, the goal-oriented mode of perception' (*Reason and Hope*, 96–7).

69. *Religion II*, 47. An important methodological point is that when Cohen deals with the terms of a correlative relationship, he insists that they must both affect each other. Hence in religion 'weder Gott allein, noch Mensch allein, der eigene Inhalt des religiösen Bewusstseins ist, sondern vielmehr der Mensch in Korrelation mit Gott' (ibid., 97).

70. Ibid. 96.

71. Ibid. 49.

72. Ibid. 47.

73. Ibid. 47–8. For *Erhaltung* (conservation) in logic see p. 26.

74. *Religion III*, 73–7. Creation is the logical, not temporal, transition from being to becoming.

75. Ibid. 476.

76. *Religion II*, 121 ff.

77. *Systematic Theology*, i. 12.

78. *Religion III*, 437.

79. *Reason and Hope*, 90.

80. Ibid. 92–3.

81. Ibid. 93.

82. Ibid. 93.

83. Ibid. 80.

84. *Religion II*, 100–1.

85. *Religion III*, 440.

86. *Reason and Hope*, 211–12.

87. *Religion III*, 185 f.

88. Ibid. 188.

89. Ibid. 441.

90. Ibid. 435.

91. Ibid. 434–5.

92. See Wolfson, *Philo*, ii. 109–10.

93. For a consideration of the manna legends in rabbinic exegesis and Christian writings see P. Borgen, *Bread from Heaven*, 2nd edn. (E. J. Brill, 1981), and B. J. Malina, *The Palestinian Manna Tradition* (Leiden, 1968). Christian exegesis was indebted to John's gospel in which the manna of the Torah is replaced by Jesus. See B. Lindars, *The Gospel of John* (Oliphants, 1972), 234 ff.

94. *Reason and Hope*, 99.

95. *Religion II*, 18.
96. Ibid. 112.
97. Ibid. 111.
98. *Religion III*, 3.
99. It is interesting to contrast Cohen's understanding of the rationality of revelation to that of Barth. In his book *Anselm*, 44 ff., Barth distinguishes between ontic and noetic ratio, but suggests there is yet another ratio, *ratio Dei*. With Cohen 'ontic', or better, ontological ratio is identified with God, whose being is the being of all logical and teleological principles. Consequently 'noetic ratio' for Cohen 'discovers' ontological ratio, and this is what revelation is. He therefore requires no third 'higher' level of reason (Barth's *ratio Dei*) in addition to the other two, because there is no diastasis between them, but perfect correlation. Accordingly Cohen has no need for a supernatural revelation to be given in order to overcome such a diastasis.
100. *Religion III*, 103.
101. Ibid. 84.
102. Ibid. 100–1.
103. Ibid. 103.
104. See Wolfson, *Philo*, ii. 94 ff.
105. See *Religion II*, 106 (the essence of God should be defined only in correlation with mankind); *Reason and Hope*, 83 (the essence of God is morality); *Religion III*, 414 (the essence of God is truth).
106. The translation of vv. 21–2 is taken from B. S. Childs, *Exodus*, 3rd imp. (SCM, 1979), 583.
107. *Religion III*, 93.
108. Ibid. 94. It should be noted that the *Midrash Rabbah* on Exodus takes the words about the passing before Moses of God's goodness to mean 'I will show thee both my Attribute of Dispensing Goodness and My Attribute of Punishment'; see *Midrash Rabbah: Exodus* (Soncio Press, 1951), 524. Maimonides likewise appeals to this passage in his important discussion of the divine attributes in *The Guide for the Perplexed*, i/54, and takes the request to see God's glory as a request for knowledge of God's essence. Philo, moreover, in one important passage, takes Moses's request to see God's glory to be a prayer for full apprehension of the essence of God's powers, to which the reply is made, 'But while in their essence they are beyond your apprehension, they nevertheless present to your sight a sort of impress and copy of their active working. You men have for your use seals which when brought into contact with wax or similar material stamp on them any number of impressions while they themselves are not docked in any part thereby but remain as they

were. Such you must conceive My powers to be, supplying quality and shape to things which lack either and yet changing or lessening nothing of their eternal nature. Some among you call them not inaptly "Forms" or "Ideas", since they bring form into everything that is, giving order to the disordered, limit to the unlimited,bounds to the unbounded, shape to the shapeless, and in general changing the worse to something better. Do not, then, hope to be ever able to apprehend Me or any of My powers in Our essence' (*De Specialibus Legibus*, i/8. 46–9).

109. *Religion III*, 129.
110. See Wolfson, *Philo*, i. 156.
111. *Reason and Hope*, 139.

3
WILHELM HERRMANN
THEOLOGICAL EPISTEMOLOGY
AND THE DUALISM OF FAITH

WILHELM Herrmann taught systematic theology at Marburg from 1879 until his retirement in 1917. It was during his professorship that the theological faculty of Marburg underwent dramatic changes. From being something of a provincial academic backwater, it became an international centre of theological learning, attracting students not only from Germany and Switzerland, but from other continental countries, England, Scotland, and America. In the summer semester of 1878 there were only 60 students registered with the faculty, but after Herrmann's appointment that number rose to 176 by the summer of 1883. After Harnack's arrival at Marburg in 1886 numbers increased even more dramatically, so that by 1888 there were 241 students of theology. With a teaching staff that was to include such giants as Weiss, Jülicher, and Otto, theology at Marburg continued to prosper until the advent of the First World War. Though the theological style of this important centre of learning was unashamedly called 'modern'—a trend which Barth later dismissed as bankrupt liberalism—the unprecedented growth of Marburg perhaps more than anything else attests to the vitality of theology there. Many able students were drawn to Marburg and among Herrmann's pupils were people such as Barth and Bultmann who became leading theologians later in the century.[1] It was roughly about the same time that Marburg became the renowned centre of neo-Kantian philosophy, with the philosophical faculty likewise enjoying an unprecedented leap in student numbers and increased international acclaim. With two such lively faculties, interdisciplinary discussion was inevitably stimulating. To appreciate Herrmann's response to the Marburg critique of religion, however, it is first necessary to consider how this appropriation of Marburg neo-Kantianism was indebted to Ritschl's theological epistemology, which decisively coloured his approach to the relations of theology and philosophy.

The contemporary trend in Herrmann research has been to divide his work into various phases. One disputed point concerns the extent to which Marburg neo-Kantianism was a formative influence or whether its impact was limited to one particular period. Although it cannot be denied that Herrmann's *Die Religion im Verhältnis zum Welterkennen und zur Sittlichkeit* (1879) shows familiarity with Cohen's early work,[2] it should be recalled that the Marburg philosophy itself did not achieve thorough systematic expression until publication of Cohen's system began in 1902. The philosophers at Marburg, moreover, only began to write books about *Religionsphilosophie* during the last decade of the nineteenth century;[3] yet whatever the history of the complex interplay between theology and philosophy at Marburg, it is clear that by the first decade of this century Herrmann had adopted the neo-Kantian *Wissenschaftsbegriff* in its entirety.[4] In Herrmann's article *Die Wirklichkeit Gottes* (1914), for example, it is stated: 'Humanity has sought truth for its life in three directions. We want to become truthful in our willing, cognition or knowing, and experience. From the first there arises morality, from the second, science, and from the third, art.'[5] Here is the tripartite division of knowledge which had been traditional since Kant and which was once more being advocated by Cohen and Natorp. Herrmann's familiarity with the theory of cognitive generation is evident from the way in which he calls the products of these three *Richtungen* 'productions' (*Erzeugnisse*).

Herrmann's indebtedness to Marburg philosophy is shown not only by his acceptance of the theory concerning how knowledge is generated by the transcendental structures of consciousness, but also by his agreement with Cohen's estimation of myth as naïve, pre-scientific knowledge:

Myth is a primitive form of science . . . Myth attempts to give an explanation of things appropriate for undeveloped consciousness. With every advance wrought by elucidative thought, mythical explanation recedes. Elucidative thought advances in ever-new forms wherever there is still the need of a surrogate for science.[6]

The kind of thought which attains *Wissenschaft* is, by contrast, *rationalistisches Denken*. Its supremacy over the *ad hoc* connections of myth is due to the fact that it has a priori rules and is governed by laws:

The law-ordered structure of reality is not a result of scientific research, but rather its presupposition. . . . The law of nature, or the conception of how the structure of nature is itself constituted by law, has become evident to our contemporary thinking as the eternal presupposition of all experience in space and time.[7]

When speaking of science or knowledge, Herrmann, like Cohen, was very sceptical about the ability of empirical intuition to contribute anything to knowledge. Knowledge of reality is achieved solely through the ideal workings of thought:

All work aimed at securing knowledge of what is real depends upon two principles. The first is that the reality known by science is a law-constituted system, a sequence of happening, that is, governed by laws. The second is that the real known to science is never completely and fully grasped.[8]

The process of coming to know reality involves work at mental tasks and never reaches a conclusion because science advances by progressively generating knowledge in a never-ending development. The development in question is determined by a priori laws and the knowledge thereby achieved has such a character that it claims absolute validity and compels universal assent (*Allgemeingültigkeit*).

Important to Herrmann's appropriation of neo-Kantian philosophy was the impetus given by Ritschl, who felt the possession of a sound epistemology was an essential prelude to any systematic theology.[9] The flavour of his epistemological style can be savoured in the following remarks from the *Theologie und Metaphysik* of 1881:

The representation of a thing arises out of the different sense-impressions which attach themselves in a certain order to something which fixes perception in a limited space. We posit the apple as round, red, and sweet because the impressions of the senses of touch, sight, and taste attach themselves to the place where the corresponding relationships of form, color, and taste are perceived. It is precisely from these relationships which converge in the same place in repeated perceptions that we focus the representation of a thing. A thing 'exists' in its relationships and it is only in them that we can know the thing and only by them that we can name it. The significance of the relation of these characteristics, ascertained through sense-impressions and expressed in the judgment, 'This thing is round, red, and sweet,' is that we get to know the subject of this sentence only in its predicates. If it were possible for us to let these predicates drop from our sight or for us to forget them, then the thing with which we were acquainted under these characteristics would also fall out of our cognition.[10]

This quotation shows, first, how Ritschl's account of knowledge had no place for Kant's thing-in-itself. There are no hypothetical entities 'behind' appearances and the object is simply a regular sequence of relations, perceived characteristics, or attributes. Secondly, however, knowledge requires judgements as well as perception, from the cognitive agent. Without perceived attributes or characteristics there could be no thing, but neither would there by any knowledge of objects were there no rational agents to value or judge the mass of perceptual material that bombards the senses and excites feeling. At its crudest this epistemology confesses 'we know the thing in its appearances' or 'know things-in-themselves as they are *for us*'. This important *pro nobis* accent in Ritschl's epistemology, though possessing certain theological advantages, encouraged confusion and lack of clarity concerning the nature of known objects.

In one passage Ritschl suggested that actual things were causes of the qualities perceived, but elsewhere his writings betray the view that things are simply mental fictions.[11] The reason for this lack of clarity in ontology is to be sought in Ritschl's misgivings about metaphysics. It seems to have been his opinion that metaphysical and ontological questions could safely be ignored once a sound scientific epistemology had been constructed. In espousing what Troeltsch called 'ontological agnosticism', Ritschl sometimes satisfied himself with an epistemology which verged on vulgar realism.

Metaphysics, according to Ritschl, examines the universal grounds of being and yields only 'elementary and formal knowledge' of things in general. This supposed science, moreover, is blind to a fundamental feature which informs all experience, for its concentration upon things in general encourages it to ignore the crucial distinction between nature and spirit. The confounding of the two realms—that of nature and that of morality, culture, or spirituality—abounded not only in the metaphysics of Absolute Idealism, but also in the philosophies of matter that flourished in Germany after the disintegration of Hegel's School. The distinction between *Natur* and *Geist*, originally embraced by Lotze in repudiation of the philosophies of matter, was to exert a formidable influence upon the course of Protestant theology throughout the remaining decades of the nineteenth century. It continued to make its presence felt in theology when idealism gave way to existentialism in the years immediately following the First World War.

Ritschl was remarkably vague over the question as to whether the distinction between nature and spirit said something about reality or whether it was simply a distinction in two different ways of knowing. His epistemological investigations often proceeded by way of unsystematic psychologizing. In one passage, for example, the origin of the distinction between nature and spirit is based upon generalizations about the ego:

... in order to elicit the distinction between the two in the realm of the subject, I recall the twofold manner in which the mind [*Geist*] further apropriates the sensations aroused in it. They are determined, according to their value for the Ego, by the feeling of pleasure and pain. Feeling is the basic function of the mind, inasmuch as in it the Ego is present to itself.[12]

Other passages, by contrast, suggest that the distinction is based not only upon the psychology of cognition but upon differences in the two sorts of knowledge and their respective methodologies. Elsewhere the distinction between *Natur* and *Geist* arises from arguments about the value of the two species of knowledge. Natural science, though it enables predictions about the course of natural events and allows human beings to control the natural order, is incapable of fashioning spiritual and moral goals even for the natural scientist. Though lacking the rigour of later epistemologies, this approach anticipated the distinctions between natural sciences and the humane disciplines which were to receive much attention from Dilthey, Windelband, and Rickert. Whatever its metaphysical, psychological, or epistemological origins, Ritschl was firmly convinced that his systematic contrast escaped the attention of metaphysics or ontology, which is 'indifferent to the distinction in value by which the metaphysician, as spirit, knows himself to be set off from all nature and feels superior to it'.[13] Scientific knowledge of nature, as well as the philosophies of matter based upon it, were consequently thought to offer no satisfactory 'world-view'. They could not frame any interpretative system of values, goals, and hopes for humankind.

It was such weighty religious issues of nature and destiny that ultimately preoccupied Ritschl's mind in his epistemological endeavours and in his criticisms of metaphysics. He was convinced that no religious interpretation of the world and its human occupants was possible without acknowledging some distinction between nature and spirit.

In all of its forms, the religious world view is established on the principle that the human spirit differentiates itself to some degree in value from the phenomena within its environment and from the workings of nature that press in upon it. All religion is interpretation of that course of the world which is always perceived, in whatever circumstances, an interpretation in the sense that the sublime power which holds sway in or over that course of the world sustains or confirms for the personal spirit its own value over and against the limitations imposed by nature or by the natural workings of human society.[14]

Correlatively, 'Theology has to do, not with natural things, but with the states and movements of man's spiritual life . . .'[15] Ritschl almost monotonously improvises upon the theme of nature and spirit. It is encountered in his discussion of different types of knowledge, when he appeals to the Kantian distinction between theoretical and practical reason, and in his condemnations of mysticism and speculative theism. His thoughts about the relations between theology and philosophy were likewise largely determined by this distinction. He suggested, for example, that theoretical judgements, as well as philosophical and scientific world-views, establish only general and special laws to explain 'parts' of the world in terms of natural causation. Religious and moral judgements, by contrast, take account of spiritual and mental life. Such judgements, unlike the partial knowledge arising from investigation of particular phenomena, are all-embracing. They are judgements about the world as a whole and, more specifically, about its total value for its human inhabitants who, as well as being of nature, are also spiritual and moral beings.

These and other arguments advanced by Ritschl are not devoid of value. God, for example, is not usually regarded as an object like natural objects; it may well be the case that religious knowledge is different in kind from that of natural science and is perhaps more akin to moral and aesthetic forms of cognition. Nevertheless much confusion arose, first, from Ritschl's tendency to deal with different types of knowledge as though they were discrete and, secondly, from his refusal to address ontological questions about the nature of known objects. This situation becomes even more invidious when philosophy is ranked alongside natural science as theoretical knowledge and when, for that very reason, it is argued that philosophical reasoning is in no position to assess the truth claims, epistemological status, or reality of alleged religious experiences and world-views. When philosophy does address problems like these, Ritschl's considered opinion was that it not only lapsed into a questionable form of metaphysics which ignored distinctions between *Natur* and *Geist*, but became pseudo-theology by attempting to make a total assertion about the nature of reality.

There is, nevertheless, evidence suggesting that even Ritschl was aware that his famous distinction made claims which were ontological in character and that theology required some sort of metaphysic if its religious assertions were not to be deprived of ontological reference.[16] Neither could he remain content with an ultimate disjunction between theoretical and religious knowledge:

> The possibility of the mixture and again the collision of the two kinds of knowledge lies herein, that they are directed towards the same object, namely, the world. One cannot soothe oneself with the peaceful decision that the Christian knowledge understands the world as a whole, the philosophical establishes the special and general laws of nature.[17]

In order to overcome any collision or antagonism between philosophy and theology, causality and teleology, scientific knowledge of the natural world and religious, moral, or aesthetic judgements, Ritschl contended that an urgent task for theology was the development of a harmonious *Weltanschauung*. This, however, proved a difficult project, for Ritschl deprived theology of the necessary philosophical and conceptual tools to accomplish such a task.

Ritschl's use of philosophical argumentation is both confused and eclectic principally because he did not first formulate a theory of cognition and then build a theology upon it, but rather propounded his epistemology subsequently, in defence of his theology. The emphasis upon 'what things are *for us*' is largely due to the influence of a very definite theological doctrine. In the following passage, for example, Ritschl's scientific epistemology is presented alongside the religious doctrine:

The elementary knowledge that spiritual life is something real is only preparatory to the knowledge of the distinctive character of the spirit in the functions of feeling, knowing, and willing—chiefly, however, in willing. Furthermore, one cannot authenticate the impact of others upon the human spirit except in the context of active and conscious sense impressions [*Empfinden*] which comprise the raw material for the articulate self-consciousness of the 'I'. This raw material is the key to all knowing and the occasion for recognizing the motives of the will. Only in this realm of the actuality of the spiritual life can one understand the actions of God which furnish the basis for religion. But since we can only perceive God in his actions towards us, which correspond to his public revelation, so it is that we perceive God's presence for us precisely in these actions.[18]

The doctrinal element at the heart of Ritschl's epistemology appears even more clearly in the following passage:

. . . what we substantiate religiously as the activity of God or Christ within us authenticates the presence . . . of the author of our salvation. . . . *Hoc est Christum cognoscere, beneficia eius cognoscere non quod isti* (*scholastici*) *docent, eius naturas, modos incarnationis contueri*. Therefore the subtance and worth of Christ should be understood in the beneficient actions upon us Christians, in the gift of the blessedness which we sought in vain under the law—not in a previously held general concept of his divinity.[19]

Aided by this Melanchthonian epistemology, Ritschl economically combined doctrines of revelation, Christ, and salvation, grounding them all in an appeal to the revelatory benefits of 'God or Christ'. These effects, being primarily a religious resource that enables Christians to face the moral tasks confronting them with resolution, are tokens of a lively relationship with God. The individual member of the Christian fellowship enjoys an unbreakable relationship with God by virtue of these revelatory effects. They alone supply knowledge of God and the resulting practical experience authenticates, validates and guarantees the legitimacy of such knowledge.

The almost positivist temper of Ritschl's vocabulary, in which revelatory benefits become the raw material of religious cognition, testifies to the cardinal importance of this approach to revelation for his entire theology:

To the degree that a man wants to be a Christian, he has this datum which he must acknowledge as given: the relationship to God which is expressed by Christ and sustained by him ... One must avoid all attempts *to go behind this datum*, that is, to determine in detail how it has come into being and empirically how it has come to be what it is.[20]

An appeal to the Melanchthon of the *Loci*, together with an epistemology that sought knowledge of God exclusively in the practical experience of God's (or Christ's) revealed benefits, became prominent features of Ritschlian theologies. Adopting such a standpoint usually involved embracing three additional theses. First, there was the denial that philosophy, natural science, or any form of theoretical knowledge that refused to adopt this revelatory and experiential basis, could articulate any general statement about the world or attain reliable knowledge of God. There was, secondly, the view that philosophy was incapable of assessing the truth claims of religious knowledge. Thirdly, despite difficulties in arguing about the nature of a cause from some alleged effect, there was a naïve theory about religious experience which maintained that God is known chiefly through introspection. By perceiving some spiritual or moral inner motions, the individual member of the Christian community comes to acknowledge that these 'effects' are divine in origin and yield intimate knowledge of the divine will. To this extent Garvie's observations about Ritschl's methodology are not without justification:

His true attitude is one of absolute scepticism as regards the ability of human thought apart from Christian faith to reach any view of the world which offers any completeness or certainty. But over against this philosophical scepticism must be placed a religious positivism. Whatever he takes away from us as illegitimate profession of philosophy, he gives back to us as a warranted assurance of religion.[21]

This position allowed Ritschl to claim certain knowledge of God's revelatory benefits which we rational agents, *qua Geist*, perceive and judge according to their value *pro nobis*, whilst simultaneously avoiding any positive ontological statement about God's relation to the world. In the end the only legitimate form of metaphysics turns out to be a Christian *Weltanschauung*:

In Christianity the revelation through God's Son is the *punctum stans* of all knowledge and religious conduct ... the acknowledgement of God's revelation in Christ yields this pre-eminent excellence of Christianity, namely, its view of the world as a rounded whole, and that the goal it sets to life is this, that in Christianity man becomes a whole, a spiritual character supreme over the world.[22]

The distinction between nature and spirit, his understanding of metaphysics and philosophy, the rejection of speculative theism and mysticism, plus his scientific epistemology, are all indissolubly bound to Ritschl's central theological motif. By appropriating the benefits of 'God or Christ' through faith, man is freed not so much from the natural law, as from the law of nature, that is, from the causally determined and necessary course of natural events, which was thought to be the content of scientific and philosophical knowledge. The great boon afforded by these revelatory benefits is that they elevate mankind to a position from which moral and spiritual 'lordship' may be exercised over the law-determined world of nature:

Reconciliation is not merely the ground of deliverance from sin's guilt, and from all evils in some way merited: it is also the ground of deliverance [Befreiung] from the world and of spiritual and moral mastery [Beherrschung] of the world. . . . the believer exercises spiritual dominion over the world in accordance with his justification through faith.[23]

Ritschl artfully combines doctrines of sin and justification, first with his distinction between nature and spirit and, secondly, with a questionable understanding of Kant's contrast between pure and practical reason. This is calculated to support the view that through justification and reconciliation one is elevated from the mechanically determined course of natural events into the sphere of God's Kingdom, which is the moral and religious purpose of the world.[24] Following this translation to the teleological sphere, worldly reality is known sub specie aeternitatis. Ritschl's estimation of reason's competence is accordingly governed by his understanding of justification by faith in its practical aspect, together with the epistemological theory which he devised for it:

The correct forms of the understanding, no less than the Scholastic forms, are subject to the truth of the principle that revelation goes beyond reason [revelatio supra rationem]. Revelation must be given so that our experience of it can be apprehended and interpreted with ontological, logical, and psychological correctness. . . . Ratio, however, is given a different meaning when the other principle is advanced that revelation goes contrary to reason [*contra rationem*]. By reason here is meant a connected world-view which interprets the order of nature and spiritual life with methods of knowledge that are indifferent to the Christian religion. The Christian view of the world is thus opposed to that produced by materialism and to those views presented in systems of monistic idealism.[25]

Though it is undoubtedly correct to suggest that traditional Christian beliefs are incompatible with materialism and monism, it may be questioned whether the opinion that revelation is contrary to reason is an adequate response to objections raised against Christian beliefs by both philosophies. Neither can the contention that revelation is contrary to reason supply sufficient grounds for the justification of religious beliefs. In addition, moreover, Ritschl's constructive doctrine of reconciliation had fatal theological flaws. His single-hearted determination to repudiate both monism and materialism resulted not only in a positivist approach to revelation, but also in a doctrine of salvation in which nature possessed mainly negative overtones. What natural science called nature—a necessary series of events causally determined by immutable laws—was something from which one needed to be delivered. Though the revelatory benefits of God were supposed to afford a spiritual and practical 'lordship' over the world of nature, nature had received such a negative status in Ritschl's theology that the mastery in question appears to have been exercised over a vacuum. This lamentable disjunction between doctrines of salvation and eschatology on the one hand and creation on the other became one of the more questionable legacies of the inheritance bequeathed by Ritschl to later generations of Protestant theologians.

I. REALITY

When Herrmann came to address the criticisms of his philosophical colleagues at Marburg, his armoury consisted of largely Ritschlian weapons. The distinction between nature and spirit, which was for Ritschl primarily an epistemological distinction, assumed more ontological overtones at the hands of Herrmann. An early writing in 1879, for example, contended that religion has privileged access to a reality which could not in principle be known by either philosophy or natural science: 'If this power over the world stands firmly to religious faith as something truly real [als etwas Wirkliches], the category of reality [Realität] has another meaning here than that used by metaphysics, since the validity of the religious object is rooted solely in a definite energy of self-feeling.'[26] In 1907, now in opposition to Cohen, Herrmann was still insisting that religion deals with a Wirklichkeit which eludes the grasp of any philosophical thought:

Man deceives his own feeling of Selfhood when he shirks the moral task, but he protects this feeling from suspicion of illusion when he decides to act in its service. It is by means of this feeling of Selfhood that we become conscious of a reality in which we live as individuals. This reality, however, can not conform with what is scientifically comprehensible.[27]

Not only did Herrmann wish to exorcize metaphysics from theology and to devise an academically respectable scientific epistemology for his discipline, he was of the opinion that the theologian need not be unduly worried about philosophical views. Provided philosophy respects the difference between things and spirits or acknowledges a distinction between 'independent knowledge' and the 'moral ideal', 'whether in other respects philosophy is deistic, pantheistic, theistic, or anything else, is a matter of indifference to us as theologians'.[28] When philosophy ignores these distinctions and ceases to respect its limits (Grenzen), as it seemingly did in Marburg Religionsphilosophie, another strategy was called for. Such a situation merited fierce anti-philosophical apologetic, such as 'God's reality lies beyond every-thing that science can prove . . . When this science which ventures to call itself Religionsphilosophie dies, faith is brought to stand upon its own feet.'[29]

Faced with such able and informed opponents as Cohen and Natorp, Herrmann found himself in an awkward situation. On the one hand he desired to welcome the mastery (Herrschaft) of the world afforded by the natural sciences for which his colleagues were busy supplying epistemologies.[30] On the other hand, however, he could not accept the Marburg philosophy in its entirety, for his own theology would then have to become Religionsphilosophie. He would be compelled to reduce religion to either ethics or feeling and cease speaking about God's reality, since the price demanded for a scientific account of religious belief was the renunciation of its traditional cognitive claims (Tran-

szendenzansprüche). Herrmann would have none of this. He fought resolutely for the *Selbständigkeit* of religion, that is, for its irreducibility and cognitive integrity. Religion, he insisted, knows a *Wirklichkeit* of a totally different order from anything encountered by philosophy or *Wissenschaft*.[31] Access to this reality is afforded soley through faith-experience and the knowledge which is thereby acquired possesses certainty (*Gewissheit*).

All this suggested to Herrmann that philosophy had very definite limits of an epistemological and ontological nature. Religion, by contrast, gained access to a reality through a special religious way of knowing. It would therefore be the height of folly for theology to become inextricably bound to some secular ontology or alien epistemology. No less than Ritschl he therefore believed that the integrity of theology demanded the exclusion of metaphysics and ontology:

For me the exclusion of metaphysics from theology implies the clear perception that methodical knowledge of the scientific kind in no way makes contact with the reality of our God. Science does, indeed, grasp nature and the eternal ground of nature—what we, through faith, recognize as a work of divine activity—but science does not grasp the supernatural God himself. When we separate metaphysics from the theological portrayal of faith, we consequently acknowledge that we come to God only because he came to us in history. In addition we also perceive that the researcher, with his science alone, does not completely arrive at knowledge of what truly is: that this entire world of science, even though its temporal existence is grounded in the eternal, passes away; that only personal beings, who have found God and do his will, remain in eternity. It is this 'dualism' of faith that we intend and affirm when we banish metaphysics from the theological portrayal of faith.[32]

Such dualism of faith was certainly not welcome to Marburg *Religionsphilosophie*, not only on account of its confessional or apologetic character, but additionally because it threatened to upset the system by advocating two major asymmetries. First, it was asserted by Herrmann that another reality existed *ausserhalb* that monism of experience which was the central presupposition of Marburg philosophy. Secondly, moreover, Herrmann's own theological epistemology contradicted the general epistemology of the Marburg philosophers. Their claim was that for human cognition *alles aufgegeben ist*, whilst Herrmann suggested that the reality (*Wirklichkeit*) encountered in the Christian religion is *gegeben* through a special experience, namely, revelation. The important implication of this was that Herrmann could not accept that identity between *Sein* and *Denken* to which the philosophers aspired. The reality of his God could not be comprehended by Cohen's category of *Wirklichkeit*, nor even by his category of *Realität*.[33]

II. LAW, PHILOSOPHY, AND WORK

Herrmann's writing of 1879 endeavoured to show with much pathos how metaphysics attempted in vain to achieve a unified conception of the world. This metaphysical quest for unity, wholeness, and totality was seen by Herrmann to arise not simply from a purely academic preoccupation with systems; but rather from deep-seated 'practical' impulses which inspire all philosophical activity. Herrmann attributed, perhaps unfairly, a soteriological quest to all philosohers, arguing that those who wrote about metaphysics hoped to solve the riddle of man's position in the world. Metaphysical systems, whether monist, idealist, or pantheist, were nothing less than futile attempts to heal the sundered existence of humanity. Herrmann, following Ritschl, believed that human life was in a precarious position being part nature, part spirit. On the natural level it seemed governed by general and special laws of causality, yet on the spiritual (that is, moral or religious) level there is the prospect of the purposeful rule of teleology. Human life, being partly constituted by nature, appears oppressed and constrained by necessary laws, but when it aspires to be spiritually alive and moral, the human being needs to feel free from the constraints of necessity and causality in order to devote itself to moral tasks. Metaphysics, therefore, when it ventures to grasp the whole, attains only one ultimate: the *Naturgesetz*, which is the sole unifying concept available to it. The Christian *Weltanschauung*, by contrast, reconciles and unifies the seemingly antagonistic realities of nature and spirit by regarding them both as being under the teleological rule of a personal and gracious God.[34]

The idea that philosophy produces only the *thought* of a law-ordered causality when it offers a general description of reality is repeated in Herrmann's later debates with Cohen and Natorp. His criticism, for example, of Cohen's *Gottesidee*, which created a harmony between various parts of the system, was that its content was merely the *thought* of a unity between logical and moral truth.[35] He argued furthermore that when a philosopher like Cohen seeks *allgemeingültige Erkenntnis* in religion, he is bound to be disappointed and will find only archaic illusion or myth; legacies, that is, of a pre-scientific era. There is nevertheless something startling in the assertion that: 'Whoever proffers the claim of *Allgemeingültigkeit* for the religious point of view, makes religion into something base . . .'[36] Herrmann's contention that religion is devalued when it is regarded as making the sort of claims which can be evaluated by philosophical criticism, may result from a belief that philosophy abstracts and distorts personal experience. The theological roots of his approach, however, lie much deeper.

Take, for example, this seemingly innocent statement about life (a key concept in Herrmann's theological vocabulary): '. . . personal life is no scientifically ascertainable fact, nor does it permit itself to be objectified'.[37] Marburg philosophy, of course, deemed objectification to be the cognitive generation of objects according to laws and the pursuit of such knowledge an *Aufgabe*, a task involving mental work.[38] It is interesting that Herrmann constantly called this procedure of objectification and generation, supposedly employed in all cognitive activity, a 'work': 'The mere resolve to work includes the notion that the things, on which we work, will, in their genesis and activity, obey the laws which our thinking can comprehend.'[39] It was by means of such work that nineteenth-century humanity gained technical 'lordship' or 'mastery' over the natural world and the systematic philosophy, which sought to clarify the fundamental structures of this scientific enterprise, was no less a work. Natural science, and the philosophy that hoped to 'ground' this knowledge through *Logik*, were furthermore forms of *Gesetzerkenntnis*. After stressing that work and law are essential to philosophical or scientific knowledge, Herrmann took the step of introducing the Reformation antagonism between faith and works or grace and law into his estimation of philosophy and natural science.

The doctrine of justification by faith through grace, apart from works of law, governs Herrmann's understanding of the relations between philosophy, theology, religion, and science from beginning to end. It is to be found in all his systematic writings. In one article, for example, Herrmann pays homage to the Kant of the Marburg School, who 'first began to uncover the origin of scientific autonomy in that thinking which itself creates the presuppositions for knowledge of its objects. We can neither exhaust the infinity of reality formed through this thinking nor escape from its law-ordered structure (*Gesetzmässigkeit*).'[40] By contrast, when Herrmann turns his attention to the theme of life, it is asserted that the religious and moral dimensions of *Leben* can neither be addressed nor assessed by the *gesetzmässig* methods of natural science or philosophy:

> ... life creates its own justification through its act. This act cannot, as such, be proved to others, since the act alone brings the acting subject into the forum of life. The attempt to procure such a justification through scientific proof must be seen as profanation from the perspective of life or religion; from the perspective of science it would involve abandonment of its moral dignity and power over things. In generally valid knowledge we comprehend the real which, to the religiously alive, always becomes God's revelation; but neither religious vitality [*Lebendigkeit*] nor the revelation offered [*geschenkt*] to man in such vitality, in any way lead to science. The autonomy of individual religious life and the independence of scientific research belong together. They are linked by their primary moral demand for truthfulness. That their unity is however inscrutable for us, is shown by the inharmonious opposition between what we experience [*erleben*] and what our thinking creates.[41]

Once again there is clear evidence of Herrmann's dualism of faith. Proof (or *Rechtfertigung*) of the scientific–philosophical variety is applicable only to the reality produced by *Gesetzerkenntnis*. Life or religion, by contrast, is justified through what elsewhere Herrmann calls the proof of faith. Religious life is bestowed (*geschenkt*) upon individuals through experience of a vivifying force (*Offenbarung*) which is self-authenticating. It is then, *sub specie fidei*, that the reality comprehended by *Wissenschaft* may become a revelation of God. Science or philosophy therefore 'justifies' only that which falls within its legitimate sphere and is accordingly blind to both justification by faith (or *Leben*) and the proof of faith. This blindness becomes particularly evident when science focuses attention upon life, religion, and morals. In other words, when profane science addresses the religious dimensions of life and culture with its law-oriented methods, it either turns religion into a form of *Gesetzerkenntnis* or finds in religious belief nothing but myth. But the other side of the dualism of faith was of equal importance. Though seemingly paradoxical, Herrmann believed this very procedure of assessing religion without the dualism of faith conspired to undermine the entire scientific enterprise. Scientific tools would thereby be used to tackle jobs for which they were not made and the resulting confusion between natural science and religion blunted those tools by compromising the integrity and *Selbständigkeit* of science.[42]

Alongside this epistemological dualism of faith, there begins to emerge an ontological dualism. Throughout Herrmann's apologetical writings there is a clear contrast between the reality generated according to laws and the experiential *Wirklichkeit* of *Lebendigkeit*. The reality of religious living was so overwhelmingly real for this theologian that it forced him to abandon the Marburg philosophy's methodological monism. No longer was everything a thought-provoking task for mental work (*alles aufgegeben ist*) because something dynamically new is given (*wird gegeben*) to human beings through revelatory experience. Herrmann's response to Cohen invariably dwells on the theme of the gratuité of *Leben* and the self-authenticating knowledge through which it is received:

Knowledge of God, which should procure for us deliverance from a life of mere semblance, does not arise from either *Logik* or *Ethik*. It is no creation of that thinking which can and should demonstrate itself pure before the critical questioning of reason. It is neither generally valid nor provable knowledge, but rather the defenceless expression of individual experience.[43]

Beyond all question of doubt the dualism of faith not only affects knowledge and methods of knowing, but reality as well. There is a sharp contrast between the objective world, generated by laws which necessarily govern the work of cognition, and the private, defenceless, but none the less, actual reality of life, religion, faith, and God.

Herrmann never tired from affirming that his dualism of faith had advantages for both religion and science. Once it was appreciated that the experiential claims made on behalf of religion could not be assessed by either science or philosophy, science could travel its own autonomous way without religious interference. Religion too, for its part, could travel the experiential path of *Vertrauen* without fearing anything from science or feeling the need to meddle in scientific affairs. Faith, indeed, might just discern the *Deus absconditus* lurking somewhere behind the law-ordered work of science. Both scientific researchers and even those poor metaphysicians, whose work results in nothing but the thought of *Naturgesetz*, could take solace from Herrmann for, in more traditional theological language, faith in the Gospel not only delivers from the curse of the law, but helps us to understand the law aright. It becomes the *paidagogos* that leads to Christ. As Luther once said: 'For the law is there in fact, without our being necessary to it, and even against our will, before justification, at the beginning of it, during it, at the end of it, and after it.'[44]

III. LIFE AND EXPERIENCE

No other words characterize Herrmann's theology better than life and experience. Whilst admittedly his earliest writings talk in a Ritschlian manner about *Geist*, words like life, experience, and vitality became more frequent. This was in part due to the increasingly popular *Lebensphilosophie*, the almost forgotten ancestor of later existentialism, but, importantly, it represented Herrmann's response to problems about the *Ich*, *Subjekt*, or experiential side of consciousness which were proving surds for the philosophies of Cohen and Natorp.

Herrmann often used *Leben* and religion as synonyms. Life, like its earlier predecessor, *Geist*, was endowed with religious and moral significance, but being primarily experienced, Herrmann perceived that words like *Leben* and *Erleben* had conceptual possibilities worth exploiting. The experience of being truly alive (*Lebendigkeit*), or of possessing an authentically moral feeling of personhood (*Selbstgefühl*), is a definite, particular, and individual experience which, as such, contrasts markedly with the general, universal, and necessary structures of reality that were being systematized by the philosophers of Marburg. It seemed patently clear to Herrmann that what ever else *das Selbst* might be, it is certainly not 'ein Erzeugnis des Denkens als eine durch allgemeingültige Gedanken festgestellte Tatsache'.[45]

The experience of 'being a self' is, to be more precise, an *Ereignis*, a significant biographical happening which each person 'has for himself alone'. The possession of a truthful, personal, or authentic *Leben* is, therefore, both a religious experience and the presupposition of morality. In order to intimate something of what this event involved, Herrmann adopted an anthropological starting-point: 'The struggling moral will of a man stands under a pressure which he himself could not overcome. He becomes free from this pressure only through an experience [*Erlebnis*] of a specific kind. Unfortunately both Cohen and Natorp too easily by-pass this predicament of the human situation.'[46] Human life, said Herrmann, lies under a moral obligation to become true, but because sin and guilt oppress the will, this task cannot be achieved by either autonomous volition or moral work. Cohen was there-fore completely wrong to suggest sin was the *principium individua-tionis* and the self a task to be worked at; forgiveness and the revelatory experience of unmerited grace create the new life which constitutes the self: 'If we understand by God a power which so affects us that we, through this experience, gain strength to overcome the world, it is self-evident that we can know this God only in so far as he reveals himself to us by his work in us.'[47] This passage clearly echoes the 'Melanchthonian' epistemology of Ritschl and maintains, against Cohen, that a vital power for overcoming the world and the bound will is actually bestowed upon humankind through a revelatory experience. It is the renewed, invigorated self, created by divine power, that alone makes any morality possible and life worth living.

Herrmann could sometimes use Schleiermacherian language to suggest how one becomes aware of this divine power that creates a moral identify for the self. Sometimes he spoke of a *Selbstgefühl* and *Anschauung*, through which one perceives both the actuality of divine working and the new life of the self. This intuitive know-ledge, though immediate, is so uniquely personal that it may be known solely in the depths of personal experience. Like the feeling about which Natorp wrote, it could not be objectified in cognition, but neither, as Herrmann repeatedly stressed, could it be subject to philosophical proof or justification.

The individual nevertheless may, and if a believer should, testify about the personal meaningfulness of this life-bestowing experi-ence to others. Theologians, moreover, have the obligation of helping the 'morally earnest' to interpret their experience aright by means of traditional biblical and doctrinal language. They therefore must portray the 'way' which leads people of good will to religion, but ultimately the individual has to traverse this path for himself and experience religion in the depths of his soul. When this occurs, the experiential event is self-authenticating because 'das Leben schafft sich seine Rechtfertigung durch seine Tat'.[48]

It is important to note how Herrmann's affirmations about faith parallel his statements about *Leben*. First, faith is self-authenticating:

> ... faith cannot defend itself. Those religious people who, none the less, attempt a defence show in so doing that they are secretly ashamed of their faith before men. In spite of this contradiction, faith firmly maintains that God performs such miracles for the faithful; for it can justify this conception to itself.[49]

Faith, secondly, is an unmerited act wrought by divine workings and not something generated through cognitive or volitional labour:

> If faith is pure trust, it is for us a free surrender which is the exact opposite of volitionary activity (the latter would be a work). Faith, at its depths, is really *our own work*, though for the sake of clarity I would prefer to say 'act'. Equally, however, it is experienced as the work of one stronger than ourselves who inwardly compels us. This experienced *union of dependence and freedom* characterizes true religion. It is in this union that there is *created* an inwardly *independent* being; it is a wholly incomprehensible event.[50]

Thirdly, therefore, though God is the active agent in creating life-giving faith, individuals who experience this event are not entirely passive. They may not work in the same sense as God does, but they do respond to efficacious grace in a comportment of humility, submission, and surrender. In short, they assent experientially to revelatory grace.

Faith, fourthly, is essentially miraculous. When Herrmann talked about the miracle of faith, he intended the word miracle to be understood in the strongest supernatural sense possible as *supra et contra naturam*: '... a miracle originates from a transcendent reality; it is therefore to be defined only in contrast with nature, though it is in the sphere of nature that it is experienced. The attempt to make miracle intelligible inevitably annuls the idea of miracle.'[51] At its most succinct, the miracle of faith is an 'over-coming of the world by the faith created by God'.[52] Faith, like *Leben*, cannot be called into being nor be assessed by the

Gesetzerkenntnis which applies to mundane reality alone. Life-giving faith, by contrast, is a supernatural creation of God and also an inner response, neither of which in principle could be objectified. Marburg philosophy, being concerned with codifying cognitive, moral, and aesthetic laws, was therefore in no position to adjudicate the epistemological validity of this personal mode of knowing. Neither, furthermore, could the reality or actuality of faith-experience be incorporated into the idealist ontology of the Marburg system, because faith arises from a reality totally different in character from the cognitive productions of thinking, willing, and aesthetic feeling. Herrmann's intensely personalist approach to faith is particularly manifest in the language he used to portray faith. Dispositional and moral similes, drawn from interpersonal relations, predominate. Faith is pure *Vertrauen* and *Hingabe*, a *Verkehr* between God and the individual. This state impinges upon moral relations between the believer and contemporaries; he aims at trusting, communing with, and respecting his fellows.

By emphasizing the transcendent, supernatural, and miraculous character of life-bestowing faith, Herrmann sought to protect religion from the moral reduction of Cohen and the psychological reduction of Natorp. In response to Cohen he insisted that morality in no way wants a supremely inactive *Gottesidee* that does not interfere with moral striving, but a gracious Lord to grant power for living. His reply to Natorp was that religion involves an actual experience of divine *Wirklichkeit* that works upon the soul and therefore surpasses the category of objectless feeling. Against both Cohen and Natorp, Herrmann asserted that faith, *Leben*, or experience of a power which creates and sustains the self, has its *Ursprung* in an act that transcends the generative powers of the neo-Kantian consciousness. Herrmann, then, far from being an accommodating liberal or naïve idealist, argued for a realist approach to religion, as well as for its cognitive integrity and irreducibility (*Selbständigkeit*). He continuously proclaimed Christian experience to be in touch with a supernaturally effective *Wirklichkeit* that was decisive for the genesis of personality, yet one which could not be assimilated by *Logik*, *Ethik*, or *Ästhetik*, or, for that matter, be incorporated into a scientific system of philosophy.

IV. REVELATION

The typically Herrmannian themes of life, faith, and experience find their systematic anchorage in the concept of revelation, which becomes synonymous with the *beneficia Christi* experienced by the believer. Revelation, as one might expect, yields no *allgemeingültige Erkenntnis*, though it does bestow personal awareness of a divine, life-giving power. Throughout all his writings, Herrmann intentionally focused upon the experience of *Offenbarung* and the divine power actual in it, so that even his own theology could never be taken as a formal 'law of faith'. Dogmas, doctrines, creeds, and articles are secondary to the personal experience of revelation, with which they should never be identified. The therapeutic work of the theologian was to call attention to the primary *Ursprung* of religion in this event of revelation, which was just as supernatural as life or faith. Apologetical therapy involved removing all obstacles to appreciating the primary experiential significance of revelation, whether those obstacles be doctrinal, philosophical, or allegedly biblical.

The situation addressed by revelation is the moral predicament of individuals and Barth himself provides a reliable summary of his teacher's theology on this issue: 'His theology stands or falls with the assertion that man must "himself" will, yet cannot; and then must "himself" experience [*erleben*] or undergo [*erfahren*] revelation.'[53] It is then that God's beneficial revelation comes to aid the weakness of the human will with an influx of divine power which overwhelms and creates new life by healing the rift between willing and nilling.

Throughout Herrmann's writings revelation has a bi-polar structure. There is first a universal anthropological axis maintaining that all human beings desire to be truthful in will and deed, yet are unable to be so through autonomous effort. It is at this point that a second, more theological polarity enters, whereby the individual experiences a supernatural power that heals the will and creates a new moral identity by gathering together the dislocated and opposing movements of the will, which, for Herrmann, was the essence of personality. This second polarity of the revelatory event, called *innere Sammlung* or *Selbstbehauptung*, was something about which Herrmann often wrote:

An man inspired by this understanding of a personal self can accomplish the inner surrender, which makes his self-affirmation [*Selbstbehauptung*] true, only when confronted by reality which he cannot produce [*erzeugen*] from within himself and which is not some generally valid state of affairs, but rather a reality he experiences [*erlebt*] for himself alone. A being who wants to be a truly alive self [*das etwas für sich selbst sein will*] draws the power for this not from something which all men see, but from the hidden resource [*aus dem Verborgenen*] by which, in free self-surrender, the personal being knows itself to be completely overcome. We seek God when we long for such a reality and when we encounter such a reality God reveals himself to us [*so offenbart sich uns Gott*].[54]

A particular crux in this concept of revelation concerns the meaning of the word self. In order to clarify Herrmann's oft-repeated statement 'we have no other means of knowing God except dass er sich uns selbst offenbart', Moltmann appropriately asked whether the 'self' in question refers essentially to God or to man. Is the 'self' or 'self-revelation' to be understood theologically or anthropologically? Moltmann correctly perceived that Herrmann intended to use the term *Selbst* both theologically and anthropologically, so that the human 'self' was defined theologically and God's revelatory activity upon the individual anthropologically:

Revelation is not instruction, and not an emotional impulse. Revelation of God cannot be objectively explained, but it can certainly be experienced in man's own self, namely, in the non-objectifiable subjectivity of the dark, defenceless depths in which we live the moment of involvement. The revealing of God in his working upon ourselves is therefore as unfathomable, as non-derivable, as much grounded in itself as the living of life, which no one can explain, but everyone can experience.[55]

The locus of divine activity in revelation is not in the first instance the law-constituted natural world of science, but the hidden depths of human *Erlebnis*. God, who acts in this submerged, but decisively crucial dimension of individual life, likewise remains hidden from science, generalities, and objectivities. His revelatory activity, however, is as personal, real, and as actual, as the individual who experiences the event: 'The non-objectifiability of God and the non-objectifiability of each particular existence or each particular "self" constituted one and the same mystery for him. The ungroundable character of God and the ungroundable character and *gratuité* of life that is lived merged for him into one.'[56]

Herrmann continually repeated how the life-giving event of revelation was an actuality that could not receive any philosophical or scientific confirmation. To *Wissenschaft*, in its varied forms of natural science, philosophy, or system, such experience remained inscrutable. Its concern was with laws, general structures, objectifications, whilst religion based upon revelation was an unmerited, individual, and personal event, experienced in the actualities of life.

Although the knowledge of revelation was held to be valid in its own way, it was none the less considered different in kind and quality from that acquired by natural science and philosophy. From this perspective it becomes easier to contrast Herrmann's understanding of revelation with that presented by Marburg *Religionsphilosophie*. Herrmann could indeed affirm, with the later Cohen, that knowledge of God had its *Ursprung* in revelation and also that it had implications for morality. Herrmann, furthermore, was in agreement with Natorp in his respect for the experiential, internal, or feeling side of revelation along with its non-objectifiability. It was argued against both, however, that an actual, divine, and life-bestowing power is effective in revelatory situations and, secondly, that this power is experienced as given or bestowed by something beyond (*jenseits*) consciousness. It is therefore a power which could neither be generated nor actualized by the cognitive or moral functions of the neo-Kantian *Kulturbewusstsein*. The new self, arising through its encounter with divine power, is certainly no *Aufgabe* to be worked at, but a gift to be received with gratitude. Herrmann consequently argued that neo-Kantian *Wissenschaft* could neither assess the cognitive claims of revelatory experience nor perceive the supernatural workings of God in that event. The active God of revelation, therefore, could not be made into a logical concept (Cohen) nor be reduced to an immanent objectless feeling that accompanies every act of consciousness (Natorp).

V. THE HISTORIC PRESENT

It is no understatement to affirm that Herrmann's theology aspired to protect the integrity and efficacy of divine activity in revelation from the sophisticated idealizations of the Marburg philosophers. His stress upon the actuality of divine power in the event of revelation, together with its anthropological and moral benefits for the individual, led him to provide a 'historic', rather than a metaphysical, foundation for systematics which was to have decisive consequences for Bultmann's theology.

In the first place it is important to understand how the historical world is ontologically different for Herrmann and qualitatively distinct from the natural world for '. . . on the one hand there is inanimate nature, but life and will, which desires to follow its own laws, gives rise to history as a new region of existence in and above nature.'[57] The distinctness of the historical world is due to the fact that it is a moral and teleological sphere. Here individuals are free from constraints imposed by a law-ordered and causally determined universe. It is a dimension of reality, therefore, in which freedom is possible and actual: 'History, as a reality [Wirklichkeit] distinct from nature, arises before us when we see something in man which can never be explained from its interrelations with other things. . . . History [Geschichte] is a world distinct from nature in which freedom should be realized.'[58]

History, secondly, is that dimension of life in which human beings are able to devote themselves to moral tasks and where a 'truthful', personal, or authentically moral Leben is to be gained or lost. This life has its own peculiar reality and, accordingly, its own very special laws, for whilst the reality of nature is founded upon the Naturgesetz, the Wirklichkeit of history depends upon the Sittengesetz and presupposes freedom. Ethics, not surprisingly for Herrmann, functioned as a philosophy of history. The Lebensbereich of history is no dead static realm, but one populated by 'living figures' and permeated with spiritual and moral energies. Here the influence of moral educators like Paul, Augustine, and Luther lives on and becomes effective in the present. Historical life is, in short, participation in a teleological community: 'History is not a disordered mass of purposeless happenings occurring in the causal nexus. It is the ever-new certainty of individual life cascading forth from the community with which we are associated through the truth and power of the same moral goal.'[59] Though each person has life 'for himself alone', he is not on that account an individual isolated from the transcendental community of moral solidarity. He has communion (Verkehr) with other free spirits when his will conforms to the same moral goal which inspired the sublime educators of humanity. It is a will for truth and personal integrity that creates history and participates in the teleological destiny of humankind:

Without this will to truth, through which humanity desires to set itself free from deadness and become truly alive, there would be no history, . . . but when that creative vitality which carries its future in its volition is lacking, then, of course, history disappears; for history is not a straightforwardly observable happening, but an act of giving shape to the future through a truthful or free will.[60]

On this account, thirdly, history is not some Kantian transcendental idea of freedom posited for the sake of moral theory, but an experiential dimension of life. History is creative act supplying a moral power to be drawn upon creatively in the task of living. Once made truly alive, the biographical situation of the individual is enriched as he or she enters into communion with a teleological kingdom of ends. No longer alone or at the mercy of natural laws that seem to govern biological life with mechanical necessity, the individual experiences fellowship with other free beings. When Herrmann speaks of history, he does so in language which is at once dispositional and drawn from interpersonal relations:

The first impulses of moral perception lead the soul to consciousness of its freedom. They do not arise, however, in the person who is isolated and alone, but in the man who is surrounded by human community. Human beings are made awake to moral knowledge in the primary happening of all historical life—in the moment, that is, when strength and wealth surrender to serve weakness and need.[61]

The desire to 'commune' morally with people, together with the disposition that gives birth to this state, form the *Urphaenomen* of history, since *Vertrauen* is the foundational experience and primary happening of historical life. Acquiring historical knowledge is like a personal revelation—an event which, in Herrmann's own phrase, 'opens the doors to moral perception'. This knowledge, having more to do with personal orientation than with learning past facts, arises from an experiential intuition (*Anschauung*) and has very little to do with detached scholarship. Only those who have 'experienced' history by communing with its moral and spiritual energies are entitled to make 'historical' judgements or to testify about its personal and teleological efficacy.

It is indeed unusual that Herrmann should speak of history in such personalist terms and his idea that both historical and moral knowledge depend upon some specific experience of freedom and communion felt in the depths of the soul is no less strange. The reason for this is that Herrmann was attempting to show how religion, the experience of revelation, makes this sort of history possible. Individuals, by virtue of revelatory benefits, are elevated from the causal nexus of nature into a sphere of freedom and ends where moral lordship can be exercised over the world:

The person who finds himself involved in the movement of history and who, through free service to others, is elevated to trust and, consequently, to moral knowledge, is on the way to religion, provided that the summons to a truth which disregards consequences encompasses these individual experiences as well.[62]

What excited Herrmann was his conviction that the vital dimension of historical living is never at a 'standstill'. Forces, powers, and vital energies pervade history and, through some electrifying religious experience, people are as it were plugged into an immediate, rich, and life-bestowing power. The individual is thereby free to direct his will toward moral goals—goals which already, in part, have been followed by others. One thus enters a network of moral and spiritual influences with which one communes.

The two inner processes (awareness of divine power and voluntary submission to it) appear united in an efficacy of *Vertrauen*. Here is the sphere in which faith in God arises in us. Here everything earthly is cast aside. Here is something supernatural given [*ist gegeben*]. Here, in the realm of moral life, of pure act, pure revelation is possible and actual . . . Real faith is completely inseparable from history, that is, from the history which faith itself has experienced.[63]

The most succinct formulation reads: 'That which in the first place makes possible both history and man a bearer of history is religion.'[64] According to Herrmann the seminal insight of Schleiermacher's youthful writings was his discovery that religion *is* history and that to find religion one must turn to history.[65] Religion, the experience of divine revelation and experiential assent to it, is possible and actual only in the historical realm of freedom and ends which transcends the law-ordered, work-produced, and causally determined world of nature. When Herrman talked about revelation being a *geschichtliche Tatsache* or of 'revelation entering our own historical realm', he was speaking about this transcendental, moral, yet experiential dimension of inner life. In this sphere it could be said that the lives of others reveal themselves to us or that the 'inner life' of Jesus is the mightiest power and most living figure of history. History, then, is that depth of individual life in which God is sought and found for '. . . it is only from events of our history that we can gain the impression that God seeks us in our temporal life and takes us unto himself'.[66] History, accordingly, means something historic in the biographical life of the individual. History is not so much concerned with an event *wie es eigentlich gewesen war*, as with moral and religious facts (*Tatsachen*) and their significance for contemporary *Leben*. In Herrmann's hands even the word fact (*Tatsache*) is transformed through his appreciation of God's self-revelation as act (*Tat*) and human response to it as being also an act or event.

Given this understanding of history as a significant event in individual life, Herrmann had to face problems about relations between the contemporary 'historic' significance of exemplary personalities and research into their past. What was crucial for Herrmann's appropriation of historical criticism, which was called by him a *Wissenschaft*, was not so much a distinction between *Historie* and *Geschichte*, as a contrast between *Geschichte* and *Natur*:

Everything past, which we represent to ourselves as being sensuously comprehensible, falls within the realm of nature. . . . anything existing at temporal or spatial distance from us, we account as belonging to nature and, whether we like it or not, we conceive this conceptually under the forms of nature.[67]

Historical criticism, in so far as it is a science, by definition gains knowledge of facts which belong exclusively to the causally determined and law-governed natural realm. The attempt in Herrmann's book to grasp what is essentially living and actual with methods applicable to learning about dead natural facts was the most pernicious mistake of *Historismus*. When reviewing

Troeltsch's *The Absoluteness of Christianity* Herrmann's consistent argument was therefore:

The science, which demonstrates what reality is like, aims at uncovering the causal connection with some other reality. What it grasps is relative. The efficacious and primary element [*das Ursprüngliche*], however, can be perceived by each individual only for himself through personal conviction.[68]

Unlike natural and historical sciences, Herrmann's *Geschichte* required a living, moral, or personal empathy with its spiritual forces because 'one can only know history in as far as one is sympathetically and actively involved in it'.[69] Herrmann, furthermore, accepted Cohen's idea about the infinity of scientific cognition and this suggested to him that at any one time knowledge is limited and open to further development. In relation to historical science this was taken to imply that its results were for ever relative, indefinite, qualifed, and open to future revision. Yet should the historian for one moment lay aside scientific research into the distantly removed past and begin to evaluate the contemporary 'historic' significance of events for present-day living, Herrmann believed that the researcher had leapt into and encountered another reality. Dead nature, in such cases, is left behind and the question becomes one of moral significance, so that even before he or she is really aware of it, such a 'scientific worker' is on the way to religion. The fruits of biblical criticism were likewise always relative and being a scientific discipline it could neither add to nor subtract from the spiritual or moral image (*Bild*) of Jesus's personality, which the historically alive person intuitively understands from the biblical sources and from his living energy active in the historic life of the Christian community. From a *religionsgeschichtlich* or *wissenschaftlich* perspective, therefore, no absoluteness could be claimed for Christianity, but 'it is perhaps different with the history which is experienced in the present by the individual'.[70]

To conclude this discussion of Herrmann's understanding of history a number of issues must be clarified, since they are of importance for Barth's earliest theological work. In the first place, when Herrmann wrote about revelation in history, he was speaking about a religious experience in the transcendent dimension of an individual's contemporary life and not primarily, it has to be stressed, in some past temporal event. Secondly, the relationship between *Geschichte* and the past is ambiguous in the extreme. The historical sphere, being bound intimately with the individual's experiential communion with life through religion and morality, is not conterminous with the spatio-temporal continuum of natural events. Historical or scientific *Arbeit*, because of its law-dependent methods, cannot reach this spiritual and moral sphere in which truly 'historic' judgements or decisions are made. It follows, thirdly, that the relationship between the natural and historical worlds is similarly ambiguous because the distinction between things belonging to nature and those pertaining to history is not merely methodological, but ontological. When the historian begins to make 'historic' judgements, he forsakes the way of science and travels the path to religion, finding therein that another reality has been given him. Consequently, and this is the fourth point, Herrmann could offer hardly any criteria for assessing the truth of historical (*geschichtlich*) claims, apart, that is, from a personal testimony about their moral and religious significance to the individual and like-minded people who have experienced the vitalities of inner history. One's appropriation of history, like the reception of faith, is a matter of personal orientation which cannot be subject to scientific proof or demonstration. Finally, it should be noted how the relation between revelation and history is discussed exclusively from within the religious circles of faith. Revelation, as a historical fact, meant for Herrmann a religious experience which has importance for an individual's present and future moral comportment. The historical dimension of revelation, however, becomes even more problematical when it takes the form of an experience that raises human beings from the law-determined sphere of nature into the realm of free spirits. On the one hand revelation is an event in the individual's life, yet on the other hand it is located in the transcendental sphere of history. Revelation therefore becomes a permanent possibility at a transcendental level, but is actually present at the 'historic' level whenever moral questions are raised.

Herrmann's great objection to neo-Kantian philosophies of religion was that they not only ignored the actuality of religion in individual life, but forgot that the moral subject is dependent upon encountering some resource given by God in history. The authentically moral self, accordingly, was not a task, but a gift sustained by grace. To the philosophers, this stress upon the necessity of something being given not only ran contrary to the basic tenets of their epistemology, but seemed at best a curious remnant of mythical thinking and at its worst, an unscientific mixture of naïve religious realism and positivism.

VI. THOUGHTS OF FAITH AND THE TASK OF DOGMATICS

An interesting feature of Herrmann's theological development is that whereas his earliest writings called the doctrinal beliefs of Christians either *Glaubensgegenstände* or *Glaubensobjekte*, from 1884 onwards, the word *Glaubensgedanken* becomes the preferred expression. The reasons for this change in terminology are both interesting and important. In the first place, Herrmann increasingly desired to stress the difference between objects that formed the content (*Inhalt*) of natural or scientific knowledge and the essentially practical content of religious or moral beliefs. Secondly, being considerably indebted to Tholuck, Herrmann always sought to proclaim the religious–experiential benefits of faith, thus protecting his theology from becoming a law of faith or theoretical speculation. Whilst he did not go as far as the Erlangen theologians, who insisted that the experience of spiritual regeneration was a prerequisite for any theological work, Herrmann nevertheless regarded theology as a form of personal testimony that witnessed to the actuality of living religion. Herrmann, thirdly, was increasingly regarded as Ritschl's successor and could hardly avoid the controversy raging over Ritschl's theories about value judgements and the keenly debated issue of whether they provided a sufficiently objective ground for the theological enterprise. His own involvement in this internal theological debate led him to pay more attention to the nature of theological language. Finally, however, a decisive factor, which without doubt prompted Herrmann to revise his technical vocabulary, was his increasing familiarity with Cohen's philosophy and his acceptance of neo-Kantian theories about the constructive nature of thought. According to Marburg philosophy being was a function of thinking, for it was thanks to the generative agency of thought that objects were objectified by laws from the intricate network of possibilities that constituted the neo-Kantian *Kulturbewusstsein*. Though Herrmann enthusiastically accepted this scientific account of epistemology, he could not agree that the supernatural reality, to which dogmas, doctrines, or creeds indirectly testify, was the result (*Erzeugung*) of human thought. Had he done so, he would have been open to the charge of Feuerbachianism and susceptible to the humanist reduction of Natorp. It was therefore imperative for him to clarify such issues as the function of generative thought in theology, the significance of objectifying-type concepts in religion, and the relation of both to the system of thought being constructed by his philosophical colleagues in Marburg.

Herrmann's notion of *Glaubensgedanken* was clearly dependent upon Schleiermacher's distinction between religion and doctrine. A writing of 1888, for example, maintained that faith, the inner experience of liberation from sin and need, has a definite experiential *Inhalt* consisting of those 'facts' which make human beings certain that God is a Father who cares for them. To faith, furthermore, belong the thoughts which express this conviction in linguistic symbols.[71] *Glaubensgedanken* are thus conceptual formulations of an experience by devout Christians. The experience in question is primary; thoughts or concepts, though arising almost spontaneously from the experience, are nevertheless secondary. Herrmann surprisingly found the language of cognitive generation (*Erzeugung*) most congenial for illustrating how a primary experience (*das Ursprüngliche*), in which relevation is received by faith, spontaneously generates ideas, thoughts, and images: 'The thought of such a being, to whom one freely surrenders, each person can and must generate within himself [*in sich selbst erzeugen*]. This he knows—that here alone his liberation from inner impurity and uncertainty is to be sought'.[72] Another passage, from *The Communion of the Christian with God*, is also instructive: 'If I am to be saved, everything depends upon my being transplanted into that inner condition of mind in which such thoughts (of redemption by God) begin to be generated in myself; and this happens only when God lifts me into communion with Himself.'[73] It is intriguing to note how Herrmann in these passages reversed the epistemology of Marburg Kantianism. Instead of thought generating reality from the tasks it sets itself, faith, being an experience in which something real is given and known, generates conceptual forms for expressing the new reality it has encountered.

Thoughts of faith are accordingly abstract conceptualizations of an intimate experience which each individual Christian has 'for himself alone'. The person who 'undergoes' God's self-revelation recognizes that his *Glaubensgedanken*, as well as those of others, are lively portrayals of faith-experience. Negatively, however, this implies that conceptualizations of revelatory experience do not contain knowledge which has pretensions to scientific validity, since their truth can only be perceived by individuals who have enjoyed existential experience of living religion:

> The thoughts of religion possess only as much truth as they are the symbols of this experience which enlargens the various directions of our own existence. . . . The truth of such thoughts can signify nothing other than that they are to the devout Christian a conceptual expression of religious experience. Their truth is the power which is manifest in them, the power, namely, which has liberated a human soul for pure surrender.[74]

All this depends, of course, upon there having been an unambiguous encounter with a potent supernatural resource which possesses such an overwhelming accent of reality that the individual is constrained to recognize its divine origin. This reality is one that the recipient of redemptive power 'can not generate from his own resources as something generally and universally valid, but which he experiences for himself alone . . . We seek God when we long for such a reality and when we encounter such a reality God reveals himself to us.'[75]

The apologetical gains resulting from this way of viewing doctrines and religious beliefs were potentially enormous. Because *Glaubensgedanken* are true inasmuch as the reality to which they testify has been experienced by the individual and consequently possess only personal, not scientific, validity (*Allgemeingültigkeit*), they are on no account *Lehrgesetze*. They are not, that is, laws of religion, analogous to the laws of scientific cognition that necessarily compel universal assent, but personal testimonies of individual experience. When Christians demand that others must accept certain propositions in order to be accounted Christian, they betray their own faith and distort its nature. Theologians, therefore, are in business not to protect, prove, and conserve authoritative dogma or even to improve ancient propositions. They should rather be showing earnestly moral people how religion is to be encountered by testimony, witness, and, perhaps, gentle persuasion. Whether or not 'religion' is adopted depends ultimately upon the revelatory encounter, which is always available in principle to aid the morally struggling will. In relation to Christological dogma, for example, a preacher or theologian should testify about the importance of God's benefits in Christ for his moral or religious life and such witness is properly expressed in *Gedanken* about Christ's divinity. The experience, however, which makes such thoughts possible and necessary is a personal encounter with the moral and historical 'fact' of Jesus's historical personality, in whose *Bild* the individual perceives the operation of God as a power for goodness and love.[76]

Christian *Glaubensgedanken* accordingly have little in common with either philosophy or the varied forms of *Wissenschaft*, since 'Between the thinking of faith and the experiential type of knowledge about the world that reaches its summit in science there exists an unbridgeable chasm for us.'[77] The chasm is ultimately due to the fact that faith has its a priori origin in a revelation of divine activity, which cannot be called into being by cognitive labour or conceptual generation: it is not a work, like those Roman Catholic practices to which Luther objected, but God's gift. Authentic thoughts of faith therefore depend not upon the autonomous functions of generative thought but upon a given revelation of divine grace.[78]

All this is particularly important to Herrmann's estimation of Cohen's *Gottesidee*. To call this idea 'God' was, in Herrmann's opinion, a massive category error. Cohen's so-called God was indeed a thought, but not a thought of faith. It was rather an abstract scientific concept, intentionally generated to connect logical validity with moral theory. That alone formed the content (*Inhalt*) of Cohen's philosophical concept of God, whilst the content of Herrmann's own *Gottesgedanken* was, by contrast, existential and moral. The God articulated in this thought is to be regarded as a redemptive energy for personal life, a *Wirklichkeit* experienced in the epiphany of a new moral self, and not a formal idea of truth.[79] The God of Marburg philosophy therefore had little in common with the God of Marburg theology. Although the scientific procedures of the former were certainly valid for generating scientific knowledge of nature with the aid of thought-posited laws, the living experience which animates the latter is supernaturally bestowed; it is *gegeben* or *geschenkt* by God. Living experience cannot be proved, confirmed, or justified by scientific procedures and neither is it a work of cognitive labour; it is a gift to be received with thanks.

Whatever theology may or may not be, Herrmann believed its task was to develop *Glaubensgedanken* in a systematic manner. This it must do if it is to speak meaningfully to the Christian fellowship and sympathetic outsiders, as well as to the academic community. Herrmann had very definite ideas about the objectives of systematic theology in respect of the first two groups:

What we must do in systematic theology remains something definite for us. We should help people who understand the legitimacy of moral thoughts to find their way to religion. For the religious community we should seek to increase awareness of life in religion. Both goals serve to clarify the inner process in which religion itself perceives its origin [*Ursprung*] to lie.[80]

Systematic theology, moreover, being as much an academic discipline as a confession of faith to insiders and outsiders, needs some method to execute its task properly and some system in order to be academically respectable. There were, however, problems with this, because the thoughts with which the theologian was concerned were different in origin, intention, and quality from the thinking that produced systems of philosophy or generated scientific knowledge of the natural world. This difficulty was considerably exacerbated by the fact that in Marburg at this time there was only one truly academically respectable methodology, namely that being fashioned by Cohen and Natorp. When Herrmann therefore thought about method and system, the system of Cohen and Natorp was the most widely accepted model and the one which came most naturally to his mind.

Perceptive readers may have noticed the key concept of Marburg philosophy, *Ursprung*, in the previous quotation, and it is not by chance that this term frequently appears in Herrmann's later writings. His way of dealing with problems of method increasingly involved borrowing technical concepts from his philosophical colleagues. He attempted to find an origin (*Ursprung*) from which thoughts of faith arose and which also justified their truth. Thus 'religion itself finds its origin [*Ursprung*] in revelation understood as a unique personal experience [*als ein eigenes Erlbenis erfasster Offenbarung*]. For the past thirty years I have endeavoured to show how religion regards the truth of its thoughts grounded only in that experience which is its revelation.'[81] Herrmann's quest for some principle of origin to ground the validity of thoughts of faith obviously owed much to Marburg philosophy, but in that case was not his theology in danger of becoming incorporated into a system of philosophy and, further, was not the integrity and irreducibility of religion thereby threatened?

The answer to these questions is an unqualified no, for in Herrmann's systematics the *Ursprung* which justifies religious thoughts is not some ideal concept, but a personal experience of God's redemptive grace. The event of revelation bestows a power for life which defines and individuates the moral self and, according to Herrmann's ethics, it is this theologically defined self that forms the origin of volition and action. Such revelatory experience becomes, in other words, the a priori condition of personal morality. Unlike the *Ursprung* of Marburg philosophy, his origin of faith was not an ideal synthesis of logical and moral a priori principles; but an actual, personal, and given experience, bestowed by a reality which is not generated by human thought.

Systematic theology, being a function of the Christian community, must speak authoritatively to that community and claim some sort of validity if it is to be taken at all seriously. Herrmann's theology, despite its reluctance to claim scientific validity, did affirm something universal, namely that 'all men' desire to be truthful in their willing, existence, or experience of life. Just as the Marburg philosophy attempted to produce a logic of pure thought, Herrmann aspired to a theology of faith which was expressed in 'pure doctrine', doctrine, that is, which being at once descriptive and normative, would portray clearly the essence of the Christian religion and demonstrate its universal validity for all Christians:

Religion itself sees in its origin [*Ursprung*] that there is a generally valid factor bound with something particular in an indivisible experience. The generally valid element is the morally necessary question of how a person can be truthful in his *Existenz*. The particular factor is the experience [*Erlebnis*] in the grasp of which the person discovers the inner freedom leading to truthful life. Because religion so regards its origin [*Ursprung*], it may not on that account concede that the thoughts which express its life [*Leben*] achieve the same sort of general validity as the thoughts of morality and science [*Wissenschaft*].[82]

The paradoxical result of Herrmann's search for pure doctrine and the generally valid element of the Christian religion was that there arose two sorts of *Allgemeingültigkeit*—one claimed by science and another claimed on behalf of the Christian community. But how, it may be asked, can something be generally valid and not generally valid at the same time? How can theology claim any truth for the *Ursprung* of religion when the only criterion of this truth is a self-authenticating experience of revelation, which is inscrutable and hidden in principle from all forms of philosophical reasoning?

The Marburg philosophers were not slow to criticize Herrmann's theology. How, it was asked, could he consistently claim that thought plays an essential role in religion and yet deny that the thoughts generated by religion could be assimilated into the system of thought they were busy codifying? Why, moreover, did Herrmann maintain that in religion alone experience is given and received, whilst for every other sphere of *Kultur* experience is constructed or generated? His answer to these and other objections was simple: the generally valid thoughts of religion were valid only within the *Lebenskreis* of religion, that is, in the transcendental, yet experienced, realm of history.

After considering the tasks of dogmatics and the nature of theology as an academic discipline, Herrmann, perhaps unwittingly, offered a theological method which was a strange parody of Marburg philosophy. Systematics, like *Logik*, had the task [*Aufgabe*] of accounting for the a priori origin [*Ursprung*] of religion, so that its conceptuality could claim universal validity. Theology, in addition, did not so much strive to demonstrate the laws which pure thinking, willing, or feeling follow, as to depict a normative pattern of religion in a system of pure doctrine. Yet despite this terminological similarity, a chasm separated the two disciplines at Marburg. Although Herrmann availed himself of the Marburg System, it was deprived of its monist and idealist ontology. The origin, or necessary a priori condition, of religion was found in a personal experience which was not *aufgegeben*, but *gegeben* or *geschenkt* by an essentially supernatural *Wirklichkeit*. It was this origin that grounded the truth of *Glaubensgedanken*—those thoughts, that is, which are generated after the experience of revelation and unfolded to produce (*erzeugen*) a pure system of doctrinal abstractions. The universal validity of such doctrine, moreover, was deemed intelligible only to those who had experienced at first hand an encounter with divine *Wirklichkeit* through God's self-revelation. This experience, being self-authenticating, required no scientific demonstration and was for ever hidden from the probings of philosophers. If Troeltsch was correct in his criticism that Herrmann attempted to overcome history with history, it is no less true to say that he also hoped to overcome philosophy with philosophy. His major premiss, that reality is given to individuals in immediate experience, was not at all philosophically acceptable, since it created a central asymmetry for the Marburg System.

The central problems are obvious. Herrmann's epistemological dualism tended towards an ontological dualism: the world generated by logical laws arose from human works, whilst knowledge of divine efficacy, by contrast, was given through revelatory experience. The former was the mechanically necessary world of nature, the latter a free and vital world of morality, history, and life. The unmerited grace of God transferred human beings from the dark dominion of causality, law, and necessity, into the luminous kingdom of ends, which was the true abode of the self. Philosophy was said to be concerned with the first, theology and religion with the second. It was not surprising, therefore, that Herrmann disputed the ability of any philosophy to raise general metaphysical questions about reality. Theology alone could give an account of reality, though only from the viewpoint of faith. All its claims and affirmations were about the experiential sphere of *Leben* and how the universe appears from this perspective.

For all his talk about ethics and morality, Herrmann failed to appreciate one element of realism in Cohen's thought. Morality, said Cohen, required worldly *Dasein* for its realization, but in Herrmann's theology the only connection between creation and *Leben* was the precariously subjective religious experience which freed the individual from the mechanistic world of contemporary *Wissenschaft*. Nature and creation were given such negative overtones that Herrmann's ethical teaching became increasingly focused upon private virtue and its discussion of public morals all the more bankrupt and devoid of content. His ethics was, to use a phrase from Jaspers, a special form of *appellierendes Denken*—an appeal calculated to awaken and call forth an invigorating self-experience. In retrospect, therefore, it must be asked whether the combination of ontological scepticism and religious positivism left Herrmann with any appropriate conceptuality for discussing actual ethical problems.[83] His apologetical responses to Marburg philosophers, which were calculated to support the integrity and irreducibility of religion, encouraged him to give the natural world a mainly negative significance. In the first place it was to be escaped from and, in the second, to be 'ruled over', though the locus of this lordship was the private world of religious experience. When the young Barth arrived at Marburg to study under Herrmann, the tendency towards *Weltverneinung* was already a sinister undertone in the latter's theology.

Herrmann's entire edifice, furthermore, depended upon there being an unambiguous religious experience from which the moral personality arose. His optimism about the steady evolution of human morality, together with his confidence that contemporary Germanic *Kultur* arose from and was dependent upon religious morality, could not endure the moral pessimism that followed the First World War. Once the link between revelation, culture, and conventional morality seemed irreparably fractured, Herrmann's theology lost its credibility. Even at his strongest, when he was at pains to insist upon the *Selbständigkeit* of religion and the objectivity of religious experience, Herrmann nevertheless bequeathed problems for his successors. The relations between faith, its object, and its conceptual expression was one such problem that preoccupied Karl Barth when he turned to dogmatics. These three, according to Herrmann, all rested upon a revelatory experience which was given to the individual 'for himself alone'. This individualist axis considerably exacerbated the problem of how systematic theology could ever aspire to a normative doctrine that claimed universal *Allgemeingültigkeit* even within the Christian fellowship. In later life, Barth found this most unsatisfactory.

It would be tedious to labour the more obvious criticisms that suggest themselves to any perceptive reader of both Ritschl and Herrmann, but there are two points of a metaphysical nature which cry out for comment. The first concerns the understanding of human existence which characterizes these authors. For Herrmann, and to a lesser extent for Ritschl as well, the essence personality was sought in the will. Volitionary activity more than anything else individuated the human being and defined his or her character. Now though it might seem one-sided to emphasize this aspect of human existence to the detriment of the rational, emotive, and psychological attributes of personality, an even greater imbalance was that the will and its activity was considered in isolation from any practical consequences. Although Herrmann affirmed that 'true willing' did indeed give rise to certain activities, by and large these activities were chiefly mental. They are more appropriately called dispositions or, if one prefers, mental character traits, that adhere to the personality. The point therefore is that the agency of the self is severely restricted. The acts of a subject are almost entirely confined to the 'inner side' of existence, and this is not completely surprising since Herrmann defined the will in opposition to the biological, organic, and social activities of human beings. Problems arise not only about the relation of the will to the rest of organic and social life, but, additionally, about the will's capacity to act in the natural world. If the agency of the self is restricted solely to the transcendental sphere of the historic, volitionary 'life' is all the more impoverished and the actions which define a self so limited that the very concept of *Ich*, *Selbst*, or *Subject* becomes severely attenuated.

A further metaphysical point arises in relation to divine activity. Although Herrmann never tired of proclaiming that God acts in the event of self-revelation, he could not ascribe any meaning whatsoever to the notion of God's acting in or upon the natural world. When Herrmann spoke of creation, for example, the primary act of divine creativity was not the creation and preservation of organic being, but the overcoming of the natural world by the faith which he supernaturally creates and graciously bestows upon human beings. Neither primary nor secondary causation are real issues in Herrmann's account of divine activity in the natural order, for the locus of God's influence is confined exclusively to the historic dimension of personal biography which was, of course, defined in opposition to nature. Once in the historic sphere of revelatory experience, the world naturally appears different from what it was before. But this is because one now lives in 'God's world', in, that is, the transcendental world revealed to faith. The only way in which God therefore acts upon the world of nature is through a primary act of elevating people from it into communion with himself. Using more traditional language, it may be said that this act, and this act alone, is an event of primary causation; but it must be noted that no other form of divine activity whatsoever is required or demanded by Herrmann's theology. In relation to the doctrine of God, it would appear that God's activity is as restricted as that of the willing subject, being confined, that is, to the transcendental sphere of history. Theologically, therefore, it seems to be the case that a major dimension of reality is given no positive relation to God and, additionally, that God's relation to natural reality is exclusively limited to a supernatural act of deliverance from it by an original creation of transcendental life. It is therefore to be doubted whether this achieves the desired 'view of the world as a whole' which, in contrast to every other metaphysical system on offer, was said to be the great gain of Christian theism.

Finally, this survey of Herrmann and Ritschl raises in an acute form a question about the significance of the doctrine of justification. The thesis that the validity of religious claims rests exclusively upon a self-authenticating revelation of God and that any other cognitive style is simply an unjustified human *Werk* to be regarded as a priori suspect, as well as religiously and epistemologically invalid, remained a positive dogma amongst Herrmann and his followers. Not only did this insufficiently examined thesis aim at neutralizing legitimate philosophical questions, it could, more grievously, become an impregnable fortress for those who sought refuge from modernity, the secular world, critical historical consciousness, and ultimately from the moral and political challenges of contemporary life.

Herrmann, however, no less than Ritschl, occasionally seemed a little unhappy with a thoroughgoing dualism of faith. He wanted to say that humankind has been seeking truth in the three 'directions' of culture, science, ethics, and art, and that 'Sie gehören alle in besonderer Weise zur Religion und sie bedürfen alle der Religion in gleicher Weise'.[84] A more relentless quest for religious truth in every dimension of culture was a challenge which the young Karl Barth accepted with enthusiasm.

NOTES

1. See G. A. Jülicher, 'Zur Geschichte der Theologischen Fakultät', in H. Hermelink and S. A. Kähler, *Die Philipps-Universität zu Marburg 1527–1927* (N. G. Elwertsche Verlagsbuchhandlung, 1927), 569–74.
2. For Herrmann's critique of Cohen during this period see O. Jensen, *Theologie zwischen Illusion und Restriktion* (Kaiser Verlag, 1975), chs. 1–3.
3. The first edition of Natorp's *Religion innerhalb* dates from 1894. Although Cohen addressed religious issues in a number of articles, his first systematic account of religion was *Religion und Sittlichkeit* (1907). Natorp published his second edition of *Religion innherhalb* in 1908, whilst Cohen continued to pursue religious topics in successive editions of the *Ethik* as well as in his *Der Begriff der Religion im System der Philosophie* (1915). Herrmann's writings throughout this period contain numerous references to both Cohen and Natorp. Particularly important are the three articles 'Hermann Cohens Ethik' (1907), 'Die Auffassung der Religion in Cohens und Natorps Ethik' (1909), and 'Der Begriff der Religion nach Hermann Cohen' (1916), all of which are published in the second volume of Herrmann's *Schriften*. Karl Barth, who arrived at Marburg in 1908, was a student there when the debates between philosophy and theology on the topic of religion were reaching a climax. It is certain that his fragment *Ideen und Einfälle zur Religionsphilosophie* was written shortly after the completion of his studies at Marburg.
4. See P. Fischer-Appelt's introduction to the first volume of Herrmann's *Schriften*, pp. xxxvi–xxxvii, 'Breiter und strenger als mit *P. Natorp* hat Herrmann sein Leben lang mit *H. Cohen* um das rechte Verständnis und die richtige Zuordnung von Sittlichkeit und Religion gerungen, während er sich den neukantianischen Wissenschaftsbergriff im ganzen vorbehaltlos angeeignet hat'. Herrmann explained in an article dating from 1907 that his work *Die Religion im Verhältnis zum Welterkennen und zur Sittlichkeit* was never republished because 'Inzwischen meine ich eine besseres Verständnis von der Religion gewonnen zu haben, und glaube ich auch der Arbeit der Philosophen ein besseres Verständnis der Wissenscahft zu verdanken' (quoted by Fischer-Appelt, pp. xxiii–xxiv).
5. *Schriften*, ii. 298.
6. Quoted by T. Mahlmann in 'Das Axiom des Erlebnisses bei Wilhelm Herrmann', *Neue Zeitschrift für Systematische Theologie und Religionsphilosophie*, 4 (1962), 16.
7. Ibid. 19.
8. Ibid. 20.

9. See the important quotation on p. 113.

10. *Theologie und Metaphysik* (1881) from P. Hefner's translation in *Albrecht Ritschl: Three Essays* (Fortress, 1972), 184.

11. For further discussion see A. E. Garvie, *The Ritschlian Theology* (T. & T. Clark, 1899), 47 ff.

12. *Die chritlische Lehre von der Rechtfertigung und Versöhnung iii: Die positive Entwickelung der Lehre*, 2nd edn. (Adolph Marcus, 1883), iii. 190.

13. Ritschl, *Theologie und Metaphysik*, 155.

14. Ibid. 156.

15. Ritschl, *Die chritlische Lehre*, 20.

16. Ritschl, *Theologie und Metaphysik*, 187.

17. Quoted by Garvie, *The Ritschlian Theology*, 73.

18. Ritschl, *Theologie und Metaphysik*, 193–4.

19. Ibid. 195, 204.

20. Ibid. 178.

21. Garvie, *The Ritschlian Theology*, 75–6.

22. Ritschl, *Die christliche Lehre*, 188–9.

23. Ibid. 332–3; Ritschl, *Theologie und Metaphysik*, 175. The biblical basis for this 'dominion over the world' is to be found in Gen. 1: 26–8, for which Luther's translation reads, 'Und Gott sprach: Lasset uns Menschen machen, ein Bild, das uns gleich sei, die da herrschen über die Fische im Meer . . . Seid fruchtbar und mehret euch und füllet die Erde und machet sie euch untertan und herrschet über die Fische im Meer'. It is important to note that Luther linked this pre-lapsarian dominion enjoyed by Adam with man's God-given faculty of reason. Ritschl is suggesting that his moral and practical *Herrschaft* over nature is again restored to mankind through justification and reconciliation.

24. Here again Ritschl seems indebted to Luther, this time to his distinction between the *regnum rationis* and the *regnum Christi*. B. A. Gerrisch summarizes this distinction as follows: 'In all his dealings with the world man's guide is reason: the world is the Kingdom of reason [*regnum rationis*], and by his God-given understanding and wisdom man is able to subdue the earth and have dominion over the beasts of the field. In his dealings with God, however, only faith can be man's guide, specifically, faith in "the Word" or in Christ: the spiritual sphere is the Kingdom of Christ [*regnum Christi*]. By judicious use of his natural capacities, a man may acquire outward or civil righteousness in the *regnum rationis*, but righteousness in the *regnum Christi* is acquired only by faith—indeed, not so much acquired *by* faith as given *to* faith, for here righteousness is not "active", but "passive".' See *Grace and Reason: A Study in the Theology of Luther* (University of Chicago Press, 1979), 25–6.

166 HERRMANN'S DUALISM OF FAITH

25. Ritschl, *Die christliche Lehre*, 23–4.
26. *Die Religion im Verhältnis zum Welterkennen und zur Sittlichkeit: Eine Grundlegung der systematischen Theologie* (Niemeyer, 1879), 118.
27. *Schriften*, ii. 100.
28. *Schriften*, i. 21.
29. *Schriften*, ii. 292.
30. A typical apologetic motif throughout Herrmann's writings is his insistence that the *Herrschaft* aquired by science and technology was a direct consequence of Luther's Reformation. Modernity began, according to him, not with the Enlightenment, but with the Protestant Reformation. The Enlightenment, and Kant in particular, were authentic successors to Luther's critique of scholasticism. Particularly interesting is 'Kants Bedeutung für das Christentum' of 1884 which is reprinted in *Schriften*, i. Views such as these called forth the wrath of Troeltsch.
31. It must be noted at this point that the word *Wissenschaft* had many meanings in Herrmann's day:

1. Generally a *Wissenschaft* is any theoretical study or discipline which makes cognitive claims. The word may therefore be applied to natural science, experimental psychology, philology, history, etc. In this context, the word can refer to either the results of such undertakings (meaning, thereby, 'knowledge') or the methods involved in the pursuit of this knowledge (hence, being roughly equivalent to the English word 'discipline').

2. Sometimes, and especially when used in connection with philosophy, *Wissenschaft* refers to the meta-scientific pretensions of various philosophies of idealism. The philosophies of Cohen and Natorp were 'scientific' in this sense.

3. The word *Wissenschaft* also covered what Anglo–American philosophy calls the philosophy of science. In Germany at this time natural science was the especial concern of philosophers like Cohen and Natorp, but psychology and sociology were also deemed important areas for philosophical scrutiny.

4. Yet another meaning of the word is any systematic presentation of a thesis, topic, or area of investigation, which need not be 'scientific' in the sense of 2 above. Theology, in serving the Church and Gospel, is thus 'scientific' when it presents a systematic account of commitment. In Herrmann's hands the borders of the scientific become blurred here, and at times *Wissenschaft* is synonymous with *Weltanschauung*.

It is to be noted that Herrmann rarely distinguished between various meanings of the word *Wissenschaft*, the result being that its meaning is at times far from clear. He furthermore had profound problems with what Dilthey and the Baden School called *Geisteswissenschaften* (humane or cultural disciplines) because the word *Geist* for him was defined almost in opposition to anything natural and capable of scientific investigation. He could not understand how a 'science' of religious and spiritual reality was possible without the experiential knowledge of faith. When German theologians talked about theology being scientific, it is important it recall the many nuances of this word for German speakers. 'Theological science' or 'scientific theology' generally sounded most impressive, but its meaning was sometimes less than scientific.

32. *Schriften*, i, p. xxvii.
33. This provides Herrmann's theology with its realism and also corresponds to Luther's understanding of faith as passive. Cohen, even at the end of his life, was most perplexed about Herrmann's appeals to God's *Wirklichkeit*, a word which had a very precise meaning in his *Logik*: 'The Unique God can have no actuality, for actuality is a concept relating thought to sensation. This relation is however excluded from the concept of God', *Religion III*, 185.
34. For a penetrating study of the understanding of metaphysics in Herrmann's early work see P. Fischer-Appelt, *Metaphysik im Horizont der Theologie Wilhelm Herrmanns* (Kaiser Verlag, 1965).
35. *Schriften*, ii. 104.
36. Ibid. 105.
37. Ibid. 215. For *Leben* and *Erleben* see pp. 140 ff.
38. See pp. 43 ff.
39. Quoted by R. Bultmann in *Glauben und Verstehen* (J. C. B. Mohr, 1964), i. 215.
40. *Schriften*, ii. 259.
41. Ibid. 261.
42. The *Gestalt* effects of Herrmann's dualism of faith are clearly seen in the following passage from *Schriften*, i. 114–15: 'If it is correct that scientific knowledge estimates the reality of each thing according to its law-ordered participation in the entire system of things, it is completely impossible to justify scientifically the opposition to natural entities according to which man defines the being of his own soul. If we become aware of the treasures of our soul and through inner composure grasp the goal of our life, it is incontrovertibly clear that this soul, being both independently sovereign and irreducible, is different from natural entities. . . . The reality known through science signifies nothing other than standing in a system of nature and thereby rendering things capable of explanation through that systematic network. In our faith, by contrast, we have confidence that God created and rules the world. If we believe that to be true, the expectation that science could furnish proof for some deeper

knowledge of the world, leading to certainty about its origin in God, would appear to be justified. In fact, however, the wisdom of former epochs laboured in vain to furnish such a proof.'

43. *Schriften*, ii. 322.
44. G. Ebeling, *Luther: An Introduction to His Thought* (Fontana, 1975), 135.
45. *Schriften*, ii. 214.
46. Ibid. 222.
47. *Prinzipienlehre*, 252.
48. *Schriften*, ii. 261.
49. *Systematic Theology* (George Allen & Unwin, 1927), 84.
50. Quoted by Bultmann in *Glauben und Verstehen*, i. 101–2.
51. *Systematic Theology*, 83–4.
52. Ibid. 69.
53. *Prinzipienlehre*, 261.
54. *Schriften*, ii. 108–9.
55. J. Moltmann, *Theology of Hope*, 5th imp. (1977), 52. Moltmann suggests that Bultmann developed Herrmann's theology of divine self-revelation anthropologically, Barth theistically. Whilst the former emphasized the 'transcendental subjectivity of man', and the latter 'the transcendental subjectivity of God', both affirmed that knowledge of God originates exclusively in his actual self-revelation.
56. Ibid. 53.
57. *Schriften*, ii. 31–2.
58. Ibid. 325.
59. Quoted in Mahlmann, 'Das Axiom des Erlebnisses bei Wilhelm Herrmann', 77.
60. *Schriften*, ii. 298.
61. *Schriften*, i. 292.
62. Ibid. 295.
63. *Schriften*, ii. 252–3.
64. Quoted in T. Mahlmann, 'Philosophie der Religion bei Wilhelm Herrmann', *Neue Zeitschrift für Systematische Theologie*, 4 (1964), 89.
65. See *Schriften*, i. 316 ff. and also Fischer-Appelt's *Einleitung*, pp. xxxvii ff.
66. *Schriften*, i. 103.
67. Quoted in Mahlmann, 'Das Axiom des Erlebnisses bei Wilhelm Herrmann', 74.
68. *Theologische Literaturzeitung*, 11 (1902) col. 332.
69. Quoted in Mahlmann, 'Das Axiom des Erlebnisses bei Wilhelm Herrmann', 74.
70. Herrmann, *Theologische Literaturzeitung*, 11 (1902), col. 332.
71. *Schriften*, i. 140.
72. *Schriften*, ii. 108.

73. *The Communion of the Christian with God*, trans. from the 4th edn. of 1903 (SCM, 1972), 42.
74. *Schriften*, ii. 109–10.
75. Ibid. 108–9.
76. This forms the *Grund* of faith, which is distinguished from the *Inhalt* of faith. For a consideration of these terms and of their importance to Herrmann's Christology see W. Greive, *Der Grund des Glaubens: Die Christologie Wilhelm Herrmanns* (Vandenhoeck & Ruprecht, 1976), 98–105.
77. *Schriften*, i. 146.
78. Greive, *Der Grund des Glaubens*, 99, comments, 'Die Glaubensgedanken sind Christi Kraft im Menschen, nicht Werk des Menschen.'
79. *Schriften*, ii. 104.
80. Quoted by Fischer-Appelt in *Schriften*, i, p. xlvi.
81. *Schriften*, ii. 208.
82. *Schriften*, i. 344. It should be noted that Herrmann used *das Wesen der Religion* and *der Ursprung der Religion* as equivalents.
83. See further H. Timm, *Theorie und Praxis in der Theologie Albrecht Ritschls und Wilhelm Herrmanns: Ein Beitrag zur Entwicklungsgeschichte des Kulturprotestantismus* (Mohn, 1967).
84. *Schriften*, ii. 298.

4

PHILOSOPHY, METAPHYSICS
AND THE NATURE OF RELIGION
ACCORDING TO BARTH

KARL Barth left university after completing his theological studies as a 'convinced Marburger' to become a *pasteur suffragant* in Geneva. Before leaving Marburg, where for a short while he had worked on the editorial staff of *The Christian World*, Barth publicly raised the issues of whether the 'modern theology', in which he and other liberals had been nurtured, was of any use for a minister's pastoral activity. Despite this momentary hesitation, he nevertheless continued an enthusiastic supporter of Marburg theology and in fact had plans to return to his 'Sion' for further studies under Herrmann.[1]

As well as his preaching, pastoral work, confirmation classes, and articles for the parish magazine, Barth was academically busy during his stay in Geneva. It was during this time, he tells us, that considerable inroads were made into Calvin's *Institutes*, which had the surprising effect of deepening his appreciation of Schleiermacher. His theology at this time, he testified, aspired to combine the best of German Idealism and Romanticism with the theology of the Reformation. It is perhaps not astonishing to hear that he read Cohen copiously during the summer of 1910.[2]

The writings examined in the following two chapters of this book represent the earliest theology of Karl Barth. They testify to the weighty influence which the Marburg School, in both its theological and philosophical guises, exercised upon their youthful author. Amongst the published works that will be quoted is the short article entitled 'Moderne Theologie und Reichsgottesarbeit' which, together with a reply to critics, was published in the *Zeitschrift für Theologie und Kirche* of 1909. Another important work pre-dating Barth's dialectical phase is 'Der christliche Glaube und die Geschichte' which, though originally a lecture delivered at a pastoral conference in Neuchâtel during the summer of 1910, was published in the *Schweizerische Theologische Zeitschrift* of 1912. Yet another shorter article, 'Ob Jesus gelebt hat?', is quite important.

It was published in his parish magazine during the Easter of 1910 and gives Barth's reactions to a keenly debated issue that rocked the theological establishment following the publication of *Die Christusmythe* by the infamous Arthur Drews.[3] A fourth article, 'Der Glaube an den persönlichen Gott', is perhaps the most confused and confusing work in the entire Barthian opus. It is uncharacteristic in that its objective is to address a series of metaphysical issues relating to classical theism and German Idealism.

Two unpublished works will also be used during the remainder of this book and it is important to say something about them at the outset. The first is a lecture given by Barth to the Société pastorale suisse de Genève on 31 May 1911 entitled 'La Réapparition de la métaphysique dans la théologie'. The second is an undated fragment which, on grounds of content, should most certainly be assigned to Barth's stay in Geneva or shortly afterwards. Neither of these works was ever published in Barth's lifetime and even the bibliography assembled by his faithful secretary, Charlotte von Kirschbaum, makes no reference to either work.[4] Busch, however, mentions both works in his excellent biography of Barth,[5] and it is hoped that both will become available to scholars, together with other unpublished early writings, in forthcoming volumes of the *Gesamtausgabe*. They are indispensable for any consideration of Barth's Marburg background.

The lecture on metaphysics is important on at least two counts. First, it yields insights into his earliest theology generally, and also gives more particular evidence of Barth's approach to the relations between theology and philosophy. He appears as an authentic, though sometimes critical, follower of Ritschl and Herrmann in their attempt to overcome philosophy with philosophy and also in their epistemological dualism which was outlined in the previous chapter. This lecture, secondly, shows how Barth, in sustaining the traditional Ritschlian critique of metaphysics, defined his position against that of the more prominent theologians of that era. He was particularly critical of people like Wobbermin and Lüdemann, but especially interesting are his criticisms of Troeltsch, who was himself an able and incisive opponent of Herrmann and all forms of Ritschlian theology. This in itself would merit careful consideration of the text, for here is the first in a series of criticisms which Barth would level at Troeltsch. Though an analysis of the text from this perspective transcends the scope of this present work, it must be said that Barth's partial adoption of Marburg neo-Kantianism not only encouraged a thorough mis-interpretation of Troeltsch's philosophical theology, but also led to a completely perverse understanding of the latter's religious a priori.[6]

The fragment of *Religionsphilosophie* is unique in the Barthian corpus, for it shows how Barth took seriously the need of theology to articulate a religious understanding of reality in relation to *Kultur*. The work, secondly, witnesses to a clear dependence of Barth upon the Marburg philosophy and also illustrates his profound respect for Schleiermacher. Thirdly, moreover, the fragment is surprisingly un-Barthian in style, with religious and philosophical issues being discussed without the usual over-whelming array of biblical images, quotations, and exegeses that characterized his later writings. Fourthly, and importantly, this writing bears clear, albeit fragmentary, testimony to some theological–philosophical synthesis of Barth's thought before the advent of what is customarily called dialectical theology. Although there are indeed traces of dialectic in this and other writings of Barth's early years, the dialectic is not of a Hegelian or Marxist variety; nor is it the sort of dialectic usually associated with the name of Barth. It is related rather to the *Dialektik* of Schleier-macher and, secondly, to the traditional Christian humanism of the *philosophia perennis* which has its origin in the humanism of the Reformers and ultimately in Augustine. Here, however, this traditional motif is clothed in the conceptuality of Schleiermacher and of Marburg neo-Kantianism.

Caution is necessary when interpreting Barth's fragment of *Religionsphilosophie* and other writings from his *Genfer-Zeit*, for until more of this material becomes available it would be misleading to suggest that these early writings warrant a complete reinterpretation of Barth's theology. It may well be the case, there-fore, that Marquardt's exuberant enthusiasm over Barth's earliest writings is a little premature. Marquardt, presumably referring to the fragment of *Religionsphilosophie*, says that 'in Geneva, Barth created a scientific–theoretical, religious–philosophical frame-work which overcame the old Kantian–Schleiermacherian opposition between "religion" and "science"—the "two kingdoms" theory of German idealism. This fragment was to govern his entire theological work to come.'[7] If, by contrast, von Balthasar's excellent hermeneutical advice is accepted,[8] extravagant claims about the long-term influence of this 'framework' will have to be provisionally suspended.

The hermeneutical procedure followed here is different from that of Marquardt, whose interpretation of Barth's earliest writings is governed by the following set of questions:

What were the inward intellectual conditions which made it possible for Barth to view public political engagement as a meaningful and even necessary part of his preaching and pastoral activity? What basic theological factors could have motivated him as a pastor to undertake concrete political efforts?[9]

Obviously Barth's later critical commitment to social and political problems illuminates his understanding of how, at that time, theology was to function in relation to the state, culture, and politics. Neither, moreover, should one ignore the wave of religious socialism and anarcho-communitarian mysticism which began to make its presence felt in Germany before the First World War. The feeling that capitalism was about to witness an apocalypse certainly helped to fashion the dialectical *Denkform* of Barth, but the prophecies of Kutter and the biblical realism of the Blumhardts were of equal importance. The point is that none of these factors, taken either individually or collectively, sufficiently explains and interprets the conceptual content of Barth's earliest writings. The nature of Barth's 'public political engagement', moreover, is open to a variety of interpretations and whatever one makes of Barth's socialism, it is certainly a socialism that owed more to the neo-Kantian tradition of socialism inaugurated by Lange than to any Marxist–Leninist sympathies. It was also oriented more towards theory than praxis.[10]

Having cautioned moderation, however, it is not being suggested that the earliest writings of Barth represent a brief halfhearted flirtation with a liberalism which meant very little to their author. This has too often been the picture of Barth championed by triumphant neo-orthodoxy and accepted with little hesitation by its adherents in Britain and America.[11] Those supporting this approach to Barth's theological development claim, with some justice, that it well accords with the master's own understanding of his work as documented in autobiographical reminiscences.[12]

Memories may well be that from which history is made, yet even if first-person memories acquire ripeness with personal, academic, and theological maturity, they are nevertheless subject to illusion, distortion, misplaced emphases, and polemical exigencies.[13]

Returning more directly to the topic of Barth's fragmentary *Religionsphilosophie*, it must be asked, first, whether Barth intended to write a full-scale book on the philosophy of religion and why, if that is the case, the work was not finished. It is clear from the chapter headings and outlines that Barth had it in mind to publish a substantial work. Furthermore it should be recalled that Barth was in Marburg when Natorp published the second edition of his book about religion in 1908. Both Cohen and Herrmann were also involved with the philosophy of religion during this period, so perhaps this embryonic theologian intended to make his public début with a first book that tackled an extremely controversial and keenly debated issue. A number of factors may explain why the work was never completed. Barth, in the first place, found himself extremely busy in Geneva, particularly when for six months the parish lacked a chief pastor. Affairs of the heart, moreover, claimed much attention and it was in May 1911 that Barth became engaged to Nelly Hoffmann. Thirdly, however, there is a curiously intriguing autobiographical statement in which Barth recalled that it was during his stay at Geneva that he gave up all plans of returning to Marburg for further studies under Herrmann.[14] Perhaps he believed he was more suited to *Reichsgottesarbeit* than to academic studies.

It is interesting to note that there is at least one counterpart to Barth's fragmentary *Religionsphilosophie*, for in 1913 the young Paul Tillich wrote a systematic theology which also remained fragmentary, principally because he reported for military service.[15] Though lacking the existentialist language which he later found in Heidegger and Sartre, it has been claimed that this early writing contains seminal insights which matured into Tillich's later system. Like Barth's fragment, it too remained unpublished during the author's life. Given this amazing similarity in form between the writings of two young men who were to become theological giants of their era, it is perhaps not idle speculation to wonder whether in Barth's case we are presented with a *Grundlage*, framework, or embryonic system, which was capable of being developed in a way altogether different from the trajectory which Barth subsequently followed.

I. THE PRIMACY OF EXPERIENCE

It is fitting to begin a consideration of Barth's earliest theology with the now famous essay 'Moderne Theologie und Reichsgottesarbeit'. Many scholars refer to this article, suggesting that Barth writes as one who was already disillusioned with the liberalism of Marburg *moderne Theologie*, for he appears to question the practical efficacy of such theology for evangelical ministry. The 'essence' of modern theology, religious individualism, and its other characteristic, historical relativism, lead to lamentable consequences. Religion knows only individual values whilst history deals with general facts which cannot be made absolute.[16] Undoubtedly Barth felt a little uncomfortable with this situation, but upon detailed examination, far from repudiating the liberal enterprise, the article concludes with a resounding affirmation of modern theology.

Barth's brief analysis of religious individualism is considerably indebted to Ritschl and Herrmann. In modern times morality, which, we are told, must form the presupposition of religion, is no longer deemed blind obedience to norms imposed upon humanity 'from the outside' by some external authority such as God or the Church. Deep moral concern is rather believed to arise from an internal truth and authority present in the inner experiential core of each individual: it is this inner passion that directs the will to noble and righteous ends. This is an obvious echo of Herrmann's teaching about the morally earnest man who is on the way to religion, but the dependence upon Herrmann becomes even more clear when Barth considers how modern theology understands the genesis of religious faith. As a direct consequence of its understanding of morality, faith, too, said Barth, is approached from the perspective of individual experience by modern theology. It is the individual who perceives how his own efforts do not lead to obedience of the moral law. Being in the predicament of wanting to be moral and not being able to attain this goal, the individual experiences the redemptive power of revelation to which he succumbs. Both moral and religious individualism consequently imply that there is no longer any 'universally valid *ordo salutis*, nor any universally valid source of revelation which one person could demonstrate to another'.[17] The only apology for religion in modern times is, in other words, Herrmann's proof of faith.

Barth next proceeds to indicate how faith arises from personal experience of a supernatural revelatory event and, not unexpectedly, how the resulting 'life' must be understood individually or, as a later generation would say, existentially:

> The Christian who succumbs to this power overcomes the world. With increasing clarity, yet in constant strife, the New prevails in his inner-life, volition, and thought. The New so affects the Christian in experience [*Erlebnis*] that his actions follow divine norms, his world becomes God's world which works for good to them that love Him. The course, however, which leads to this overcoming of the world must spring from the Christian's own faith. No other can give it him. Christianity knows no normative injunctions and there is no normative Christian world view.[18]

Though the historical relativism of modern theology might at first sight seem completely incompatible with faith when religion is approached from such an intensely personal or individual perspective, Barth contended that this was not the case. He, like Herrmann, believed the only morality compatible with religion was one which demanded personal intellectual honesty and an uncompromising devotion to truth. This implied that theologians should subject the historical sources of the Christian religion to ruthless investigation with tools supplied by *allgemeingültige Wissenschaft*, even though it places them in an intolerable situation. On the one hand, that is, the Christian theologian enjoys a truth which makes him free that arises solely from a personal encounter with the efficacious power of God and not from acquaintance with some universally valid piece of scientific information. The science, on the other hand, which critically investigates historical sources, has the effect of making all historical events relative. Neither in the realm of nature nor in that of spirit are there absolutes for science. The theologian, therefore, who is indebted to the New Testament witness for that experience which supplies inner strength, peace, and which elevates him above the world into communion with God, is forced to regard the very same Testament as a collection of books in no way different from other collections of ancient religious documents. When

Christianity is examined from this historical perspective it becomes only one amongst many other religious phenomena. Jesus, likewise, appears as a religious leader in no way different from others because the critical methods employed in historical research of the New Testament are precisely those that would be used to investigate the religion of Zoroaster or Avesta.[19] The dilemma thus facing Barth is simply this: the modern theologian is under a religious and moral obligation to investigate Christianity with the techniques of historical science, yet when that is done, the absoluteness, which his personal faith demands, disappears. In this situation two things remain for the modern theologian: knowledge of the past and its relativity plus his own personal faith.

In the final section of his article Barth endeavours to demonstrate how religious indiviudalism and historical relativism are not ultimately irreconcilable for a believing theologian. In the first place the theologian has to accept the legitimacy of both historical criticism and religious individualism, but being someone who has experienced religious faith himself, the theologian is entitled to raise the question of how far the ideas and concepts of the past are adequate expressions of *his own personal faith*. Such 'coming to terms with the thoughts of the past', or the dialogue between faith and history, is the task of a lifetime. There is no immediate and easy solution, says Barth, but, it is hoped, the problem of personal faith and history will achieve resolution as one matures in moral insight, commitment, and experience.[20] The following encouraging words, however, which may be regarded as Barth's own earliest theological agenda, were calculated to affirm the value of religious individualism, modern theology, and its continuing dialogue with historical criticism, philosophy, and science: 'religion is . . . experience conceived in a strictly individual fashion and we deem it our duty to come to terms, clearly and positively, with the general human culture consciousness [*Kulturbewusstsein*] on its scientific side.'[21]

From the earlier discussion of Herrmann's theology it should be evident that Barth's approach to the challenge of historical relativism depends upon the distinction between faith (revelation experienced as something absolute in the contemporary life of individuals) and thoughts of faith. Historical research throws up past thoughts of faith and makes the theologian painfully aware of their historical, social, and cultural relativity. Barth, however, as a true liberal of Herrmann's school, employs a religious value judgement to assess these past formulations of faith. They are judged, that is, from the vantage point of contemporary religious experience. The absoluteness, which present faith-experience possesses for the individual, therefore becomes the criterion by which all past conceptualizations of faith are judged.

In a response to two senior critics Barth attempted to clarify some of the issues he had raised. He strongly affirmed the necessity of *Individualismus* in both religion and ethics, since a return to *Theonomie* had been rendered impossible by Kant and the Romantics. Unlike Troeltsch, who argued that training and tradition were more important for morality than some vague feeling of individual freedom, Barth maintained that there was not, and should not be, any escape from *Autonomie*. The idea that some eternal authority like God or the Church should compel moral rectitude was, in Barth's opinion, pernicious and danger-ous. In agreement with Cohen, Barth affirms autonomy to be the transcendental principle, the *ratio cognoscendi*, of the moral law.[22] This, however, led to problems over reconciling the demand for radical individual autonomy with the absolute moral law which, by definition, had to be universally valid for all. Barth's very unsatisfactory answer took the form of a cursory appeal to Schleiermacher's moral theory, but the generalization which followed is truly amazing. Inasmuch as a moral act originates in the depths of individual subjectivity, only the individual is able to judge the ethical value of his actions![23] This highly unsatisfactory discussion about autonomy is due to the fact that Barth was attempting to amalgamate two fundamentally incompatible accounts of the moral subject. The first, and more theoretical, was that of Cohen's *Ethik*, in which radical human autonomy was the primary prerequisite of all morality. The second, however, was indebted to Herrmann's musings about the genesis of moral volition, according to which an experience of revelatory power was the a priori condition of morality, for without an influx of divine energy, the will supposedly remained rent asunder and impotent. The degree to which these approaches were basically incom-patible exacerbated the problems confronting Barth.

After this defence of *Individualismus* in morality, Barth had more success when he turned to religion. In the first place he accepted a suggestion from his critics who urged that religious individualism is in fact limited in Christianity, where Jesus Christ is the authority and norm for personal religion. After conceding this Christological proviso, he stated his position more clearly by once again quoting Schleiermacher. On this occasion he appealed to Schleiermacher's exegesis of John 1: 14:

Whatever Christ may say about himself would represent no Christian truth were it not instantaneously verified through . . . affection [*Affektion*]. *This is, and remains for me, what is the primary cause [das Urpsrüngliche] of Christiantiy. Everything else is simply derivative.* The manifestation of Christ which affects in a certain manner is authentic revelation and also objective.[24]

Though a seemingly strange response to the problems about the universal validity and objectivity of personal religious experience, it is not too difficult to perceive here the Melanchthonian-type epistemology upon which Herrmann and Ritschl placed much stress. Barth, moreover, was at pains to insist that the affective power of revelation is truly objective, in the sense that it originates in God and not in the individual's emotive or cognitive activities. Affection, he suggests, is normative for Christian faith-experience, especially when the latter is construed in strictly personalist terms, and it even takes precedence over the conceptual formulations of such experience in dogmas, doctrines, or traditional exegesis, precisely because it is immediate, personal, and caused by God. It is nevertheless conceded that one pressing theological task is the communication of this inner, but none the less objective, state of being (*innere Tatsächlichkeit*) through norms and appropriate theological language; yet the norms must not be those old 'external norms' of Protestant orthodoxy.[25] Barth, in other words, was attempting to preserve the objectivity of efficacious revelation without recourse to a propositional understanding of revelation, hoping to achieve thereby some synthetic balance between the subjective pole of individual faith-experience and the more objective pole of divine revelation through Christ. Once again there is evidence of an unresolved tension which also characterized Herrmann's theology: how could an essentially private experience be construed as possessing *Allgemeingültigkeit* for all Christians?

When clarifying his thoughts on historical relativism, Barth once more agreed with his seniors that relativism is mitigated by an 'absolutizing' value judgement, which is made by the 'subject' of living religion who appropriates history according to its value for contemporary religious experience. This is a brief summary of Herrmann's reply to Troeltsch, and Barth quite innocently recommends that this procedure should govern the relations between religion and *Wissenschaft* in general. The point is repeatedly hammered home—apart from their synthesis in the faith-experience of the individual, both the approach which proceeds by way of value judgements and that which relies on the scientific procedures of historical criticism are irreconcilably opposed. The co-existence of both nevertheless becomes possible and actual when the subject, who makes the relativizing historical judgement, is identical with the 'subject' of living religion:

> The individual elevates from the flux of history that absolute norm which becomes redemption and conquest [*Überwindung*] for his life—rather much more, this norm grasps, redeems, and conquers the individual. Only in the 'affection' of this inner experience [*Erlebnis*] lies that which is normative, objective, and eternal, for everything expressed in either thought or word intrinsically belongs and returns once more to the relativizing flux of history.[26]

An example of what this might mean in relation to a contemporary theological issue is afforded by Barth's discussion of whether Jesus lived. He does not shy away from saying that Christianity would be an error of two thousand years' standing if Jesus did not walk upon this earth,[27] and he is convinced that facts regarding the death of Jesus and those relating to his influence upon contemporaries are historical certainties. Yet, despite such certitude, it would be fatal to make the *Grund des Glaubens* dependent upon academic rejoinders to sceptics such as Drews:

> The ground of our faith is, and continues to be, *independent* of proofs and counter-proofs. Scientific proof affords a certainty which always remains only highly probable. The certitude of faith, by contrast, I compare with the fact that we breathe and therefore live . . . The ground of faith . . . cannot be proved, and what can be proved is not the ground of our faith.[28]

Barth is confident that faith is not a matter of appropriating and assenting to some external facts (*äussere Tatsachen*) of history, but rather it is trust and confidence in the God who calls humankind from darkness into his own wonderful light. Faith, once again, as with Herrmann, is primarily construed as experiential assent to an inward epiphany of divine grace in the hidden depths of individual experience: 'faith is a mystery and it is bestowed [*ist geschenkt*] upon us'.[29]

As it is with us now, so was it with Jesus, for in the historic realm of inner affection, space and time no longer count. On the basis of contemporary faith-experience, Barth feels entitled to make some most un-Barthian remarks about the inner life of Jesus:

> The ground of faith is Jesus. This means that such confidence, which makes us free from wickedness, and such obedience, which makes us free for goodness, are possible and actual because something like the life [*Leben*] of Jesus was possible and actual amongst mankind . . . The 'Life of Jesus', which is the ground of faith, or that which signifies God's revelation for us, is not the series of external facts about him that were handed down . . . Rather the ground of faith is the personal, inner, *Leben* of Jesus. I understand by that his human portrait [*Charakterbild*] which presents itself to us as complete obedience to God, total love of brethren, and, therefore, as utter self-denial that will not even halt at death, because the way to life passes through death. If, when we are faced with this portrait, it becomes clear to us who *God is* and what we should *become*, it is then that we *believe*, then we *have* the guarantee and anchorage we need in order to become free and joyous people. This guarantee becomes neither weaker nor stronger through whatever scholars have to say pro or con the certainty of Jesus's *external* life.[30]

In a manner resembling the soteriology of early Arianism, Jesus appears here as the eldest of many brethren.[31] The inner life of freedom and obedience, which marks the *Charakterbild* of Jesus, is now, through God's gracious revelation, given to individual experience in the present. Jesus was the first to have this particular life-form; now it is eternally available to the faithful. Looking at the same phenomena from a different perspective, it could also be said that the a priori condition of 'our' enjoying a fully Christian *Leben* is the 'fact' of Jesus's life. Moreover, it is argued that because 'we' actually enjoy the said benefits, they must have originated in 'something like' the revelation of God in Jesus's life, for without this our own religious experience would be inexplicable.[32]

The same stress on religious individualism which marked *Reichsgottesarbeit* therefore characterizes the article about Jesus. There is, for example, the link between religious individualism and the inner experience of divine revelation or, using more Schleiermacherian language, the experience of being affected by an efficacious agency. This almost pietistic approach to faith experience distinguishes many of Barth's early writings; interestingly enough, the article concludes with quotations from Tersteegen and Arendt.[33] It is in a similar vein that Barth replies to critics of *Reichsgottesarbeit* by affirming the essence of Protestant religion to lie in a completely inner act of faith (*Glaubensakt*), which eludes even the most adequate theological conceptualizations and remains inaccessible to the most painstaking scientific researches.[34]

Four important points arise from this brief review of three early writings. In the first place, Barth consistently saw religion as involving an inner synthesis between the religious individual and God through the more immediate, internal, and intimate modalities of life, experience, or affection. The quotation from Schleiermacher, in which objective revelation affects the individual and so becomes actual and verifiable in personal experience, is of immense importance. This epistemological style, which has already been encountered in the claim made by Ritschl and Herrmann that knowledge of God originates solely from the revealed benefits of Christ, enjoyed the status of an axiom amongst contemporary theologians. The fortunate term 'relationism' was coined by Hans Frei to describe the understanding of faith and revelation that characterized the liberal theology of this era. His comments deserve quoting in full:

It is taken for granted that God has indeed revealed himself to man and that the relationship established in his self-revelation is a given, indissoluble state or condition, a sort of *nexus* of divine–human contact. On the one hand one must not endeavour to go beyond this *nexus* for knowledge of God; on the other hand one may rely altogether and unquestionably upon it as the point of departure, objective and enduring through time, for all Christian life and inquiries of theology. ... *that* revelation is fact, that there is an indissoluble relationship, or synthesis in which it is realized or posited—all this is beyond question and the indisputable starting point for all theologizing.[35]

The tenets of relationism are accepted without hesitation by Barth's pre-dialectical writings. A later Barth, in loyalty to his Reformed tradition, strove to protect the sovereignty of God over the grace of revelation and human response, but there is no doubt whatsoever that the *givenness* of divine–human relatedness in faith and revelation formed the *Voraussetzung* of his earliest theology. Although such divine–human contact in a personal experience of religious faith was taken to be an indisputably given fact by Barth himself and by many other modern theologians, the recipient mode of this divine–human nexus was discussed. It was asked whether this state is realized psychologically, as those who followed Schleiermacher affirmed, or more objectively in the 'coincidence of historical events and their inward appropriation',[36] as Herrmann sometimes affirmed. Whichever alternative was adopted, however, the relational premiss remained intact, as did the contention that the truth of the divine–human nexus was, when actualized or experienced, self-authenticating. Throughout the remainder of his book the term relationism will be reserved for this given, indissoluble cathexis of faith and revelation in immediate experience. This is because some British and American scholars, who were familiar with the 'relationism' of liberal theology, referred to this assumed givenness of divine–human relations, in which faith is posited with revelation and revelation along with faith, as 'positivism'. For the sake of clarity this latter term will be avoided as far as possible until the concluding chapter.

A second consideration arises from Barth's approach to historical relativism. The assertion that relativism is itself relativized by an individual's absolute value judgement might seem to give greater credence to thoroughgoing relativism, but the theological point Barth attempted to make was that only the existential experience of divine–human relatedness may claim absoluteness. Furthermore, though Herrmann said a chasm existed between scientific criticism of history and the contemporary 'historic' experience of faith, Barth was more concerned to indicate that one and the same subject makes historical judgement as well as the 'historic' decision of faith. On that account he was not at all happy with a thoroughgoing dualism betwixt the two. Yet despite this reservation, Barth eventually sided with Herrmann because some personal revelatory experience is essential for encountering God in 'history', or, in other words, it is the individual, who is affected or touched by divine efficacy in the present, who perceives an absolute and religiously compelling dimension in past records of faith-experience. This internal approach to problems raised by 'external history' is a direct consequence of relationism, for the relational nexus was deemed to be an eternally enduring state which transcended time and space, though it could, admittedly, be realized in finite individual experience at any moment. When such a miraculous event occurred, however, its locus was inner experience and that, too, transcended the forms of space and time. The foundation of faith, which historical criticism could not in principle effect either positively or negatively, is therefore 'grounded' in the eternal efficacy of God's revelation, together with personal awareness of that efficacy. This way of addressing history and religious experience, as well as raising obvious philosophical questions, had doctrinal consequences which Barth often preferred to ignore. It could well be asked, for example, what Christological doctrines refer to. Are they primarily statements about divine activity in the individual, with Christ being a type or exemplar of a particular religious life-form, or do they refer to some divine being who eternally and essentially participates in divine life? The article about Jesus studiously avoided metaphysical affirmations concerning Christ's status as well as judgements about the significance of his historicity ('external life') for the Christian faith.

Barth's earliest writings testify, thirdly, to what became a long-standing concern about the nature of doctrine and, more particularly, its validity. This question bothered Barth early in his career and troubled him again in the 1920s when he was preparing to embark upon dogmatics. The problem of the *Allgemeingültigkeit* of doctrine was a legacy of Herrmann's work, where there was an unresolved tension between a personalist approach to revelation and the necessity of proclaiming a particular individual experience as the universally valid way to religion. The problem was aggravated for Barth and Herrmann because they relied on Schleiermacher's principle that conceptualization (*Reflexion*) is not only secondary, but also distortive, in that it fragments immediate awareness.[37] Barth, even in *Reichsgottesarbeit*, perceived that pupils from less liberal schools of theology seemed to have been better prepared for, and more successful in, evangelical labours, attributing this, in part, to the powerful battery of norms and doctrines which were proclaimed as universally valid. Liberals had only the defenceless proof of faith. To rectify this situation it was conceded that an urgent task for modern theology was the formulation of normative concepts to express inner religion more adequately.[38] Such concepts, however, had to be far removed from propositional and rationalist approaches to revelation, as well as being kept distinct from the sort of universal validity which marks natural science, philosophy, and historical criticism. This problem was only satisfactorily resolved for Barth when he later formulated the theory that dogmatic thinking is *Nachdenken* in obedience to given revelation. Then, however, revelation no longer meant the immediacy of divine–human relatedness in religious experience.

Finally, the quotation which might be said to represent the agenda for Barth's earliest theology deserves emphasis.[39] Coming to terms with the general *Kulturbewusstsein*, the relationship, that is, between theology and culture, was affirmed by Barth to be one of the major tasks confronting theology. This meant that theology should not only take seriously the contemporary role of religion in the socio-cultural situation, but also enter into dialogue with every aspect of culture. Moreover Barth stressed that this dialogue should be particularly directed to addressing *Kulturbewusstsein* on its 'scientific side'. What else could this have meant in the Marburg of 1909 than debating with that science which claimed to portray *Kulturbewusstsein* critically and systematically, namely the scientific philosophy of Cohen and Natorp?

II. BARTH AND MARBURG NEO-KANTIANISM

Bonhoeffer, who always expressed profound indebtedness to Barth's commentary on Romans 'despite its neo-Kantian eggshells', offered an acute observation concerning Barth's theology and the conceptuality of Marburg Kantianism which it frequently employed: 'Barth makes use of the philosophical language of neo-Kantianism, yet he also knows the blurring effect which such conceptuality involves: it never gets to the heart of the matter. For this reason it is rash to call him a neo-Kantian.'[40] The point is telling, for despite his reading of Kant, Cohen, and Natorp, Barth had no intention whatsoever of becoming a philosopher. He did, however, want to be a theologian and, indeed, a theologian who subscribed to the goals and methods of modern theology. Inasmuch as this was his objective, he could not fail to assimilate Herrmann's approach to theology and philosophy, as well as his teacher's critique of Marburg *Religionsphilosophie*.

From the very beginning it must be stressed that Barth's knowledge of Marburg philosophy was not second-hand, mediated to him through Herrmann. During his studies at Marburg he attended lectures delivered by the philosophers and his private library contained books written by both Cohen and Natorp.[41] Investigating the earliest writings themselves, however, is perhaps the most reliable way of discovering the degree to which Barth was familiar with Marburg neo-Kantianism and its highly specialized conceptuality. Throughout them, for instance, Barth, like Herrmann, divided knowledge into *Logik*, *Ethik*, and *Ästhetik* and this classification immediately raised the issue of where religion fitted in. Did religious cognition basically belong to logical or scientific knowledge, as the few supporters of Hegelianism contended; was it perhaps to be chiefly associated with ethics, as those who followed Kant and Cohen affirmed; or was religion perhaps more akin to aesthetic experience, as Natorp and Schleiermacher seemed to suggest? This question was central for anyone who wished to write about *Religionsphilosophie* from a neo-Kantian perspective, but perhaps these well-tried solutions to the problem of religion and its place in the system of knowledge were not the only ones. Interest arose in the exciting possibility, which was most attractive to the younger generation of theologians, that religion might penetrate every dimension of knowledge and culture and yet, somehow, transcend them all. This was the possibility which Barth began to explore in his preparatory notes for a book of *Religionsphilosophie*.[42]

In agreement with Marburg philosophy, Barth called the three dimensions of knowledge *Richtungen*, showing thereby that they arose from the three cognitive operations of consciousness; one writing expressly speaks of the three *Funktionen* of *Kulturbewusstsein*.[43] His words thus show familiarity with the theory of cognitive generation which was essential to the ontology and epistemology of Marburg Kantianism. Barth's writings from his time as a student and his period in Geneva accept two further tenets of Marburg philosophy, the first being that all knowledge is generated in accordance with necessary laws and the second that such knowledge is 'generally valid', meaning thereby, universally and necessarily true.

What is not clear is the degree to which Barth understood the important concept of infinitesimal analysis which Cohen made into the paradigm of systematic thought. There is, however, one passage which suggests familiarity with the Marburg claim that knowledge is based upon mathematico-logical patterns of thought: 'Leonardo da Vinci, Copernicus, Kepler, Bacon, Gassendi, and Newton began the era of experimental science by embracing, either covertly or intentionally, the presupposition of Platonic epistemology: οὐδεὶς ἀγεωμέτρητος εἰσίτω,—everything real must be knowable mathematically.'[44] These words accord not only with the mathematical character attributed to logical thought by the Marburg Kantians, but also with the claim that their philosophy fulfilled and perfected what Plato was seeking to express.[45]

Barth's acceptance of the universal validity of *Gesetzerkenntis* has already been mentioned, but it is necessary to stress this because it exercised formidable influence over his estimation of philosophy. The only sort of cognition which deserves the epithet 'scientific', he believed, was one which is governed by laws: 'scientific apprehension is called *knowing*. Clearly this knowing . . . is only made possible through the type of *thought* which reconciles and orders its own contents.'[46] Barth contended that from Descartes onwards philosophy became more interested in the process of knowing than in the metaphysical status of known objects, more interested, that is, in the *Gesetzlichkeit* of things than in things themselves.[47] Having appreciated how profane knowledge is essentially ordered by cognitive laws, Barth then proceeded to adopt Herrmann's apologetical interpretation of this notion by calling into play the dialectic of faith and works, which his mentor had already imposed upon the Marburg understanding of *die Geseztlichkeit* of knowledge and reality.

What seems to have attracted Barth most about the Marburg philosophy is what Ollig termed its 'operationalism', according to which reality is not a static given to be copied in the process of cognition nor known through essentially passive sense intuition. It rather results from creative acts wrought by the epistemological subject who 'realizes' or 'actualizes' the latent possibilities of consciousness which thought itself posits a priori. Words like realization and actualization figure prominently in Barth's conceptuality, especially when he turns his attentions to *Religionsphilosophie*. The notion of a never-ending, incessant actualization of culture by thought was deeply attractive and one of the questions Barth felt compelled to ask was that of its ultimate *Woher?*; the question, that is, from whence thought, volition, and feeling derive their creative energy.

A further facet of Marburg Kantianism characterizing Barth's early writings is its thoroughgoing transcendentalism. He believed that all scientific knowledge depended upon necessary laws and, moreover, that such laws were posited a priori by thought: 'nature ... for us is culture consciousness understood as an a priori structure that thoroughly pervades the possibilities of consciousness.'[48] Barth's adoption of Marburg transcendentalism is particularly clear in a discussion of post-Kantian metaphysics:

> Kantian idealism proved the truth of scientific, moral, and aesthetic experience through the discovery of reason's a priori. This a priori precedes all experience not psychologically, but virtually, and makes everything we call experience accessible and possible for the spirit. Such a priori experience is the necessary and objective form of all the being and becoming which is contained in reason.[49]

Transcendentalism, or the understanding that all experience and valid knowledge depend upon a priori knowledge and experience, is a stance meticulously observed throughout Barth's fragmentary *Religionsphilosophie*.[50]

To summarize the discussion so far, Barth believed the a priori structures or possibilities of consciousness alone to supply the indispensable cognitive foundations for finite experience in space and time. Not only did he deem it essential for objective experience, but its deep structures, which thoroughly pervade the a priori possibilities of consciousness, issue in actual knowledge when they are actualized by generative thinking. Barth's transcendentalism, moreover, went all the way with Cohen in supposing that this a priori structure was not dependent upon the psychophysical constitution of the human organism, but rather posited as a *sui generis* transcendental nexus. It was stressed by him, moreoever, that this foundation of knowledge is to be regarded as having been posited by *autonomous* human reason—there was nothing divine or specially religious about it. One point, however, separating Barth from Cohen and Natorp was his interpretation of Marburg philosophy as being solely concerned with epistemology. When speaking of this philosophy, Barth makes hardly any reference to the ontological correlate of its theory of knowledge, namely that reality consists of thought-produced relations. The reasons for this interpretation are to be sought first in his indebtedness to the Ritschlian inheritance, which often treated philosophy as being primarily epistemology. Secondly, however, there were deep theological reasons why the ontological thesis of Marburg philosophy could not be accepted. It suffices for the moment to note that Barth believed Marburg philosophy to be primarily an account of how knowledge is attained, and agreed, furthermore, that its resulting theory of knowledge was scientific and objective, not in anyway concerned to provide metaphysical information about transcendent realities.

When referring to the epistemology he had embraced, Barth was often at pains to stress the importance of autonomy for the cognitive enterprise. This has already been encountered in the discussion of *Reichsgottesarbeit* and its sequel, where it was noted how Barth conceded to Cohen that radical *Autonomie* was the *Grundgesetz* of ethics and morality.[51] Barth also agreed with Cohen that *Autonomie* characterized the entire *Methodik* for acquiring scientifically valid knowledge and governed pre-eminently the work of philosophy. He saw such autonomy as the decisive contribution of Enlightenment criticism to Western culture, representing a triumph for human freedom and dignity: 'Autonomy is the *critical* tribunal which consciousness discovers in its own *law pervaded structures*. Once this step in spiritual evolution has been reached there is no retreat.'[52]

Barth's hearty commitment to autonomy possessed a threefold significance. In the first place he felt that once knowledge had been decisively liberated to follow its own paths it could no longer be forced to accept propositions foisted upon it by some alien authority, whether it be Church, State, Bible, or God. Once such autonomy had been claimed for science, cognition had to develop freely, constrained only by its self-posited laws, principles, and possibilities, which alone ought to govern the creative generation of knowledge. Autonomy, secondly, possessed a cultural and historical significance according to the early writings of Barth. He dated the awakening of autonomy with the beginnings of experimental science, as marking a culturally liberating break with the *Zwangskultur* of the Middle Ages. Once the quest for knowledge was no longer obstructed by supposed authorities, freedom, liberty of conscience, and respect for the rights and dignities of the individual were inevitable. Like Herrmann, Barth believed these values were actively nurtured by the religious revolution of Protestantism and argued that such laudable cultural values, being decisive for the modern era, had to be fully appreciated, welcomed, and embraced by everyone—especially by theologians and practitioners of religion. Thirdly, Barth argued that it was high time for the implications of autonomy to be recognized by the churches. The Church should no longer force people to accept 'truths' solely on the grounds of magisterial or alleged biblical authority.

Once I have become critically clear as to what my reason is able to achieve, that is, what it *can assimilate*, I cannot, and may not, then revert to accepting solely on grounds of authority, thoughts whose truth content I cannot in the least rationally establish. The notion of authoritative statements deriving from a hierarchical institution becomes untenable, as also do the notions of an authoritative canon, authoritative thoughts, statements, and narratives—even though an angel from heaven had brought them.[53]

A theological theme that further colours Barth's appropriation of Marburg neo-Kantianism follows from this. In his lecture on metaphysics in theology it was argued that the movement which made science 'atheistic' in fact owed its inspiration and momentum to religion.[54] It was not irreligion, but religion, said Barth, which sowed the seeds of modern free thought. Such recognition, affirmation, and welcome of *Autonomie* compares favourably with Bonhoeffer's statements about a world come of age which no longer requires a 'God-hypothesis' to fill in cognitive gaps. It should be obvious, therefore, that when Barth refers to religion in his early writings there is no hint of the unbelief, hubris, or idolatry of the commentaries on Romans. At this stage of his career he was keen to stress the beneficial contributions of religion to Western civilization and especially to the *Kultur* prized, honoured, and nurtured in German universities. The relation between religion and culture in these writings is consequently positive and one involving mutual support.

A final point of some importance concerns Barth's approach to the perennial neo-Kantian problem with the *Subjekt*, *Ich*, or ego, which seemed to disappear in the vast transcendental network of cognitive functions in Marburg philosophy. Cohen, it will be recalled, resolved the problem through his moral philosophy by presenting the moral personality as a task or goal to which volition and action should aspire. Personality for Cohen, consequently, was not a metaphysical entity given to *das Subjekt* prior to volition and action. In his religious writings a decisive moment for the teleological genesis of an ego was the growing awareness of moral claims which the presence of the Thou precipitated; for only the correlation of Thou and I, the recognition of the other as a moral being with rights and obligations, was thought to render meaningful any talk about subjects.[55] Herrmann objected most strongly to this, since his *Lebenstheologie* aspired to a theological definition of the self. The morally earnest person, not being able to achieve his practical goals, becomes so crippled with guilt and torn apart by the constraints of nature and its laws, that the will seemed impotent and indecisive. Upon becoming aware of failure and weakness, the individual's moment of need is answered by an experience of God's self-revelation which, being a life-bestowing power, raises the person concerned above the world into communion with God. This experience, therefore, *gives* new life to the individual and inspires both will and action to noble ends.[56] Natorp's approach to the problem differed from both. He sought the essence of personality in that non-objective and immediate modality of feeling, which humanized the more objective, alien, and abstractly formal functions of consciousness.[57]

Barth's sympathies veered naturally towards Herrmann's theological anthropology and the following was taken to be an axiom concerning the individual's *ewiges Lebendig-Werden*: 'it is not posited, and indeed cannot be posited, in the psychological factors of logical thinking, ethical willing, or aesthetic feeling'.[58] In similar vein a writing of 1914 stressed that the subject, the very essence of personality, is grasped neither by the 'transcendental discipline' of philosophy nor for that matter by the more empirical discipline of psychology:

The concept of the personality is indispensable to the transcendental and psychological approaches, yet for both it is something impossible to establish. *Logic* and *ethics*, as transcendental–critical disciplines, encounter at their very foundation not only the problem of truth (which finds its solution in their mutual relatedness), but also the problem of the subject—the question, namely, of who thinks and who wills. It is impossible for them to give a positive answer to this latter problem without applying a concept of substance outside the limits of spatio-temporal experience in a manner which transgresses the foundational law of the critical method.[59]

Barth is here dealing with two problems which he found in Cohen's philosophy. The first is that of truth which, as he suggested, is resolved in neo-Kantianism by the mutual related-ness (*Aufeinanderbezogenheit*) of logic and ethics. There can be no doubt to whom Barth was referring, for a footnote adds that this was the meaning of Cohen's concept of God. The second foundational problem he detected in German Idealism was that of the subject. Barth argues that logic demands a subject who thinks and that ethics requires a willing subject, yet neither empirical psychology nor critical idealism seems capable of giving a satisfactory account of that concept. He makes his point with a somewhat cursory appeal to a section of Kant's *Critique of Pure Reason*.[60] Barth points out that any recognition of a thinking and willing subject by the transcendental method of philosophy would contradict its own foundations, because the category of substance would have been used illicitly; it would have been applied to an object which transcends the forms of space and time. His point is simply that a personal centre of consciousness creates grave asymmetries for the Marburg System yet, on the other hand, that philosophy was incomplete without one.

Barth felt that the presence of a subject was absolutely essential for both philosophy and theology, and he justified the validity of that concept by giving it the status of a *Grenzbegriff*: 'The transcendental method must accept the thought of personality as a limitative concept, but only as a limitative concept, as a thought which cannot be executed, but which nevertheless cannot be dispensed with.'[61] This valiant attempt to rescue personality from the dissolution it suffered in Marburg philosophy led Barth to place the concept of personality at and beyond the boundary of scientific or critical knowledge. His understanding of *die Grenze* was accordingly different from that of Natorp, for whom the only 'limits' of knowledge were those logical possibilities posited by thought for the generation of knowledge and, secondly, the frontiers of contemporary knowledge which were always receding.

The concept of *die Grenze* is so important for Barth's early work that further comment is warranted. For obvious theological purposes Barth wanted to arrive at a position similar to that of

Herrmann; he needed, that is, to speak of a subject which was responsible for willing and acting, but which also could be a possible recipient of revelatory experience. By suggesting that the concept of personality was a 'limitative concept', he sought Kantian authority to secure its validity. Kant had argued that ideas such as the *Ich* as a thinking soul, the world as a totality, and God as the author of reality, are legitimate regulative principles 'of the systematic unity of the manifold of empirical knowledge in general, whereby this empirical knowledge is more adequately secured within its own limits', but not constitutive principles, 'for the extension of our knowledge to more objects than experience can give'.[62] It was therefore deemed inadmissible by Kant to use these three ideas speculatively, in order to acquire knowledge of super-sensible (that is, metaphysical) entities. Such ideas, being merely empty thoughts, could not be regarded as providing any objective knowledge, though as heuristic tools they encourage the understanding to construe experience as being an interrelated system of the sort that can be investigated by natural science. In several early writings Barth appealed to this Kantian distinction between heuristic (or regulative) and constitutive principles in order to secure the validity of certain concepts felt to be indispensable for religion and theology. With regard to the problem of personality, he spotted an *Ich*-shaped lacuna in Marburg philosophy which afforded an entrance for 'religious individualism'.[63]

This brief exposition of philosophical conceptuality in Barth's early writings should be sufficient to indicate his appreciation of the prevailing philosophical temper. Barth did not accept the Marburg system in its entirety, neither did he want to be a philosopher. He never troubled himself with a reasoned criticism of that philosophy; rather it was accepted at face value as offering a satisfactory account of how scientific knowledge arises and of how such knowledge is justified or shown to be universally valid. His interests were always primarily theological and he only bothered to criticize the philosophy of Marburg when it was felt to misrepresent the nature of religion. Barth's appreciation of the primacy of experience in religion, moreover, involved an element of realism in his theory of religion, which constrained him to confess that something *ist gegeben*, thus necessarily forcing a rejection of Marburg ontology and its logical monism.

Neither Barth nor his teacher understood why the experience of God's self-revelation, which seemed so real and self-evident to them, was exceedingly problematical for Cohen and Natorp. They did not realize that were Marburg philosophy to adopt the account of religious experience offered by Marburg theology, the former would have to abandon its radical idealism.

III. BARTH'S CRITIQUE OF METAPHYSICS IN THEOLOGY

There is at least one juncture where the earliest theology of Barth exhibits substantial continuity with the work of Ritschl, and that is his criticism of metaphysics in theology. The characteristics of Ritschlian methodology—the distinction between nature and spirit; the reduction of the competence of philosophy to epistemology; the faith that Christianity alone offered a well-rounded *Weltanschauung*; and the acceptance of Melanchthon's soteriological principle as being the only epistemological premiss with which theology may operate—regularly appear in Barth's early writings.[64] In a lecture concerned with an unwelcome reappearance of metaphysics in theology, that was delivered to a pastoral congress at Geneva during the early summer of 1911, Barth expressed Ritschlian disquiet at a new trend amongst contemporary theologians which sought to reinstate metaphysics to the theological agenda. He passionately believed theology was signing its own death warrant by wooing metaphysics in order to bolster its epistemological claims and the explicit objective of his lecture was to discredit this trend. Three theologians in particular were accused of contributing to the suicidal metaphysical revival—Lüdemann, Wobbermin, and Barth's *bête noire*, Troeltsch. Since the first two theologians are not widely known outside Germany, it might be helpful to say something about their work before considering Barth's criticisms.

Lüdemann held a chair at Berne, and Barth, having studied there before going to Marburg, was acquainted with his views from lectures, articles, and books.[65] Lüdemann's numerous articles, usually published in the *Protestantische Monatshefte*, along with his book, *Das Erkennen und die Werturteile*, testify to his especial concern with epistemology. In such writings he attempted to clarify the nature of value judgements and to indicate how they operated in different spheres of knowledge. This, of course, represented no great innovation to those familiar with the writings of Ritschl and his followers, but Lüdemann did not stop with epistemology. Value judgements, he argued, can and do produce knowledge about the nature of reality (*Seinserkenntnis*) precisely because judgements of a valuing nature presuppose that the agent making such judgements has some knowledge about the nature of being. It was therefore his conviction that an important task for philosophical theology involved a rational justification of its ontological base.[66] Lüdemann himself supported a modified version of proofs for divine existence based upon intuitive self-consciousness (*Selbstanschauung*) and though it would be tedious to comment at length upon the unlikely and unconvincing course of his arguments, the significance of his work lies, first, in the recognition that Christian truth claims require justification, though he conceived such justification somewhat narrowly, limiting it to a questionable procedure of 'proving'.[67] Secondly, however, his plea for ontological clarity was important and completely justified. Despite special pleading from the disciples of Ritschl, Lüdemann was not convinced that epistemology could be restricted to technique and discussed without any reference to ontology. It was his belief, therefore, that many claims made by Christian theism did in fact require metaphysical commitments, the self being one amongst many, from which there could be no escape.

Wobbermin was one of those theologians whose achievements were obscured by the upheavals of dialectical theology. It was he who pioneered the discipline of *Religionspsychologie* in Germany, making himself responsible for the German edition of James's epoch-making book about the varieties of religious experience. He was also responsible for a massive shift in the discussion of faith and history, suggesting that the distinction between *Geist* and *Natur* was theologically less important than a distinction between *Historie* and *Geschichte*. His systematic distinction was to have a profound impact upon exegesis and doctrine later in the century.[68] Wobbermin eventually acquired a chair at Göttingen, where Barth later joined him, and ultimately became an object of polemic in early volumes of the *Church Dogmatics*.[69]

A passion which characterized the writings of this truly inter-disciplinary scholar was his resolute determination to controvert

secular philosophies and ideologies which he regarded as fundamentally incompatible with Christian beliefs. In *Monismus und
Monotheismus*, for example, he dealt with such issues as Haeckle's
scientific *Weltanschauung*, Christianity and Darwinism, the
implications for theology of atomic theory, and contemporary
monism, particularly that advocated by the celebrated author of
the *Christ Myth* in his *Der Monismus dargestellt in Beiträgen seiner
Vertreter* (1908). This intellectual giant, who kept abreast of
developments in psychology, natural science, and philosophy in
both its popular and academic guises, fell foul of the young Barth
because he insisted that 'Theologie ohne Metaphysik sei unmög-
lich'. By metaphysics Wobbermin meant '*a definite orientation
towards a total view of the world and an integrated attitude to life*. More
precisely such an orientation points beyond the entirety of what is
immediately given to us, beyond, that is, the world we discover
empirically.'[70] Such words to one, like Barth, who was schooled in
modern theology, were anathema. Wobbermin therefore joined
Lüdemann and Troeltsch as a dangerous reactionary to be
defeated by a truly modern theology.

    Turning to Barth's contribution to the debate, it is important
first to clarify what he meant by metaphysics. From the outset he
stressed the scientific character of metaphysics, because its goal
was to answer the question, 'of whether there is an object which is
known, a necessity which is known, a reality which is known;
whether we can grasp ultimate, supreme, truth by means of the
theoretical faculty which works with and reflects our own spirit'.[71]
Barth attached great significance, first, to the claim that metaphysics could attain ultimate truth about the nature of reality and,
secondly, to the affirmation that such truth can be attained by
rational means alone. Metaphysics, said Barth, is a scientific
procedure which has a unitary method and, if this is accepted,
there is only one valid form of metaphysics. He stressed repeatedly
throughout his lecture that in principle there could be no other
way to the Absolute than that laid down, posited, or presupposed
by the scientifically uniform method of metaphysics.[72]

    After emphasizing the scientific and methodologically uniform
character of the metaphysical enterprise, Barth proceeded to ask
how such a science could be used in theology. This he regarded as
a methodological crux because 'Religion, which is the object of
theology, claims itself to represent, possess, and reaffirm the

Absolute; to be the absolute, supreme truth'.[73] From the very beginning, therefore, a methodological dilemma is set up between the science of metaphysics, which claims to attain the Absolute, and religion, which proffers similar claims. Barth's discussion therefore focuses upon the logical dissonance of two rival and mutually exclusive paths to truth. In this situation, therefore, 'we would have two different ways of attaining the Absolute: not only the way of faith, belief, revelation, inspiration, or whatever term we use to designate what is properly called religious experience, but also the purely theoretical way of . . . metaphysics'.[74]

In order to clarify the issues further, Barth distinguished between two species of metaphysics, the first of which, 'consistent metaphysics', is found in Origenism, neo-Platonism, and Hegelianism. Here Barth was really characterizing a central feature of Hegel's philosophy, according to which religion indeed possesses truth, though only in an imaginative, pictorial, or representational form, whilst philosophy, being the absolute science, has truth as system: 'Religious belief is only a comprehensible and popular form of the metaphysical science which is accessible to . . . the philosopher. . . . theoretical interest in the Absolute made the exponents of consistent metaphysics see in religion itself a quasi-science of the Absolute which was not, however, perfect.'[75] Were theology to embrace the programme of 'consistent metaphysics', not only would religious belief become theoretically superfluous, but additionally a dualism between popular religion and the metaphysical insights of a cultured elite would be sanctioned. Being deeply committed to the primacy of personal experience in religion, as well as to the understanding that religion represents a *sui generis* form of knowledge and reality, Barth could not accept either consequence:

Religion lives from the revelation which is not immanent and general, but actual, historic, and individual. Religious life is primordially a receptive life. Through it we reach supreme truth because we ourselves are touched by supreme truth: for we *receive* it and do not *make* or *do* something. To transform this supreme truth into a science would be the same as removing its principle, that is, the revelation, which a person does not work at as he works at science, ethics, or art, but which he *undergoes* and *accepts*.[76]

Here is not only the immediacy of divine–human relatedness in revelation which characterizes the thesis of relationism, but also a contrast between scientific knowledge and religion. The former is regarded as having been manufactured or constructed, whilst the latter is a freely given gift bestowed by divine grace. Both themes, of course, distinguished Herrmann's theology, but more importantly the quotation clearly illustrates a tension between realism and idealism which is all pervasive in Barth's earliest writings. Idealism is accepted as a valid epistemological style for what Barth elsewhere called the 'transcendental discipline' of philosophy, whilst realism is seen to be demanded by religious experience. The contrast between cognitive work and unmerited grace, moreover, involves the dialectic of faith and works which marked Herrmann's apologetic labours.[77]

This first genus of metaphysics thus aspires to find the Absolute by purely theoretical and rational means. A second form of metaphysics, 'inconsistent metaphysics', offers an alternative approach. Here the Absolute Object is recognized as having been given to the individual through revelatory experience, but now metaphysical science aims at proving what experience has already encountered.

It is a matter of verifying this religious given by the methods of science. One must demonstrate the reality of this Reality. . . . One must prove the God that has already been found; not, however, God in his entirety, for there are some mysteries of the divinity which are accessible only to faith, that is, by revelation—for example, the Trinity and Redemption. However, certain of his qualities must be proved, not least among them his existence. That is the task of metaphysics which, according to this programme, is not a competitor, but a companion or, to employ a famous phrase, a handmaid, of both religion and theology.[78]

Theologians who followed this procedure did not for one moment doubt the existence of God, but a very definite objective apparently prompted their 'proving': 'This is the programme of scholastic metaphysics: *to prove the Absolute Object which is found by other means, that is, in religion, in order to give a scientific character to theology*.'[79] The emphasized statement is of considerable importance, for it shows how Barth accepted Herrmann's belief that revelatory experience is self-authenticating. Being grounded solely *autopistia*, revelation so conceived neither requires nor admits any proof or reasoned justification whatsoever. Religion, therefore, needs no handmaid, but should theology nevertheless invite assistance from the science of metaphysics, the consequences are grievous. The handmaid becomes a tyrannical mistress who distorts the true nature of religion by transforming it into something over which she may exercise complete control.

Barth detected inconsistent metaphysics in post-Kantian philosophy where the Absolute was no longer an object μετὰ τὰ φυσικά but instead appeared πρὸ των φυσικῶν in the guise of an a priori. The Absolute is accordingly found in consciousness and theology is transformed into a science of religious experience:

Kantian idealism proved the truth of scientific moral, and aesthetic experience by discovering the a priori of reason. ... It is easy to understand that the idea had to develop of finding analogous criteria for the truth of religious experience. Finding these criteria means demonstrating the scientific character of theology, that is, the necessity of its object in the universe of the spirit.[80]

Barth suggested that Schleiermacher's *Gefühl* may be viewed as procuring an a priori for religion and, of course, he was certainly aware that Troeltsch had spoken of a religious a priori. Whenever a quest arises for some a priori to endow theology with a scientific character, hoping thereby to render its claims more credible, the whole objectionable procedure invariably revolves around 'the question of general support . . . to verify the special Christian given [*la donnée chrétienne spéciale*]. Before Kant, one proved God. After Kant, one proved religion.'[81]

Both types of metaphysics, therefore, have the effect of blinding theology to the fundamental fact that the Absolute is legitimate in religion alone. Its validity, that is, depends upon its being a conceptual expression of experienced religion:

Religion has always shown itself to be a generative force [*une force procréatrice*] in the domain of thought, action, and art. What it generated in all these areas claimed always to be absolute values, not in themselves, but in their religious quality. ... religious thought is not absolute *qua* thought, and has no desire to be absolute, except as *religious* thought. Religious thought maintains its absoluteness by means of its genetic connection with the Absolute. ... Once this genetic rapport is interrupted, religious thought is petrified and transformed into pure fancy or mythology.[82]

When theology therefore speaks of an Absolute or makes absolute claims, it does so purely symbolically, because its concepts or doctrines are simply ciphers of immediate religious experience.[83] Here Barth is relying on Herrmann's distinction between faith and thoughts of faith and upon his perception that religious immediacy is always fragmented and distorted by conceptual reflection. A fatal category mistake therefore occurs whenever the word Absolute is used without reference to the experience from which it arises and which it also simulates.

Barth conceded that this criticism is rendered difficult when authentically religious thought encounters a non-religious, scientific, or philosophical form of thought

which also knows supreme and ultimate givens or believes it knows them. It claims that these givens are results of deductive work accomplished by the theoretical spirit. It is at the moment of this clash between religious and non-religious thought that religious thought easily turns into proving thought. It is then that the symbol of the Absolute reveals a tendency, more or less clear, to become the science of the Absolute.[84]

Such symbolic reification was believed to mark the writings of Wobbermin, Lüdemann, and Troeltsch. Though severely critical of this trend, Barth condescended to view it sympathetically, for it arose from an individual's psycholgocial need to explain the relations between two forms of thought—autonomous philosophy and religious theology. It nevertheless remained axiomatic for Barth that the scientific truth of philosophy could not confirm, justify, or demonstrate the truth revealed to experienced religion. When a theologian, no matter how laudable his intentions, is constrained by some psychological pressure to introduce metaphysics into theology

religious truth, in the process of being translated into religious thought, has entered into the terrain proper to science. In order to prove religious truth one has to transform religious thought into scientific thought. One must extend the position of the first by applying the methods of the latter. It is in this way that the older metaphysics proved scientifically the reality of God in the world and it is also in this way that the new metaphysics proves the reality, that is, the necessity, of religion in the universe of spirit.[85]

Though a little critical of Ritschl, Barth recommended his opponents to re-read this theologian and listen once more to his salutary warnings and lessons. They would then perceive that the whole enterprise of using metaphysics as a scientific support for religion precipitates the destruction of theology.[86]

Constraints of space forbid a thorough examination of the more specific objections levelled at Lüdemann and Wobbermin, but the general critique of metaphysics in theology is worth noting, for it follows those well-trodden paths through the undergrowth of metaphysics cleared by Ritschl and Herrmann. In the first place Barth reaffirms Ritschl's objection that metaphysics confounds and confuses the distinction between nature and spirit:

The concept of God, which speculative science formulates, is indifferent to the battle in which the individual is engaged with his natural environment. . . . The supreme cause, the teleological principle, the entity found by means of the ontological proof, is not God, for the reality of God is, objectively, an act which we undergo that subjectively raises the soul. This act and raising do not presuppose the theoretical harmony of spirit and nature as established in the metaphysical concept of God. On the contrary, it presupposes the practical conflict between the two, which does not . . . exist a priori, but in life and history. Religion is really this life struggling in history. . . . The essence of the God of living religion . . . is his love which searches for us and sustains us in our practical conflict.[87]

A second criticism of this 'propping up' of religion and theology with metaphysics is that religion is perverted by an unacceptable 'intellectualism'. God becomes a mere idea, an empty thought lacking actuality, and religious knowledge, instead of being saving knowledge, becomes a fascinating conceptual game. Knowing such a God is simply a matter of logically deducing attributes which thought posits along with its metaphysical concept of deity. Consequently a further implication of using metaphysics in theology is the *spekulative Fälschung* of religious doctrine. Such impieties wrought by metaphysics are particularly evident 'in these abominable discussions about the "true" divinity of the Saviour, which have been diverting the understanding of the gospel again and again right up to our own time'.[88] The words following this sentence in Barth's French text are somewhat obscure, perhaps the edited version of the *Gesamtausgabe* might eventually cast some light on them, but Barth's argument seems to be as follows: the truth of Christ's divinity is his 'equality' with the Father, yet the religious significance of this equality is forfeited when a metaphysical concept of deity is foisted onto God, for then Christ has to be predicated with all the metaphysical attributes enjoyed by the metaphysical God. The attributes which Barth particularly stresses are those of God's 'non-limited character', 'eternity in time', the qualities of *causa sui* and *causa omnium*, as well as omnipotence and omnipresence. In addition to the alleged misrepresentation of Christ's person and work, Barth makes a general point of considerable importance concerning the validity of metaphysical statements about divine attributes. They are devoid of any cognitive value except when they are construed:

1. as regulative ideas, as *Grenzbegriffe* of science.
2. as expressions and symbols that are accessories of the religious life, but which mean *nothing* for the constitutive and essential knowledge of God and have *no* constitutive and essential importance for that practical elevation of the soul which is the essence of religion.[89]

By contrast the decisive epistemological and soteriological principle upon which Barth's relationism and his critique of metaphysics depends is stated quite unambiguously: '*Melanchthon* once expressed this very well: "Hoc est Christum cognoscere, beneficia ejus cognoscere non quod isti docent, ejus naturas, modos incarnationis contueri." *Beneficia ejus cognoscere*—that is the principle of knowledge not only for Christology, but for religious thought in general.'[90] Perhaps enough has already been said about the use and abuse of this principle in modern theology to render further comment superfluous.[91]

Before leaving Barth's discussion about metaphysics in theology, his misgivings about the religious a priori deserves some attention. Though he conceded that Troeltsch regarded the religious a priori as not being essential to his system of *Religionsphilosophie*, Barth thought it was. He generously acknowledged there to be some genuine religious elements in Troeltsch's work, but nevertheless claimed that his religious a priori obscured the experiential actuality of religion: 'what is the use of dressing up the reality of religious life with a metaphysics which resembles very much in its details the Gnostic systems of the second century and which, in short, is not a metaphysical theory but a mythological analogy of religious thought?'[92] Similarly, but with less polemical ferocity, Barth used the word 'perverse' to characterize this attempt at placing 'religion on a par with cognition, volition, and feeling, in the form of a religious a priori as a generally valid, that is, transcendentally necessary, form of consciousness and so to incorporate it into *Kulturbewusstsein'*.[93] The following is a more detailed exposition of what is taken to be Troeltsch's method:

According to him, actual religious experience would be virtually preceded by a general form, a necessary idea, a priori; one, that is, which is immanent in consciousness, just as there is an a priori of science, morals, and art. This rational norm would be found by means of a critical analysis of religion, of its psychology and history. By demonstrating this norm, which is at once a priori, psychological, and historical, one would have demonstrated the reality of religion in the life of the spirit.[94]

Barth's lecture, in conscious opposition to Troeltsch's mythical way of proceeding, states the legitimate meaning of the a priori for critical philosophy, which

does not ask the question: is there such a thing psychologically as science or morality? But rather: if there is such a thing, what is its necessary and thus a priori form, its *ratio cognoscendi*? . . . it asks, quite simply, what is the disposition of the scientific or moral spirit and it is in this disposition that it finds reality.[95]

It has been noted how Barth regarded cognition as a work by which knowledge is generated from the possibilities of the neo-Kantian *Kulturbewusstsein*. In this passage the cognitive consciousness of Marburg philosophy is construed as a necessary transcendental synthesis and its various 'dispositions', that is, directions or *Richtungen*, are believed to constitute reality. The fundamental mistake of Troeltsch's religious a priori lies in its being a poor parody of this truly scientific methodology. At most it merely proves the psychological reality of religion for *Kulturbewusstsein*, but by supposing there to be religious a priori, from which religious knowledge is generated, Troeltsch unwittingly turned religion into a purely human psychological act in which divine efficacy played no part. He consequently ignored what Barth deemed essential to religious faith: experience of God's self-revelation through immediate awareness of Christ's benefits. Faith was accordingly turned into work by Troeltsch's futile attempt at cognitive justification.[96]

Barth's war against the religious a priori was fought with the aid of three further weapons. On the basis of the sweeping claim that pure critical philosophy is concerned only with epistemological technique and not with ontology or metaphysics, there is the assertion that the a priori belongs exclusively to science, morality, and art. Establishing an a priori, therefore, 'is not intended to be more than it is: a simple method of searching for truth, not truth itself'.[97] Barth secondly offered a criticism concerning the religious legitimacy of a supposed religious a priori:

> Religion cannot be included in this system of the a priori because religion is truth, reality, actualization; because it is the principle which generates history and not merely an a priori norm. Religion cannot be a transcendental function because it is not a method of living, but the very life of the individual. Religion cannot be put side by side with science as a function of consciousness . . . because it does not represent a function, but the functioning of the consciousness which is lived.[98]

A third criticism arises from Barth's own approach to the relations between religion and culture. Establishing an a priori for religion as a mere appendage to the three other directions of consciousness perpetuated, thought Barth, an untenable distinction between faith and knowledge. Religion, as he wrote elsewhere, does not desire to be confined to just one direction of culture or knowledge: it much more wants to be the *Realitätsbeziehung*, the force, that is, which binds the religious individual to culture in the immediacy of religious life.[99] To say more than this would be to anticipate the next chapter, the subject of which is the theory of religion that pervades the earliest writings of Barth.

To conclude this discussion of metaphysics, religion, and neo-Kantianism in Barth's writings, the following observations should help pave the way to the exploration of his systematic theory of religion. The fact that Barth disputed the legitimacy of meta-physics in theology should not be taken to imply that he had no ontology, for he did have a very definite ontology which was realist—as far as religion was concerned. The trouble with Barth's assessment of philosophy was its lack of rigour on the one hand and its reliance upon an apologetic strategy involving neo-Reformation polemics on the other. The legitimacy of this strategy was never questioned. His way of approaching philosophy was, first, to reduce it to epistemological technique and, secondly, to contrast its epistemological idealism with the realism felt to be necessary for religion. The attempt to combine idealist epistemo-logy with the rudiments of realist ontology accounts for the numerous terminological contortions to be found in Barth's earliest writings. The possibility that the Marburg machinery of generation might not be right never occurred to Barth, and neither did the possibility of a realist metaphysics. He normally combated opponents with a common-sense appeal to religious beliefs, experiences, and revelations, claiming them to possess such an overwhelming degree of reality for the religious individual that religion must be something real and true in order for it to have been experienced in the first place. This realism, moreover, spilled over from immediate experience and became predicated to the more abstract theological conceptuality that was believed to be sanctioned by the same experience. The typically Herrmannian premiss, according to which revelatory experience is self-authenticating, was made to support this plea and to reinforce the irreducibility and cognitive integrity of religion in the face of philosophical criticism. A second tension begins to emerge in Barth's understanding of religion. Religion is seen predominantly as an intimately personal experience of being related to God on the one hand, yet on the other it is presented as a creative force active in culture and history. There thus arises an obvious imbalance between Barth's personalist approach to religious revelation and his desire to see religion active in the intersubjective forum of culture. It was the great task of his fragmentary *Religions-philosophie* to find some positive theory of religion that could do justice to both emphases. Barth's relationism, thirdly, held unforeseen theological dangers. The understanding of the individual's relatedness to God as a synthesis involving divine power and religious feeling, which had to be accepted as given and beyond question, might have the unfortunate consequence of imprisoning God in his grace. Though Barth constantly reiterated that religion was not a human work but an unmerited divine gift, God was as indissolubly bound in the relational nexus as the individual who accepts or 'undergoes' the experience of revelation. Finally, Barth's advocacy of the primacy of experience, plus his total exclusion of metaphysics from theology, encouraged him to view religious language as a cipher of such experience. This, however, aggravated the question of criteria. Why, for example, need one utter thoughts of faith which ostensibly affirm the divinity of Christ, when religious language is ultimately concerned with one truth, namely, the relatedness of the individual to God? The questions Barth later asked himself about the objectivity of doctrinal language and also about the place of the Word of God in theology, arose directly from unresolved tensions in his earliest theology.

NOTES

1. Barth left Marburg on 18 Aug. 1909 to begin work in Geneva on 18 September. He preached his farewell sermon to the congregation at Geneva on 25 June 1911.
2. See E. Busch, *Karl Barth* (SCM, 1976), 56–7.
3. See further J. Weiss, *Jesus von Nazareth, Mythus oder Geschichte*, and B. A. Gerrisch, 'Jesus, Myth and History: Troeltsch's stand in the "Christ Myth" Debate', *Journal of Religion*, 55 (1975), 13–35.
4. 'Bibliographia Barthiana', in *Antwort: Karl Barth zum siebzigsten Geburtstag* (Evangelischer Verlag, 1956).
5. Busch, *Karl Barth*, 57–8, 59.
6. Barth, though never friendly towards Troeltsch, during the winter of 1908–9 copied the lectures on *Religionsphilosophie* which Troeltsch delivered the previous summer. As well as Troeltsch's theological, epistemological, and historical criticisms of Herrmann's work, it should be recalled that he favoured the Baden School of neo-Kantianism to that of Marburg, principally because he believed the latter did not take historical phenomena seriously and offered an anti-realist philosophy of history which he regarded as metaphysically and methodologically questionable. Amongst the many rejoinders to Troeltsch, Herrmann's review of *Die Bedeutung der Geschichtlichkeit des Jesu für den Glauben* in *Theologische Literaturzeitung* 11 (1902), and Häring's 'Ein Wort zu "Glaube und Geschichte" und zum "religiösen Apriori" ', *Christliche Welt*, 24 (1910), 245–9 are particularly instructive. For an account of the relations between Troeltsch, Herrmann, and Barth, see W. Groll's fine monograph, *Ernest Troeltsch und Karl Barth—Kontinuität im Widerspruch* (Kaiser, 1976). It is worth mentioning in passing that the later *Zwischen den Zeiten* circle, though far from being a homogeneous body of thinkers, found a unifying factor in their total opposition to Troeltsch and to everything he stood for. See further on this C. Gestrich, *Neuzeitliches Denken und die Spaltung der Dialektischen Theologie* (J. C. B. Mohr, 1977).
7. From F.-W. Marquardt's 'Socialism in the Theology of Karl Barth' in G. Hunsinger (ed.), *Karl Barth and Radical Politics* (Westminster Press, 1976), 70.
8. 'We can interpret and explain his later works in terms of earlier

writings, tracing the former back to the root ideas from which they sprang; or else we can relate the earlier works to the later ones, regarding the latter as the full development of the former. There is no question of choosing one alternative to the complete exclusion of the other . . . any attempt to bypass Barth's earlier thought, to regard it as a thing of the past and to concentrate solely on his later works, can only lead to a very incomplete understanding of them' H. V. von Balthasar, *The Theology of Karl Barth* (Holt, Rinehart, & Winston, 1971), 43, 46.

9. Marquardt, 'Socialism in the Theology of Karl Barth', 70.

10. One of the most mature and probing accounts about the nature of Karl Barth's political views is contained in two works by W. R. Ward. See 'The Socialist Commitment in Karl Barth', in *Studies in Church History*, 15 (Blackwell, 1978), 453–65, and *Theology, Sociology, and Politics: The German Protestant Social Conscience 1890–1933* (Peter Lang, 1979).

11. See e.g. T. F. Torrance's *Karl Barth: An Introduction to his Early Theology* (SCM, 1962), 33–4: 'Barth admits he was once a liberal theologian, even an enthusiastic one in his youth. . . . Although his university training threw him into the prevailing philosophical and scientific discussion pursued within the tradition of the eighteenth and nineteenth centuries so that he was forced to think within its universe of discourse, yet from the very start he felt deeply uneasy about it—it could not meet his theological hunger, for nowhere could he find a theology with radical clarity about its own positive task, but only one where the nature and function of theology were blurred through the subsidiary task of coming to grips with the spirit of the age. . . . Barth's deep uneasiness was backed up by his inquiring mind which insisted on reflecting upon the questionableness of this whole proceeding.'! Von Balthasar, who was more sensitive to Barth's intellectual background, also speaks of Barth's early writings as bearing the 'outward trappings of liberal theology', implying that the intention of his earliest theology, its substantial *Inhalt* or *Gehalt*, somehow transcends the inessential liberal form in which it was temporarily imprisoned. Von Balthasar, *The Theology of Karl Barth*, 179.

12. For an example see Barth's 'On Systematic Theology', *Scottish Journal of Theology*, 14 (1961), 224 ff.: 'To the prevailing tendency of about 1910 among the younger followers of Albrecht Ritschl I attached myself with passable conviction. Yet it was not without a certain alienation in view of the issue of this school in the philosophy of religion of Ernst Troeltsch, in which I found myself disappointed in regard to what interested me in theology, although for the time being I did not see a better way.' Between 1908 and 1912, however,

the Barth of history was well aware that Troeltsch's *Religions-philosophie* not only issued from Ritschl's School, but also departed from it radically and, moreover, decisively repudiated those who, like Herrmann, continued to support it. Barth's unpublished lecture on metaphysics in theology in fact firmly castigates Troeltsch and his supporters for forgetting the lessons Ritschl had taught them! An examination of Barth's early writings does not support the view that his commitment to 'modern theology' was 'passable'—for nearly a decade it was enthusiastic and whole-hearted.

13. An example of this is the view which Barth preferred to take about his break with liberalism. He liked to date this from that 'black day' when the 'Manifesto of the Intellectuals' appeared in Aug. 1914 (Busch, *Karl Barth*, 81). A close examination of his contemporary writings, however, casts doubt as to whether this incident produced the decisive and instantaneous break which Barth would have us believe—see particularly the two works by Ward cited in n. 10 above.

14. Busch, *Karl Barth*, 58.

15. The text is reproduced in Appendix I of J. P. Clayton's *The Concept of Correlation: Paul Tillich and the Possibility of a Mediating Theology* (De Gruyter, 1980).

16. *Reichsgottesarbeit*, 317–18, 319.

17. Ibid. 318.

18. Ibid.

19. Ibid. 318–19.

20. Ibid. 320.

21. Ibid. 321.

22. *Antwort*, 481.

23. Ibid. 481–2.

24. Ibid. 482.

25. Ibid. 482–3.

26. Ibid. 483–4.

27. *Jesus*, 2, col. 2.

28. Ibid. 3, col. 1.

29. Ibid. 3, col. 2.

30. Ibid. 3, col. 2–4, col. 1.

31. See R. C. Gregg and D. E. Groh, *Early Arianism: A View of Salvation* (SCM, 1981), chs. 2, 5.

32. The debates following the work of Drews left a profound impression on the younger generation, so much so that the issues raised continued to haunt people like Bultmann and Tillich. It is interesting to compare Barth's way of tackling the problem with Tillich's in the second volume of his *Systematic Theology*. Though not relying in the same way as Barth on the distinction between inner and outer history, his answer to the question of what faith can guarantee with

respect to the factuality of that event called Jesus the Christ recalls the early appeal to the *Grund* (foundation) of faith. His aesthetic analogy, between the biblical picture and the actual human life from which it may have arisen, additionally recalls some of the thinking about the *Charakterbild* of Jesus which is to be found in Kähler, Herrmann, and the early Barth. His discussion is a little more sociologically oriented than Barth's, but not much more.

33. On Barth and Pietism see E. Busch, *Karl Barth und die Pietisten* (Kaiser, 1978).
34. *Antwort*, 484.
35. 'The Doctrine of Revelation in the Thought of Karl Barth 1909–1922: The Nature of Barth's Break with Liberalism' (Ph.D. thesis, University of Yale, 1956), 27, 33.
36. Ibid. 27.
37. See p. 80. In his *Antwort* (p. 484) Barth significantly quotes the famous words 'Spricht die Seele, so spricht ach die Seele nicht mehr'.
38. *Antwort*, 482–3.
39. See p. 177.
40. *Gesammelte Schriften*, v. 221.
41. For books by Cohen and Natorp in Barth's library see Appendix I.
42. Not only did this concern Barth, but also other young theologians such as Bultmann and Tillich. See the former's 'Religion und Kultur' (1920) in J. Moltmann (ed.), *Anfänge der dialektischen Theologie* (Kaiser, 1963), ii, and the latter's *Über die Idee einer Theologie der Kultur* (Reutler & Reinhard, 1920).
43. *GUG*, 5.
44. Ibid. 16.
45. For this claim see Natorp's *Platons Ideenlehre: Eine Einführung in den Idealismus* (Felix Meiner, 1903).
46. *GUG*, 4.
47. Ibid. 16.
48. Ibid. 55.
49. *Metaphysics*, 6.
50. *Religionsphilosophie*, 4: 'In den Aktualisierungen des logischen, ethischen, ästhetischen a priori konstatiert die Vernunftkritik das Auftreten eines der Methodik jener Bewusstseinsrichtungen ebenso inkommensurablen wie unentbehrlichen Elements: die Idee.'
51. See p. 178.
52. *GUG*, 17.
53. Ibid.
54. *Metaphysics*, 4.
55. See pp. 82 ff.
56. See pp. 140 ff.
57. See pp. 60 ff. and 74 ff.

58. *GUG*, 5.
59. *BPG*, 25.
60. *KDRV*, A341/B399 ff.
61. *BPG*, 25.
62. *KDRV*, A671/B699.
63. It should be noted that Barth in fact returns to a more authentically Kantian position, in that he aimed to restore the hypothetical possibility of noumenal objects or things-in-themselves because it seemed to make room for faith and its beliefs, whilst simultaneously denying knowledge. The Marburg School from the outset laboured to overcome this 'inconsistency' in Kantian idealism. This shows how naïve Barth was to accept the Marburg account of epistemology whilst ignoring its ontological implications or—even worse—believing there to be none.
64. See pp. 127 ff.
65. Busch, *Karl Barth*, 33–4.
66. See e.g. *Das Erkennen und die Werturteile* (Heinsius, 1910), 231 ff.
67. See 'Vom "Beweisen" überhaupt und in der Theologie insbesondere', *Protestantische Monatshefte*, 9 (1910), 361–80.
68. 'Geschichte und Historie in der Religionswissenschaft', *Zeitschrift für Theologie und Kirche*, Supplement (1911).
69. See Busch, *Karl Barth*, 133; *CD*, i/1. 210 ff., 217 ff., 232 ff.; and also the earlier critiques of Wobbermin in *Die christliche Dogmatik, Gesamtausgabe*, ii/14 (1982), 74–5, 79 etc.
70. *Monismus und Monotheismus: Vorträge und Abhandlungen zum Kampf um die monistische Weltanschauung* (J. C. B. Mohr, 1911), 118.
71. *Metaphysics*, 2.
72. For the various meanings of *Wissenschaft* see ch. 3 n. 31 above. Not all metaphysicians would agree with Barth. Compare, for example, the words of Peter Strawson: 'Metaphysics has a long and distinguished history, and it is consequently unlikely that there are any new truths to be discovered in descriptive metaphysics. But this does not mean that the task of descriptive metaphysics has been, or can be, done once for all. It has constantly to be done over again'. *Individuals: An Essay in Descriptive Metaphysics* (London, 1959), 10.
73. *Metaphysics*, 2.
74. Ibid.
75. Ibid. 3.
76. Ibid. 3–4.
77. See pp. 136 ff.
78. *Metaphysics*, 4–5.
79. Ibid. 5.
80. Ibid. 6.
81. Ibid.

82. Ibid. 7–8.
83. For the concept of cipher see K. Jaspers, *Chiffren der Transzendenz* (Piper, 1972), and *Philosophie* (Springer Verlag, 1932), iii.
84. *Metaphysics*, 8.
85. Ibid.
86. Ritschl, according to Barth, established an untenable dualism between belief and science. Barth, however, in his lecture ends up in an analogous position.
87. *Metaphysics*, 10–11.
88. Ibid. 12.
89. Ibid.
90. Ibid.
91. See pp. 127 ff. and 163 f. etc.
92. *Metaphysics*, 14.
93. *Religionsphilosophie*, 3–4.
94. *Metaphysics*, 14.
95. Ibid.
96. Barth, I believe, was indebted to Häring's review of Troeltsch in the *Christliche Welt*, 24 (1910). Since it is something of a gem, his characterization of the religious a priori and his comments are worth quoting: 'Religion has its seat in the primordial disposition of reason: look within thyself, there shalt thou find religion as the central and fundamental law of thy life . . . "From the outset" religion lies in our spirit as something "original", completely independent of all historical experience and of anything which is "added" "a posteriori" to that which was original; our religious reason is the source, norm, and ground of certainty in religion . . . On the other hand, however, religion does not live by virtue of the creative activity of our spirit, nor is it sufficient to view the creative power of our spirit as God's act in us . . . The way religion operates is the opposite to such creative being [*Schöpferseins*], it is reverent dependence, a thankful allowing of ourselves to be created by the God who is actively creative in history and whose living act quiets the deepest need of our spirit' (cols. 1107–9).
97. *Metaphysics*, 15.
98. Ibid. 15–16.
99. Once more Barth's position is very close to the understanding of the relations between religion and culture in Tillich's early writings.

5

REVELATION, CULTURE, AND DIALECTIC

ELEMENTS OF A THEORY OF RELIGION

WITH the abolition of metaphysics as a *Hilfswissenschaft* for theology, neither Barth nor other modern theologians of his era found they could rely exclusively upon traditional biblical or doctrinal language when writing theology. Either unwittingly or intentionally, increasing use was made of theories of religion as an alternative to the discredited science of metaphysics. As far as Marburg theology was concerned, an additional impetus to formulate a general theory of religion came from the debates with Cohen and Natorp, for even Herrmann could agree with these philosophers that Christianity belonged to the genus of religion. An articulate theory of religion, it seemed, was useful for challenging reductionists and essential to theology as an academic discipline. Serving the purposes of an epistemological grid, some general account of religion offered the prospect of enabling theologians to find their bearings on the cognitive map of contemporary culture. This very interesting move, in which a theory of religion begins to replace both natural theology and general metaphysical descriptions of the world from a theistic perspective, was not an explicit methodological goal as far as Herrmann was concerned; it was, rather, an inevitable consequence of his apologetic concerns. Barth, by contrast, was more single-minded in his quest for a theory of religion, and a coherent approach begins to emerge clearly in his early writings. This chapter will uncover three elements that were central to his developing theory of religion. They are encountered in his theology of history, in an explicit theoretical objective to find a scientifically acceptable way of addressing religion in relation to culture and prevailing academic trends, and in a special form of dialectic which pervades his early writings.

Before considering Barth's earliest systematic theology, it is essential to begin with Christology because no Christian theologian, however committed to devising a general theory of religion, could afford to ignore it, although the young Barth himself was capable of being quite iconoclastic when he turned to Christology. In his Genevan days he said of the Chalcedonian Definition, for example, 'If Jesus were like this, I would not be interested in him'; yet such statements were always balanced by more pious thoughts, such as 'if Christ begins to live in *us* ... that is the beginning of Christian faith'.[1] Precisely the same sentiments were expressed in an article about Christian faith and history, on this occasion with verses from Silesius's *Der Cherubinische Wandersmann*: 'Wird Christus tausendmal zu Bethlehem geboren, und nicht dir: du bleibst doch ewiglich verloren.'[2]

No modern theologian, including the young Karl Barth, wished to dispense with Christology—nor could they, for the special religious epistemology developed by Ritschl and Herrmann absolutely depended upon an appeal to the benefits of Christ which were revealed in Christian religious experience. This was the legitimate starting-point not only for Christology, but for theology in general. Again and again Barth, true to form, cites Melanchthon, welcoming 'the systematic specification of the programme already established by Melanchthon in his famous: *hoc est Christum cognoscere, beneficia ejus cognoscere*'.[3] With such systematic dependence upon the benefits of Christ one urgent problem arose, first, from Drews's contention that contemporary theology spoke in ways suggesting that its Christ principle, idea, or image (*Bild*), had little relation to Jesus—even if such a figure ever existed. Secondly, the new content bestowed upon Melanchthon's words required some clarification concerning the relations between soteriology, Christology, and revelation. Both problems, moreover, were aggravated by a third, for they had to be considered in the context of the increasingly thorny issue of the New Testament criticism which was busy unearthing a Jesus in many ways alien to the urbane piety of nineteenth-century Lutheranism. Even if Schweitzer's thoroughgoing eschatological Jesus was not quite right, he nevertheless stated a truth about early twentieth-century theology: 'He comes to us as One unknown.'

I. HISTORY AND CHRISTIAN EXPERIENCE

The relational thesis stated that all knowledge of God is dependent upon his self-revelation which itself was imprecisely related to Jesus Christ, whose benefits were experienced by the individual believer. The figure of Christ therefore became a sort of filter through which divine revelation *occurs*. Despite its attractiveness, formidable difficulties were soon encountered by this approach. The prohibition of metaphysics, though promising many apologetic gains, effectively precluded any ontological statement about the relation between Jesus Christ and the eternal God who was affirmed to be his 'Father'. As a direct result of this lack of clarity on the one hand and the axiomatic status of Christ's benefits on the other, it is sometimes very difficult to ascertain whether the Christological statements of the modern theologians were primarily theistic or both theistic and anthropological at the same time. To put the matter as plainly as possible, was it being affirmed that the objectivity of Christological doctrines rested ultimately upon a self-authenticating experiential synthesis involving God, the individual, and a Christ image, or was it the case that these statements purport to state something about the figure to which they seem to refer? When Herrmann confessed that he found God personally present in Christ,[4] this 'thought of faith', whatever its theological deficienies, expressed something essential about his relationism.

The synthetic character of the relational stance consequently renders precarious any superficial judgement about the alleged Christo-centricism of Ritschl, Herrmann, or, for that matter, the early Barth, since the three elements of the nexus—God, the individual, and a Christ figure—were equally important. A close examination of contemporary statements about the essence of Christianity will confirm this point. The heart of Christianity was, according to Herrmann, 'the communion of the Christian with God'. With Harnack too something similar emerges. The essence of Christianity for him lay in God the Father, his heavenly kingdom, the infinite value of the human soul, and the higher righteousness of evangelical love.[5] Barth was closer to Herrmann, finding the essence of religion in the practical elevation of the soul to God.[6] In view of the fact that each element of the relational synthesis was of equal importance, it is perhaps better to affirm that these theologies were Christo-morphic in character with the symbol, image, or *Bild* of Christ receiving the status of a cipher or conceptual simulator of personal religious experience. If this is so, the Christ cipher was none the less indispensable and axiomatic, since it represented both the origin (*Ursprung*) and goal (*Zweck*) of the Christian religion. Yet even here there arose an uneasy tension between methodology and theology. The relatedness of the individual to God, which was held to be the aspiration of religion in general, need not necessarily be portrayed Christologically. Barth, for example, could state his understanding of religion quite clearly without such terms: '*In intuition [Anschauung], in beholding God's efficacy [Wirksamkeit], in faith in moral obedience, the feeling [Gefühl] which is effected by God—justification and election—becomes fact.*'[7] When the transition from a general theory of religion to a dogmatic discussion of the Christian religion occurs, the same experience, to which the words above supposedly refer, is treated Christologically. Christology enters, almost as a *deus ex machina*, through an appeal to Melanchthon: '*Ecce cognitio Christi justificatio est, cognitio autem sola fides est*. That is, the religious beholding [*Schauen*] of Christ, seeing the efficacy [*Wirksamkeit*] of God in him, *is* justification. Thus this beholding, and only this, is Christian faith.'[8] The tension between general methodology and Christian doctrine was increasingly felt by Barth, to the extent that he irrevocably disowned the approach embraced by his early theology. In the earliest writings themselves, however, he consciously aspired to resolve this tension by means of a theological definition of history.

It has already been emphasized how Christ was the symbol through which revelation *occurs* because the present tense of the verb possessed supreme importance. The relational thesis espoused by Barth maintained that divine–human togetherness was always available to individuals. It was, using his later phrase, a 'permanent possibility' always available in principle to human beings—which is not entirely surprising since experience of Christ's revelatory benefits was deemed essential to the definition of being human. Though widely accepted by many theologians, this stress upon the contemporaneity and actualism of God in revelation was directly responsible for two difficulties. In the first place, if experience of God's gracious revelation is indeed a possibility capable of being realized at any point in time, how does this understanding of divine availability relate to the epistemological–soteriological principle that linked divine revelation exclusively with Christ? When one is forbidden to speak of a pre-existent or 'metaphysical' Christ that is, there emerges the problem of reconciling the idea that relatedness to God is always available throughout history, with the view that knowledge of God is based solely upon an experience of Christ's benefits. Furthermore, if the significance of the word 'Christ' is felt to depend upon its being predicated to someone who lived long ago, namely Jesus of Nazareth, is it not implied that there was a time when Christ's benefits were not? Would not this contradict the tenets of relationism? Herrmann avoided such problems by refusing to probe what he called the 'genesis' (*Entstehung*) of faith, but the difficulties did not disappear on that account. A second set of problems arising from the transcendentalism of relationist theology concerned the recipient mode of communion with God. The question here was simply whether divine–human relatedness is solely experienced in the modalities of *Gefühl*, *Erlebnis*, *Offenbarung*, or whether history could mediate this experience. If the latter was to be affirmed, could it be done so without forfeiting the claim that standing in relation to God is an immediate actuality? Barth, like Herrmann, was unwilling to discuss the first set of problems, but most eager to deal with the second. He did so by approaching history with a theological theory of religion.

Throughout the essay on faith and history Barth meant the religious experience which *contemporary* Christians enjoy when he referred to faith. The concept of history he therefore formulated was one demanded by this *Tatsächlickeit* of Christian experience. Any problems encountered, such as relations between *religionsphilosophisch* and doctrinal approaches to history, Christology and history, or even between the 'historic' present and past history, were all addressed from the perspective of contemporary religious experience as defined by the relational thesis. In Barth's own words, his task was

to indicate the special religious and, correlatively, the unique theological method by virtue of which there exists an absolute relation to absolute history, by virtue of which faith and revelation exist; the method, that is, of the factual genesis [*Entstehung*] and preservation [*Bestand*] of Christian experience of God in history. I stress: what follows concerns the appropriate portrayal of an *actual state of affairs*, namely the relation of faith to history as present in actual Christian awareness [*im wirklichen christlichen Bewusstsein*].[9]

Just as Herrmann's theological approach to history rested upon an indissoluble correlation of faith and the historic dimension of life, Barth from the outset assumed that faith and revelation were internally related to history. The most radical and astounding formulation of this relationship between history and faith was articulated in his lecture on metaphysics: religion is the principle which generates history![10]

Since so much depended upon the Christian consciousness and its experiential contents, it is important to probe Barth's understanding of faith a little further. The following quotation offers a psychological description of the *Glaubensvorgang*—the way, that is, in which religious faith affects individual psychology. It must be stressed that this analysis is supposed to be a non-dogmatic, more phenomenological, discussion of religious faith, and it serves as a very good introduction to the theory of religion which will be unfolded in the course of this chapter:

Faith is experience of God [*Gotteserlebnis*], immediate consciousness of the presence and efficacy of the super-human, super-mundane, and, therefore, absolutely superior power for life [*Lebensmacht*]. The believer lives, experiences, senses, feels, and knows that he lives and is *being made* to live. According to the psychological manner in which faith operates therefore, passive and active characteristics of humanity coincide. It has as much to do with the elevation of the individual to the trans-individual, as with the ingression of trans-individual life into the individual. In that elevation [*Erhebung*] and in this ingression [*Einsenkung*] the believer experiences *that which relates him to reality and reality to him* [*Realitäts-beziehung*] or his eternal reception of life [*ewiges Lebendig-Werden*]. We are not concerning ourselves here with the question of whether this experience is truth or illusion: we simply state that this experience is not posited, and cannot be posited, in the psychological activities of logical thinking, ethical willing, or aesthetic feeling.[11]

At the centre of this approach to faith lies the dual experience of elevation and ingression. The former was previously encountered in the definition of the essence of religion—the practical elevation of the soul to God which is, of course, an echo of a traditionally Ritschlian theme, whereby believers ascend to the teleological kingdom of ends in order to exercise lordship over the world. The more active psychological condition is called, as in Schleiermacher's work, *schlechthinige Zielstrebigkeit* whilst, not surprisingly, the more passive disposition is absolute dependence.[12] Equal emphasis is placed upon both, so that Ritschl's teaching about the teleological kingdom, which becomes the objective and active

moment of the *Glaubensvorgang*, is artfully balanced by the more
subjective and passive moment of dependence.

Having depicted the two leading psychological characteristics of
the religious consciousness, Barth next observes how something
spectacular happens when both are present. The individual then
experiences his *ewiges Lebendig-Werden*, whereby religious energies
begin to pervade, animate, and penetrate consciousness. Precisely
because religion is a dynamic force—a *Lebensmacht*—which
convulses interior life, it diverts consciousness from immersion in
its mundane environment and from preoccupation with abstract
possibilities. Consciousness is then so overwhelmed by religious
experience that it becomes aware of a wider, richer, and more vivid
reality. The relationism espoused by Barth is therefore more of a
momentum than a merely substantial or static bond between two
relata. This dynamic thrust, towards what Barth will call a 'total
actualization' of consciousness,[13] is reflected in the other word
chosen to characterize the coincidence of the active and passive
states in religious awareness—*Realitätsbeziehung*.[14]

In view of the traumatic effect of religion upon consciousness, it
would be most interesting to discover what precisely this dynamic
force actualizes. Barth's answer is at once astounding and
revealing:

Within the entire expanse of consciousness faith is the historical element
par excellence. It is quite different from the cognitive apparatus which
assesses validity in logic, ethics, and aesthetics. For here intersect two
problems which lie on completely different levels . . . the problem of the
Ich, the individual, and individual life, and the problem of law-
structured consciousness, human culture, and reason.[15]

Barth's point is that faith humanizes and historicizes *Kulturbewusstsein*. This must not be interpreted in a Heideggerian sense
to mean that religion endows consciousness with awareness of
temporality. Rather, because history is internally related to faith's
experience of revelation, it is being affirmed that the vitalities of
revelation transform all the abstract and theoretical possibilities of
the neo-Kantian *Kulturbewusstsein* into actual, real, and concrete
experiences for the individual. The ideal epistemological functions
of consciousness thereby become actual cultural artefacts which
can be experienced as such by a living or 'actualized' subject.
Barth at this point is exploiting the neo-Kantian embarrassment

about the *Ich* or *Individuum*—the manifest antagonism between the ideal epistemological subject of philosophy and the conscious awareness of everyday life. Religion, as the historic moment *par excellence*, is therefore not the 'Moment' of Barth's dialectical writings, the 'Now' when eternity enters history and almost abolishes finite time. The historical moment of which Barth speaks here is the bestowal of a relationship with God which brings the individual to fullness of life in culture. Since this relation is a moving force or an operative momentum, it penetrates and convulses even the abstract possibilities of *Kulturbewusstsein*. It forces them, moves them, thrusts them forward into actualization, and simultaneously humanizes and vivifies them:

Through the regulative, heuristic, boundary-conceptual element of faith (which ultimately does not belong to the problem-provoking tasks of reason, but rather to the problem of individuation), the abstract possibility of *Kulturbewusstsein* is actualized and transformed into concrete reality. This means that through the momentum of faith culture consciousness becomes historic [*geschichtlich*]. Faith and the historicity of culture become synonyms.[16]

It is important to appreciate that history for the early Barth had more to do with actualization, with which it is almost equivalent, than with temporality. History is the overwhelming presence of reality in the infinite depths of personal experience:

Contrary to how it must at first appear, faith is in no way bound to the form of intuition called time [*Anschauungsform der Zeit*]. In the *Realitäts-beziehung* of experience of God there is no time. Just as the passive and active attributes of humanity meet in this experience . . . so the past (the genesis of faith's experience) and the future (its perdurance and consummation) are present each moment in this very experience of God.[17]

This collapse of temporal distinctions in faith-experience is a correlate of Barth's insistence that religion is neither experienced nor grasped cognitively through philosophical categories like Kant's *Anschauungsformen*, which are merely formal, abstract, epistemological concepts. It is also a direct consequence arising from the transcendentalism which his relational approach to religion required. From the perspective of the relational consciousness there never is a time when the individual is not 'always already with God'.[18] Divine–human relatedness is therefore a reality available to humankind at any time, though not in finite time. In the trans-historical event of revelation such relatedness is awakened and actualized in the individual:

The characteristic relationship to history in Christian experience of God is essentially not a relation to something past and gone, but rather it possesses ... the distinctive marks of contemporaneity. 'Jesus Christ, yesterday, today, and the same for ever'. This passage from Hebrews is the correct articulation of the *religionspsychologisch* state of affairs.[19]

The psychological analysis of religious consciousness thus discovers two dynamic processes: elevation and ingression. Consciousness, when affected by religious forces, is thrust forward to actualization. On the one hand the abstract cognitive mechanisms of the neo-Kantian consciousness are now stimulated to produce the tangible goods of culture. On the other, the formal epistemological subject becomes transfigured into a 'fully alive' individual who is capable of experiencing God, the world of culture, and other individuals in vivid immediacy. Though it is the individual consciousness that undergoes these various transformations, it is not left isolated and alone, for it experiences the totally new 'trans-individual' social world of culture, religion, and history.[20]

Following his psychological investigation of faith and history, Barth proceeds to analyse the same topic from a 'historical–critical' perspective and offers a résumé of the meaning of faith from New Testament times to its degeneration in Protestant orthodoxy. The whole discussion is introduced by the question, 'Where do we authentically and authoritatively find that intuition [*Anschauung*] which establishes faith?'[21] Barth most fully approves of the answer allegedly given by Paul:

Did Paul ever know Christ 'according to the flesh?' In any case, he declares 'not to know him thus now' (2 Cor. 5: 16), rather *being in Christ, that* is new creation (2 Cor. 5: 11). This life in Christ, the power of God, or the gospel he preaches, is for Paul no complex of tradition, it is his gospel which was 'taught and received from no man, but through a revelation of Jesus' (Gal. 1: 12). Admittedly this revelation, either completely or in part, had been handed on to him through the medium of oral or written tradition; however what he received and what he passes on, is nevertheless *his* gospel and not Peter's gospel. For 'the Lord is the *Spirit*' (2 Cor. 3: 17) and 'whoever is joined to the Lord, the same is one Spirit with Him' (1 Cor. 6: 17). 'I live no longer as myself; it is Christ that liveth in me' (Gal. 2: 20).[22]

Barth's comments on this catena of Pauline quotations reveal what he takes to be Paul's answer to his question:

Paul carries the foundation and authority of his faith in himself. 'In the heart' God lets 'dawn the radiant ascent to the knowledge and glory of God in the face of Christ' (2 Cor. 4: 6). 'Into the heart' has come the Spirit who makes intercession for us and who searches out all things (Rom. 8: 26–7; 1 Cor. 2: 9f.). Hence it is no rhetorical flourish but the expression of an immediate inner state of affairs when Paul comes forward as 'an ambassador in Christ's stead' (1 Cor. 5: 20).[23]

This preponderance of Pauline texts mentioning spirit and heart is taken to imply that Paul was a supporter of Barth's relationalism: the *Anschauung* which grounds faith is present in the experience of the believer, that is, in the Christian consciousness. It is further claimed that Reformation teaching about the *Testimonium Spiritus Sancti internum* has a similar meaning.

Sharply opposed to this understanding of faith is Protestant orthodoxy, *Biblizismus*, and Roman Catholicism. These have one obnoxious thing in common, namely a synergism which all too easily obscures the divine, miraculous, and gracious action of God in bestowing faith by supposing that human beings take an active part in their conversion. Originally, of course, the synergistic controversy was a conflict about the human will—its state after the Fall and its possible role in conversion. Barth was not at all interested in this aspect of synergism; instead he eagerly sought to refute the view that intellectual assent is a decisive moment in the genesis of faith. It is synergism of reason, rather than will, that claimed his attention. In Protestant orthodoxy, as well as in Thomism, therefore:

the appropriation of salvation . . . becomes a co-operation, a *synergein* of God and man; God brings grace, man brings faith. One hand clasps the other . . . Here historical salvation stands objective *vis-à-vis* man. Man now stretches forth his hand, now he appropriates and possesses something he did not have before. Moreover because salvation stands confronting him in the form of a rational 'Word of God', the most essential psychological factor in the process of conversion is rational assent.[24]

This polemic is calculated to stress, first, that faith is neither propositional assent to revealed truths nor a feat demanding cognitive labour, but rather an experiential happening. Barth, secondly, is at pains to emphasize that his form of relationism should not be construed as a 'co-operation' between human faith and divine revelation. The two are indeed present as a nexus in the actual state of divine–human relatedness, but the Christian consciousness would seem to require divine initiative in establishing this factual state of affairs. In faith, consequently, there is a real divine 'ingression' and a miraculous 'elevation' of the individual. All this is clinched by a 'philosophical' argument which contends that faith cannot withstand the onslaughts of modern autonomy when viewed as intellectual assent coerced by biblical or magisterial authority. Even were such a questionable approach to faith possible in the early twentieth century, it would lead to intellectual dishonesty and a regressive retreat from the liberal values of enlightenment.[25]

Several interesting points are then discussed in a *religions-philosophisch* investigation of faith and history, but as a prelude it is important to begin by clarifying what *Religionsphilosophie* meant for Barth. It is a topic of some importance which will have to be addressed again in more detail. For the moment, however, it must be stated that 'philosophy of religion' is often a misleading translation of this word. Although some contemporary English-speaking philosophers have approached the objectives of philosophy of religion more constructively than was previously the case to supply, for example, a reasoned justification of religious belief or a religious *Weltanschauung* for modern man, by and large the emphasis in Anglo-American philosophy of religion has fallen upon analysing epistemological and metaphysical problems presented by any religious system of belief. Barth in his Genevan days would certainly not have recognized this to be *Religionsphilosophie*. Being intimately related to systematic theology, this discipline for Barth was constructive and synthetic. It resembled what David Tracy has called 'fundamental theology', though perhaps 'foundational theology' better conveys Barth's intentions.[26]

At the heart of Barth's *religionsphilosophisch* investigations there lies a sympathetic interpretation of Schleiermacher's words, 'Piety . . . considered purely in itself is neither a knowing nor a doing, but a determination of feeling or of immediate self-consciousness':[27]

Thereby the peculiar character [*Eigenart*] of religion is perceived with a clarity which was never achieved in classical poetry and which was obscured in the writings of other Romantics. Knowing and doing here, feeling, life, and experience there. Culture-consciousness here, self-consciousness there. I repeat and emphasize that religion does not deal simply with another problem, but with a problem of a totally different order. There the discussion is about the objective and abstract possibility of consciousness, the a priori *Gesetzlichkeit* of knowing and doing, here with religion the discussion centres on the knowing and doing *subject*, the thinking and willing *individual*—in short, on the actuality of *man*.[28]

The word *Eigenart*, a term used by Cohen to designate the special characteristics of religion distinguishing it from logic, ethics, or aesthetics, immediately betrays Barth's intention. He is anxious not only to defend the irreducibility and cognitive integrity of religion, but also to specify how it operates in the individual by contrasting it with the abstract transcendental mechanisms of the neo-Kantian *Kulturbewusstsein*. Dynamic religious energies therefore operate at a totally different level from the more scientific functions of consciusness—hence the series of contrasts between the *Gesetzlichkeit* of cognition and the awareness enjoyed by a personal centre of consciousness. Barth, however, praises Schleiermacher's characterization of religion precisely because it did not rest content with an absolute dualism between 'science and experience' of the sort he encountered in Ritschl, as well as in Herrmann's 'dualism of faith'. But how, exactly, is such dualism overcome if religion and the cognitive functions of consciousness operate at completely different levels? Persevering with his contrasts, an answer begins to emerge:

There knowledge of a thing-in-itself is excluded and any heteronomy in the concept of obligation prohibited: true knowledge is knowledge of appearances alone, and good will is simply one's own will. Here is the knowing and willing man who, *in that* he knows, stands in the midst of the thing-in-itself, and who, *in that* he wills, stands under absolute heteronomy. In this immediate operation of *actual reality* on consciousness [*Bewusstseinswirklichkeit*] ... we have before us the phenomenon which was characterized as *Realitätsbeziehung* in our pyschological investigation.[29]

Leaving aside the amazing words about standing in the midst of *Dinge-an-sich*, Barth contends that experience of supernatural energy transfigures ideal and abstract operations of conscious-ness into real experiences. Just as it was previously affirmed that religious energies historicize or actualize *Kulturbewusstsein*, the same is now said in the language of realism. The transformation of the ideal and abstract into the actual and immediate thus occurs on three fronts. In the first place, the formal epistemo-logical subject is thrust into authentic personal existence. Secondly, the previously abstract possibilities of culture-consciousness become actual, and, thirdly, are experienced by the individual as possessing an overwhelming degree of reality. When Barth suggested that religion was a *Lebensmacht*, the word 'power' should therefore be interpreted to mean operative momentum.

The central effect of religion is continually affirmed to be *Realitätsbeziehung*, and since this term occupies pride of place in Barth's theory of religion it is important to attend to what is said about it. The following passage mentions two attributes of the *Realitätsbeziehung* which arises from the presence of revelation and faith in the individual:

> It is both individual and trans-individual, self-certainty and certitude of God in one. Its relationship to consciousness is that of a principle of actualization, because it is the regulative principle. It enables the law-ordered and a priori possibilities of thinking and willing to become actual thoughts and decisions. It is like the Platonic *Idea*: we are in the cave with our backs to the fire, but in its light we see the light.[30]

The psychological operations which were previously character-ized as 'ingression' and 'elevation' are here given a more precise content. Theologically they refer to the ingression of divine revelation—interpreted primarily as an operative power that gives awareness and vitality to consciousness—and to faith, an individual's existential relationship with God through all that is real, true, beautiful, and good in culture. This experience of reality is therefore the light and life which revelation brings to the world. Without it there are only shadows—as formal and as abstract as Cohen's logical conceptuality. When an individual 'undergoes' revelatory experience, it is not so much a divine being that is encountered, but a vital resource which actualizes authentic selfhood in and through a culture claimed by God.[31]

Barth, continuing to extol the religious *Realitätsbeziehung*, compares it once more with Schleiermacher's famous definition of piety:

And indeed this *Realitätsbeziehung* 'considered purely in itself' is 'neither a knowing nor a doing', neither a thought nor a decision, but immediate, unanalysable, irrational, personal and individual vitality [*Lebendigkeit*]. The peace of God is higher than all reason. From this perspective it is possible to offer a religious–philosophical justification of what was simply presupposed . . . namely, the absolute difference in kind between immediate awareness and reflection about it, between faith and thoughts of faith.[32]

Religious revelation, the encounter of consciousness with God, is irrational in the sense that it is neither called into being nor generated by cognitive, volitional, or aesthetic labours and cannot, moreover, be justified by them. It is a totally supernatural act because it originates in God and occurs at a 'different level'; the historic level of actualization, realization, and individuation. Even more forcefully it is stressed that the experience in question so transcends the normal functions of the neo-Kantian consciousness, that it cannot be conceptualized by them. Any theoretical attempt to grasp the reality of faith and revelation causes the actuality of the experience to disappear so that one is left with mere thoughts, dim echoes, or shadows of reality. This, in short, is nothing less than a return to Plato's cave after intellectual and spiritual illumination by the light.

The belief that reflection somehow shatters and disintegrates an original perception—a belief which unites Herrmann, Natorp, and the young Barth—was something they learned from Schleiermacher. One of the most important passages testifying to this belief about reflection occurs in the first edition of Schleiermacher's *Reden*. Since Oman's English translation of Schleiermacher's *Speeches* was based on a later edition, there follows a translation of the decisive passage:

Intuition [*Anschauung*] without feeling [*Gefühl*] is nothing and can possess neither legitimate foundation [*Ursprung*] nor authentic efficacy [*Kraft*]. Feeling without intuition is also nothing: both are only something if and because they are originally [*ursprünglich*] one and undivided. This first mysterious moment . . . but that I could and dare express it or at least give some intimation of it without profanation! It is as fleeting and as transparent as the first mist which the dew breathes upon flowers awoken by the dawn, shy and tender as a maiden's kiss, holy and fruitful as a bridal embrace. It is not merely like, it is itself all of these. ... I lie on the breast of an infinite world. In this moment [*Augenblick*] I am its soul, for I feel all its powers and endless life as my own. In this moment it is my body, for I pervade its sinews and limbs as my own and its innermost stirrings are moved by my spirit and whim as though they were my own! The slightest shock, and the holy embrace dissolves; then intuition stands before me as a fractured form. ... This moment, when intuition and feeling are united, is the highest bloom of religion. If I could create it in you, I should be a god—but may holy fate pardon me, for I have had to disclose more than Eleusinian mysteries. It is the moment of birth for everything living in religion.[33]

In a less romantic vein, but with equal passion, Barth claims Schleiermacher's account of religion as his own, by explaining how two factors are involved in *individuelles Lebendigwerden*. Though these may be distinguished conceptually, like Schleiermacher's moment they are united and undivided in actual experience. When an individual awakens to life there is 'the taking up into consciousness of an efficacy [*Wirksamkeit*] and the effects wrought within consciousness by this efficacy'.[34] Here once more we meet the ingression of revelatory powers and the spontaneous arousal of existential life (that is, faith). The first is said to correspond to Schleiermacher's *Anschauung*—the intuitive or contemplative stance in which one is 'passive'—and the second to his *Gefühl*, a state in which consciousness is aroused, active, and actualized. Such an account of the effects of religion is eminently compatible with the language of affection to which Barth appealed in his reply to critics.[35] Unfortunately, however, it will have been noticed that the relationship between objective ingression and subjective elevation is perilously close to cause and effect. This was something which bothered Barth greatly during and after his break with modern theology. Throughout his later career he insisted that Schleiermacher—and by implication his own early theology—construed the relation between revelation and faith as cause and effect on the one hand, and as reciprocal on the other.[36]

Returning to the Genevan Barth and his Schleiermacher, what he later called the *Indifferenzpunkt* of Schleiermacher's theology (that is, the coincidence of intuition and feeling) was then regarded as the presence of the Infinite in and to the finite. Barth once more explains himself in language savoured by the *Reden* as well as by the technical language of Marburg philosophy:

To our reason, to our objective consciousness that is, what is finite in nature and history is a problem-provoking task [*ist aufgegeben*] because only that which is finite can be pursued intellectually; yet *in* the finite there is a Whole, an Eternal, an Absolute. This Infinite in the finite occurs as an unfragmented activity and reveals itself each moment to our immediate self-consciousness.[37]

Barth later recalled how his earliest objective in theology was to combine the best of German Romanticism with the theology of the Reformation. Here, plainly, is the Romantic side. How, one wonders, could this be united with the Reformation cry 'by faith alone'?

An ingenious, yet almost perverse attempt is made to interpret all this talk about the Infinite in the finite, the historicization of *Kulturbewusstsein*, and the actualization of culture, in terms of the more traditional language about justification by faith. According to Barth's Luther, faith was not a means of procuring justification because the latter was not an object to be reached for and taken. Rather, 'as you believe, so you have' or, according to Barth's own formulation, 'in the act of faith *is* the object of faith—it is not first to be brought into existence *per fidem*'.[38] In order to protect his own form of relationism from being interpreted synergistically on the one hand, or from being incorporated into the immanent functions of *Kulturbewusstsein* on the other, it is strenuously affirmed that this 'factual state of affairs' originates in divine grace:

The sinner *is now* justified, for through the justifying judgement God has established a personal relation [*persönliche Beziehung*] and communion between himself and the sinner. The foundation of this personal relation with God, however, does not first need to become effective through the faith of man: the efficacy [*Wirksamkeit*] lies with God and not with man, but *because and in that this efficacy is effective, man believes*. . . . The relationship between subject and object in the *Realitätsbeziehung* of an individual's coming to life may be described from the perspective of Schleiermacherian religious philosophy, together with the Reformation approach, as follows: *in intuition, in beholding God's efficacy, in faith, in moral obedience, the feeling which is effected by God—justification and election—becomes fact*.[39]

Before continuing with the Reformation side of Barth's theology there is one point which needs addressing. If it is true that some divine power actualizes the potentialities of consciousness and individuates a person, how are these boons to be related to the traditional benefits of Christ, from which alone awareness of divine–human intimacy arises? The transition from a theory of religion based upon cultural, anthropological, and psychological considerations, to a specifically doctrinal account of soteriology and Christology is aided by a question: 'How do faith and intuition, in which the *Realitätsbeziehung* of religious life is actual, come into existence? For it is something which must *come into existence*, it may *not* be *presupposed* as given along with the general concept of man.'[40] What is now being asked is whether the efficacy of God can be mediated through history. The answer is that of course it can; because all that has been affirmed about religion and its vitalities used the vocabulary of act, realization, and actualization. The point is simply that whenever the individual encounters the activity of God, the 'totally different plane' of history has been encountered—different, that is, from the cognitive apparatus attributed to consciousness by the neo-Kantian thinkers of Marburg:

We are not concerned with reason, but with the individual. Unlike the former we have to do not with the transcendental, general, and law-structured possibility of ideal occurrences, but with concrete, unique, actual occurrences, in short, with *history* . . . the individual finds the revelation, which he perceives and appropriates through religion, in humanity, that is, in history. The creative principle, however, through which the intuition arises, is love—the personal and inner experience of pure surrender and pure empathy with others.[41]

It is interesting to note how Barth's relationism becomes more complex at this juncture. Not only is there a nexus or experiential synthesis between the single one and his God; now divine–human relatedness involves three participants: God, the individual, and other individuals. These others, to whom one is also related through the efficacy of divine grace, are encountered in history, that is, in the immediacy of experience. Since all three elements converge when historic immediacy dawns, it seemed inappropriate to enquire which element of the Christian consciousness enjoyed precedence. In the actualized or, as a later generation would say, 'existential' moment of faith, all three are simultaneously present. This experiential convergence is what Barth meant by *Geschichte*. Then, as in Schleiermacher's second speech, the Infinite is experienced and perceived in the finite and it is this ecstatic moment of inwardness, when an infinite world or *Universum* is vividly real, that constitutes history. In this transcendent dimension of depth there is a threefold relation involving divine revelation, individual faith, and communion with other actualized beings.

Having thus introduced history, it is not too difficult to find an entrance for Christology. In Christian experience 'Christ is the efficacy of God upon us and, for that reason, the source and material of our religious intuition'.[42] Barth's dogmatic discussion about faith and history astonishingly turns out to be nothing more than an analysis of the relation between faith and Christ that exists in the 'Christian consciousness'. It is from this perspective that Barth introduces his Christology and does so dialectically: '*The methodology of the Christian faith recognizes only a Christ outside ourselves. It knows no Christ in himself. It knows only a Christ within us.*'[43] A Christ *an sich* is a purely 'object-Christ', examples of this being the metaphysical Christ of ecclesiastical doctrine or the Jesus who is made into a religious founder and great prophet by the naturalized consciousness of historicism. The relational consciousness of Christians, by contrast, recognizes only a Christ who is 'outside ourselves', the Christ, that is, of *Anschauung*. This Christ, the Christ in whom divine power is active, represents an efficacy which is to be taken into consciousness, yet inasmuch as this efficacy is really active, Christ in us becomes our *justification* and *Leben*. His benefits, in short, are felt and spontaneously give birth to the feeling of faith. The two are, of course, one operative process, though Barth is very careful to ensure that the *Christus in uns* does not become simply an anthropological datum or an immanent *Erzeugung* of the cognitive consciousness:

This effective Christ in us is 'objective'. The circle is thereby closed which we began with the statement that faith knows only a Christ external to us. The truth of feeling, *justificatio*, or life, depends upon his being external to ourselves and the truth of intuition, *fides*, or experience, depends upon his being within us. *The Christ external to us is the Christ within us. Effective history is effected faith.*[44]

The emphasized sentences are crucial to the whole argument. The relation between faith and history—or what is much the same thing, the relation between faith and Christ—is precisely the same relation that exists between that which effects (the intuited efficacy of God in Christ) and that which is thereby effected (the felt benefits of Christ). As far as the actualized Christian consciousness is concerned, the two are inseparable. The objective and the subjective, or the historical and the psychological moments of faith, are one and undivided; wherever one is present, so is the other. As long as both elements are taken as given, as being posited along with the existence of a Christian consciousness, it would be no hard task to suggest that one requires the other.

The tandem relationship between history and faith is put forward with the utmost seriousness and Barth offers several intriguing statements about it. He says, for example, that 'efficacy presupposes a qualitative homogeneity of that which effects and that which is to be effected',[45] suggesting thereby that the whole momentum of religion depends upon a qualitative homogeneity of intuition and feeling; faith and justification; Christ without and within; the objective and subjective; and, finally, the historical and the psychological. When all coalesce in one operative momentum a *Universum* is then experienced: the Infinite in the finite, something trans-individual and something individual. It is in this dimension of effective history that the life of Jesus is intuitively understood and experienced. His 'inner life', being a unique datum of the Christian consciousness, could in no way be grasped by an abstract scientific consciousness that selects or orders merely dead historical facts. Through the operation of divine grace the efficacy of this life enters and convulses consciousness into total realization. Methodologically speaking, therefore, the effective Christ of history, the Christ upon whom justification depends, is simply posited along with intuition or faith: 'Faith does not stand over against history, on the contrary, it is simply the extension or apprehension of history in the life of the individual ... We have presupposed faith as simply a given fact and, from that perspective, found history posited along with faith.'[46]

Barth, it is to be noted, does not shy away from the more radical consequences which might arise from the synthetic relatedness between the effective historical Christ and the community whose life *is* the inner life of Christ:

> Christ's righteousness becomes my righteousness. Christ's religion becomes my religion. He becomes me . . . Faith shows its historicity by exhibiting itself as a developmental process in the life of the individual . . . effective history is effected faith. The Living Man is mediated to humanity through men who are becoming alive. The concept of history, intuitively perceived in faith, consequently expands. What we previously understood as an apparently isolated fact at the turn of the aeons, becomes a fact that is effective throughout the centuries. *The Jesus of history becomes the resurrected and living Christ in the community of Christ*.[47]

Such Christ-monism is accepted most heartily by Barth and one is at a loss to find parallels to this soteriological style which could well be termed rampant Arianism. Perhaps its closest counterpart is the soteriology of the more extreme Pietists, whose writings the early Barth was so fond of quoting. What he later said of Schleiermacher, therefore, is no less applicable to his earliest Christology: 'When Schleiermacher speaks of Christ and Christians and their mutual relationship, what he primarily has in mind is neither one nor the other, but one single concept embracing both, namely the 'composite life' of humanity, the history of human nature.'[48]

The article concludes with the interesting observation that other ways (that is, that of Troeltsch) of relating faith to history were not acceptable because they wrongly assumed the relation to involve *Gegenüberstellung*, mutual opposition. The methodological principle he supports, by contrast, is one that construes this relationship as being that of *Ineinanderstellung*, mutual coinherence—with the important proviso that this relation exists in the Christian consciousness and nowhere else. The *innere Methodik* he recommends is one deemed to be demanded by the allegedly 'factual state of affairs' encountered in the Christian consciousness.

Barth, having adhered to the principle of radical *autopistia* throughout his essay, never once stepped outside the inner 'factual state' of the Christian consciousness. Questions relating to the genesis of faith, to its actual appearance in chronological history (and not, that is, in 'effective history'), were methodologically superfluous and manifest *non sequiturs*:

We for our part do not consider giving any further attention to the question of the genesis of the factual state of affairs which comes into existence with faith. Not, that is, because faith itself is the genesis, the genesis of the reality of life, actualization of the a priori functions given in the possibilities of consciousness, but rather because the question about the genesis of the genesis of faith would be as meaningful as the question about the truth of logical truth.[49]

A number of characteristics clearly emerge as one encounters Barth's theory of religion. Religion was seen to be a force that actualizes the human potential. The great advantage this approach possessed for Barth was that it overcame the dualism between faith and knowledge that marked the Ritschlian inheritance. Though Ritschlian thinkers indeed claimed that their theologies offered an interpretation of the world as a 'rounded whole', Barth at an early stage perceived the weaknesses of such theories. The sacrifice demanded by their religious interpretation of reality was, as Barth indicated in his essay, founded upon a dualism of idealism and realism. On the one hand there was science, nature, law, and the cognitive subject; religion, history, freedom, and experience on the other.

The uneasy tension between idealism and realism was an issue of which Barth became acutely aware; indeed it was intensified by his own theoretical approach to religion precisely because it embraced the idealist account of cognition offered by Marburg philosophy. The conceptual problem facing Barth was how to make the transition from the ideal epistemological subject of neo-Kantian philosophy to the experiencing centre of consciousness, which Westerners are apt to call the 'I'. It was religion, said Barth, which performed this office. Revelation, being attributed with such an overwhelming degree of reality and actuality—ultimately becoming the most real thing anyone is likely to encounter—individuated the formerly abstract subject of idealism into an autonomous living centre of experience. This had the effect of creating a *Universum* of experience by realizing abstract potentials. No longer isolated and imprisoned in abstractions, but living in a historic world, a world in which all the possibilities of consciousness have been actualized and claimed for God, an entire new totality is revealed to the believer. The individual now communes with God and others through whatever is good, true, and beautiful in culture. Religion truly bestows *die Realitätsbeziehung* to the individual and his world. The conflict between idealism and realism was thus focused upon consciousness, the abstract and formal network of cognitive functions portrayed by the philosophies of Cohen and Natorp on the one hand, and the actualized consciousness enjoyed by recipients of revelatory experience on the other. Had the vocabulary of existentialism been available to Barth, no doubt he would have used it.

In retrospect the very promising move from metaphysics to a theory of religion as a preamble for theology was robbed of its impact because it was conceived so very narrowly by Barth. He relied too heavily upon the conceptuality of Schleiermacher and defined religion exclusively in terms of Christian religion—and Protestant religion at that. That other religions and different Christian traditions might lend greater precision to a theory of religion, was a thought Barth never entertained. Instead he stuck to his relationally construed 'Christian consciousness' and never for one moment left it. The weaknesses are particularly evident in his *religionspsychologisch* discussion of faith and history. Given the contemporary situation, in which nobody was entirely sure as to what psychology was or by what methods it ought to proceed, perhaps Barth could be forgiven. His very generalized psychological investigations, however, centred on an hypostatized entity called the Christian consciousness, the two leading processes of which turn out to be psychological counterparts of justification and faith! All this testifies to a certain methodological blindness. The Christian consciousness, established by revelation and faith, the content of which was a lively 'real' relationship between the individual, God, others who commune with him through Christ, and the truly positive values of culture, was assumed to be a datum: a fixed synthesis or factual state of affairs, which had to be accepted as given and completely beyond all question. Establishing or justifying the truth of this synthesis would be as fruitless and as futile as enquiring into the truth of logical truth. The discipline called religious philosophy at Barth's hands became simply a matter of analysing the Christian consciousness into its component elements, showing their interrelatedness, and then demonstrating their interdependence. All this was anchored in the contention that revelatory experience of God, which established the Christian consciousness, was self-authenticating. Realism has here lapsed into vulgar realism, though to give Barth his due he openly admitted that religious actualization was indeed irrational and unanalysable.

The approach to religion adopted in Barth's article, though aspiring to claim all that was noble in culture for Christ, led to tensions between theology, methodology, and actual cultural analysis. The account of how Christ's benefits actualized the possibilities of consciousness was as unconvincing as it was unlikely. That justification by faith was somehow responsible not only for music, poetry, and art, but also for the advances in natural science, the growth of Western humanism, liberalism, and autonomy as well, might just receive some confirmation from cultural anthropology, yet even so the relational synthesis could not guarantee that Protestant religion would retain its formative role in Western culture. Neither did it justify optimism about the continued evolution of Christian civilization. Barth's theory of religion, therefore, though laudable in intent, was exceedingly anachronistic. The real *Universum* it aspired to portray was more at home in a privileged suburban canton of Switzerland, than in an increasingly secularized and industrialized Germany. Christ, it must be added, was certainly not identified with culture *überhaupt*, but he was identified with the internalized culture that possessed reality for the Christian consciousness. Whether God might be efficacious in culture *ausserhalb* this entity or even judge of both, the young Barth did not deem worthy of consideration. A more thorough and less confused analysis of this topic was to have been undertaken in his book on *Religionsphilosophie*.

The writings of Barth so far considered were at their weakest when they discussed history. All the criticisms arising from Herrmann's notion of the historic are valid here, so it would be tedious to repeat them. However, it is important to note how the binding of relationism with the *Ineinanderstellung* of faith and history was already becoming difficult to affirm for a number of reasons. There was in the first place a fateful ambiguity about the relation between *Geschichte* and time. Barth's history remained on a 'completely different' plane from the time and finitude it transcended. His history was a transcendental 'permanent possibility' on the one hand, but experienced contemporaneously by the individual on the other. This affirmation was already losing plausibility through exegesis. Barth had ample opportunity of reading and hearing Johannes Weiss who, since at least 1892, had argued that the Kingdom of God proclaimed by Jesus was not a contemporaneous, individual, religious experience, but one objective Messianic Kingdom—something like a treasure which comes from heaven.[50] In the theology of history set forth by *Christian Faith and History*, the Kingdom of Heaven gives way to the vivid *Universum* of experienced reality, whilst the power of the Kingdom becomes a dynamic principle of actualization which incessantly and eternally stimulates the nascent possibilities of culture. One fails to grasp precisely what this had to do with the teachings and life of Jesus as depicted in the less homiletical and more critical writings of Schweitzer and Weiss. Barth never liked Schweitzer, and whatever uncomfortable questions he or Weiss asked could safely be ignored. The history which interested Barth was the 'effective history' attributed to the life of contemporary Christian consciousness and which supposedly characterized the trans-temporal 'inner life' of Jesus in precisely the same way. Between the two there subsisted an eternal qualitative homogeneity. Time was swallowed up in 'history', eschatology in religious experience.

Barth's approach to history, secondly, was exceedingly deficient in cultural analysis. Though a few scholars such as Herrmann and Harnack saw everything in modern culture arising from and remaining dependent upon the Reformation, others, like Troeltsch, were convinced that Englightenment criticism, industrialization, and the concentration of the working population in towns, were more radical breaks with the past and more decisive for modernity than the events of the Reformation. Even in academic circles, furthermore, Christianity was losing any self-evident character it may have possessed, with interest increasingly being focused more upon religion in general than upon traditional Christian doctrines. When the fifth World Congress for Free Christianity and Religious Progress took place at Berlin in 1910, leading speakers offered papers on the psychology, sociology, philosophy, and phenomenology of religion. Barth wrote as if none of this was happening, yet the 'Christian consciousness' and the axiomatic methodology corresponding to it seemed to the prevailing academic temper less absolute, more enigmatic, problematical, and but one interesting religious phenomenon amongst many others.

Finally, the way Barth established the absoluteness and eternity of Christian history depended ultimately upon an appeal to a factual state of affairs, namely to that very abstract entity called the 'Christian consciousness' and its dogmatic contents. In opposition to Herrmann's monotonous insistence upon the historical 'fact' of Christ—and the same would equally apply to his pupil's historic *innere Tatsächlichkeit*—Troeltsch, with some justification, contended that this 'fact', like all other historical facts, 'given first only in the form of reports, can only be established by historical research. Faith can interpret facts; it cannot establish facts.'[51] This elegantly encapsulates the issue, for both Herrmann and Barth did confess that faith created facts and also produced history. Troeltsch, being firmly opposed to this *autopistia* conception of history, denied one could gain immediate and privileged access to the personality or inner life of Jesus in a manner which totally avoided the mediations of history and society. The additional apologetical conviction of Herrmann and Barth, which effectively maintained that this inner life of Jesus was incapable of being questioned, let alone substantiated, by historical research, appeared to Troeltsch as special pleading on the grounds of miracle; a strategy that seemed no great improvement upon eighteenth-century apologetic.

In view of these points it is no surprise that Troeltsch replied with these words after receiving a copy of *Christian Faith and History* from its author:

Dear Reverend Sir, Many thanks for kindly sending me a copy of your article on faith and history which, nevertheless, was primarily directed against me. In the years of my youth I, too, deemed such a position possible, but now it strikes me as untenable and as being at best effective for Orthodoxy alone. I also understand the feeling of superiority with which a standpoint like this despises such tentative probings as my own, but I am quite happy to bear it. Yours faithfully, E. Troeltsch.[52]

II. *RELIGIONSPHILOSOPHIE*: REVELATION AND CULTURE

So far Barth's views on a number of interrelated issues have been presented. It is now time to draw these threads together, as Barth did himself, with a systematic account of *Religionsphilosophie*. As a prelude, however, it is necessary to anticipate one possible objection to this procedure. The thoughts of the young Barth were gleaned from a wide variety of occasional writings, articles, and lectures, but the book of *Religionsphilosophie*, in which he planned to offer a theory of religion to serve as a theoretical foundation for systematic theology, was never published. Since all that remains of this project is fragmentary writing containing chapter outlines, notes, and footnotes, it may well be objected that it is perverse to attempt a systematic presentation of Barth's 'modern theology' when the author himself did not complete the task.

At the risk of overstating a reply, it must be affirmed that at least six recurring themes in these early works justify attributing a synoptic view on religion and theology to their author. They are distinguished, first, by a consistently executed approach to methodology and epistemology. Throughout these writings the thesis about faith and revelation to which Frei gave the fortunate term relationism is encountered. This appears in the methodology of appealing to the Christian consciousness and its relational contents as the primary datum for both religion and theology. It was deemed a factual state of affairs, which a theologian had to accept as a given datum and which must not be transcended through empirical, scientific, or speculative endeavours to probe the *Entstehung* of its *Tatsächlichkeit*. Regarding epistemological questions, the integrity of the Christian consciousness was made to depend upon an appeal to immediate religious experience, which itself was accounted a self-authenticating actuality bestowed upon humankind by God's revelation through the beneficial work of Christ. Barth furthermore stressed that sound methodology and reliable epistemology were not simply aids to the academic predicament of theology; but that they also possessed crucial practical importance for evangelizing contemporary society.

The writings also give evidence of a consistent polemical

objective. Under this heading belongs Barth's robust and sometimes ill-judged argumentation directed against everything
Troeltsch stood for, as well as his relentless passion to exorcize
metaphysics from theology in order to stress the personal,
immediate, and religious character of faith-knowledge. The
polemic against anything that reeked of a real or imagined
religious a priori, that threatened to naturalize religion by
incorporating it into the intricate network of cognitive possibilities
immanent in the neo-Kantian consciousness, belongs to this
category. Thirdly, moreover, a coherent theory of religious
language and, along with that, a precise understanding of the role
of conceptualization in theology distinguishes Barth's earliest
writings. This refers, of course, to the disjunction between faith
and thoughts of faith which Barth inherited from Herrmann.
Reason or conceptualization (*Denken*) was thought to be legitimate and even essential to religion, provided it faithfully mirrored
the inner experience of faith and revelation. Such thought,
however, forfeits all legitimacy when it severs itself from religious
actualities such as life and experience. This happens, for example,
when Christological doctrines become frozen by propositional
orthodoxy, when faith is considered a matter of rational assent,
and when authentically religious thought is perverted by speculative development in the interests of some metaphysical system. In
such cases a massive category error occurs and religious thought is
abused in the service of alleged scientific purposes or other more
illicit ends.

The conceptual homogeneity of Barth's early writings provides
incontrovertible evidence of unity in content and expression.
There is clear dependence upon the philosophical and theological
terminology of Schleiermacher, Herrmann, and, to some extent,
Ritschl. Though key concepts such as *Geschichte*, *Leben*, *Erleben*,
Offenbarung, and *die Religion* might be encountered in the writings
of any contemporary theologian, when their meaning is ascertained from specific contexts it is obvious that Barth's usage was
similar to that of his teacher. Herrmann's theology, moreover,
owed much to the *Reden* of Schleiermacher, and Barth also used
the language of feeling, intuition, affection, and dependence.
Alongside this romantic and vitalist vocabulary there are also
traditional doctrinal affirmations drawn from the Protestant
Reformers. Particularly prominent is the appeal to the soterio-

logical and Christological principle of Melanchthon, which Barth used for precisely the same apologetical purposes as Ritschl and Herrmann. A further source of conceptual homogeneity is due to Barth's explicit use of philosophical terminology drawn from German Idealism in general and from the Marburg School in particular. The latter provided him with a philosophical vocabulary and, imporantly, with an appreciation of the nature, goals, and methods of human knowledge. If the foregoing pages have shown anything, they certainly testify to the complex interplay and mutual criticism of theology and philosophy at Marburg. Barth was at home with this philosophy; though admittedly neither he nor Herrmann gave unqualified assent to it, especially when Cohen and Natorp trespassed upon religion and espoused a seemingly anti-realist and reductive *Religionsphilosophie*. The cogency of this particular philosophy was nevertheless affirmed, especially its epistemological tenets, which were accepted as a universally valid account of cognition in every dimension of knowledge, apart, that is, from historic, religious, and personal knowledge of reality. Despite Marquardt's comments concerning the nature of Barth's earliest theology, it must be mentioned at this point that there appears hardly any evidence of socialist ideas and vocabulary. As far as these writings are concerned, Barth exhibits little interest in either Marx, Lenin, or even Hegel. Though he believed religion to be important for social culture, his concern was with how religion makes culture 'come alive' when individuals encounter divine revelation. That reality and culture might need to be changed, and changed, perhaps, through revolutionary struggle, is a thought that never seems to have crossed Barth's mind. His discussion of social ethics is weak. When generalizations are advanced on such topics, he either offers truncated remnants of Cohen's neo-Kantian socialism or, more often, focuses upon the 'pure *Gemeinschaft*' of religious experience, to which revelatory power elevates the individual. Regrettably Barth's earliest *Ethik* is no great improvement on Herrmann's. His interest in ethics was primarily theoretical and apologetic, being concerned to demonstrate how its postulates require a religious definition of the individual. As with Herrmann the result is a *Gesinnungsethik*, bothered more about personal moral sentiment than concrete consequences of maxims and actions. On the basis of available evidence, I must therefore respectfully dissent from Marquardt's exposition, which sees social and political praxis as the unifying theme of Barth's earliest theology.

This leads to two final considerations. Without forcing Barth's theology into some artificial mould, it can be said in the first place that a unity of purpose informs his early works: 'Religion . . . is experience conceived of in a strictly individual fashion, and we regard it our duty to come to grips, clearly and positively, with the general human culture-consciousness on its scientific side.'[53] Barth, in other words, was attempting a theology of culture, an undertaking which in later years he viewed with much suspicion. Though he was to argue that any theology of culture inevitably reduced both God and his revelation to anthropology, Barth's earliest writings studiously sought to avoid this consequence. His skirmishes with Marburg *Religionsphilosophie*, the emphasis upon personality, personal culture, immediate religious awareness, and his understanding of religion as the dynamic force that actualizes abstract possibilities of *Kulturbewusstsein*, can be interpreted in no other way than fashioning foundations for a *Kulturtheologie*. Finally, three major early writings—the lecture on metaphysics, the article on faith and history, and the fragmentary outline of a *Religionsphilosophie*—present a coherent theory of religion which is most adequately comprehended in Barth's own words about religion being *die Realitätsbeziehung*. It is hoped that the meaning of this decisive word and the theoretical project associated with it will become clear.

A. THE NATURE OF *RELIGIONSPHILOSOPHIE*

Barth planned to publish a work entitled *Ideen und Einfälle zur Religionsphilosophie*, but since this word should not be confused with contemporary philosophy of religion, it might be helpful to consider the nature of this discipline for German theologians in the first decade of the present century. A good guide to Barth's understanding of the discipline is provided by those writings of *Religionsphilosophie* with which he was familiar. First, of course, were the writings of Cohen and Natorp on the topic of religion. For these scholars the central objective of *Religionsphilosophie* involved finding a place for religion within the confines of their system. This was achieved by considering the nature of its cognitive claims, its relation to the three principal 'directions' of the neo-Kantian *Kulturbewusstsein* and, finally, its importance for

nurturing culture and personal morality. In addition, furthermore, neo-Kantian philosophies of religion were not without
prescriptive and polemical elements. Both Natorp and Cohen
deemed a healthy religion essential for the well-being and
continued vitality of culture, yet both proclaimed that the future
efficacy of Western religion depended upon a massive revision of
its traditional theology. Natorp was perhaps the most radical, for
he counselled theologians to develop a theology of pure spirituality. He recommended them to take leave of God and other
transcendent objects by avoiding reifying metaphysical objectifications. No longer needing to defend illusory supernatural
objects or events, theologians were thereby liberated to devote
themselves to a poetics of pure inwardness and a robust
humanism. They could then investigate the spiritual resources
that lend vigour, moral passion, and authenticity to the individual,
whose primary duty was to contribute to the further development
of culture. Cohen, though less radical than Natorp, advised
theologians to concern themselves with the *Eigenart* of religion, its
unique characteristics, that is, which enrich morality and are to be
uncovered by hermeneutical idealization of scriptures, traditional
doctrines, and theologies. Even here radical revision was manda-
tory if the humanist vision of religion was to triumph in contemporary society. Authentic religion, said Cohen, occurs in the
correlation between human endeavour and eternal ideals, the
realization of which was dependent upon autonomous work, hard
work, and not upon an influx of supernatural energy or the
gracious actions of a divine being.

The neo-Kantians therefore provided Barth with some assessment of what a philosophy of religion should accomplish. He, in
offering his own account of religion, would accordingly need to
consider the nature of religion—whether it belonged predominantly to ethics, logic, aesthetics, or whether it was somehow
related to all three. Next he would have to discuss whether religion
enjoyed a unique rapport with a reality which could not properly
be reduced to other forms of culture and cognition. This, in turn,
required some consideration of the cognitive character of religious
beliefs, of how they may be established and what they refer to.
Another major task demanded that Barth should arrive at some
notion of how religion might be accommodated to the prevailing
philosophical temper. Since the Marburg philosophy presented

itself as science *par excellence* and presumed to adjudicate on all issues of reality and epistemology, he would consequently need some articulate account of faith and reason, when reason meant the scientific *Denken* defined by the logic and architectonic of Cohen's system. After discussing all these issues, it would have to be enquired whether the outcome compelled theological revision and, if so, to what extent. This obviously involved some estimation of the function of theology and its relation to what Barth called the 'lived religion' of the present, as well as a critique of traditional doctrine. Finally, and decisively, the main task, which encapsulated all others, was descriptive and prescriptive. Any philosophy of religion would have to investigate the relations between religion and the culture that was honoured and prized in the German-speaking universities. This demanded a thorough estimation of the value of religion for culture, along with a frank discussion of whether its offices were regressive or progressive. If religion at times seemed culturally regressive, it would have to be shown that this was due to a perverted religion and that a more enlightened religion was beneficial for nurturing and conserving humanitarian values. An element of prescription would accordingly result from the preceding evaluations that could well terminate in proposals about how religion should organize itself in order to retain a formative role in culture and how theologians might best supply modern man with a credible religious ideology. In short, therefore, the task of *Religionsphilosophie* was nothing less than a theoretical account of how religion operated in culture, together with a critique of theology, and an evaluation of future prospects.

Though such tasks were interesting and challenging, this approach to *Religionsphilosophie* imposed severe limitations. The first is obvious. The meaning of culture was to a great extent already determined by the Marburg System. That philosophy claimed to offer a scientifically articulate account of culture and saw itself as a sort of microcosm that revealed the inner heart, dynamism, and value of culture with a clarity, definitiveness, and scientific precision that never before was achieved. On the one hand culture was therefore regarded as a complex but interrelated whole, the absolute value of which had been philosophically demonstrated by the neo-Kantians. On the other hand, however, it was the most profound attribute of authentically human spiritual life (*Geistesleben*). In the words of Natorp, culture was that infinitely advancing creative deed of object formation, through which mankind created itself and its world, by fundamentally and indelibly imprinting the stamp of its spirit on its creations.[54] Such a concept of culture obviously had inbuilt value judgements regarding the nature and destiny of humanity, social ethos, and especially the virtue of idealism. As a consequence any theory of religion indebted to the Marburg account of culture was bound to be highly selective and overdetermined in the direction of Germanic Idealism. The claim of the Marburg System to represent actual cultural analysis was thus highly tendentious because the whole edifice, though fascinating, at times profound, and sometimes tediously abstract, made little use of sociology and often lacked any historical or comparative perspective. The nearest Cohen and Natorp came to actual cultural analysis was by way of Cohen's 'encyclopaedic psychology' and Natorp's 'reconstructive psychology', both of which were less than value-free disciplines. The theory of religion issuing from Barth's attempts at *Religionsphilosophie* shared these deficiencies. It remained highly conceptual, dependent upon the methodology of the Marburg School, and lacked any empirical analysis of the sociology or psychology of religion.

There was another problem connected with this approach to *Religionsphilosophie*, which has perhaps already suggested itself to perceptive critics, concerning differences in perspective. Cohen and Natorp wrote as philosopher kings or guardians of culture and accordingly viewed religion from that perspective. Barth, by contrast, was not a philosopher and never intended to become one. He was, however, a Protestant theologian deeply committed to the religious values of the Reformation and even his earliest writings exhibit confessional themes distinguishing his Reformed stance from Herrmann's Lutheranism. No one, not even the early Barth, could write theology in a confessional vacuum, and he was interested in a theory or philosophy of religion only inasmuch as it enabled him to write and practise theology. Like Clement's Gnostic Christian he could say of philosophies and theories of religion 'I embrace worldly culture as a younger maid and a handmaid', but to the Christian religion and its theology 'thy knowledge I honour and reverence as a full-grown mistress'.[55] For him, both philosophy, and theories of religion indebted to it, were fully subordinate to the biblical religion of the Reformation, which he believed to be founded upon revelation. This, however, only intensifies the problem of why Barth should even have bothered with *Religionsphilosophie*, especially since his theories assumed the Christian consciousness and its relational contents to be self-authenticating. Indeed it was explicitly stated by him that rational thought could not add to the special methodology of the Christian consciousness and even on occasions might thoroughly obscure this unique experiential datum. In reply it has to be recalled how at this stage of his career Barth attributed a whole internal *Universum* of culture to his Christian consciousness. Whatever was therefore good, beautiful, or true in culture was claimed by God and drawn into the internal synthesis. His belief in the self-authenticating impact of revelatory experience, moreover, impinged upon his apologetical strategy. It was his sincere conviction that once the full virtues of experienced religion had been depicted in all their glory, their appeal would be immediately apparent and so precipitate the conversion of philosophy and culture. It was therefore an evangelical imperative to devise a theory of religion which would portray the full efficacy of faith and revelation, in contrast to the more truncated neo-Kantian versions, and its highest aspiration was to convert those who supported such accounts to a true and more efficacious form of religion of the sort found in Schleiermacher, the writings of the Reformers, and contemporary religious experience. Barth, in other words, hoped to evangelize the philosophy of Marburg and claim it for Christ. He also perceived that systematic theology, as well as biblical, doctrinal, and dogmatic material, required some methodology to lend form, coherence, and structure to its objectives. A general theory of religion would therefore be particularly welcome if it enabled theologians to speak intelligibly to other religious beings and provide an overview or general pattern according to which systematic theology could organize itself without recourse to outworn metaphysical preambles or untenable proofs. This desire to devise what will be called a foundational theology,[56] thus owed more to a distinctively confessional and theological orientation than to any neo-Kantian theory of religion, since its objective was to supply systematic theology with a general overview, idea, or pattern, focused upon man as a religious being. As will be seen presently, Barth's own foundational theology relied heavily upon Schleiermacher's notions of philosophical theology and philosophy of religion.

It has been suggested so far that Barth's understanding of *Religionsphilosophie* was shaped in the first place by neo-Kantian theories of religion and secondly by the desire to articulate a foundational theology. Neither of these, it must be added, was equated by Barth with systematic theology or *Glaubenslehre* proper; though both might indeed contribute to the organization of the latter. At this stage, however, it is important to consider a more polemical factor which possibly contributed towards Barth's emerging notions of *Religionsphilosophie*. What was to have been his first major academic work addressed an issue which was keenly debated and highly topical. A consideration which doubtless must have added impetus to Barth's labours was an awareness that his earliest and most despised *bête noire* was likewise busy with *Religionsphilosophie*. Troeltsch, as well as writing numerous articles on the topic, often lectured about *Religionsphilosophie*, and in the winter of 1908 Barth made a copy of the lectures on *Religionsphilosophie* which Troeltsch had delivered at Berlin during the previous summer. He was also probably aware that Troeltsch planned to write a book on the philosophy of religion and it is interesting to note that Troeltsch intended to publish his lectures on *Religionsphilosophie* which were delivered in 1912. Around the time Barth was writing his own brief outline, therefore, unofficial copies of Troeltsch's lectures were being circulated and Barth probably heard rumours about their publication. It is highly probable that Barth's first work was not only to have been a scientific critique and rejoinder to the works of Cohen and Natorp, but also a head-on confrontation with Troeltsch's philosophy of religion. What more spectacular introduction to the theologically literate public could have been available to a young 'modern theologian'? Barth, I suggest, would have subjected Troeltsch to the sort of methodological criticism encountered in the lecture on metaphysics, arguing that his entire approach naturalized the religious consciousness to such a degree that no room was left for even his reconstructed religious teleology. It is ironic that neither work was published.[57]

Barth's own philosophy of religion was to have begun with a general prolegomenon, the three chapters of which would have dealt successively with the concept of *Religionsphilosophie*, its history, and tasks. Though there are notes for only the first and third topics, it is nevertheless possible to discover in some detail how Barth set to work on what I have called foundational theology.

Although Barth's fragment never directly quotes Schleiermacher's famous prolegomenon to theology, the *Kurze Darstellung*, his introductory notes concerning the concept and tasks of *Religionsphilosophie* were to some extent modelled upon it. Schleiermacherian *Religionsphilosophie* was a discipline more akin to sociology of religion than to what today is accounted philosophy of religion. It first of all involved explicating the notion of religious community. Demanding comparison, as well as historical research, it had to show not only the common features of religious communities, but also their differences, by paying especial attention to their distinguishing social styles and theological divergences.[58] Schleiermacher, secondly, divided theological study into three main disciplines with philosophical theology forming its root, historical theology its body, and practical theology its crown. The first discipline, philosophical theology, must not be confused with the more general discipline of *Religionsphilosophie*, though it used the varying patterns of religious social ethos discovered by philosophy of religion in order to present:

(*a*) that perspective on the essence of Christianity, by which it can be recognized as a distinctive mode of faith, and, simultaneously, (*b*) the form which the Christian community takes, and (*c*) the manner in which each of these factors is further subdivided and differentiated. Everything that belongs to these three undertakings, taken together, forms the task of philosophical theology.[59]

Whereas *Religionsphilosophie* was concerned to arrive at a general theory of religion, this quotation shows how philosophical theology was specifically concerned with the Christian religion.

Thirdly, when dealing with either philosophy of religion or philosophical theology, Schleiermacher's procedure was neither straightforwardly empirical nor speculative, but critical and so in a very real way it anticipated both Weber and Troeltsch. The method of *Religionsphilosophie* recommended by the *Kurze Darstellung* is not far removed from the critical and comparative study of religion which proceeds by typifying the various forms of religious community that have existed in history, with Christianity being recognized as one such type. The special task of philosophical theology within theological study, then, would involve a critical portrayal of the distinctive marks, nature, or essence of that type of religious community which may legitimately be called 'Christian'.

Instead of adopting Schleiermacher's distinction between philosophy of religion and philosophical theology, Barth placed his own form of *Religionsphilosophie* at the root of the theological tree. This was contrary to Schleiermacher's objectives, for it effectively defined all religion in terms of the Christian religion. Furthermore, whereas Schleiermacher's two forms of philosophical research were critical exercises in typification—classifying the different forms of religion according to their religious beliefs and social ethos—Barth's orientation was more conceptual and less historical. *Religionsphilosophie*, he maintained, is a discipline that 'grounds' the possibility of a science of religion. Barth, in other words, was very close to neo-Kantianism at this point because he adopted the typically Marburg way of justifying any cognitive enterprise by establishing its a priori possibility as a necessary principle of cognition. Though this might seem very much like a concession to Troeltsch's religious a priori, Barth's 'grounding' of religious knowledge found the necessary a priori condition for a scientific account of religion in the ubiquitous Christian consciousness.

Importantly, and quite uncharacteristically, Barth followed Schleiermacher in the controversial step of affording philosophy of religion methodological priority over doctrine. The point of departure for philosophical theology, according to the *Kurze Darstellung*, 'can only be taken above Christianity in the logical sense of the term, that is, in the general concept of a religious community or fellowship of faith'.[60] This methodological *über*, to which some, including the later Barth, have taken much exception, may be interpreted in an entirely innocent manner. Since the objective of philosophical theology was to attain a critically informed typification of historical Christianity, and not to offer a complete *Glaubenslehre* or systematic theology, it is quite natural that this enterprise should be logically prior to a complete explication of Christian believing. Schleiermacher, in other words, was inviting erstwhile theologians to take an overview of Christianity, on the understanding that a critically informed study of various religions results not in some global, common denominator, or universal religion, but rather in sharper criticial awareness of the distinctiveness of Christianity as a religion. Some idiosyncratic notion of religion in general and Christianity in particular has not thereby simply been dreamt up, for the theologian's estimation of the distinctiveness of Christianity in fact arises from critical immersion in its history, theology, and ethics. For a theological generation wrestling with pluralism on the one hand and global theologies on the other, Schleiermacher's approach has much to commend it.

The methodological *über*, moreover, offered an overview or foundational systematic pattern in yet another sense. Schleiermacher believed it essential for the theologian to have some general notions as to what Christianity is about before starting to write or speak about Christianity in a systematic manner. Naturally such a general overview should not arise from eccentric a-historical musings, but rather be controlled by theological, historical, and exegetical studies. If systematic theology is at all desirable, it seemed indispensable to have a critically informed general idea, pattern, or programme to follow. The discipline of philosophical theology, therefore, is simply an exercise in mental housekeeping. Being a sort of conceptual clearing-house, it promotes a critically informed overview of distinctively Christian beliefs and practices. To this extent it is not difficult to see why 'everyone's philosophical theology essentially includes within it the principles of his whole theological way of thinking'.[61]

Barth, then, subscribed to this methodological *über*, but his approach was less historically and sociologically oriented. *Religions-philosophie* for Barth first proceeds transcendentally by grounding the possibility of religious knowledge, but, secondly, by supplying foundations for a science of religion, it also becomes an introduction to the basic principles of *Glaubenslehre*. This seems to be Barth's version of the role which Schleiermacher assigned to philosophical theology of portraying the essence of Christianity. In Barth's own words, the philosophy of religion defines the 'object of faith, which *Glaubenslehre* then explicates'. The difference between Barth and Schleiermacher is that the former was so influenced by the neo-Kantian concept of science, especially its transcendental method of 'grounding' the possibility of any cognitive enterprise, that the methodological *über* is not defined heuristically, as it was with

Schleiermacher, but transcendentally. Barth hoped this procedure would demonstrate the truly scientific character of Christian theology, support its integrity as an academic discipline, and establish the cognitive legitimacy of its claims. All this, of course, stands in perfect accord with the explicitly avowed intention, first proclaimed in *Reichsgottesarbeit*, of coming to terms with the prevailing *Kulturbewusstsein* on its 'scientific side', or of assessing religion and theology in the light of neo-Kantian philosophy and its understanding of scientific method.

The concept of *Religionsphilosophie* which Barth was endeavouring to formulate also accords with another theme of *Reichsgottesarbeit*. Though all this talk about transcendental procedures, grounding possibilities, and the scientific status of religious conceptuality might seem narrowly academic, Barth, like Ritschl and Herrmann, passionately believed that a sound methodology was supremely important for the mission of the Church in contemporary society. His fragmentary notes about the philosophy of religion therefore emphasize that *Religionswissenschaft* has a practical dimension because its objective was to prepare ordinands and future leaders of the Church. In this respect Barth endorses Schleiermacher's views on the importance of practical theology and simultaneously affirms what Schleiermacher called the 'positive' character of theological science: 'Theology is a positive science and its constituent elements form a cohesive whole only through their common relation to a particular mode of faith or to a particular mode of being conscious of God.'[62] It is important not to confuse this positive character of theology with positivism. By 'positivism' Schleiermacher meant studies that are predominantly neither empirical, speculative, nor theoretical, but, through their concern with the historical and contemporary experience of identifiable social groups, serve important practical functions. The best analogy to the positive character of theology would therefore be the study of jurisprudence and law. That discipline too has historical and social dimensions, but it is also concerned with the practical needs of litigation and with training future solicitors or barristers. Barthian *Religionsphilosophie* therefore had the essentially practical objective of explicating the geography of religion in relation to the contemporary cognitive map. By indicating how religion functioned in contemporary culture, clerics would be able, by studying Christianity in this

way, to gain the necessary insight to labour effectively in the first
decades of a new century.

It is now essential to examine how Barth proposed to establish a
science of religion and with it the cognitive integrity of its object.
The following words begin to clarify his intentions: 'As the
philosophy of religion stands above [*über*] religion, the philosophy
of religion is scientific, i.e. methodological reflection on the fact of
religion which is somehow present to the scientific consciousness.'[63] Barth's approach here is a strange amalgam of transcendentalism on the one hand and an almost positivist appeal to the
fact of religion on the other. The opening words promise a
transcendental grounding or justification of religion, but instead
of establishing the logical *Ursprung* of religion, Barth appeals to the
fact of religion which, he contended, is 'somehow present to the
scientific consciousness'. The difference between Barth's procedure and that employed by Cohen and Natorp becomes immediately apparent when one recalls how for these philosophers the
object of cognition was constructed through ideal generation and
objectification. In contrast to this approach, in which an object *ist
aufgegeben*, Barth effectively maintains that the object of religion is
already *gegeben* to consciousness and is neither constructed nor
generated. Instead of embracing the operational definition of
thought which characterized Cohen and Natorp, Barth reduces
thinking to merely reflecting what has already been given.
Thought, therefore, is no longer creative and constructive, but
representational and reflective.

Barth's procedure becomes even more clear in the following
passage:

An object cannot be defined if it does not exist. Religion, however, *as an
object*, can only be present in the religious consciousness of the one who
philosophizes about religion; *since in all historical existence only the raw
material of living religion is here present*. You'll never attain it, save you know
the feeling . . . The particular religion, which shapes the presupposition
of the philosophy of religion, forms the correct methodological point of
departure.[64]

Once again a neo-Kantian transcendentalism, which seeks to
ground a science by establishing its a priori possibility or
antecedent presuppositions as logically necessary, is combined
with a common-sense appeal to the self-authenticating facts of the

religious consciousness. The most important fact, of course, is the experience of being immediately related to God, and the quotation from Goethe's Faust, 'Wenn ihr's nicht fühlt, ihr werdet's nicht erjagen', is indicative of the entire enterprise. It need hardly be said that such a naïve, indeed almost positivist, appeal to given 'raw material' and to an already formed object of religious cognition, would be completely unacceptable to philosophers such as Cohen and Natorp. There is nothing here that would convince them that the facts, objects, or experiences, which Barth will presently explicate, are given directly to consciousness by the deity without having first passed through the generative fire of thought.

In view of this radical departure from the architectonic of Marburg Kantianism, Barth would obviously need to offer some assessment of the neo-Kantian approach to *Religionsphilosophie*. Presumably such a critique was to have been undertaken in the third chapter of his prolegomenon by defining the essence of religion in relation to culture, meaning thereby, the intricate network of logical, ethical, and aesthetic objectifications that characterized neo-Kantian *Kulturbewusstsein*. This issue was crucial for any philosophy of religion and four options were available to Barth, as to other contemporary philosophers of religion. He could have associated religion with one particular *Richtung* of consciousness, perhaps regarding it primarily as the paradigm of all human knowledge, or, second, as a form of social ethics, or, third, as an aesthetical mode of cognition. Instead, however, he took a fourth option which was also advocated by the earliest writings of Paul Tillich. Rather than systematically reducing religious cognition to one branch of knowledge, Barth aspired to relate religion to all three aspects of culture. How such a vision of religion is established philosophically was to have been the leading theme of his book.

Barth therefore begins to define his own philosophy of religion more precisely by contrasting it to the theories of other scholars, the three most important being those offered by Natorp, Cohen, and Troeltsch. He is able to agree with Natorp that religion should never be portrayed as a regressive force which iconoclastically threatens to destroy culture or the social values of liberal enlightenment it was believed to promote. Its relationship to the humanitarian values of culture must rather be shown to be positive, supportive, and formative. To this extent religion 'must be placed in an internal and *necessary* connection with those other forms of consciousness' and such an internal and necessary connection will turn out to be what Barth called *die Realitäts-beziehung*.

What a positive relationship between religion and culture should not involve is explicated by reference to Troeltsch. Though Barth's book was to depict religion as a supernatural resource that animates the interior life of culture and nurtures its values, he was aware of its dangers. Bringing religion into contact with the neo-Kantian *Kulturbewusstsein* might imply a reductive interpretation of religion by turning it into an immanent or natural function of the human spirit. Could theology therefore be protected from becoming anthropology and its supernatural revelation from being rendered unnecessary? Barth believed it could, because his new theory, unlike that of Troeltsch, did not 'incorporate religion into culture-consciousness'. He therefore systematically excluded Troeltsch's mistake of placing 'religion on the same footing as cognition, volition, and feeling in the form of a religious a priori as a generally valid, that is, transcendentally necessary form of consciousness'; but had not his way of establishing the scientific character of theology in fact adopted the very same procedure?

There are three points to be made here. First, Barth's objections to the religious a priori arose from his belief that Troeltsch's programme completely naturalized religion by incorporating it into the vast network of internalized culture that formed the neo-Kantian transcendental synthesis. He consistently argued that Troeltsch naturalized religion to such a degree that it was deprived of any supernatural origin in divine revelation. Troeltsch, in other words, mistakenly equated the redemptive efficacy of religion with the efficacy of generative thought and thereby rendered implausible from the outset any connection between religion and the miraculously bestowed benefits of Christ. Barth's early criticisms of Troeltsch and his later ruthless attacks on Schleiermacher are remarkably similar: both naturalized religion. Secondly, the contention that religion should be placed 'in a necessary connection; with all forms of consciousness, but not as 'a transcendentally necessary' form of consciousness, testifies to an unresolved tension between methodology and theology in Barth's early theology. He desired to arrive at a scientific account of religion by using the conceptual tools of neo-Kantianism on the one hand, yet, on the other, to convert or transfigure both Marburg ontology and epistemology by an epiphany of supernatural revelation. The tension is neatly encapsulated by the way in which his book was to proceed. The first chapter dealt with religion *innerhalb* culture, the second aimed to offer an account of religion as an individual experience, and the third aspired to the impossible task of speaking about religion '*ausserhalb* culture'—a near meaningless phrase devoid of any possible religious or philosophical content. Not surprisingly, it is at this point that the fragment breaks off. It must be appreciated, thirdly, that Barth's interpretation of Troeltsch was highly biased. He was deeply committed to Herrmann's theology of revelation—something to which Troeltsch strongly objected—but furthermore Troeltsch was consistently interpreted through the thought forms of Marburg neo-Kantianism and these, even if Barth wanted to understand him properly, had a very distortive effect. After much abstract argumentation and heavily transcendental conceptuality from Barth, it is somewhat ironic to hear him complaining that Troeltsch turned religion into a dead 'necessary objectivity', instead of truly depicting its glories as 'an individual, infinite, and diverse revelation of life'!

Natorp's understanding of religion, claimed Barth, was closer to 'actual' and 'lived' religion than anything dreamt up by Troeltsch; though the cogency of Natorp's approach could not entirely be accepted either, for it placed religion firmly *innerhalb* the limits of humanity, whereas, as we have seen, Barth aspired to place it both *innerhalb* and *ausserhlab* culture. Against Natorp, who advocated a pure spirituality of feeling and aesthetic humanism devoid of any distortive theistic objectifications, Barth stated that 'religion has no desire to be considered as a mere accompanying emotion; rather it wants to be reality relating, whilst, according to Natorp, this reality relation completely exists only within the actualizations of consciousness as such'.[65] The criticism is simply that Natorp had a defective ontology, because reality for him and the other philosophers of Marburg was generated by operative thought without any assistance from God. Barth nowhere attempts a reasoned refutation of Natorp's logical monism, but, speaking on behalf of the religious consciousness, straightforwardly asserts that religion relates humankind to a much wider, supernatural reality—like the experiential *Universum* about which he wrote in 'Christian Faith and History'. Natorp's understanding of religion was therefore deemed inadequate precisely because it did not faithfully reflect the unique factual datum which Barth called 'the actual religious consciousness'.

Criticisms of Cohen are brief and sketchy. His rationalizing *Religionsphilosphie* excluded not only mysticism, but more grievously 'real religion', from the 'constitutive actualization' of consciousness and his concept of God was therefore nothing more than a *Grenzbegriff* for logic, ethics, or aesthetics. The force of Barth's criticism is that Cohen's philosophical God was merely an abstract conceptual construct, an empty rational symbol of truth, generated to create harmony for a system of philosophy. Cohen's God, it will be recalled, 'entered philosophy' only after the main section of the system was complete, but Barth preferred to see the dynamics of religion actualizing, converting, and renewing culture from the very outset. Cohen's radically idealist stance, moreover, was impossible for Barth. He wanted to speak about religion as a personal experience which arose directly from a revelation of divine actuality, whereas for Cohen religious experience seemed highly ambiguous and very problematical. Ideas possessed more reality for him than the *Wirklichkeit* to which Barth and his teacher appealed. Yet again one is able to perceive how the actualism and realism demanded by the theologians of Marburg created asymmetries for the philosophers and how the idealist science of the philosophers, which the theologians felt constrained to use, ill suited their confessional allegiancies and commitments to a life-bestowing self-revelation of God.

It is hoped that these remarks will be sufficient to convey some indication of Barth's prolegomenon to the philosophy of religion, but before continuing, the sequence of Barth's fragment deserves attention. The first chapter was to have discussed 'religion within culture as a feeling of complete direction', the second, 'the feeling of complete direction and the individual' (or, more simply, 'religion as individual experience'), whilst the third aspired to the very problematic task of discussing 'religion outside culture' as a feeling of complete dependence. The fourth and final chapter promised an account of religious symbolism, together with some thoughts about the concept, objectives, and methods of *Glaubens-lehre*. Leaving the final chapter to one side, it is interesting to note how the others follow a threefold pattern which is already familiar from the Christological discussions of 'Christian Faith and History'. There, when Barth drew attention to God's supernatural activity of revealing Christ's benefits to the Christian consciousness, it was argued that the Christian faith demanded a conceptual distinction between (a) a Christ principle active within consciousness, (b) an effective Christ idea which transcends consciousness—one, that is, which is defined theistically and supernaturally—whilst, (c) it was insisted that the two coalesce in a vivid singular occurrence where they are 'one and undivided'. A similar sequence distinguishes Barth's analysis of the 'religious consciousness' generally— without, that is, any reference to Christ—and also his psychological description of how religion operates in the individual.[66] What occurs here is a curious form of dialectic, the nature of which will be revealed in the section about dialectic in the early Barth. In the projected book of *Religionsphilosophie*, this dialectical pattern would have been used to explicate the relations between religion and culture.

B. RELIGION IMMANENT IN CULTURE

Any attempt to specify how religion functions *innerhalb* culture, would no doubt be influenced by Natorp's account of religion *innerhalb der Grenzen der Humanität* and Barth, though anxious to retain a real rapport between the believer and the transcendent God who, in some sense, remains *ausserhalb* culture, believed this philosopher offered a more authentic account of 'lived religion' than anything found in the writings of Troeltsch. His indebtedness to Natorp is immediately apparent in the title of the first chapter: religion within culture is a feeling of complete direction (*schlechthinniges Richtungsgefühl*). Feeling, for Natorp, was an objectless psychic dynamo. Though situated in the inaccessible and abysmal depths of inner being, it was nevertheless the agency responsible for the genesis of art, science, and morality. As well as objectifying the absolute values and glories of culture, it was the inner, restless, and creative feeling of religion that lent authenticity to the individual and unified his diverse creations into an experiential totality. Barth likewise claimed that religious feeling was the agency which created culture, and his neologism, *Richtungsgefühl*, implied that the three transcendental functions of consciousness, along with their associated scientific, ethical, and artistic objectifications, were ultimately dependent upon religious energies. Religion, being the feeling that gives 'complete' (a Schleiermacherian word) direction, is therefore not only the agency through which culture is generated; it supplies the necessary energy to fuel the teleological momentum of culture. From the outset Barth did not simply tack the additional *Richtung* of religion onto the three neo-Kantian dimensions of culture and knowledge, but rather implemented his programme of discovering an internal and necessary relation between religion and those spiritual resources which give birth to culture.

1. *Ideas*

From the very beginnings of Islamic, Christian, and Jewish philosophy, theologians believed their scriptures testified to the belief in ideas. However these ideas were defined, that they existed and that they formed an ideal order or reality, were presuppositions which shaped the form, content, and structure of Western religious thought until comparatively recent times. Though at this stage of his career, Barth was either not interested in patristic philosophy or knew very little about it, ideas were of cardinal importance to his own *Religionsphilosophie*.

The first chapter of Barth's projected work would begin to unveil his own theory of religion which had centred on the neologism *Realitätsbeziehung* ever since the article on Christian faith and history where it was favourably compared with a Platonic idea. His first chapter would accordingly argue for the validity of that idea and offer a more detailed account of its nature. We are therefore told how any transcendental critique of cognitive reason, such as the one advocated by the neo-Kantian philosophers of Marburg, begins by positing an 'indispensable element' at the root of the three directions of consciousness which generate science, ethics, and art. This Barth calls 'the Idea', whilst Cohen termed the first principle of knowledge and reality 'the Origin' (*Ursprung*). Barth is, however, careful to warn readers that should an idea be pressed to yield 'constitutive transcendent knowledge', the result would be the sham knowledge exposed by Kant's antinomies of pure reason.

This reference to Kant is important, for Barth's approach to 'the Idea' proves to rely upon an eclective synthesis of Kantian, Platonic, Schleiermacherian, and neo-Kantian philosophy. In the first place, Kant defined ideas both negatively and positively. On the negative side ideas were 'pure concepts of reason'. They have no essential reference to anything intuited through the senses, and hence, to 'objective experience', because no representation of finite sensate experience could possibly correspond to an idea of reason. Kant, secondly, signalled out for criticism three ideas in particular, namely the cosmological, psychological, and theological ideas. These ideas, being pure creations of thought, transcend all possible experience and offer no objective knowledge, yet, thirdly, and some would say paradoxically, Kant desired to find some positive meaning for these three ideas—indeed his *Critique of Pure Reason* would be heavily dependent upon them. It was argued that their validity lay not in their supposed ability to afford knowledge of alleged transcendent realities (such as an immortal soul or a purposive world governed providentially by a deity), but rather in their function as regulative or heuristic principles. They suggest to the understanding that the mind should be viewed *as if* it were a simple substance, the world *as if* it were a totality, and the natural order *as if* it had a single, highest, and all-sufficient cause beyond itself in a self-subsistent, original, and creative rationality.[67] By a sophisticated and intriguing route, these three ideas became none other than the postulates of practical reason in Kant's second critique. In his first critique, however, their legitimacy rested upon their being construed as heuristic or regulative principles that encourage empirical research in its quest for complex, but interrelated unities in the natural order. The ideas of Barth's *Religionsphilosophie*, therefore, were claimed by him to be regulative in the Kantian sense.

As well as being familiar with this notion of ideas, Barth knew about Platonic ideas from his patristic studies, and, to complicate matters even more, was aware of the transformation Platonic ideas underwent in the writings of Marburg philosophers. These philosophers turned the ideas of Plato into the a priori 'presuppositions' or 'hypotheses' upon which all scientific knowledge, including the Marburg System itself, was thought to depend. They became what Cohen called the *Ursprung* of knowledge and being.[68] The important point arising from this is that despite appealing to Kant's heuristic use of ideas, Barth, writing under the influence of Marburg philosophy and, as will be seen,

Schleiermacher, in fact used ideas constitutively in order to acquire knowledge of transcendent, super-sensible objects. Ideas are therefore construed by him platonically and realistically, as causes of culture, principles of valid knowledge, eternal exemplars of particular goods embodied in culture and, finally, to form the essence of what is truly real. To anticipate the discussion a little, 'the Idea' is even experienced, with a supernatural revelation, and not dialectical reason, revealing its existence and nature. The relation between the mind that generates culture and the ideas which animate it, not surprisingly becomes that of Platonic participation.

Returning, however, to its allegedly regulative use, 'the Idea' recommended by Barth,

means for logic, ethics, and aesthetics the *reality relation*. In this sense the Idea is the thing-in-itself. The search for truth and truth itself are identical. Without this reality relating principle, a culture consciousness remains singular, empirically it would not come into existence at all, and additionally the theory of reason ('hypothesis') cannot dispense with it.[69]

In a note appended to the main body of text, *die Realitätsbeziehung* is explicated by a reference to *Glaubenslehre* §3, 4 where Schleiermacher affirmed piety to be neither knowing nor doing, but a *Bestimmtheit* of feeling. Piety was nevertheless related to both because it 'stimulated knowing and doing', so that whenever piety has a predominant place in consciousness it 'will contain within itself one or both of these'.[70] Schleiermacherian piety, therefore, is equated by Barth with the object-forming, yet objectless modality of feeling about which Natorp so romantically wrote. Religion is a sort of dramatic impetus that energizes and convulses consciousness, thrusting it forward into what Barth termed 'total actualization'.[71] It needs hardly to be said that religion so conceived stands in positive, necessary, and internal relation to culture because it realizes to the maximum both the possibilities of cultural development and the human potential for life.

The teleological dynamism attributed to religion in the individual spirit and, consequently, *innerhalb* culture generally, represents Barth's own interpretation of Schleiermacher's characterization of Christianity as being a 'teleological religion', 'one, that is, which is determined in the direction of *activity*, in which the consciousness of God is entirely related to the sum-total of the *states of activity* in the idea of the Kingdom of God'.[72] Without religion, Barth argues, culture would lose its teleological momentum and become atrophied. Lacking the dynamism of actualizing religious energy, which the religious consciousness knows to be divine power, culture would not come into existence at all. Neither would there be a self-conscious subject to experience the varied forms and delights of culture or to be an agent through which culture is created. The individual, that is, through whose *Geist* culture is constructed, would remain 'singular', a non-actualized or solipsistic entity—a theoretical point or mere potentiality lacking potency for actualization—and therefore severed from all reality. The *Realitätsbeziehung*, to which Barth refers here, is religion as a dynamic principle of actualization that gives birth to the individual and to culture. It is religion as the efficient and final cause of whatever is true, good, and beautiful in the world of culture.

But what, exactly, to use Scholastic terminology, is the 'material cause' of the reality relating principle, of what does it consist? Admittedly it must at least be an energizing divine powr, but is it at all possible to be more precise? At first sight Barth's equation of 'the Idea' with the thing-in-itself is perplexing and not at all promising. The article about Christian faith and history, however, had already referred to the person in whom religion was truly actual as 'the knowing and willing man who, *in that* he knows, stands in the midst of the thing-in-itself'.[73] On the basis of various passages from Schleiermacher's *Reden* it became evident that the experience of reality meant the presence of a *Universum* at the auspicious 'moment' when intuition and feeling were united and unfragmented by conceptual reflection. But what things-in-themselves did Barth have in mind when he referred to them in this and other passages? Throughout his early career one leading *Ding-an-sich*, that claimed the attentions of his teacher and occupied a central position in his own theology since *Reichsgottesarbeit*, was *das Individuum*; that autonomous being which nevertheless was capable of experiencing revelation, acquiring scientific knowledge, and creating its own moral ideals. Recalling Kant's trinity of ideas, as well as the contents attributed to relational Christian consciousness by Barth, it is no surprise to discover that the remaining two things-in-themselves are God and the real world, the latter meaning the cosmic totality or *Universum* in which the individual finds itself as a result of experiencing revelation—the 'trans-individual' kingdom of a culture claimed for God. There then break through into consciousness the full immediacy and glories of reality relating experience, which is 'individual and trans-individual, self-certainty and certainty of God in one. Its relationship to consciousness is that of actualization, because it is the regulative principle . . . considered "purely in itself" this reality-connecting principle is . . . immediate, unanalysable, irrational, personal and individual vitality.'[74] The entire forum of internalized culture is therefore drawn into the great locus of synthesis, the religious consciousness, to become the third element of Barth's *Universum* alongside God and other converted individuals. This explains why Barth used the word idea in the singular instead, like Kant and Plato, of referring to a plurality of ideas: they all achieve a synthesis in the relational religious consciousness. Any distinction between them is merely conceptual and abstract, for originally, in the moment of universal experience, they are 'one and undivided'.

Though the chapter on religion immanent in culture was not to discuss the implications of this theory for systematic theology (since that was to be the especial concern of the final chapter), it is not difficult to guess how the transition would be made. As well as bestowing momentum and teleological direction to culture, Barth, during the course of his exposition, mentions that the process of actualization gives form and shape to life (*Lebensgestaltung*). *Leben* and *ewiges Leben* were important themes in Herrmann's theology, and Barth's article on faith and history equated *Leben* with the *justificatio* of Reformation theology. It is therefore probably the case that the fourth chapter of his book would have equated the vitality resulting from the presence of religious energies in culture and in individuals with the benefits of Christ, which were so highly valued by Ritschl and Herrmann.

2. *Truth and Divinity*

Having offered an account of the internal, necessary, and positive relation between culture and religion, Barth intended to round off his chapter by affirming the value of his astounding vision of religion *innerhalb* culture with some very important words about truth. Since any interpretation of his *Religionsphilosophie* would be singularly incomplete without consideration of his thoughts about truth, the following passage merits comment: 'All *substantial content of truth* [*Wahrheitsgehalt*]—in the critical sense—in logical knowing, moral willing, and aesthetic feeling, is religion or *consciousness of God*.'[75] This equation of the presence of truth in the three actualized dimensions of culture with awareness of God is indebted once more to Schleiermacher's *Christian Faith*. Barth's article on faith and history had already embraced Schleiermacher's psychology in which two principal functions of consciousness, one active and spontaneous, the other more passive and receptive, were termed 'elevation' and 'ingression'.[76] Though the *Glaubenslehre* itself argued that these two psychological attributes of self-consciousness were most aptly termed 'the feeling of freedom' and 'the feeling of dependence', Schleiermacher pressed his analysis further, by suggesting that these two functions of consciousness were each dependent upon a common third factor. The question of their whence (*Woher?*), the question, that is, of their origin and efficacy, was found by him to lie in a feeling of absolute dependence which was the way, or rather, mode, through which human beings feel related to God. In Schleiermacher's own words:

When our proposition equates absolute dependence and relationship [*Beziehung*] with God, this is to be understood in the sense that the Whence of our receptive and active being, which is posited along with this self-consciousness, is to be designated by the expression 'God'. This for us is the true and original meaning of that expression.[77]

Schleiermacher argued that along with passive and active states of self-consciousness there must be postulated (*mitgesetzt*) a third factor upon which the very existence (*Dasein*) of these attributes depends. The relation between the three is not, however, simply due to some sophisticated dialectical play with concepts, for the three are dynamically related in actual experience. They are, that is, modes of response and awareness. Barth in similar fashion was trying to suggest that the *Woher?* of his *Kulturbewusstsein*, the origin of its teleological efficacy, that is, comes from an energy which is divine.

Barth, no less than Schleiermacher, was anxious to emphasize that his account of the immanent activity of religion was no mere *Beziehung* of concepts and cognitive functions, but a relation realized predominantly in personal experience. To this extent, therefore, *die Realitätsbeziehung* is bestowed upon consciousness through a sort of revelation through which it encounters a divine efficacy operating in its own experience and activities. Hence Barth's way of connecting the reality relating principle to the other dimensions of the neo-Kantian consciousness was also anticipated by Schleiermacher:

> Feeling oneself to be absolutely dependent and consciousness of being in a relationship [*Beziehung*] with God are one and the same, because absolute dependence is the fundamental relation [*Grundbeziehung*] which must include all others in itself. According to this exposition, the last expression includes God-consciousness in self-consciousness in such a manner that the two cannot be separated from each other. . . . To this extent it may be said that God is given [*sei uns gegeben*] to us in feeling in an original way. When, therefore, we talk about a primary revelation of God to man or in man, this is what is always meant: along with the absolute dependence, which characterizes not only human, but all temporal existence, there is also given to human beings immediate self-awareness of this absolute dependence which, for these beings, becomes an awareness of God.[78]

Just as Schleiermacher's romantic mixture of dialectic and psychology affirmed that all other relations and activities of consciousness are included in the *Grundbeziehung* of divine–human intimacy, so Barth argued that all the relationships which characterize the complex neo-Kantian network of logical, ethical, and aesthetic operations are experienced in their absolute immediacy, vitality, and splendour when it is perceived that a divine energy inspires their momentum and reveals itself in these ceaseless operations. The various cultural goods actualized by divine efficacy working in consciousness are consequently partial refractions of that activity and each in its own way is a partial embodiment or actualization of the divine splendour from whence (*Woher*) they arise. The consciousness through which scientific, moral, and aesthetic culture illumines a dark age is a consciousness which lives, moves, and has its being in God. That full depth of being, from which all truth proceeds, is the Truth which lies in God and comes into the world with a sheer excess of vitality that graciously nurtures truth in culture. These incarnate or actualized configurations of truth, beauty, and goodness in human culture, at their most profound, original, and creative dimension have a depth of meaning that is divine (*Wahrheitsgehalt*).

Lest it be thought that Barth here advocates some natural theology, it should immediately be said that his procedure is not so straightforward. His philosophy of religion was to offer a theory of religion, along with what I have called a critically informed perspective, overview, or foundational pattern concerning the nature of Christianity, both of which would be singularly useful for writing a *Glaubenslehre*. As yet, the question of revelation has not been directly encountered, but the assumption that something must be given—whether it be a divinely originating *Lebensmacht* or the 'fact' of religious actualities working in consciousness prior to any scientific reflection—would lead one to expect revelation figuring somewhere in Barth's presentation. The role assigned to revelation becomes particularly clear in the projected second chapter concerning the individual's experience of religion, and also in Barth's highly original schema of truth.[79] It might not be immediately apparent that Fig. 1 depicts not so much the hermeneutical circle of faith, as an ellipse with two foci, which a later Barth would prefer to have been 'a circle with one centre' because the ellipse inevitably 'turns the Christian relationship of man and God into an apparent human possibility'.[80] His earlier

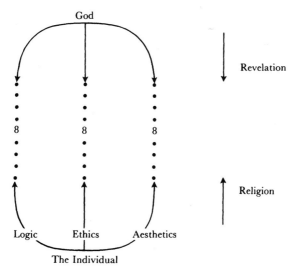

FIG. 1 Barth's Schema of the System of Truth

theological method, by contrast, seems to have been quite
enthusiastic about Schleiermacherian ellipses with their equal and
opposite foci.

Since the schema of truth would doubtless occupy a pivotal
position at the heart of Barth's system of *Religionsphilosophie*, it
deserves detailed commentary and the following pages will argue
that its approach to truth represents in the first place an interpretation of Cohen's *Gottesidee*. Next it will be shown how Barth's
interpretation of Cohen was itself considerably indebted to a very
traditional resource supplied by the *philosophia perennis*, though
this perennial leitmotif was artfully blended with themes from
Reformation theology and the more romantic elements of
Schleiermacher's thought. A comparison between Barth's fragment and some early unfinished musical score may be a helpful
analogy for interpreting his fragmentary outline, for he
bequeathed posterity a score which was only partially realized in a
series of articles, lectures, and notes. Careful attention to detail,
style, and sources would enable but a tentative reconstruction.
Though interpretation, rather than reconstruction is the more
modest objective of the following remarks, it is hoped they might
none the less encourage some appreciation of that harmony
between German Idealism, Romanticism, and Reformation
theology which Barth himself claims to have heard.

God as truth. That is a thought expressed in Cohen's philosophy, for it was his concept of God that bestowed harmony upon
his system by internally relating its principal divisions. Barth was
thoroughly familiar with Cohen's very ideal concept of deity;
indeed his fragment alluded to Cohen's Faustian remark, 'The
quest for truth, that alone is truth'. It is interesting that these
words were written by Cohen in a discussion of Lessing, who once
told a pointedly ironic and somewhat anthropomorphic parable
about God. In it the deity, like an oriental despot, was to grant a
favour to his humble petitioner who was invited to chose one of
two gifts. His right hand held the gift of all truth, but the left
offered a perpetual exploration and quest for truth that inevitably
led to error and illusion. The choice of the intercessor was
unequivocal: it was for the gift offered by the left hand, 'Father,
grant me that. Absolute truth is for Thee alone.'[82] Cohen's
rationalizing analogical interpretation is at once eager and
telling:

The quest for truth, that alone is truth. The method alone by means of which logic and ethics both together—not one by itself alone—become productive is this integrating and unitary method which accomplishes and guarantees truth. If one has to distinguish between two hands, one would be logic, the other, ethics. Both, however, are what they are, by virtue of the same method. The efficacy of this 'by virtue of' is what we account as truth. Truth consists in the unitary method of logic and ethics. Truth cannot be revealed as a datum.[82]

This idealization is a wonderful example of Cohenian hermeneutics. They are governed, completely and absolutely, by his system of philosophy. For Cohen there could be only one truth: the truth of system, which was always advancing, discovering, and infinitely generating new truths. There was, therefore, no Hegelian Absolute Truth; all truth is seeking, as dynamic and operative as thought itself. The unitary 'integrating' method of Cohen's philosophical calculus testified to this ever-unfolding truth, as, he believed, did his entire system. Since truth, for Cohen, infinitely develops through the productive agency cognition, there is no absolute truth outside the system of philosophy which even hypothetically could be revealed by a deity and function as a datum upon which other truths are based—a contention which Cohen was being urged to adopt by his theological colleague, Herrmann. Though truth is relative to the body of actualized truths at any one time, this did not, according to Cohen, carry the implications of relativism. The foundations or first principles of both cognition and reality (*Denken und Sein*) retained absolute, and not relative validity, and Cohen did not equate truth with validity. If, however, truth was to interrelate the infinite evolution of knowledge and reality, it was best exemplified methodologically by the idea of God, which gathers together and unifies the incessantly developing *Richtungen* of consciousness.

Barth's reactions to the deity of Cohen's *Ethik* which, being a sign of truth, binds ethics and logic into a teleological unity, are scattered throughout his early writings. Rather than entering the system of truth to create systematic harmony as it were through the back door, Barth would have preferred to see Cohen's deity active from the very beginning. To this extent, he insisted that the deity of *Religionsphilosophie* should not be posited by human thought at the end of its cognitive labours, but rather, to use Cohen's somewhat disaparaging term, should be accepted as a primary 'datum' from the outset. It is in this light that Barth's references to the unfounded ground of thinking and willing should be interpreted in that very difficult article about belief in a personal God. God ought to be the first principle (*Ursprung*) of knowledge and reality:

> To question the foundation of 'reality' as such is to affirm it at the same time. The suspension of space and time immediately implies dominion over space and time. The 'unfounded' becomes the ground for the foundation of what is thought and willed, the pure deduction to pure origin (*Ursprung*). It is the truth and validity which rests in itself—the truth and validity of the a priori—that manifests itself here as the positive component of the concept of God.[83]

It might be helpful at this juncture to recall how in patristic times there were three interpretations of Platonic ideas available to the Fathers. An Aristotelian-type explication construed them to be real incorporeal and self-subsistent beings, with one idea, that of the Good, being identified with God. Another interpretation, originating probably with Albinus, deprived the ideas of their self-subsistence and they become divine thoughts, whilst a third, that of Philo, accounted the ideas to be an intelligible order contained in the logos. These, according to Philo, were initially divine thoughts but later created into real beings by God. Cohen's last book of religious philosophy seems to have made the totality of ideas into thoughts of God, just like the second interpretation, with the deity therefore becoming a divine principle of origin. Barth anticipated Cohen in this move, but he should not be credited with originality on that account, for such a religious interpretation of Marburg philosophy had already been advanced in the doctoral thesis of his philosopher brother, Heinrich Barth.[84] In his fragment Karl Barth did not use the word 'origin', but he did affirm that the (Kantian) problem of reason and the (religious) problem of God correspond to each other as 'reciprocally related totalities' because, it would seem, the first principles of logic and ethics have their ultimate, true, and transcendental origin in divine rationality and righteousness. The a priori is no longer the necessaary universal condition of knowledge it was in Kant nor, for that matter, merely an a priori from which religion might be generated. It is rather the great principle of origin which engenders the truths and goods of culture. God, therefore, in ways now obvious, is the Idea of ideas and Being of all beings, the totality of which is truth.

In view of this it may well be asked what has become of all the talk about religious experience, history, faith, and revelation, which so forcefully marks much of Barth's early writing. In the system of *Religionsphilosophie* did he abandon his passionately held thesis about the primacy of experience in favour of religion of reason? At this point it is necessary to recall Barth's schema as shown in Fig. 1, with its descending arrow symbolizing revelatory ingression and its ascending arrow, representing the individiual's religious response to divine efficacy, that travels upwards together with the actualized configurations of culture. The concept of revelation is pivotal in several crucial respects, for first of all it facilitates the transition from a purely transcendental concept of God as truth to a more actualist focus on divine immanence. Revelation, secondly, solves the epistemological problem of how God is known because Barth's deity, unlike Cohen's, is actively present in consciousness prior to any reasoning and is not merely discovered by proofs, posited by dialectic, or deduced by autonomous reasoning. It was the same concept, thirdly, that enabled Barth to combine the radically ideal God of Cohen with the realist approach to divine–human contact in personal experience which characterized his approach to faith and religious experience.

The following passage clearly indicates how Barth, along with an idealist concept of deity as truth and transcendental ground, also offered a realist definition of truth as the immediacy of divine–human togetherness in religious experience. First there is a quotation from Cohen's *Ethik*, which gives Cohen's explanation of how Hegel's erroneous notion of the Absolute arose; Barth then offers his own comments:

H. Cohen well says 'The concept of the Absolute arose as an expression of despairing humility in the depths of the human spirit at the self-induced irony of human reason. Since all being depends upon foundations supplied by reason, there arises a profound desire for a ground independent of this foundation.' The authentic rationale of critical idealism, which concerns the foundation of thinking and willing, is cancelled with this 'despairing humility' and 'profound desire', thus making room for the problem of religion: *inquietum est cor nostrum, donec requiescat in te. In te* speaks of immediate religious perception [*Empfindung*] and thereby places the Sublime as a Thou before the I.[85]

Here, obviously, is a religious and experiential understanding of truth, which now lies in the inner, hidden depths of personality where a human *Ich* experiences its relatedness to the divine *Du*.

The allusion to Augustine conveniently leads to an explication of traditional and perennial motifs that enriched Barth's thought. In a footnote to the text of Barth's fragment, there is a reference to Schleiermacher's understanding of revelation as the original fact which lies at the foundation of any religious communion. Schleiermacher's discussion of revelation at this juncture was neither empirical nor naturalistic, for he expressly stated that the word revelation presupposes divine communication and declaration. To this extent he saw a divine causality in the original fact from which a religion arises. Revelation, moreover, acts primarily on self-consciousness: it is not originally and essentially doctrine. Towards the end of his postscript, when discussing the truth claims of various religions, the following statement is made:

Perfect truth would mean that God made himself known as he is in and for himself. Such truth, however, could not arise outwardly from any fact—indeed, even if it did in some incomprehensible way come to the human soul, it could not be grasped by that soul and retained as a thought; and, if it could not in any way be grasped and retained, it would not become efficacious [*wirksam*]. Any proclamation of God, which is to be operative [*wirksam*] upon and within us, can only express God in his relation [*Verhältnis*] to us. This represents no subhuman ignorance concerning God, but rather the nature [*Wesen*] of human limitation in relation [*in Beziehung auf*] to him.[86]

By deflecting human rationality away from the blinding possession of Absolute truth—the sort of truth, that is, which Lessing preferred not to receive—Schleiermacher was not thereby advocating a thorough theological agnosticism. He rather affirmed that any 'proclamation' or revelation which is to become efficacious and truly engage consciousness can testify to God only inasmuch as it speaks about his relation to human beings, and not about the deity as he might be *an und für sich selbst*.

The perception that divine beauty is so overwhelmingly magnificent that it is essentially incomprehensible to finite beings has traditionally been accompanied by the associated belief that religious truth for finite beings lies in the awareness of grace operative in the human soul. Both motifs have enjoyed a long and venerable history in some Christian and some Jewish thought;

both also appeared in the modern theology supported by the young Karl Barth. They inform, for example, the epistemologies which lauded the soteriological principle of Melanchthon, in which God was not to be discovered by the metaphysical speculations of philosophers, but in the benefits of Christ experienced by the believer. This 'inner experience' was, for them, the truth to which 'thoughts of faith' very imperfectly testify. The internal or spiritual encounter of human beings with God, the communion of the Christian with God, was the historically momentous event of personal revelation which formed the non-objectifiable essence of being human.

The quest for truth, to which both Lessing's parable and Barth's 'profound desire' refer, has often been depicted as an interior pilgrimage that culminates in an inner apocalypse when the soul encounters the God within: *noli foras ire, in te ipsum redi, in interiore homine habitat veritas*. In Augustine's philosophy the interior journey towards an encounter with God was influenced by the distinction between knowledge of the world and knowledge of self or, as the Germans would later say, the epistemological distinction between *Natur und Geist*. Whilst knowledge of external reality involved the mediation of sense perception, the second species of Augustinian knowledge was attained more immediately, through introspection. This contrast between mediated and immediate knowledge implied to Augustine that the latter was superior and closer to truth than the former. No less interesting is the way in which rationality received a theological interpretation from Augustine, with reason becoming graceful reason and consequently almost synonymous with religious belief and true religion.

Return within yourself. Truth dwells in the inner man. If you find that you are by nature mutable, transcend yourself, but remember that in doing so you must transcend yourself even as a reasoning soul. Make for the place where the light of reason is kindled. What does every good reasoner attain but Truth? Yet Truth is not reached by reasoning, but is itself the goal of all who reason. . . . It has to do no seeking, but you reach it by seeking, not in space, but by a disposition of mind, so that the inward man may agree with the indwelling truth with a pleasure that is not low and sensuous, but supremely spiritual. . . . Reasoning does not create Truth, but discloses it. Before it is discovered it abides in itself; when it is discovered it renews us.

Augustine's theology of truth was in no way impervious to what Kant later called 'practical reason'. The inner itinerary of the soul

demanded moral purification and its encounter with divine grace
was such that divine power not only precipitated moral orientation
but, in virtue of the love apprehended by faith and poured by the
Holy Spirit into the human heart, inspired good works spontaneously to arise and beautify the world.[87]

This theology of reason was eminently compatible with the
concerns of *moderne Theologie* during the last decades of the
nineteenth century and the first decade of the twentieth. The
contrast between knowledge of natural objects and immediate
knowledge of spiritual realities would resemble to late nineteenth-
century theologians the methodological distinction between
Welterkenntnis and *Leben*, *Erleben*, or *Geschichte* that was popular
amongst the followers of Ritschl. It would also seem to support the
concern expressed by Herrmann and Barth about the individual's
moral personality which they believed the Marburg philosophy
inadequately addressed, principally because it lacked their realist
appreciation of life-giving energy and divine efficacy. The
Augustinian stress upon the affective nature of true (Christian)
religion, furthermore, might lend apparent support to the
relationist thesis, according to which a 'qualitative homogeneity'
subsisted between the 'affection' experienced in revelation and the
efficacy of divine grace. It is therefore not at all surprising that
when theologians like Barth felt they could no longer rely on either
traditional proofs for divine existence or even upon metaphysics,
recourse was made to the traditional motif of proof from awareness
of grace.

A most sensitive and succinct summary of what has sometimes
been called the Augustinian proof from existence, though it is
perhaps better termed 'the proof from presence', was afforded by
Martin D'Arcy. Augustine, he explained, having established the
existence of a supra-sensible world,

is free to concentrate on the two objects of his predilection, God and the
soul. The soul comes first in order of demonstration, and the method he
follows has a striking resemblance to that of Descartes . . . The gist of it is
that truth exists, the soul exists, therefore God exists. Between each of
these truths there is scarcely any interval; strike one chord, and the others
immediately respond.[88]

Given, however, the dynamism characterizing Barth's account of
the divine efficacy which actualizes consciousness and gives

direction to culture, this traditional motif of proof from presence inevitably received a more dramatically dialectical form than anything found in Augustine and his immediate successors.

One favourite quotation, scattered liberally throughout Barth's earliest writings, was 'Thou wouldest not seek me hadst thou not already found me', which may seem a faithful interpretation of the scriptural promise 'Ask, and it shall be given you; seek, and ye shall find; knock, and it shall be opened unto you. For everyone that asketh receiveth; and he that seeketh findeth; and to him that knocketh it shall be opened.'[89] It may just be possible to see in this passage some general instruction on prayer or, alternatively, it might lend support to the conviction that God is 'always already' with the soul, inspiring the quest for himself before any conscious 'finding' occurs. It is, however, perhaps more correct to interpret such passages of scripture by Jesus's proclamation of the Kingdom. God would remain the 'giver' and the 'opener' but, according to the exegesis of Manson:

The blessings of the new age are not the fruits of 'progress' or 'evolution': they are the result of an act of God in history, his response to human needs and longings. . . . The thing to be sought is the Kingdom of God, which, being found, is the satisfaction of all human needs (Luke 12: 31). The door to be knocked at is the door which gives entrance to the Kingdom of God.[90]

Manson's exegesis would certainly not support an Augustinian-type proof from existence nor see in the logia a dialectic of seeking and finding, according to which the 'seeking' depends upon a prior transcendental 'having' of divine relatedness, with the 'finding' consequently becoming an experiential realization of this 'having'. Yet that is precisely what Barth did affirm with his language of seeking, desire, and actualization. Even more contrary to Manson's exegesis, the energies of interior grace create the fruits of culture and give momentum to social and moral evolution.

This traditional motif of inwardness, however, was mediated to the young Karl Barth through Schleiermacher and Herrmann, so the proof from existence became a proof from the religious consciousness. This methodology, it must be stressed, is found nowhere else in Barth's later writings except, that is, in polemical references to 'theological Cartesianism'—a methodology which instigates much criticism in the *Church Dogmatics*.[91] An earlier

Barth, by contrast, made copious use of 'theological Cartesian-ism'. Numerous references to Augustine, Luther, and Melanch-thon, as well as his own amazing 'Im Glaubensakt ist das Glaubensobjekt', were made to support the idea that prior to either seeking or finding there was a transcendental 'having' or, to use a word from his later works, an *Anknüpfungspunkt*, between God and human consciousness which, being a 'permanent possibility', was for ever available to human beings. Revelatory experience simply actualized this latent, but eternal, possibility.

'Calvin' and 'Kant' are thus made to agree because Barth found many echoes in Calvin of the *philosophia perennis*: 'If we regard the Spirit of God as the sole fountain of truth we shall neither reject the truth itself, nor despise it wherever it shall appear unless we wish to dishonour the Spirit of God.' With Calvin, however, the lesser temporal truths of culture are nowhere near as stable, enduring, and as spiritually beneficial, as the incarnate truth of Christ who, for the sake of humanity, died and wrought a work of atonement. As with many Reformers, Calvin's Augustinianism was modified by the new emphasis placed upon the benefits of Christ. The presence of truth and grace in the soul was therefore refracted through the prism of Calvin's doctrines of atonement and election.[92]

The religiously realist emphasis upon truth within soul and the transcendental truth of idealism, like Romanticism and Reforma-tion theology, revelation and reason, religion and culture, and much else besides, became 'reciprocally related totalities' because they all acquired unique synthesis in the 'religious consciousness', which divine revelation engendered and which had to be accepted as a self-evident datum for any theological account of reality.

3. Revelation, Ideals, and the Individual: Existential Participation

With Barth's account of 'religion as an individual experience', we return once more to the familiar territory of religious indivi-dualism. This section of Barth's book promised to achieve two objectives, the first of which was to offer some account of indivi-duation, and the second to suggest how the 'religious individual' relates to culture. Both themes were really two aspects of one over-arching concern, because Barth believed the presence of reality relating revelation gave impetus to what he called *Lebensgestaltung*. This section of his book would probably suggest that both individual life and the emergent configurations of culture received their vitality from the efficacy of divine grace. Life, therefore, is first bestowed upon individuals in virture of efficacious revelation and, working through them, spontaneously actualizes the varied goods of culture.

The Platonic words idea, illumination, and participation figure frequently in Barth's preparatory notes and though at first glance they might seem out of place, they accord well with Barth's allusions to Plato's parable of the cave in his article about faith and history. According to Barth's interpretation the human predicament was analogous to imprisonment. Being incarcerated in the dark world of abstract possibilities, humans are severed from all connection with reality and are therefore aware only of images, shadows, or distorted refractions of truth, beauty, and goodness. When, however, they turn to the life-bestowing idea, light is seen and experienced. What were previously mere abstract possibilities—promises and intimations of what man and his dark world could become—start to become actualized by the creative energy of light. At that ecstatic moment of personal illumination, when the immediate vision of divine splendour and creativity dawns and makes its golden epiphany in consciousness, the human being is not so much deified by divine energy, as thrust into ceaseless actualization of what will become the truths, beauties, and goods of culture. Value and potency are thereby graciously bestowed upon the darkness of deficient actuality and upon a consciousness which, being previously ignorant of reality, was dreaming shadowy dreams of what might be, whilst imprisoned in a transcendental sleep of supreme lethargy. When the vision of the sun radiates its energy, the enlightened consciousness becomes alive, invigorated, and actualized. Having been fired with something of the divine creativity, not only do individuals 'eternally become alive', the energy they receive also sets culture upon its teleological momentum. In the moment of illumination one stands in the midst of the thing-in-itself and experiences what more prosaically might be called 'ultimate reality'—meaning for Barth, relatedness to God, to one's own authentic inner being, and to other actualized beings. Then, indeed, a whole new cultural *Universum*, permeated with rays of divine splendour, is overwhelmingly present and inescapably real.[93]

The fragment of religious philosophy is less lyrical in portraying its vision of divine actualization:

Kulturgestaltung materializes only where the Subject of the normal culture consciousness, in virtue of illumination by the *Idea* present in it, participates in the 'reality' of the (critically understood) thing-in-itself. μέθεξις of Plato . . . individuality is, by virtue of μέθεξις in the dignity of the Idea, the subject of concrete, actual, cultural awareness. *The subject of the Idea, the subject of actual cultural awareness, the subject of the factual pattern of life, is the individual.*[94]

Barth's outline for this chapter, only a portion of which it was possible to reproduce, makes three further points about 'the Idea'. First, it transcends the neo-Kantian *Kulturbewusstsein* and, secondly, lacks the general validity attributed to the Kantian forms of space and time, as well as to categories like causality. Thirdly, Barth repeatedly stresses that illumination by 'the Idea' is responsible for transfiguring the abstract, non-actual, transcendental subject of philosophy into an existential centre of consciousness which is capable of enjoying communion with God through the goods of culture.

The actualization, illumination, or transformation wrought by the light therefore results from a participation of the subject in 'the Idea'. The word participation was obviously taken from Plato, who used μέθεξις and its cognates in various ways. Participation in Plato's philosophy could refer to the immanence of the idea in the particular or, secondly, as a synonym for *eikon*, *mimesis*, or *homoioma*, it suggested that ideas were exemplars and efficient causes of particulars. Finally, Plato also claimed that ideas participate in each other.[95] Because of the wealth of meaning attributed to the word participation, it is far from clear precisely how particulars participated in their Platonic ideas. These universals remained essentially changeless and eternal; being located in the heavens, they were far removed from their finite embodiments, particulars, and individuals. Though ideas were indeed affirmed to be the exemplary and final causes of particular entities, the nature of the participation was never made precise by Plato.

Barth may have encountered Platonic participation in his patristic studies or may have had direct knowledge of Plato's writings, but it is unlikely that he intended to correct contemporary philosophy with a platonizing account of Cohen. Rather he desired, more simply, to highlight the intimacy with God which the believer experiences in revelation. This sort of experiential knowledge was most important to Barth and Platonic knowledge, being more than knowledge about particular things or intellectual awareness, because it involved an orientation of the entire person in order to participate in the realm of ideas, suited his purposes quite well.[96] The transcendental subject of Marburg philosophy, according to Barth, remained a mere possibility, completely deficient in actuality until it was actualized by the efficacy of divine revelation. God, consequently, was primarily a *Lebensmacht*, a vitalist resource that actualized abstractions and personalized the impersonal. When that power for life was encountered, consciousness became fully alive and the most appropriate name for this dramatic awakening was revelation.

With an alternative, more philosophical vocabulary, Barth was simply articulating something utterly familiar to all students of Herrmann's theology. His triad of idea, illumination, and participation matches Herrmann's triad of divine *Wirklichkeit*, *Offenbarung*, and *Leben*, all of which are present in the historic experience of Christians. Furthermore the similar triad of ingression, elevation, and their pregnant synthesis in the religious consciousness had played a central role in the philosophical and psychological discussions of religion in the article about faith and history. The word participation, therefore, which announces the dynamic interpenetration of divine revelation and human response, refers simply to divine causality and creativity, through which there arises an authentically sentient subject who has received energy from God to actualize the merely latent possibilities for acculturation.

At the heart of the necessary and positive relation between religion and culture lies Barth's own brand of relationism which was attributed *an sich* to the 'religious individual'. The religious consciousness arose from the interpenetration of ingression and elevation, beholding and feeling, receptivity and spontaneity, objectivity and subjectivity—all of which pivot on the sheer presence of theistic energies or, in more traditional language, of efficient grace. Platonic participation, understood as an activity in which divine efficacy 'effects' or 'affects' consciousness, was central to Barth's entire early theology: 'efficacy presupposes a qualitative homogeneity of that which effects with that which is to be effected.'[97]

Before considering how Barth might have used his theory of religion in systematic theology, two points merit comment. The revealed idea was first denied the universal validity which Kant claimed for the forms of intuition and the categories. This clearly shows the eclectic, uncritical, but consistently theological manner in which Barth's earliest writings appropriated the philosophies of Kant, Plato, and Marburg neo-Kantianism. The regulative ideas of Kant were turned into things-in-themselves, the Marburg transcendental ego into the religious consciousness permeated with supernatural energies, and though it was correctly said that Platonic ideas transcend space and time, Plato nevertheless attributed to them the universality of which they were deprived by Barth. This denial of universal validity is, I believe, a logical outcome of Barth's methodology. He, like Herrmann, credited theological conceptuality with only a relative validity, whilst simultaneously claiming absolute validity for the individual's experience of revelation. It therefore seemed logical to deny that such thoughts of faith could be justified by a less affective mode of knowledge. Additionally, moreover, since the truth of both revelatory experience and the thoughts that imperfectly reflect it depended upon the experience in question being given, and not created in the course of cognitive work, the sheer givenness of revelatory experience was afforded the status of a datum. This 'factual state of affairs', the genesis of which depended utterly upon an actual divine ingression into consciousness, became the axiom upon which all theological knowledge, ontology, and methodology were built. Any other point of departure, such as that advocated by Troeltsch or the history of religions school, was simply religiously illicit and cognitively futile. Barth, in short, first deprived philosophical terminology of its rational or metaphysical content. He next proceeded to define such terminology theologically and, having thus transformed it into a 'thought of faith', then applied his general critique of theological language. It became, therefore, not only secondary, but also distortive.

A second consideration briefly raises the question of how successfully Barth's theology of culture accommodated traditional Christian beliefs, particularly those relating to the revelation of God through the teachings, ministry, life, and sufferings of Jesus.

Precisely the same criticism could be made about Barth's earliest work which he himself later made of Schleiermacher's theology, namely that 'Jesus of Nazareth fits desperately badly into this theology of the historical "composite life" of humanity'.[98] This important issue will receive due consideration in the following section.

After his commentary on Romans, never again did Barth return to the notion of *methexis* to explicate either the nature of divine–human contact in revelatory experience or the relation between culture and the supernatural energizing power that bestowed actuality upon it and its human subjects.[99]

C. CULTURE AND THE CHRIST

The notes bequeathed us by Barth for the third chapter of his book had the near-impossible objective of making affirmations about 'religion outside culture', which he characterized, not surprisingly, as a feeling of complete dependence. This section will therefore discuss what Barth could have possibly meant by the phrase 'religion outside culture' and then consider how the final chapter might have applied the theory of religion developed throughout the book to systematic theology or *Glaubenslehre*. Finally, before turning to the fascinating topic of Barthian dialectic, some assessment of the entire project will be offered.

One of the most persistent criticisms which Barth later made of Schleiermacher—and, in criticizing Schleiermacher's theology, he was simultaneously criticizing his own early attempts at *Kultur-theologie*—was that the two foci of the theological ellipse tended to become one. This criticism implied that Schleiermacher (and his own early theology) could not effectively speak either about God or his revelation in Christ because theologies of culture such as these projected onto God fanciful anthropological and ideological concerns, as well as their own humanist preoccupations. Their deity, in other words, was simply the prevailing *Kulturbewusstsein* writ large. This criticism was most decisive for Barth's subsequent campaign against liberalism. It lies beneath his polemic against 'Cartesianism' in theology, theologies which mistakenly suppose that an *Anknüpfungspunkt* between God and the individual exists prior to the epiphany of revelation, those who suggested that response to God was a 'permanent possibility', and much else beside. As well as this methodological criticism, the chief theological objection to this style was not so much that it sanctioned the cultural status quo with the trappings of piety but, more grievously, that it compromised the sovereignty of God. God, it was argued, was so bound by cultural necessity to bestow revelation, that his sovereign freedom was impaired. God's self-revelation became so intermingled with a revelation in the human self and its culture, that the two became indistinct. Being thus bound by cultural necessities and imprisoned by his own grace, God was no longer free to be what he is *an und für sich selbst*.

It would therefore be most interesting to enquire whether these later criticisms effect Barth's earlier theology. Did it, that is, offer insufficient protection to the transcendence of God and thereby endanger divine objectivity? This question, I believe, was to have been discussed in the third and fourth chapters of Barth's *Religionsphilosophie*. The phrase 'religion outside culture' was probably calculated to stress the truly objective and supernatural character of divine ingression which constituted one pole of revelatory experience. Whatever the previous chapters had affirmed about the teleological activation of culture and humanity, the third and final chapters would endeavour to show how such benefits were 'utterly dependent upon God'. It was therefore Barth's clear intention to exclude systematically the possibility that the historical 'composite life of humanity' might be 'really after all fundamentally self-sufficient'.[100] This intention to ward off the possibility that God might simply become an anthropological datum, achieves clear expression in Barth's methodology from start to finish. The revelatory experience, from which the Christian or religious consciousness arose, was almost monotonously presented as being given or bestowed by a *Lebensmacht* 'from the outside'. Even the philosopher of religion commenced his reflections with the datum or 'raw material' of the religious consciousness, a central component of which was its dependence upon supernatural resources. I have no desire to labour this point. It was essential to his early theology informing, for example, his criticisms of synergism, Cohen, Natorp, the supporters of theological metaphysics like Wobbermin and Lüdemann, and not least the vitriolic censures of Troeltsch.

A more profitable question is whether there was a conflict between Barth's intention and the manner of its execution. Did the way in which he wrote about supernatural revelation somehow obscure the 'objectivity' of God and was that objectivity veiled, if not assimilated, by the *Universum* of human culture? Here it should be recalled how Barth's stress on divine actualism, his dependence upon the tradition of spiritual inwardness, and his general critique of theological and metaphysical language, made it most difficult to apply what neo-Kantians called 'objectifying' statements to God. His exclusively actualist or soteriological approach to revelation, moreover, accepted Schleiermacher's notion that theology could speak validly about God only inasmuch as its affirmations were about how God 'effected' or 'affected' human consciousness and its apprehension of the world. Unlike the doctrine of revelation in the trinitarian sections of the *Church Dogmatics*, such actualism systematically excluded affirmations about God *an sich*. Theological language was therefore 'somehow' related to God, but because concepts, metaphysics, or objectifying language were deemed secondary and distortive, no precise account of religious language was needed or required. Barth's single-minded determination to stress the utter gratuité, givenness, and actuality of divine grace did not however lead to mystical rapture, but, like the German mystics Susa and Eckhardt, veered off in the direction of activity. His vision of God, the *Lebensmacht*, inspired a response more like Martha's than Mary's.

A particularly acute example of the way in which Barth's focus on the sheer actualism of God effected theological language is afforded by his earliest Christology. The early Barth made some very disparaging remarks about the metaphysical Christology of Athanasius and its static concept of nature. No greater welcome, however, greeted the more 'scientific' and less dogmatic accounts of Jesus offered, for example, by Schweitzer, Weiss, and the history of religions school. His doctrinal discussion of Christology in 'Christian Faith and History' was completely functional with three seemingly paradoxical statements highlighting the actuality of God in Christian experience. The Christian consciousness, claimed Barth, experiences a Christ active in it who bestows life, but also experiences this beneficial presence as coming 'from without'. In actual faith experience, of course, the two coincide: the outer and inner Christ are 'one and the same'. Barth's resolute focus on the work of Christ was so intense, moreover, that it prompted him to deny any meaning to affirmations about Christ *an sich*.[101] The purpose of these remarks is not just to indicate how such doctrinal innovation falls short of Nicene orthodoxy, but rather to show how Barth's actualism, in which act and function almost entirely usurp being and presence, made it impossible for him to speak about God or divine activity in which the Marburgers called objectifying language. If I am not very much mistaken, Rudolf Bultmann, another theologian from Marburg, likewise laboured under the limitations and constraints imposed by this completely functionalist approach to theological language.

This leads conveniently once more to the problem of anthropological projection which seems to have exercised Barth's mind so much in later years. The ugly word *ideenprojicierend* is in fact found in Barth's notes and he had no qualms whatsoever about using it. Since his entire philosophical investigation of religion was calculated not only to explicate the positive, necessary, and indispensable relation between religion and culture, but equally to affirm the irreducibility and *sui generis* nature of religion, he was quite confident that revelatory experience was no cognitive generation created by human work. Even more surprisingly, Barth could make positive use of the word 'projection' because it was the very nature of divine energy to actualize consciousness by stimulating knowing, willing, and feeling. That the projections, actualizations, or objectifications of culture might reflect something of divine *Wirklichkeit* in humanity was only to be expected and accounted a positive gain. Human beings, therefore, produce science and technology, learn to order their social and political existence with equity, and create sublime art, rapturous music, or profound poetry, precisely because all these truths and the values embodied in them, arise from a divine energy which forever inspires human creativity. Wherever truth, beauty, and goodness are encountered, they are inevitably radiant with divine grace. When the young Barth had occasion to speak about Feuerbach he argued that this sort of vision was untouched by his facile naturalizing criticisms.[102]

Problems with the objectivity theological language was the price demanded by Barth's approach. In his early theology religious language is almost entirely metaphorical or, using his own word, *Symbolbildung*. The word 'almost' is used intentionally, because the 'raw material', from which all theologizing and religious thought arises, was the believer's personal experience of revelation in which he knew himself to be related to God. This sort of objectivity, religious dogma, or, if you will, axiom, is the one thing needful in Barth's earliest writings. It is present whenever reference is made to the Christian consciousness which, one has to say, like Herrmann's 'fact of Christ', appears monotonously throughout. The traditional doctrinal, biblical, and dogmatic conceptuality of Protestant Christianity was by no means jettisoned, but interpreted as an intricate symbolic system. The theologian imaginatively orchestrated this vast array of themes, whilst being careful not to obscure its essential leitmotif, namely the relatedness of God to the individual and his culture in revelatory immediacy. Had Barth written the final chapter of his *Religionsphilosophie*, one would therefore expect the resulting *Glaubenslehre* to have resembled some romantic symphony, in which one theme is heard through a startling variety of textures, resonances, and harmonies.

When this exposition of Barth's fragmentary *Religionsphilosophie* began, it was suggested that its objective was to arrive at a theory of religion and, having achieved that, to press on with a critically informed overview of the Christian faith, both of which would be singularly useful preliminaries to writing a *Glaubenslehre* or systematic theology. The question therefore arises how Barth would have related the two exercises. It is no difficult undertaking to suggest how this might have been achieved because something very similar was accomplished in the article about Christian faith and history.

The transition from *Religionsphilosophie* to *Glaubenslehre* simply centred on the concept of revelation. A philosophical study of religion in general resulted in a revelation of God as the operative *Woher*, from whence arises awareness of divine immanence in consciousness. In the Christian religion, by contrast, the 'divine causality' present and efficacious in revelation is filtered through those benefits of Christ which were especially valued by the neo-Protestant tradition to which Barth belonged. The energy of God in the Christian religion is therefore indissolubly bound to the experience of Christ's benefits. Just as the ingression of God's vitalist power functioned as a principle which actualized religion and culture in general, the ingression of Christ's benefits in the Christian consciousness was a principle that actualized Western culture, particularly the culture nurtured and valued by German universities such as Marburg. It was not Cohen's *Gottesidee*, but rather the Christian Logos of God that became the principle of actualization and individuation:

The religious beholding of Christ, seeing the efficacy of God in him, *is* justification; thus this intuition, and only this, is Christian faith. . . . Christ's righteousness becomes my righteousness, Christ's religion becomes my religion, He becomes me. . . . Faith evidences its historicity by exhibiting itself as a developmental process in the life of the individual . . . effective history is effected faith.[103]

It is perhaps inevitable that these reflections on culture and Christ terminate with history. Barth's projected theology of culture had the effect of turning all history into an internal history that was animated by the benefits of Christ. The outcome was that the Ideas of Plato, Kant, and Marburg neo-Kantianism were assimilated by the efficient causality of revelation through Christ. Truth, the totality of ideas, became that depth of religious awareness which the Christian experiences through revelation, and reality was the ecstatic moment of revelation when the whole *Universum* of internalized culture is experienced in its immediacy as being related to God through Christ and his benefits. The Christ proclaimed by Barth's earliest theology was not only the agency through which neo-Kantianism was to be converted to what Augustine called 'true religion', but also a reflection of the actual efficacy of God in converting culture from the time of Plato to the era of neo-Kantianism. Any weaknesses lie ultimately with the final judgement of history.

One thing which Barth's earliest theology intentionally ignored was the critical study of history, especially that being practised by theologically and critically aware scholars such as Weiss, Schweitzer, and Troeltsch. That the tradition of Western religion to which Barth himself belonged might unexpectedly discover a rather disturbing Christ, one, that is, who was actual in Jesus of Nazareth and who every now and again became the disturber, usurper, and judge of Western culture, was a possibility studiously avoided. It was through the hideousness and banality of a world war that Christ rendered untenable the other, more accommodating, Christ.

The theme of acculturation, its benefits and necessary sacrifices, together with the equally perennial theme of the role performed by God or the gods in this process, have marked both sacred and secular theorizing from the Epic of Gilgamesh to Freud. They permeate Western, Semitic, and Oriental literature. To what extent the theological theories of the early Barth encapsulate a credible aetiology of this theme, the author of this book, like the petitioner of Lessing's parable, cannot say. What, however, can be offered is a contrast between the vision of the young Barth and that of Cohen. For the former the redemptive Logos incarnate in Christ was the principle of actualization responsible for whatever is true, beautiful, and good in Western culture. Indeed it is probaly the case for this philosopher that Western culture would not exist were it not for the benefits of Christ. Cohen, by contrast, though equally concerned to relate whatever is true, beautiful, and good in human culture to God, adopted a rather different approach. His most profound conviction about culture and reality was that 'the nearness to God is my good'. In a similar fashion Moses, after outrageously requesting knowledge of God's inner being, was instead promised a vision of God's activity in the world and its history: 'Behold, there is a place by Me . . . but My face shall not be seen.' To those who were perplexed about how philosophy and religion or culture and faith should relate to each other, Maimonides explained that the 'place' promised by God in Exodus meant 'a certain degree of contemplation and intellectual intuition (not of ocular inspection), in addition to its literal meaning "place"—viz., the mountain which was pointed out to Moses for seclusion and for the attainment of perfection'.[104]

It is from these somewhat demanding intuitions that we turn to the less taxing issue of Barth's dialectic.

III. DIALECTIC

One sure generalization about the history of philosophy is that dialectic has meant many things. A review of the history of this word from its earliest use, when it simply meant the art of debate, to the more intricate dialectics of Absolute Idealism and dialectical materialism, would raise legitimate doubts whether any one definition of the term could possibly do justice to the varied dialectical types. There may, however, be one feature which most dialectical styles have in common and this centres on their intention to solve riddles. These may be of a purely formal and conceptual sort, but they could equally be riddles of ontology. The resolution of the first order more formal and conceptual riddles need not necessarily lead to a resolution of the second order ontological problems, yet a persistent strain in the history of philosophy has affirmed this to be the case. Socratic dialectic, for example, seems to have involved a simple rule of inference: if p implies not p, then not p is true (that is, p is false). This simple rule of inference was brought to bear on summary definitions or unexamined beliefs, primarily concerned with morality. With Plato's *Republic*, however, dialectic, which is the culmination of philosophical training, now leads to knowledge of the unchanging essence of things and terminates in knowledge of the supreme form of the Good. Such knowledge offers an ontological panorama, though it still remains far from clear how ideal forms relate to particulars and whether the resulting ontological riddle is at all resolved conceptually. If, however, the *Seventh Epistle* offers authentic evidence for Plato's views, it would seem that his deepest and most cherished philosophical conviction, which was, of course, the theory of forms, could not find adequate expression because of the weaknesses and limitations of language. It is acquired only through illumination, though intellectual training and asceticism were indispensable preliminaries. The riddles of ontology were, it would seem, resolved experientially by the epiphany of illumination, which was as real and as indescribale as Schleiermacher's moment when feeling and intuition were immediately present and unfragmented by conceptual reflection.

There is a second feature of much dialectic which, though less universal than the first, nevertheless deserves attention. Dialectic was often motivated by soteriological concerns and it is here that the words of Kolakowski are particularly revealing:

If the aspiration of philosophy was and is to comprehend intellectually the whole of Being its initial stimulus came from awareness of human imperfection . . . Philosophical interest centred on the limitations and misery of the human condition—not in its obvious, tangible, and remediable forms, but the fundamental impoverishment which cannot be cured by technical devices and which, when once apprehended, was felt to be the cause of man's more obvious, empirical deficiencies, the latter being secondary phenomena. The fundamental, innate deficiency was given various names: medieval Christian philosophy spoke of the 'contingency' of human existence, as of all other created being.[105]

Here ontological problematic was to the fore. The tensions which were perceived to exist between finitude and the aspiration, if not religious hope, for some answer, healing, or remedy to the impoverishment of contingency, could perhaps be resolved through a philosophical or rational response to finite reality. The theme of ontology consequently merged with that of theodicy which, as Weber argued, is essential to any soteriological view of the world.[106] In these forms of dialectic the tension between contingency and true being parallels another ancient philosophical dilemma: the relation between parts and whole. Should, perhaps, contingency be viewed from the perspective of the whole? How precisely do the imperfections of existence relate to the rationale of reality? How, furthermore, is such rationale to be discovered? This set of questions, which may broadly be termed soteriological, informed much dialectic and answers were found in the creating and redeeming God of Christianity, Plotinus' one, mystical deification, deity as the coincidence of opposites, the Absolute Spirit's trajectory through consciousness, and so forth.

A further feature characterizing some, though not all dialectical approaches to reality, developed from the second dialectical style. The impetus that necessitated a leap from soteriological reflection upon contingency to a unified ontological vision was sometimes intensified. No longer did tension exist between parts and whole, contingency and true being, deficiency and healing, but opposition, if not contradiction. Along with this radicalization there sometimes arose an intensification of oppositions. Not only did opposition and contradiction between parts and the whole exist, but the parts themselves came to be regarded as recalcitrant, antagonistic, and contradictory. A resolution to this extreme dissonance was called for, and in the writings of Causanus it was the deity that resolved the riddle of oppositions according to which this philosopher classified existence:

I call this the Greatest Something, beyond which there can be nothing greater. This surpassing abundance belongs to One alone. The greatest coincides with unity, which is also entity. If this unity is absolute—without qualification and limitation—then it is clear that nothing can be opposed to it. The Absolute, therefore, is the absolute unity of all things and everything exists in it . . . But since nothing is opposed to it, it immediately coincides with the least and therefore exists in all. Since it is absolute, it is also in actuality every possible being, for all derive from it and it derives nothing from things.[107]

Along with these two dialectical and more speculative styles there came into being a curious form of conceptual argumentation. The desired resolution of opposites or, alternatively, the eschatological satisfaction of soteriological yearnings, was somehow reflected in the sequence of argumentation. There is a curious back and forth, a hither and thither, between contingency and real being, impoverishment and fulness, the parts and the whole that the particular philosophy was attempting to uncover. To this extent, the very philosophical portrayal of reality was felt to recapitulate or re-present in conceptual terms what was hoped to be happening *in re*.

When it is suggested that dialectic is present in Barth's early theory of religion, it is not being proposed that his dialectical *Denkform* was influenced by one particular philosopher. It is rather the case that the two sets of problems which occupied his attention the most—the relation between revelation and individuals and the relation between religion and culture—lent themselves to a dialectical approach. Because these two problems already enjoyed a venerable history in both theology and philosophy long before Barth was exercised by them, it should not be surprising to learn that he took over various traditional motifs when they suited his purposes. This final section argues that before the birth of what came to be called dialectical theology, Barth already employed two forms of dialectic. One was traditional, the other less traditional and boldly speculative.[108]

The first pattern of dialectic has systematic connections with both Barth's relationism and his appropriation of the Augustinian tradition through reading the Reformers and also, to a lesser extent, Schleiermacher. It resembles the 'more inward way' recommended by Augustine in the *Confessions*, *De Trinitate*, and many other writings, which involved an introspective exploration in order to discover the God within. This interior quest, of course, was not value free, but governed a priori by faith in reason, which Augustine defined theologically, and by the principle that 'the truth which has not yet become luminous to our understanding be still held fast by faith'.[109] The turn inwards resulted in the perception of human beings as transient, finite, limited, and weak, but also in awareness of God, the truth, who is infinite, eternal, impassible, and strong to save. The tension between these perceptions was resolved both theologically and experientially. On the one hand, there was the doctrine of grace and, on the other, the vision of 'that which truly is'. In the rapture of vision the soul is no longer in the exile of finitude and corruption, but by divine favour elevated to her homeland to be where her Creator is.

This Augustinian tradition which is, as Kolakowski correctly maintains, a species of dialectic, informed the writings of Calvin, Melanchthon, and Luther. There was with these, however, a new emphasis, for grace became almost exclusively related to the benefits bestowed upon the elect by the crucified and reconciling Christ.[110] Although Calvin could still affirm with Augustine that 'Nearly all the wisdom we possess, that is to say, true and sound wisdom, consists of two parts: the knowledge of God and of ourselves' he was more emphatic in his insistence that 'God would have remained hidden afar off if Christ's splendour had not beamed upon us. ... We obtain salvation ... when we know that God is our merciful father, because of the reconciliation effected through Christ (2 Cor. 5: 18–19), and that Christ has been given to us as righteousness, sanctification, and life.'[111]

The appeal to Melanchthon's soteriological principle, which distinguishes the writings of Ritschl, Herrmann, and the early Barth, is obviously indebted to the Augustinian dialectic of inwardness and presence. This approach, it must be acknowledged, held an obvious attractiveness for theologians of the late nineteenth and early twentieth centuries. They were painfully aware that rational proofs for divine existence were not only philosophically suspect, but unable to deliver the theistic goods a theologian might expect from them. Their problems were compounded because theistic metaphysics was out of vogue and in any case seemed an extremely hazardous venture offering very mixed blessings. Added to this was their awareness that philosophy— even idealism—increasingly regarded itself as an autonomous discipline in no way dependent upon or answerable to theology and religion. Those theologians who did not explore the possibility of a truly dialogical theory of religion to replace the more traditional metaphysical preamble to theology, began instead to develop theologies appealing to personal religion, feeling, affection, will, the Christian consciousness, morality, *Leben*, and, in the

twentieth century, existence. Barth's approval of religious individualism and his apologetic welcome of *Autonomie* are to be seen
against this background.

If there is anything novel here, it lies in the manner with which
our theologians appropriated the tradition. It was introduced into
the methodological and epistemological debates which were so
important to the then modern theology, but sadly, and despite the
effort to crown the Reformation with laurels that belonged to
Kant, the appeal to the experienced benefits of Christ was an
impossible partner for either Kantianism or Marburg philosophy.
With Herrmann and the young Karl Barth, the category of
Offenbarung was reserved solely for this 'inner method'. In
attempting to argue for the irreducibility and integrity of theological terminology, they pointed to revelation as the only act of
God which could be spoken about and, simultaneously, as a real
experience for individual consciousness. Both were deemed facets
of one real event—or, in Whiteheadian language, of an actual
occasion—which, in the opinion of these theologians, gave
sufficient justification for speaking about the *Wirklichkeit* of God.
Indeed, the experience itself was regarded as self-authenticating
and altogether 'heterogeneous' to anything that philosophy,
reason, and history might discover. This implied that theology,
the object of which for the early Barth was religion, could never
leave the solid rock of faith experience, that is, the Christian
consciousness and its relational contents. If theology was a
science, it was a science *autopistia*, a science of pure faith. In
Barth's earliest writings the Christian consciousness was aware of
its relationship to the divine power that animated and sustained
it. He thought a homogeneity existed between that which effects
and that which is effected, assuming thereby that a synthesis of
divine and human existed in consciousness. It was a synthesis
which was a-temporal, but also experienced. When problems of
history or Christology were encountered, Barth would do little
more than equate God in history with God in consciousness,
attributing the immediate awareness of its 'historic' life to the felt
benefits of Christ. Several texts have already been cited to
illustrate this, but there is an additional one. It is taken from
Belief in a Personal God and is offered as a conclusive argument
against Feuerbach's reduction of religion to anthropological
projection:

A thought of God which is held to come into existence through the projection of human self-consciousness into a transcendent dimension cannot in any way attain the reality of God—much less exhaustively depict this reality. The thought of God authentic to religion cannot be projected from ourselves, but only the reflection of a fact which is created in us. This fact is the *life from God* which is bestowed upon us through our *connection with history*. This inner state of being conditioned through history is religious *experience*. In it we have God and because of it we are able to speak of God.[112]

The second form of dialectic found in Barth's early work comes clearly into view when a number of conceptual pairs are presented as polar opposites. In *Belief in a Personal God*, for example, Barth distinguishes between two approaches to personality, the first of which is transcendental and critical, undertaken by the philosophical disciplines of logic and ethics, the second of which is more empirical and uses the methods of psychology. Neither approach, however, adequately grasps the nature of personality. With the methods of ethics and logic, 'when we view this unity of thinking and willing in a thinking and willing subject from the *transcendental* side of its character, we arrive at the notion of a totality, of an entity unlimited in its functions; for thinking and willing, viewed transcendentally, have their limit only in an ideal that lies in infinity'. With the psychological or empirical approach, by contrast, 'there inevitably arises the notion of something unique, particular, and limited; of an entity with a limited and circumscribed mental capacity'. Barth adds that as far as these approaches to the problem of personality go, 'it is obvious that both are true and not true, according to the sense in which the concept of personality is used'. Neither idealism nor psychology, it is asserted, could arrive at the most blatantly obvious of facts: 'the thought of personality which, for us, is the most certain thing that is known, namely that *I* think and will, that *I* am spirit'.

There follows this most intriguing suggestion about personality: 'When we attempt to penetrate deeper into its nature we must hold firmly before our eyes the authentic place for the thought of personality, which is in the empty space between logic and ethics and psychology . . .'[113] From the transcendental method of idealism Barth gains a concept of personality as *Geistsein*, whilst from psychology he arrives at the notion of personality as *Individualität*. What deserves attention is not so much the meaning which may be attached to this notion of personality, but rather the method employed; for by the use of dialectic Barth resolves the two apparently irreconcilable methods and their contrary perceptions of personality. When the spiritual and individual–psychological dimensions of personality are united in experiential immediacy:

> We stand before the substratum of the concept of personality, the transcendental and psychological character of which we have not become familiar with. We thus stand before the *I*. Taken by itself this concept can signify nothing other than the pure subjectivity of which we are immediately aware and which we must conceive, both transcendentally and psychologically, as the presupposition of these two activities of consciousness. In the pure subjectivity of the immediately experienced I, both sides attain the unity of *personality*: spiritual being as the act of consciousness and individuality as the particular form of this action. The concept of personality signifies the unity of thinking and willing in an individual. Both are included in an individual. The statement which best expresses this reads: I *think* and *will*, and *I* think and will. In the unity of both statements the concept of personality stands exactly at the limit of the transcendental and psychological forms of investigation.[114]

The two aspects of personality are resolved not so much conceptually, as experientially, for it is claimed that spirit and individuality are united in actual experience. It is argued, furthermore, that such an immediate awareness of personality has to be presupposed by the two methods of investigation.

These passages have been quoted at some length not to illustrate with yet more examples Barth's early fascination with personality and religious individualism, but rather to introduce the second form of dialectic found in his earliest writings. Examples could be multiplied. In 'Christian Faith and History', for example, there is the systematic sequence of *Anschauung*, *fides*, *Erleben*, and the receptive mode of religious consciousness (*das Aufnehmen einer Wirksamkeit ins Bewusstsein*), paralleled by the sequence *Gefühl*, *justificatio*, *Leben*, and the spontaneous mode of religious awareness (*das durch diese Wirksamkeit im Bewusstsein Gewirkte*).[115] In the very same writing, moreover, there are other formulations of what seem to be contrary pairs—faith and history, active and passive, *Erhebung* and *Einsenkung*, along with the contrast between a psychological–philosophical approach to religion and a dogmatic presentation of the Christian religion. Yet another ubiquitous pair in this and other writings is the contrast between the law-structured scientific functions of consciousness and first-person awareness of reality which has an autonomous centred self as agent and recipient of experience. A particularly remarkable contrast occurs in the diagrammatic system of truth with God and individual as polar opposites.[116] From the side of God descends the supernatural power of revelation which actualizes possibilities for culture and individuates personal life. Upwards, from the individual, there ascends a religious response and the actualized functions of *Kulturbewusstsein* in logic, ethics, and aesthetics. At the centre there is a strange no man's land, the sphere of synthesis represented by arrows, dots, and the 'B' sign. The entire diagram was calculated to illustrate the contention that two seemingly opposed problems, the *Gottesproblem* and the *Vernunftproblem*, are reciprocally related totalities. The region in between, the area of synthesis, relatedness, and participation was particularly important to Barth. It was the moment when a *Universum* was present to resolve all tensions not so much conceptually, as experientially.

It is evident that this employment of dual formulations profoundly effects the presentation of Barthian arguments. In one of his earliest writings, for instance, Barth detected a certain tension between the application of historical criticism, which results in relativism, and the value judgement of faith, which was believed to mitigate relativism by claiming absolute significance for a particular historical event. The tension was resolved in the following manner:

The coexistence of both becomes possible and true through the identity of the subject who adopts the necessarily relativizing scientific approach to history with the living individual of religion. The individual elevates from the flux of history that absolute norm which becomes conquest and redemption for his life . . . Only in the 'affection' of this inner experience, however, lies that which is normative, objective, and eternal.[117]

The point of interest here is the conviction that these antagonistic and contrary phenomena acquire *Einheit* through an *Identität* which lies in the experience of the subject.

It is not only the use of dual classifications that is important, but their dialectical resolution. This is not a dialectic of the Hegelian variety, in which the power of the negative cancels out a previous argument, proposition, relationship, or historical moment, only to raise the *Sache* onto a higher level and so on, until the advent of absolute knowledge; it is, rather, a dialectic of intuited identity. The desired resolution of contraries is not attained through reasoning, but experience by the subject in immediate awareness of that great experiential synthesis or *Universum* which precedes the bifurcation of reality that inevitably results from reflective thought. After Kant, idealism was much occupied with the quest for a transcendental ground upon which all being and truth was believed to rest. Varying answers were given to this quest for a first principle or ultimate foundation with the *Ich*, *Natur*, or Absolute Mentality being leading candidates. The later idealism of the Marburg School developed a purely methodological ground, namely the ideal coincidence of thinking and being in the transcendental *Kulturbewusstsein*. This second form of dialectic in Barth's writings would seem to owe little to Fichte, Schelling, or Hegel; its inspiration came from Schleiermacher.

Although Schleiermacher is read, if not appreciated, in Britain, it is usually the Schleiermacher of the *Reden* and *Glaubenslehre* who claims most attention. All too often the more technical and very difficult *Dialektik* is ignored. R. R. Niebuhr, who was certainly acquainted with this work, said with much justification, 'it is essential to Schleiermacher's position to affirm that all rational activity, both knowing and doing, is an expression of the absolute ground of consciousness, and the *Dialektik* devotes considerable attention to the postulation—as over against a demonstration—of such a ground'.[118] Schleiermacher regarded dialectic as a prolegomenon to philosophy as systematic knowledge and it was absolutely crucial on two accounts. Philosophy, being systematic knowledge, had the task of interrelating the varied forms of knowledge—empirical, aesthetic, religious, and moral; dialectic therefore seemed indispensable for attaining the ideal of an integrated account of human knowledge. Secondly, moreover, because the point of identity Schleiermacher sought—the identity of knowledge and ethics with being—could not be directly known, dialectic was best suited to intimate where a point of identity was most likely to be discovered. The transcendental ground of being and knowledge, which his system aspired to intimate, never manifests itself to thought as absolute knowledge, but it was deemed necessary none the less to *presuppose* such a foundation, since without it there would be no system and no reality. The postulation of such a transcendental foundation was therefore thought to be epistemologically necessary, but as well as being the epistemological ground of knowing and willing it functioned ontologically, by representing an identity of thinking and being, willing and being, and, finally, the ideal and the real.

The certainty that such a transcendental ground existed, however, came to consciousness by means other than conceptual thought. Through dialectic one may only intimate indirectly the supreme something upon which knowledge, reality, truth, and life rest, but religious awareness was affirmed to have a particular rapport with the transcendental ground of reality. Proposition 215 of the *Dialektik* maintains: 'Accordingly we now also have the transcendental ground only in the relative identity of thinking and willing, namely in feeling.'[119] The comments on this proposition are most important for our theme:

Since the transcendental ground relates to both thinking and willing, it must be posited for both alike. However we have no other identity of both than feeling, which is the last end of willing and the first cause of thinking; but it is always a relative identity—first close to one, and then to the other. We may say that with our consciousness there is also given us the awareness of God as a component element of our self-consciousness, as well as of our consciousness of external things.[120]

The relative identity of knowing and willing, their transcendental ground, is something felt and, furthermore, it is important to mark the word 'relative' which qualifies identity. *Gefühl* is a philosophical concept and as such issues from reflective thought. The absolute identity, or the transcendental ground of reality in general, transcends even its philosophical presentation through the concept of feeling. Hence the philosopher, in order to intimate something about this, is forced to use dialectic:

thought and will on the one side and immediate self-consciousness on the other are dialectically related. Neither is in principle nearer to the transcendental ground. Both are needed to execute that final synthesis which lies beyond both and beyond expression, as the fulness of eternity present to the inwardness of temporal being.[121]

Whatever might be said regarding his dialectic and transcendental ground, it is clear from Schleiermacher's work that it was not the *concept* of God, but rather the God experienced by self-consciousness who was the transcendental ground or ultimate point of identity to which philosophy imperfectly aspires.

The curious, strained, and yet clear blending of epistemology and ontology with religion is particularly clear in proposition 216: 'We know about the being of God only in ourselves and in things. In no way do we know a being of God outside the world or a being of God in itself.'[122] The comments begin with these bold words:

The being of the ideas in us is a being of God in us, not inasmuch as they fill a moment of consciousness as definite conceptions, but in so far as they express in everyone in exactly the same manner the essence of being and, consequently, the being of God in human nature. In their certitude they express the identity of the Ideal and the Real which is posited in us as neither something singular nor yet as genus. Thus even the being of conscience within us is a being of God.[123]

Here there is not only religion and epistemology but also ontology. God's being does not lie outside the world, neither is it known as it might be in and for itself. God is rather present and effective as the ground of human consciousness in its varied forms: 'Hence God—since he is the ruling unity of both elements in the fluctuations of consciousness—is given to us as a constituent element of our nature. The innate being of God in us forms our true nature, for without ideas and without moral sentiment we would degenerate to the bestial.'[124] Consciousness, therefore, is not enclosed within itself nor pathologically preoccupied with awareness of its God; it is open to a universal totality and, for this reason, Schleiermacher contends that 'both ideas—God and the world—are correlates'.[125] The commentary continues:

But they are not identical. For in thought divinity is posited as unity without plurality, but the world as plurality without unity; the world fills both space and time, God is spaceless and timeless; the world is the totality of opposites, the divinity is the negation of all opposites. One cannot be conceived without the other. The world cannot be thought about without God . . . and also God cannot be thought about without the world.[126]

The three elements involved in Schleiermacherian dialectic—the epistemological requirement of transcendental ground, the religious motif of a God active, innate, and present with consciousness, and, thirdly, the ontological thesis that contemplates an ultimate totality of reality involving God and the world—should help to explain that joyous passage of the *Reden* which Barth always regarded as one of the most important passages in the entire opus of Schleiermacher. In that sublime moment when the polarities of intuition and feeling are not sundered by conceptual reflection, there is awareness of an infinite world.[127]

This form of dialectic, which may be termed a dialectic of the transcendental ground or a dialectic of relative identity, obviously pervades the earliest writings of Karl Barth. It might be surprising to hear that Barth's dialectical *Denkform*, certainly as far as the early writings go, was more influenced by Schleiermacher than by Hegel. All the polarities encountered in them (for example, between faith and history, transcendental and psychological methods, faith and thoughts of faith, science and actual life) are all resolved through dialectic in a transcendental ground. It is a ground, however, that is experienced and felt in consciousness— especially the religious consciousness. Barth's embryonic system of *Religonsphilosophie* saw in such experience, which was not amenable to any form of direct communication but only to indirect intimation through reflective thought and concepts, the dynamic, vitalist, and actualizing force of religion, *die Realitätsbeziehung* in short. It is then that one participates in a power which connects the various 'directions' of consciousness with a totality under God, not conceptually, but experientially and vitally.

The Marburg philosophy also represented a moment in the dialectical presentation of reality. The transcendental ground upon which it rested, the ideal identity between thinking and being in the *Ursprung* of pure thought, together with its theory of generation, according to which being is ceaselessly generated from the thought-posited possibilities of consciousness, is related, by Barth's own form of dialectic, to another, higher, more religious transcendental ground.

Barth's early writing was critical of the separation of *Glauben* and *Wissen* which he detected in Ritschl's writings. Herrmann's 'epistemological dualism' intensified this separation and, moreover, its precariousness was being mercilessly criticized by Troeltsch. Barth aspired to overcome such dualism with his dialectic of a transcendental ground. There could be no absolute antagonism betwixt religion and scientific knowledge, for in the final analysis both rested upon the same transcendental ground.

That ground itself, however, could only be experienced and not justified or demonstrated. It *had* to be presupposed as the ground of cognition and being, as well as of idealism and realism, but only in religious intuition and feeling did it reveal itself to consciousness.

It should be noted that the two forms of dialectic—the traditional dialectic of Christian humanism and the more speculative dialectic of the transcendental ground—could be fused together because Barth defined his transcendental ground theologically. The supreme *Anknüpfungspunkt* of both was the Christian consciousness. Since the second, more speculative transcendental ground was held to be religious in character, it seemed compatible with the first. The transcendental ground of Barth's dialectic, therefore, became defined by the relationist stance which characterized his neo-Reformation appropriation of Augustine. Everything achieved synthesis, not conceptually, but experientially in that great organ of synthesis, the Christian consciousness.

The tension between realism and idealism has been said to mark acutely Barth's earliest writings; it was also suggested that his entire epistemology depended upon a realist appreciation of divine–human relatedness which was held to be actual in the Christian consciousness. This actuality was given or bestowed to human experience and the concept of revelation synthetically bound human consciousness with the Deity. Revelation, thus conceived, wrought dramatic transformations upon the functions of the Marburg *Kulturbewusstsein*. When revelation was experienced through the benefits of Christ, the formal epistemological subject of idealist philosophy experienced an individuating power that bestowed life. It was likewise this power that actualized the abstract possibilities of *Kulturbewusstsein*. By bringing the abstract, formal, and ideal categories of Marburg Kantianism into dialectical contact with real religious forces, it was hoped that the penultimate polarity of the Ideal and the Real would achieve synthesis in the consciousness of the 'religious individual'.

Would this sort of approach have become untenable even if the First World War had not intervened? An attempt at a synthesis along these lines was bound to fail. Not only was its religious realism and actualism anathema to the radical idealism of Cohen and Natorp, the whole edifice, which rested upon the self-authenticating experience of the Christian consciousness, was culturally anachronistic as well as philosophically questionable. Barth's later reading of Overbeck would have suggested that this sort of *Kulturtheologie* could be no more. Barth, in addition, attempted to synthesize too much and the tools at his disposal were unsuited to the issues he chose to address. Such intransigent problems as historical relativism, the nature of historical criticism, the relations between theology and philosophy, the place of Christ in Christian theology and, finally, the relations between God and the world of nature, society, and science, indeed needed thoughtful attention. These problems, however, could not be properly addressed without recourse to a critical analysis which was prepared to distance itself from the Christian consciousness. This Barth refused to do. Philosophical and theological problems could not be simply classed into polarities and then said to achieve satisfactory synthesis in religious experience. That was no answer, even if the questions had been taken in earnest, which one sometimes doubts. This procedure amounted to sweeping such problems under the ubiquitous and convenient covering of the Christian consciousness, which in principle was inaccessible to conceptual analysis.

It is impossible not to be astounded or even overwhelmed by the sheer conceptual complexity of Barth's early writings. Concepts from modern theology, the Reformers, Plato, Kant, Schleiermacher, Cohen, and Natorp jostle side by side and the relation between them is often far from clear. Is this simply a sign of academic immaturity, or is such conceptual elasticity an inevitable outcome of Barth's dialectical *Denkform* and his appeal to self-authenticating religious experience, the justification of which occurs on the far side of conceptual reflection? Here is a night in which all cows are black; very black indeed.

In addition to the very many philosophical criticisms that could be made of Barth's early dialectic, there is a decisive theological criticism of which Barth himself soon became aware. The constant cathexis between the divine and the human in consciousness seriously compromised the freedom and sovereignty of God. God was a prisoner of his power to save, with his revelation binding him to believers in an a-temporal and eternal relationship of effector and effected. He was no longer free to have mercy on whom he will, to have compassion on whom he will, neither was he free to harden or judge.

Are these two forms of dialectic thus abandoned in the phase of Barth's writing which is customarily called 'dialectical'? The answer is both yes and no. Yes, because Barth utterly, completely, and irreversibly forsook his relationist approach to revelation. Once this went there was no eternal locus of synthesis in consciousness, for even the most religious consciousness was deprived of its 'permanent possibility' for receiving revelation. Divine–human relatedness, religion and culture, faith and thoughts of faith, reason and religion, theology and philosophy— all these now lacked an *Anknüpfungspunkt* in the religious consciousness.

No, because the desire for a transcendental ground, one which had theological, epistemological, and ontological significance, was still thought to be the indispensable presupposition of faith, theology, philosophy, and reality. No longer, however, was it located in religious *Bewusstsein* and *gegeben* in revelatory experience along with that consciousness. The great principle of origin, the epistemological *Ursprung* of knowledge and the ontological foundation of worldly reality, excluding, of course, sin, was now placed beyond (*jenseits*) being and becoming, beyond even consciousness and, ultimately, all that is involved in the great antitheses of sin and time. Now the High Word of God himself could alone give knowledge of the Divine Order and did so in the form of a revelatory address which provoked a crisis and forgave sins. No longer did one stand in the midst of the thing-in-itself, once addressed and summoned by the Word, rather one stood 'inside' the knowledge of God and of the last things. Such a happening was held to be a real and miraculous revelation which lifted one into that strange new world to which the Bible testifies. Dialectic, with its no and yes, could not call this event into being: that was God's *Sache*, dependent upon his sovereign grace and mercy. All the theologian could do was to employ dialectic as a prolegomenon to the apocalypse of revelation. Dialectic, to use a familiar Barthian image, was like the finger of John the Baptist which, in Grünewald's painting, points to the Crucified. The problem of personality, which fascinated Barth so much in his earliest writings, is still present. No longer, however, is the *principium individuationis* dependent upon a vitalist power that actualizes the ideal possibilities of *Kulturbewusstsein*. The subject is much more born *anothen* and, through such birth, becomes not so much a citizen who participates vigorously in the cultural and social life of this world, as a subject of God's eschatological kingdom.[128]

NOTES

1. E. Busch, *Karl Barth* (SCM, 1976), 54.
2. *GUG*, 57.
3. Ibid. 58.
4. Note Ritschl's telling words 'God or Christ' on p. 130. Herrmann is also on record as having said 'Gott ist Jesus'; see P. Fischer-Appelt's introduction to Herrmann's *Schriften*, p. xxxiii.
5. *Das Wesen des Christentums* (J. C. Heinrich, 1900).
6. See pp. 000 ff.
7. *GUG*, 53.
8. Ibid. 55.
9. Ibid. 4.
10. See p. 204.
11. *GUG*, 5. Although Barth's statements about psychology reflect the confusions and uncertainties about psychology that clouded the writings of the Marburg philosophers, in no way did he disparage psychological investigations of religion at this stage of his career. In *BPG* Barth called psychology an empirical discipline, and contrasted it to the transcendental disciplines of logic and ethics. His fragment on *Religionsphilosophie* interestingly raised the possibility that a 'transcendental psychology' might appropriately portray individual experience. In this psychological discussion of faith and history, Barth endeavours to describe the experiential side of the *Glaubensvorgang*, but as the quotation shows there is no disengaged phenomenological seeing, since this psychological discussion is already determined by both his own theology and the theories of Schleiermacher.
12. *GUG*, 6. *Schlechthinige Zielstrebigkeit* is sometimes translated 'absolute teleology', but 'striving towards a goal' perhaps conveys Schleiermacher's meaning better.
13. *GUG*, 59.
14. This word, probably a neologism coined by Barth, is difficult to translate, but any rendering should do justice to the productive force of the suffix. H. Frei's thesis ('The Doctrine of Revelation in the Thought of Karl Barth, 1909–1922' [Ph.D. thesis, University of Yale, 1956], 37), 'reality relatedness', and the translation in

Marquardt's 'Socialism in the Theology of Karl Barth' in G. Hunsinger (ed.), *Karl Barth and Radical Politics* (Westminster Press, 1976), 70, 'connection to reality', do not adequately convey the dynamic and productive nuances of the word. For further exegesis of this term see pp. 256 ff.

15. *GUG*, 6.
16. Ibid.
17. Ibid. 6–7.
18. The phrase is not Barth's, but Rahner's. For a critique of transcendentalism in Rahner's theory of faith see J. B. Metz, 'An Identity Crisis in Christianity? Transcendental and Political Responses', in W. J. Kelly (ed.), *Theology and Discovery: Essays in Honor of Karl Rahner* (Marquette University Press, 1980).
19. *GUG*, 7. God's eternity consequently becomes *geschichtlich* in the moment of faith.
20. For Barth the ideal order of culture and morality acquires concreteness and historicity, not primarily through praxis or political activity, but through the energizing power of religion. This is in marked contrast to Cohen, for whom the ideal ordering of social relations is realized by an active moral striving that furthers a teleological correlation between the 'I' of the individual and the 'Thou's of neighbour, society, and state.
21. *GUG*, 7.
22. *GUG*, 7–8. 2 Cor. 5: 16 received much scholarly attention from history of religions analyses of Paul's Christ. Barth was obviously aware of the debate. See e.g. W. Wrede's 'Paulus', *Religionsgeschichtliche Volksbücher*, 1 (1905), 5–6, A. Jülicher 'Paulus und Jesus' (ibid. 1 [1907] 14), and J. Weiss, *Paul and Jesus* (Harper, 1909).
23. Ibid. 8.
24. Ibid. 12–13.
25. Ibid. 17–18.
26. See pp. 240 ff.
27. *GUG*, 50.
28. Ibid.
29. Ibid.
30. Ibid.
31. For Barth's comparison of *die Realitätsbeziehung* with Platonic Ideas and his interpretation of Plato's parable see pp. 259 ff. and 272 ff.
32. *GUG*, 50–1.
33. *Reden*, 47–8.
34. *GUG*, 51.
35. See pp. 179 ff.
36. See *Schleiermacher III*, 452: 'Action and reaction, object and subject, outer and inner, the *effect* of the whole and *openness* towards that

effect: both meeting as a singular occurrence [*Indifferenzpunkt*] representing the whole [*das Universum*], which is made possible through the mystical inclination of the human soul.'

37. *GUG*, 51.
38. Ibid. 52.
39. Ibid. 52–3.
40. Ibid.
41. Ibid. 54–5.
42. Ibid. 59. In order to understand Barth's Christology, it is necessary to bear in mind the following equations and correlation which are advanced in the essay:

    1. First equation: *Anschauung* = *fides* = *Erleben* = a receptive (objective) moment of consciousness (*das Aufnehmen einer Wirksamkeit ins Bewusstsein*).

    2. Second equation: *Gefühl* = *justificatio* = *Leben* = a spontaneous (subjective) moment of consciousness (*das durch diese Wirksamkeit im Bewusstsein Gewirkte*).

    3. Correlation: in an actualized 'Christian consciousness' there is an experiential moment when 1 and 2 are undivided. This is the infinite world or *Universum* of Schleiermacher.
To anticipate Barth's dogmatic discussion, the external Christ corresponds to 1, the internal Christ to 2. The existence of the actual 'Christian consciousness', however, depends upon both having been experienced and posited. Since the two correlate in one actual experience and momentum (3), the distinction between them is only conceptual and abstract. Such actualism, in which attention is focused exclusively upon the soteriological effects of revelation in Christ, explains why Barth denied knowledge of any Christ *an sich*. The fully divine Christ of Athanasius, the Hellenistic *Kurios* of Bousset, as well as the more historically conditioned reconstructions of Jesus as a religious prophet, founder, or leader, have no place in the 'actual Christian consciousness', which is aware solely of the operative Christ of justification. In more traditional dogmatic terms, it may be said that this actualism results in the person of Christ being entirely subordinate to or, better, assimilated by, the work of salvation.
43. *GUG*, 55.
44. Ibid. 58 (emphases added).
45. Ibid. 59.
46. Ibid. 64–5.
47. Ibid. 63, 66.
48. *Schleiermacher IV*, 416.
49. *GUG*, 72.

50. *Jesus' Proclamation of the Kingdom of God* (SCM, 1971), 133.
51. *Writings*, 198.
52. Quoted in W. Groll's *Ernst Troeltsch und Karl Barth: Kontinuität im Widerspruch* (Kaiser, 1976), 34.
53. *Reichsgottesarbeit*, 321.
54. See p. 62. For an excellent discussion of *Kultur* in German thought at this time, see J. P. Clayton's *The Concept of Correlation: Paul Tillich and the Possibility of a Mediating Theology* (De Gruyter, 1980).
55. *Stromateis*, i. 5, 32.
56. The notion of 'foundational theology' is close to Tracy's 'fundamental theology', the defining characteristic of which is 'a reasoned insistence on employing the approach and methods of some established academic discipline to explicate and adjudicate the truth-claims of the interpreted religious tradition and the truth-claims of the contemporary situation . . . The major discipline usually employed is . . . philosophy or the "philosophical" dimension of some other discipline.' D. Tracy, *The Analogical Imagination* (SCM, 1981), 62.
57. Troeltsch lectured on *Religionsphilosophie* in 1908, 1912, and 1915– 16. The reason his lectures were never published is likely due to the utter failure of the *Glaubenslehre* and the increasingly popular dialectical theology which had no patience with his complex epistemological musings.
58. *Kurze Darstellung*, 23.
59. Ibid. 24.
60. *Kurze Darstellung*, 33, and *Religionsphilosophie*, 1.
61. Ibid. 67. By contrast compare the lively words of *Schleiermacher IV*, 396: 'This white flag, which the theologian must carry as an apologist, means, of course, that he must, in so far as he is an apologist, as Schleiermacher yet again clearly states, take his point of departure (standpoint) above Christianity (in the logical sense of the word) in the general concept of the community of religious people or believers. As an apologist he is not a Christian theologian but a moral philosopher and philosopher of religion.'
62. *Kurze Darstellung*, 1.
63. *Religionsphilosophie*, 1.
64. Ibid. 3.
65. Ibid. 4.
66. *GUG*, 5 ff.
67. When the ideas were illicitly used the psychological idea resulted in paralogisms, cosmological ideas in antinomies, and theological ideas in erroneous ideals. See J. Bennett's exposition in *Kant's Dialectic* (Cambridge University Press, 1974).
68. For the Marburg interpretation of Plato see particularly P. Natorp's

Platons Ideenlehre and F. Rosenzweig's interesting comments in *The Star of Redemption* (Routledge & Kegan Paul, 1971), 20 ff.

69. *Religionsphilosophie*, 4.
70. *Glaubenslehre*, §3, 4.
71. *GUG*, 59.
72. *Schleiermacher IV*, 389.
73. *GUG*, 50.
74. Ibid. 50–1.
75. *Religionsphilosophie*, 5.
76. *GUG*, 15f.
77. *Glaubenslehre*, §4, 4.
78. Ibid.
79. *Religionsphilosophie*, 5.
80. *Schleiermacher IV*, 385, 415. One mitigating concession in Barth's later criticism of Schleiermacher's theology struck me as being singularly important, even as an undergraduate when preparing a paper for Ulrich Simon's seminar on Barth. It was Barth's contention that with a better doctrine of the Spirit 'a genuine proper theology could be built up from such a starting point', ibid. 411.
81. Frome *Eine Duplik in Werke XXIII*, ed. J. Peterson and W. von Olshausen (Berlin, 1925–35), 58–9.
82. *ERW*, 91.
83. *BPG*, 72.
84. It is here that I would like to pay tribute to the work of Heinrich Barth and to the importance of the dialogue between him and his brother, Karl, which lasted into the era of dialectical theology, but which then ceased. Heinrich's thesis, *Descartes Begründung der Erkenntnis* (Max Drechsel, 1913) depicted Descartes's philosophical method as an imperfect forerunner to that of the Marburg School. In the course of his thesis, as well as offering a neo-Kantianizing interpretation of Descartes, he managed to highlight the Augustinian accents of Descartes's thought, which resulted in an intriguing blend of neo-Kantianism, Cartesianism, and Augustinianism. Karl certainly read his brother's thesis and referred to it in a footnote to his article about belief in a personal God. It is to be regretted that those scholars interested in Karl Barth's censure of 'theological Cartesianism' have paid little attention to Heinrich's thesis, for there they would find 'theological Cartesianism' in its most pristine form! It should also be added that Heinrich's passionate interest in Plato's philosophy, which bore fruit in the early writing, *Das Problem des Ursprungs in der Philosophie Platons* (Kaiser, 1921), also exercised influence upon his brother during the dialectical phase of this theology.
85. *BPG*, 75. The same quotation appears in *Romans II*, 21. Barth, it

should be mentioned, was indebted to Cohen for the 'I–Thou' contrast, as also was Buber.

86. *Glaubenslehre* §10, *Zusatz*.
87. *De Vera Religione*, xxix. 72–3; *De Spiritu et Littera*, xxxiii. 59.
88. 'The Philosophy of St. Augustine', in *A Monument to St. Augustine* (Sheed & Ward, 1934), 164–5.
89. Matt. 7: 7–8. For the dialectical motif of finding, seeking, and having in Barth's early writings see e.g. *GUG*, 57, and the later Tambach lecture of 1919 in *Gotteswort*, 34, 66.
90. T. W. Manson, *The Sayings of Jesus* (SCM, 1957), 81.
91. For 'Cartesianism' in theology see e.g. *CD*, i/1. 198 ff. ('The Word of God and Experience') in the translation by G. W. Bromiley and T. F. Torrance, *Church Dogmatics* (T. &. T. Clark, 1975).
92. *Institutes of the Christian Religion*, Book II, ch. ii. 15.
93. *GUG*, 50 ff.
94. *Religionsphilosophie*, 6.
95. For a fuller discussion see D. L. Balás, *Metousia Theou: Man's participation in God's perfections according to St. Gregory of Nyssa*, Studia Anselmiana, 55 (Rome, 1966), 2 ff.
96. For a consideration of the importance of this conception of knowledge to the tradition of Christian spirituality see A. Louth, *The Origins of the Christian Mystical Tradition* (Clarendon Press, 1981).
97. *GUG*, 59.
98. *Schleiermacher IV*, 385.
99. But see the very interesting polemical passage in *CD*, i/2. 789–90.
100. *Schleiermacher IV*, 385.
101. *GUG*, 55 ff.
102. *BPG*, 88 ff.
103. *GUG*, 55, 63.
104. *Guide for the Perplexed*, i/8.
105. L. Kolakowski, *Main Currents of Marxism: The Founders* (Clarendon Press, 1978), 11.
106. See ch. 9 of N. Weber's *The Sociology of Religion* (Beacon Paperbacks, 1964).
107. *De Docta Ignorantia*, ch. i, 2.
108. Barth's dialectical period is usually dated from his commentaries on Romans until the publication of the *Christian Dogmatics*. This is the opinion of Busch, Torrance, Zahrnt, von Balthasar, and many other authorities.
109. *De Trinitate*, ch. viii, 1.
110. See J. Moltmann's *Theology of Hope* (SCM, 1977), 60 f.
111. *Institutes of the Christian Religon*, Book I, ch. i, 1 and Book III, ch. ii, 1–2.

112. *BPG*, 89.
113. Ibid. 25–6.
114. Ibid. 29.
115. See pp. 229 ff.
116. See Fig. 1 and pp. 263 ff.
117. *Antwort*, 483–4.
118. *Schleiermacher on Christ and Religion* (SCM, 1965), 102.
119. *Dialektik*, 151.
120. Ibid. 151–2.
121. Frei, 'The Doctrine of Revelation in the Thought of Karl Barth', 241.
122. *Dialektik*, 154.
123. Ibid.
124. Ibid. 155–6.
125. Ibid. 162.
126. Ibid.
127. *Reden*, 47–8.
128. See Appendix II.

6

REVELATORY POSITIVISM
CONCLUSIONS AND CLARIFICATIONS

THE following conclusions, though aiming to offer some general assessment of Barth's earliest writings, have as their chief objective the task of enquiring whether they furnish evidence of revelatory positivism, but since a verdict on this issue will depend upon clarifying what precisely the indictment implies, it is first necessary to examine the use of this phrase in recent theology. Before examining what revelatory positivism may have meant for Bonhoeffer, I have chosen to begin the investigation with Schillebeeckx and Macquarrie.

The word *Offenbarungspositivismus*, used to characterize a certain theological style more or less associated with the writings of Barth, has enjoyed privileged status in theological polemic. Often, though, the content of this charge has not been made specific. Schillebeeckx, for example, in his justly acclaimed experiment in Christology, wrote:

More or less parallel with the Reformed *kerygma* theology of K. Barth and especially of R. Bultmann, who set up in opposition to the liberal–historical quest for Jesus in the nineteenth century, from around 1910–1960 Catholic theology too, reacting against modernism, was dominated by *Le donné révélé* [title of a well-known work by A. Gardeil]. In so far as this entails a predetermined and as it were positively interpreted, revealed given, many now regard it with suspicion.[1]

What, precisely, warrants this suspicion? It transpires that the suspicions in question are not essentially different from those criticisms which Troeltsch raised in connection with the theologies of Herrmann and other members of Ritschl's School. Since the days of kerygma theology, Schillebeeckx contends, theologians have become increasingly aware of the socio-cultural factors which inform and, to some extent, define cognition in any given epoch. Knowledge in general, and religious knowledge in particular, is not exempt from being conditioned by the linguistic, historical, social, and political matrixes in which such knowledge is valued and pursued. Sociologically speaking, therefore, at any given time a complex network of human concerns and interests renders the quest for knowledge desirable, useful, and plausible.

Such insight into the cultural and historical relativity of knowledge, Schillebeeckx believes, implies that theology ought to reassess the way in which it has interpreted revelation during the past few decades. He does not raise the issue of whether Christianity has a revelation and neither does he concern himself with the philosophical questions of whether a revelation can be received or how it may be recognized; rather he indicates his thorough dissatisfaction with the way the criticized theologies construe the nature of revelation's givenness:

What is reality for faith is set in the midst of history, is itself an intrinsic part of man's history, is itself history and culture. Revelation and the cultural-cum-historical expression of it are not to be had separately. Revelation is always partly given in ... the whole formed by generally accepted asumptions, expectations and ideologies, which none the less (and that is the Christian view) change inwardly in and through the fact that they become the wave-beat of revelation.[2]

It is striking to note how uninformative are Schillebeeckx's allusions to revelatory positivism. Here, it seems, theology is as little exempt from the sociology of knowledge as are its concepts of revelation. One wonders whether any reader not inhabiting the professional linguistic world of academic theology is given any substantial notion of what a 'positively interpreted, revealed given' is, or what the adoption of such a position might entail. It must therefore be asked whether phrases such as these, which obviously allude to Bonhoeffer's indictment, function as complex, but useful, signalling devices. When directed to professional colleagues and other knowledgeable readers, such signals inform them about the author's general intentions. Schillebeeckx, by using the phrase 'positively interpreted, revealed given', informs his readers that the problems under discussion will not find resolution by recourse to the presuppositions or methods of a recent theological movement. Those who have ears to hear and possess the requisite knowledge, will indeed hear and react either positively or negatively to this form of signalling.[3] These words are not in any way intended to disparage Schillebeeckx's important contributions to Christology; but rather to illustrate how allusions to Bonhoeffer's charge are often polemically loaded. No matter how necessary and useful such shorthand conveyances of intention might be, there is the attendant danger of jargon and, consequently, of an imprecise use of terms and phrases as vehicles to express general attitudes.

Another theologian who has mentioned theological positivism in connection with Barth's work is John Macquarrie. Anyone who, like Macquarrie, writes a thorough history of recent religious thought, will be aware that positivism is used primarily with reference to a specific corpus of philosophical beliefs. This, however, immediately presents any historian of ideas with formidable problems in defining positivism, for it is a complex genus uniting thinkers as diverse as Compte, Mach, and Ayre.[4]

Macquarrie highlights the following characteristics of positivism which

at once restricts and extends the claim on behalf of the sciences. It restricts this claim by denying that the sciences give us any knowledge of ultimate reality. They provide knowledge only of the connection and order of phenomena. It extends the claim of the sciences by denying that there is any knowledge outside them. In particular, there is a condemnation of metaphysics in any form.[5]

These two features are particularly evident in logical positivism, which made scientific language the norm of what can be said meaningfully about the world and consequently rendered meaningless other types of language—including theological language that did not satisfy this criterion. It is interesting that Macquarrie not only includes the philosophies of Compte, logical empiricism, and logical positivism amongst the secular philosophies of positivism, but some forms of neo-Kantianism as well.[6]

When Macquarrie considers positivism in theology, he first does so in relation to a 'definite positivist tendency' in Ritschl's theology, betrayed by remarks like 'I, too, recognize mysteries in the religious life, but when anything is and remains a mystery, I say nothing about it'.[7] It is not only such reserve that warrants the epithet of positivism, but primarily the use of ethical, to the exclusion of metaphysical, categories in theology. Macquarrie therefore makes it clear that the hallmark of positivism in theology is not so much subscribing to the canons of some secular positivist philosophy, as a systematic opposition to and the exclusion of metaphysics from theological writing and method.

Something similar emerges from his discussion of Karl Barth's alleged theological positivism. Barth's commentary on Romans, acknowledges Macquarrie, wrought a revolution in theology. Its subject-matter became the Word of God, its stance was one of complete obedience to that Word, and its questions, answers, concepts, goals, and methods were seen as being determined by that very same Word.[8] Immediately before his discussion of Barth, Macquarrie offers acute observations about another revolution that occurred just before Barth became appreciated by English speakers which profoundly altered the ethos of British philosophy. A new analytical direction provided philosophy with a more modest programme. As a direct consequence of Russell and Moore, the task of philosophy henceforth became that of analysing conceptuality statements about the world. Investigation of empirical fact was left to the natural sciences, whilst the quest for a Bradleian Absolute or for knowledge of transcendent reality was proclaimed to be a fruitless and illusory undertaking. No longer did philosophers deem it their duty to justify those statements about God, the world, and the soul which for centuries were regarded as ultimate. This philosophical revolution moreover coincided with what Macquarrie calls a 'laicizing' of culture. Consequently philosophers were no longer subject to the sort of cultural pressures which previously required them to pronounce on religious issues.[9]

Macquarrie hints that the increasing popularity of the Barthian revolution, particularly, one might add, in Britain, to some extent represented a theological reaction and response to this philosophical revolution. Despite their profound differences, these two movements, the secular one that led to positivism, the other which demanded total obedience to the Word, nevertheless shared some common features:

Both the philosophical movement and the theological one are disillusioned with the pretensions of speculative reason to grasp the being of God and the supersensible, and are united in their uncompromising rejection of metaphysics. For this reason, the theological movement has sometimes been called 'theological positivism'. Again, on both sides we can see a quest for autonomy, for a distinctive field where philosophy or theology, as the case may be, can reign in undisputed freedom.[10]

Though thoroughly aware of the many differences separating these two revolutions, Macquarrie focuses upon one characteristic essential to both, namely the resolute objection to and explicit rejection of metaphysics. His discussion frankly acknowledges other methodological features that testify to positivism in theology, such as a quest for autonomy (presumably, what Barth and Herrmann called *Selbständigkeit*), scepticism about the ability of reason to fathom 'ultimate' questions and, with reference to Ritschl, an almost Wittgensteinian silence touching matters mystical, yet the sign of theological positivism throughout his analysis is chiefly related to the rejection of metaphysics. If this, then, is to be the criterion of theological or revelatory positivism, it must be affirmed that Barth's earliest writings show him to have adopted such a position from the outset.

Although neither Macquarrie nor Schillebeeckx systematically develop their thoughts on theological positivism, they were signalled out because each represents a special type of criticism and both therefore help with a preliminary clarification of the positivist indictment. First, Schilleebeeckx's criticisms were obviously indebted to Bonhoeffer's *Offenbarungspositivismus* and therefore invite us to look once more at Bonhoeffer's criticisms of Barth's theology. Secondly, though Macquarrie's references to theological positivism were no doubt influenced by Bonhoeffer, I believe him to be more indebted to a well-established tradition in British scholarship which, since the critical expositions of Ritschl's theology by Garvie and Orr, has used the word positivism in connection with the exclusion of metaphysics from theology.[11] More provocative from the point of view of these conclusions is Macquarrie's exposition of Ritschl's positivism which refers to the influence of neo-Kantianism upon him; this philosophy is termed a positivist philosophy by Macquarrie. Since earlier chapters of this book have shown there to be a surprising degree of continuity between Ritschl and Barth's earliest writings, there is a potentially fruitful avenue for investigation here. Though it is perhaps a little misleading to call Marburg neo-Kantianism a positivist philosophy, it is true to say that Barth was utterly familiar with it and felt sufficiently competent to use its technical conceptuality.

One further clarification resulting from this discussion arises from the observation that when theologians speak about theological or revelatory positivism, the word is often being employed in a specialist sense. Apart from the rejection of metaphysics, it has little in common with its meaning in more secular contexts, though Macquarrie's observation, that positivism flourished in theology at times when philosophical positivism was fashionable, is important for appreciating trends in British theology during the past fifty years. There is certainly nothing at all wrong in giving a word like positivism a specialist meaning in theology, but in that case it would be incumbent to specify its meaning and indicate clearly what the adoption of such a position entails. Having said this, it is to Bonhoeffer's *Offenbarungspositivismus* that we now turn.

I. BONHOEFFER'S INDICTMENT

After reviewing the voluminous secondary literature which interprets Barth in the light of Bonhoeffer's criticisms, it is easy to gain the impression that Bonhoeffer's 'revelatory positivism' offers no real key to an understanding of Barth's theology and that the critical impact of the charge depends rather upon reading one's own evaluation of Barth's theology into Bonhoeffer's words.[12]

The passages which mention *Offenbarungspositivismus* in Bonhoeffer's papers and letters are few in number. One such passage reads:

Barth was the first theologian to begin the criticism of religion, and that remains his really great merit; but he put in its place a positivist doctrine of revelation which says, in effect, 'Like it or lump it': virgin birth, Trinity, or anything else; each is an equally significant and necessary part of the whole, which must be swallowed whole or not at all. That isn't biblical. There are degrees of knowledge and degrees of significance, which means that a secret discipline must be restored whereby the *mysteries* of the Christian faith are protected from profanation. The *Offenbarungspositivismus* makes things too easy for itself by establishing, as it does in the last analysis, a law of faith, thereby mutilating what is—by Christ's incarnation!—a gift for us. In place of religion there now stands the church—obviously that itself is biblical—but the world is in some degree made to depend on itself and left to its own devices—that's the mistake.[13]

A review of comments from distinguished scholars such as Prenter, Storch, Gollwitzer, Pannenberg, Ott, and Bethge shows they are not in agreement about the interpretation of Bonhoeffer's words. There is no scholarly consensus, first, as to what Bonhoeffer meant and, secondly, as to how his criticisms relate to Barth's theology. This is not surprising given the nature of Bonhoeffer's remarks.

First—and this observation was made by Barth himself— Bonhoeffer's criticisms were not developed systematically and his remarks are very fragmentary and sketchy. Criticism coming from an informed and sympathetic theologian like Bonhoeffer naturally invites attention; yet Barth's observations were substantially correct. Bonhoeffer's remarks are piecemeal and suggestive, not precise and lucid, but whether, on the other hand, this point warranted Barth's total and, perhaps, unduly dismissive response, is another question.[14]

There is, secondly, another point stressed by Ott and others.[15] Barth was not the only person implicated in Bonhoeffer's criticisms, for *Offenbarungspositivismus* was a trend detected by Bonhoeffer in the theology, preaching, and social witness of the Confessing Church. Once again Bonhoeffer's words lack precision, though it is patently clear that the indictment was calculated to affect the Confessing Church more grievously than Barth. Bonhoeffer criticized this community because it had in fact *forgotten* the Barthian approach (presumably referring, I would suggest, to the critique of religion in the commentaries on Romans) and, even more forcefully, because it had *gone beyond* Barth's own brand of positivism by lapsing into conservative restoration.[16] This aspect of the charge therefore renders questionable any attempts to extend Bonhoeffer's criticism into a wholesale condemnation of Barth's opus, especially when they ignore the historical *Sitz im Leben* of his remarks which were patently more disapproving of trends in the Confessing Church than in Barth's theology.

In the third place there is a problem about continuity. Bonhoeffer's very important earlier criticisms of Barth were of a different magnitude. Bonhoeffer, it seems, was stimulated and excited by Barth's condemnation of religion and *Kulturtheologie* in the commentary on Romans ('despite its neo-Kantian egg-shells'), yet, remaining loyal to his own Lutheran heritage, Bonhoeffer expressed grave reservations about Barth's more Reformed emphasis on *finitum incapax infiniti*. Such an emphasis, he believed, when stressed too strongly, could result in a negative understanding of divine freedom. God, that is, could be spoken of in ways suggesting that he is free of the world, rather than being, as

Bonhoeffer constantly proclaimed, free for it. This observation is often acutely linked with a thorough criticism of Barth's transcendentalism. Bonhoeffer believed Barth's stress on the otherness of God was adversely influenced by the epistemology of idealism in general and, more particularly, by that of the Marburg philosophy.[17] How, then, do these criticisms relate to the later charge of *Offenbarungspositivismus*? The problem about continuity becomes intensified even more when the Barthian side of the equation is examined. At the time that Bonhoeffer wrote his letters Barth had already moved away from his position in *Romans II*. During his work on Anselm, Barth formulated a conception about the nature of theology and its language which he consistently executed in the *Church Dogmatics*, the earlier volumes of which Bonhoeffer had read.[18] Were Bonhoeffer's criticisms therefore directed at a particular understanding of revelation which he detected in Barth's later theology? These questions of continuity may not be insoluble, but they do present interpreters with formidable obstacles to any straightforward generalizations about either Barth's theology or the nature of Bonhoeffer's criticisms.

A weighty consideration must furthermore be borne in mind by anyone wishing to use the artillery of Bonhoeffer's *Offenbarungspositivismus* to storm the methodological foundations of the Barthian fortress. Bonhoeffer's last criticisms of Barth are related to themes which have an alluring, though enigmatic character. In the passage quoted, for example, Bonhoeffer desired a 'secret discipline' to protect the mysteries of Christianity from profanation. What such a discipline might involve is not apparent in his correspondence from prison: it can only be teased from the texts by rigorous exegesis and speculatively developed by the theological imagination. Something similar has to be said about another theme which is also linked to the indictment of *Offenbarungspositivismus*, namely Bonhoeffer's projected 'non-religious interpretation' of Christianity. This again is an enticingly attractive theme, but as far as Bonhoeffer's papers go it is an undeveloped motif and one that remains very problematical. It should therefore come as no surprise to read both Barthians and death of God theologians citing Bonhoeffer's 'non-religious interpretation' in support of their respective positions.

In view of these considerations it might be urged that the term

'revelatory positivism' is best deleted from the theological diction-
ary. An alternative option, however, is that of redefining the term,
so as to distance it from Bonhoeffer's very problematical usage.

II. BARTH ON SCHLEIERMACHER'S 'POSITIVISM'

In polemics Barth could always give as much, if not more than he
received, and it is therefore salutary to note that he too used
positivism polemically in criticism of Schleiermacher. Investigating this will reveal something of Barth's attitude to his earlier work
and additionally promote clarity when dealing with revelatory
positivism generally.

It is important to distinguish the words 'positivism' and
'positivist' from the word 'positive', which was used by Barth in
theological contexts as both a noun and an adjective. When using
it as a noun, Barth followed the already well-established custom of
making it refer to a group of pastors and theologians who, at the
end of the nineteenth century and the beginning of the twentieth,
were traditionalist confessional theologians, united by their
rejection of Ritschlianism and the sort of modern theology taught
in Marburg by Herrmann. For Barth the archetypal positivist of
this sort was in fact his own father, Professor Fritz Barth, who went
to Berne at the invitation of a group of confessional or 'positive'
theologians in 1889. Anyone wishing to savour Fritz Barth's
'positive' theology may do so by reading his edifying book entitled
Die Hauptprobleme des Lebens Jesu: Eine geschichtliche Untersuchung.[20]
Barth also regarded the faculties of Halle and Greifswald, both of
which were mentioned in his article *Reichsgottesarbeit*, as being
positive and filled with Positives. A second group of Positives
mentioned in Barth's later work refers this time to the infamous
German Christians who were very much in favour of 'positive Christianity'.[21] With Schleiermacher's allegedly 'positivist'
methodology, however, we are on totally different ground.

Previous pages have already quoted Schleiermacher's famous
postscript to the tenth section of his *Glaubenslehre*, to which Barth
himself referred approvingly in a footnote of his projected work on
Religionsphilosophie.[22] That section of the *Glaubenslehre* had portrayed revelation as a principle of 'divine causality' effective in the
original fact from which a particular (or positive) religion takes its

genesis and which, moreover, is deemed responsible for the efficacy of that religion in history. Concerning this particular passage of Schleiermacher's work, the following comments were offered by Barth in 1927:

There we are given a definite statement of the correlative concepts of the 'positive' and the 'revealed'. At its most succinct the positive for Schleiermacher is the individual or individualized, revelation, on the other hand, is the individualizing in every religion. It is the 'original fact' [*Urtatsache*] which gives specific form to this specific religion. Obviously the latter is the same element which in the *Reden* is called 'the central insight'. Schleiermacher laid stress on the term 'original event' [*Urtatsache*]. Revelation does not teach, it acts [*sie wirkt*]. It produces a 'total impression'. . . . The complete truth of a revelation would presuppose a publication of information by God himself, yet how could such a publication be possible objectively or comprehensible subjectively? What makes a revelation is not that it is true, but that it is effective [*dass sie wirksam ist*]; not that it presents God as he is in and for Himself, but rather that it presents God in his relation to us, or that revelation effects [*auswirkt*] that relation. Revelation is the foundation [*Grund*], the 'causality' [*Causalität*] of a specific modification of our self-consciousness. Wherever religion is, there is revelation—not to be deduced psychologically but easily deductible historically as the beginning of the life-process of this religion. Upon revelation thus understood depends also the 'lofty arbitrariness' of Christianity which Schleiermacher defended against Schelling. For Christianity is in this sense a positive religion, a religion of revelation.[23]

It is essential to note how Barth does not deny that Christianity is a positive religion, in the sense that it is based upon a historic revelation of God. What, however, Barth does object to is how the positive character attributed to revelation was explicated by Schleiermacher with the language of causality and efficacy.

Essentially the same criticism is found in Barth's discussion of Schleiermacher's understanding of religion as Life. Whereas Barth's earlier theology had itself depicted God as a *Lebensmacht* and human *Leben* in culture as a gracious benefit of Christ, he now offers these critical remarks about equating religion and its life with consciousness of absolute dependence or with consciousness of standing in relation (*Beziehung*) to God:

Feeling is the centre, dominant over knowing and doing, because it is understood at its depths as religious feeling or because it is the feeling of absolute dependence. As consciousness of absolute dependence, religion must be understood as life ... In human self-consciousness, the consciousness of this Other is included, posited, revealed (*eingeschlossen, gesetzt, offenbart*]. In so far as self-consciousness is fundamentally consciousness of the Other that absolutely determines it, it is therefore conscious of a Whence? [*Woher?*], of a foundation for absolute dependence, of the absolute necessity for self-consciousness being as it is. The actualization of self-consciousness in this manner [*Aktualisierung des Selbstbewusstseins in dieser Richtung*] is religious devotion, precisely because this determining Other, the Whence? of absolute dependence, is truly God. Such actualization is therefore really actualization of the God-consciousness. One can even dare affirm that 'God is given to us in feeling in an original way'—given [*gegeben*] manifestly as the non-objective cause [*Ursache*], the effect [*Wirkung*] of which is everywhere *objective*, yet the feeling is *objectless* in distinction to knowing and doing. In so far as Schleiermacher, despite this reservation (i.e. the cause—God—is not objective, whilst the effect—the feeling—is objectless) sought to render comprehensible the givenness [*Gegebensein*] of God's being in feeling with the category of cause and effect, the preponderance of naturalism in his description of the religious life appears to be substantiated.[24]

This passage has been quoted at length because as well as allegedly being an exposition of Schleiermacher, it is at the same time a devastating criticism of Barth's own earlier theology. What this passage objects to is, first, the manner in which Schleiermacher conflated revelation with faith in the concept of life (something which Barth himself often did in his earlier writing) and, secondly, Schleiermacher's naturalism. The force of this second criticism is that Schleiermacher (or the early Barth) construed the relation between revelation and faith (or, it might be added, 'ingression' and 'elevation') as being both reciprocal and causal, the result of which was the 'actualization' of life. Evidence of such naturalism was also found by the later Barth in the *Reden* where religion is said to belong to the nature of man and depicted as a tendency, force, drive, instinct, or *Richtung*, analogous to chemical or organic processes.[25]

It is surely the case that Barth is as much criticizing his own earlier relationism as Schleiermacher's theology. His own earlier theology affirmed a homogeneity to exist between that which effects and that which is to be effected, so that when the two operatively came into contact *Lebensgestaltung* occurred. His writings also refused to make affirmations about God's being *an sich*, but nevertheless rendered God's *Gegebensein an sich* comprehensible by directing attention to the effects which divine activity wrought upon human consciousness. These precipitated a 'total actualization' of culture and bestowed an experience of universal relatedness (*die Realitätsbeziehung*) involving the self, others, and God through the medium of actualized culture and history.

It will also be recalled that Barth's earliest theology always demanded that the Christian consciousness and its relational contents should be taken as a given factual state of affairs and accepted almost as a datum. In 1927 he criticized Schleiermacher for adopting a similar procedure:

Schleiermacher in his first letter to Lücke could not assert strongly enough that his analysis of the Christian self-consciousness was intended 'very simply and honestly to be wholly empirical', that he wanted to present 'actual experiential facts' and not states of consciousness preceding experience. This assertion was certainly justified, for in sections 3–4 of the *Glaubenslehre* he established the basic nature of feeling. He did indeed establish this datum of religious life as being a datum in the literal sense: as something given [*als eine gegeben*] and not as some non-given entity such as an a priori or *Geist*. He dealt with it throughout, both theoretically and practically, like an object of a *positive science*.[26]

Schleiermacher's methodological mistake according to this quotation lay not in the assumption of given revelation, but rather in locating the given datum in religious experience (or in the Christian self-consciousness). Although it is conceded that Schleiermacher's datum was, like his own earlier datum, neither an a priori nor an immanent generation of spirit but a singular occurrence, it is alleged that Schleiermacher's approach to systematic theology transformed the experiential data of religious revelation into an object amenable to scientific explication. This, it must be acknowledged, was precisely the relation between the givenness of revelation and the science of *Religionsphilosophie* recommended by Barth's fragment. This procedure is now said to naturalize both consciousness and its religious experience. The following words are therefore significant:

In the final analysis did he think of the religious life as a third entity above the antithesis of spirit and nature, above the Kantian antithesis of transcendental and empirical? On the basis of his assumptions as a whole, one must suppose that he did so. Actually his positivism [*Positivismus*], as he himself affirmed, consisted in the preponderance of the presuppositions and methods of the natural sciences with which he approached this object.[27]

In the late 1920s, therefore, it was Barth's considered opinion that Schleiermacher's theology was not only vulnerable to the dialectical critique of *Kulturtheologie*, but fundamentally defective because of its alien and naturalizing methodology. The sheer actualism of divine revelation when expounded in categories perilously close to cause and effect, together with the assumption that some revelation in religious experience forms the unique datum for both philosophical and theological investigations, yielded sufficient evidence to call Schleiermacher a positivist.

This methodology, furthermore, was not merely suspect formally, for treating Christian revelation as a datum and its grace as an efficacy that wrought a total actualization of consciousness was believed to involve a profound material error: 'By the emphasis Schleiermacher places upon religion as being posited and presented, as the finite capacity for the infinite [*finitum capax infiniti*], the infinite life [*vita infinita*] is pushed into the sphere of the given and posited as present.'[28] In view of these formal and material errors, it seemed no longer legitimate for theology to have its methodological foundation in the given factuality of revelation which was posited as being present in the Christian consciousness. It was likewise illegitimate to make dogmatics into a scientific-type investigation of such a hypothetical and ambiguous datum.

It must be stressed that these criticisms of Schleiermacher's positivism revolve around the contention that the two poles of his theology ultimately became one. Substantially the same criticism is repeated in relation to Schleiermacher's Christology: Christ and believers become fused into one hybrid process. Since the relation between revelation and faith was thus deemed to be causal on the one hand and reciprocal on the other, the previously welcome synthetic *Universum* appeared highly questionable in retrospect: the Infinite ingression seemed to forfeit its infinite character by becoming instead a mere psychological datum, possessing no more theological significance than, say, an itch or magnetism (Barth's own analogies). It is therefore the case that if these criticisms of Schleiermacher's positivism are accepted, Barth's own earlier theology is susceptible to exactly the same objections.

III. APPEALING TO THE GIVEN
LOSSES AND GAINS

It is perhaps now evident that Barth's later criticisms of Schleier-macher were not so much directed against the assumption that the religion of Christianity, being based upon a historic revela-tion, confronts the theological enquirer as something given, but rather against how this given was supposedly received and how the relation between revelation and human response was expli-cated. Conceptuality so perilously close to cause, effect, and reciprocity offered insufficient protection to the objectivity of Christian revelation according to Barth's later estimation. Its actualism, it was argued, severely restricted the range of theo-logical affirmations about God and this inevitably resulted in highly questionable reconstructions of traditional Christian doctrines, particularly those relating to the person of Christ.

Barth's earliest theology adopted an account of theological language similar to the one criticized. Theology took its bearings from the relational contents of the Christian consciousness. These were its given data. Theology was seen to involve reflection upon this entity called consciousness and aspired to make the 'thoughts', that almost spontaneously cascade from its 'historic' experience, exceptionally vivid and overwhelmingly attractive to the present generation. A later Barth, after his book about Anselm at least, continued to regard revelation as given and theology to be faithful *Nachdenken* in obedience to this divine gift; but then, however, revelation was deemed given in an entirely different way from the earliest writings and, as far as its content was concerned, the revelation was primarily revelation of God, as it were 'in and for himself', and not therefore a revelation of eternal divine–human relatedness in which two foci are equally indispensable. God *an sich* now enters the theological circle as the sovereign revelation, revealer, and revealedness; what is thereby made manifest is the Triune Being of God. Such revelation obviously has its 'effects', but these are secondary and do not constitute revela-tion nor enter the revelatory constellation. To God alone belongs the glory and the efficacy of his manifestation.

In retrospect the long complicated story of the relations between the philosophy and theology of Marburg, as well as its sequel in Barth's later reactions to the approach he adopted as a young man, is the story about a conflict between cognitive styles in which there were neither victors nor vanquished.

A. COGNITIVE STYLES

Barth and Herrmann believed the general tenets of Marburg philosophy to offer a satisfactory account of how knowledge arises. Ignoring its monist tendencies, that philosophy was interpreted as being primarily epistemology, yet three features of the Marburg philosophy continued to cause particular difficulties. First was its ontology, according to which being was deemed to have been constructed by human cognition. A second characteristic that also proved a surd for the theologians arose from the manner in which truly valid cognition was afforded to only three types of knowledge: logical, ethical, and that concerned with the creation and appreciation of beauty. This highly formalized appropriation of the Platonic triad of truth, goodness, and beauty appeared to exclude all religious beliefs from the realm of knowledge. Since religion was thereby denied any obvious cognitive value, Cohen's earlier writings advocated a hyper-Kantianism which reduced it to ethics. Natorp by contrast found authentic religion in the inaccessible depths of inner experience which nevertheless lent shape and form to the objectifications of the human spirit. Neither philosopher had much patience with dogmatic religious beliefs: following the path of ethical reduction or indeed that of a thoroughly humanist aesthetic, they preferred to indicate the beneficial functions of an enlightened religion for acculturation and personal development. A third and perhaps even greater obstacle for supporters of traditional religion was a direct consequence of Marburg Idealism. The only foundation, *arche*, or *pincipium* of knowledge and reality was logical thought which, being self-moved and ceaselessly active, was the one thing necessary to both cognition and the construction of reality. Acquiring knowledge was not a matter of discovery or exploration, but rather an ordered construction and endless generation of the eternal first principle—thought. This, along with their resolute anti-intuitional stance, encouraged the philisophers to believe that thought required nothing to be given to it for the creation of reality and knowledge. Logically therefore neither given revelation, religious experience, nor the received authority of tradition, could be accounted any value for acquiring knowledge of some hypothetical reality transcending thought. The thing-in-itself had disappeared, and along with it the traditional ontological referrents of theological concepts.

In the debates between Marburg philosophy and Marburg theology there emerges an interesting contrast between various cognitive styles. Marburg philosophy adopted a cognitive style which was one of construction. This radically idealist epistemology, according to which being and knowledge were functions of thinking, was resolutely opposed to realism and also to an alternative cognitive style in which the quest for knowledge was seen to be more of a discovery, whereby knowledge of extramental reality is explored through experimentation as well as through concept formation. The alternative style of exploration was deemed irrational by these philosophers, primarily because it created severe asymmetries for their system: it would have demanded realism instead of an idealist logical monism, and the admittance of some intuitive or empirical element into their epistemology instead of conceptual generation and objectification. Among the Marburg theologians, by contrast, there arose yet another cognitive style; that of donation. Reality and knowledge of reality are neither generated nor discovered but given, in this case supernaturally by God through revelatory experience. The sheer gratuité of this experienced *Realitätsbeziehung*, to use Barth's own word, was stressed by emphasizing its self-authenticating nature, 'Wenn ihr's nicht fühlt, ihr werdet's nicht erjagen'. This distinctively theological style of cognition offered the prospect of great gains for the theologians.

In the first place an appeal to a given experiential dimension of reality had the effect of introducing a needful element of realism into the systematic thought of Marburg. Being theologians, and not academic philosophers, neither Barth nor Herrmann offered a reasoned critique of Marburg Idealism. Instead they asserted that reality confronts consciousness as an external environment, of which one is actively aware. To the specifically theological orientation of Marburg theologians this meant, first, that awareness of religious verities implied a reality had been given and received. Additionally it was felt that the intricate network of possibilities and functions, which characterized the Marburg consciousness, was irreconcilable with first-person awareness of oneself and of one's environment. For these thinkers it was revelatory experience that bestowed life (Herrmann) or actualized the subject (Barth). The legitimacy of this existentialist protest against a thorough-going idealism, in which individual identity was dispersed over a complexity of transcendental functions, operations, and possibilities, was indeed acknowledged by Cohen and Natorp. Their valiant but ultimately futile effort to incorporate this very human consciousness into their systems has been noted. It is perhaps ironic that even these thoroughgoing rationalists turned to religion for a principle of individuation: Natorp to a modification of Schleiermacherian feeling and Cohen's later writings to guilt, forgiveness, and the work of reparation.

This cognitive style of donation, secondly, offered the prospect of an anti-reductionist account of religion at a time when the autonomy of both religion and theology was being threatened by the prevailing cognitive ethos. To this extent the plea entered on behalf of religion by Herrmann and his pupil recalls Bradley's acceptance of the claims made upon philosophy by religious consciousness: 'In the religious consciousness we find the belief, however vague and indistinct, in an object—a not-myself; an object, further, which is real. An ideal which is not real, which is only in our heads, can not be the object of religion.'[29] Appealing to the given experiential contents of the religious consciousness offered a way of escaping from the tyranny of epistemology and the meta-scientific pretensions of Marburg philosophy by promising the prospect of an irreducible religious dimension of reality and autonomy for the discipline of theology. Neither Barth nor Herrmann was so foolish as to think that theology itself was the means whereby access to religious reality is to be found; theology rather 'showed the way to religion' and became a prelude to the apocalypse of personal revelation. The thesis that the personal experience of revelatory reality was self-authenticating and donated to consciousness implied that theology should proclaim religious knowledge of God to be encountered in affective modes of cognition entirely different from those of science and even scientific theology. The remarkable contrast between justification by faith and the philosophical justification of cognitive beliefs was likewise believed to lend a certain autonomy to the discipline of theology. With Barth's earliest writings the autonomy of theology was construed quite radically. The Christian consciousness which claimed his attentions not only represented an irreducible reality, but dictated the methods of theology: it was to reflect that 'unique methodology' whereby Christian faith arises in consciousness (or, what is much the same, in history). Theology, therefore, possessed an autonomy that derived from a reality external to consciousness which miraculously revealed itself when it bestowed its benefits to establish the Christian consciousness.

Finally, the affirmation that reality and meaning is bestowed upon human beings by a supernatural efficacy transcending consciousness permitted a restoration of tradition. The important tradition here was, of course, that of the Protestant Reformation and Pauline Christianity. Though neither Barth nor Herrmann were lovers of 'external authority', it so transpired that given revelatory experience was eminently amenable to being portrayed with received language about justification, the benefits of Christ, faith, and the Kingdom, principally because these were built into 'the given, factual state of affairs' from the very beginning. When Barth focused upon the Christian consciousness, therefore, he encountered a synthesis founded upon a given revelation, in which God's actualizing power (revelation) was joined by cathexis to personal experience (faith) resulting in life (justification) being experienced to the full. Here a comparison with Natorp helps to sharpen the contrast. His pure spirituality, it will be recalled, demanded a radical purification of religion by severing itself from all objectivities and renouncing its claim to enjoy intercourse with some transcendent reality. When Barth and Herrmann appealed to the self-authenticating efficacy of revelation, they asserted that such efficacy was divine in origin and execution. Without some supernatural efficacy they urged that no Christian consciousness would exist, because that very state of affairs depended upon an ingression of revelation. Since there was such a factual, given state of affairs, it seemed common sense to suppose that a miraculous revelation established and preserved it. In contrast to the merely functional authority of Natorpian religion, the religion of Barth and Herrmann claimed an 'inner authority' that spilled over to those biblical, doctrinal, and systematic 'thoughts of faith' which were ciphers, albeit indispensable ones, for communicating Christian experience. The authority of tradition was thus derivative and dependent upon experiential verification, yet it was nevertheless presented as making claims, though only indirect ones, about the God whose revelation established the consciousness that almost spontaneously generates such quasi-traditional 'thoughts of faith'. A certain objectivity was thereby bestowed upon the religious language most congenial to modern theology and the result, if not a complete restoration of traditional Christian theism, was that theologians felt sufficiently confident to write about a God who acts upon consciousness and whose activity is filtered into consciousness through experience of Christ's benefits. With God, the individual, Christ, redemption, and justification so anchored in the experiential authority of a consciousness invigorated by God, theology, it seemed, could restore a number of traditionally important theistic claims to the pure spirituality and agnosticism of neo-Kantian religion.

The cognitive style of Marburg theologians pleaded for a realism and an actualism which were both noticeably lacking in the writings of their philosophical colleagues. This accent of realism and actualism, however, was believed to arise from the religious experience of revelation—and that alone. Karl Barth aspired to convert neo-Kantianism to Christ by transferring his benefits into the operative centre of Marburg philosophy. Thought no longer actualized its possibilities by virtue of its innate dynamism; the revealed actuality of God rather actualized the subject, who then received power to construct a cultural order in which truth, beauty, and goodness would continuously become incarnate. Like the Israelites who left their Egyptian captivity laden with spoils of silver, gold, and raiment for worship of their God, the neo-Kantian philosophy of culture was raided for religious purposes in order to show how true religion alone gives birth to a culture radiant with value and meaning.[30]

Converting a philosophy is not, however, the same as converting an entire culture and even the 'spoils' of the young Barth were ultimately found distracting. Along with the theological and methodological gains promised by the cognitive style of Marburg theology costly losses were also incurred, some of which soon became apparent to Barth; others continued to exact formidable concessions from even a more mature Barth.

In the first place the realism with which Barth and Herrmann wished to endow the philosophical world-view of Marburg Kantianism was severely limited. Since Barth believed the experience of revelation, and that alone, created what he termed *die Realitätsbeziehung*, anything occurring 'outside' Christian experience was devoid of reality. Like Cyprian who urged that salvation is not available outside the Church, Barth's earliest writings effectively proclaimed there to be no reality outside the Christian consciousness. Even the existential Subject, about which Barth and Herrmann wrote so much, was devoid of reality until it experienced the revelatory ingression that actualized it. Barth never speculated much about the nature of existence apart from the overwhelming experience of reality received in revelatory experience, though one unpublished writing suggests that without the experience in question all that remains of the subject are abstract psychological processes.[31] Without the experience of revelation through Christ's benefits, it must be assumed that there is nothing but formal possibilities devoid of any potency. Troeltsch accurately characterized this position when he criticized Herrmann for reducing everything outside the hypostatized and artificial entity of the Christian consciousness to utter *Sehnsucht* — mere aspiration, fantasy, or impotent longing.

Revelatory experience in Barth's earliest theology is therefore responsible for the existence of the individual, history, and culture 'because religion is truth, reality, actualization'. This claim goes far beyond the anonymous theism of Karl Rahner and it is not a doctrine of creation. A theist may well wish to claim that divine grace works anonymously by inspiring human beings to create beauty, organize their societies with equity, and search for truth wherever it is to be found, but this, unfortunately, is not what Barth's earliest writings were suggesting. His point was rather that these values are first created and then perceived as values only when and where a specific religious experience occurs. It is only within the *Universum* of Christian experience that culture is actualized, real, and of positive worth. This approach was an inevitable outcome of his methodology. Since theology or even *Religionsphilosophie* proceeded by straightforward reflection upon the factuality of the Christian consciousness—along with its relations to God, other actualized beings, and historic values already converted to revelatory energies—the young Barth could do no other than put to one side the question of how truth, beauty, and goodness might manifest themselves to minds not defined by the revelatory synthesis. A hypothetical and abstract consciousness like this could not receive any theological evaluation, for it was not internally related to the synthesis that claimed Barth's attention. This methodological resolve to bracket off anything not internally related to Christian religious experience had the unfortunate result of leaving the world and its culture to their own devices, consigning them to the shadowland of semblance, resembling that inhabited by Plato's cave-dwellers.

The early Barth, it need hardly be said, was not terribly interested in theories of culture other than that offered by the Marburg philosophy which he sought to convert. Only after he became disillusioned with the optimistic and evolutionary beliefs about Germanic culture that arose with the advent of a world war, did the weaknesses of his theoretical attempts become evident. The great critic and sceptic, Overbeck, was then read retrospectively and the prospect of a Christian culture became the preserve of eschatology. From henceforth religion 'is not the sure ground upon which human culture safely rests; it is the place where civilization and its partner, barbarism, are rendered fundamentally questionable'.[32] Culture was effectively ousted from Christian consciousness and even a less dialectical Barth was sceptical whether voices and lights, other than those encountered in biblical revelation, might testify to God, though admittedly the music of Mozart was a unique exception.[33]

The quest for a non-reductive account of religion suffered similar shortcomings. The reality revealed to Christian religious experience was so absolutized that any other possible reality became not only relative, but insignificant and attenuated to an unprecedented degree. The revealed experience of a divine energy, which bestowed a totally new vivid *Universum* and animated religious consciousness, became the only reality about which a theologian could write. The price demanded by this absolutization of revelation was that all other realities were ontologically down-graded and robbed of value. Instead of Natorp's logical monism or monism of experience, Barth's earlier writings offered a revelatory monism or monism of religious experience. Only that which was internally related to the Christian experience of revelation possessed reality. The absolute *Selbständigkeit* attributed to the Christian religion by the theologians not surprisingly affected their estimation of theological method. The constructionist account of Marburg philosophy demanded that *alles aufgegeben ist*; by contrast the theology of the early Barth asserted *alles gegeben ist*—as far as religious reality was concerned. Revelatory experience not only gave birth to a truly invigorated reality completely different in kind, quality, and nature from any other so-called realities, but enjoyed a mode of cognition totally different from any other. The exciting proposal of a *Religionsphilosohie*, whereby ties of continuity, as well as accents of discontinuity, between theology and secular disciplines would be investigated, turned out in the end to emphasize an utter discontinuity between religious cognition and the cognitive styles of *Kulturbewusstsein*. Such discontinuity was particularly acute when the theologians addressed historical questions. In place of the epistemological tyranny of the Marburg system, a new cognitive imperialism was claimed for religion. Much confusion nevertheless obscured theological writing, because the apologetic stance adopted by Barth and Herrmann had no desire to belittle the scientific achievements of their philosophical colleagues. The way out of this impasse for Herrmann was through his infamous 'dualism of faith' which relied upon the very strange contrast between cognitive 'law-determined' labour and justification by faith through grace. His younger pupil, by contrast, adopted a more single-minded approach. Unhappy with the dualism between religion and science advocated by Ritschl and his immediate successors, the young Barth sought a dialectical synthesis between the two. This fascinating procedure, which would no doubt interest structuralists, involved classifying contraries into binary pairs and then affirming them to achieve harmonious synthesis provided—and this was the weakness—the individual had truly enjoyed the benefits of revelatory experience. The individual's religious consciousness alone was the organ of synthesis which experientally resolved all problems of religion and culture. The cognitive claims made on behalf of religious revelation received even greater force and, it must be acknowledged, became increasingly discrete and *sui generis* in relation to all other cognitive enterprises, through the assertion that revelatory knowledge was self-authenticating. I do not wish to dwell upon the philosophical and moral implications of any belief however passionately held—whether it be religious, political, economic, or social—that is said to be self-authenticating; the textbooks offer many formidable criticisms. In theology this ploy had the unfortunate effect of sanctioning one particular epistemological style and condemning all others. The offhand manner with which the young Barth regularly dismissed Troeltsch is perhaps indicative of the imperialism that almost inevitably results from this style. This, it could be argued, not only impoverishes theology through infatuation with one particular method, but also limits the number of exciting alternative possibilities that a theologian might want to explore. As far as all other approaches are concerned, they are told to 'like it or lump it'. The austere consequences arising from the realism of Marburg theology and its quest for autonomy were exacerbated by a determination to ignore metaphysics.

In relation to the third gain—the restoration of tradition—it is to be noted how yet again the Marburg style of cognition had the effect of making one confessional stance absolute. A particularly apt example is afforded by Marburg Christology. The famous phrase which Melanchthon judiciously removed from later editions of his *Loci* was used to sanction a thoroughly functionalist Christology, a metaphysical agnosticism about relations between the deity and the world, as well as to make absolute the exclusivist claims of one Christological tradition. By contrast Christianity has found a threefold significance for Jesus Christ, with his ministry and teachings, for example, being valued as a pattern to answer the question of how life should be shaped morally. Whether the pattern in question was seen to involve near literal imitation, monastic humility, social criticism, or revolutionary activity, the Christ of the Gospels has certainly provided moral inspiration to generations of disciples. Christ, moreover, has been hailed as the founder of a new society, the Church, in which the values of faith, hope, and charity are nurtured, affirmed, practised, and constantly renewed through liturgical worship, teaching, and sacramental contact with his grace. Finally, the figure of Christ has been looked upon as the divinely appointed 'mercy seat' in whom is present the grace of God to forgive sin, justification for those who lack experience of grace, as well as energy for a new life of faith. Though all three aspects of Christ have been valued throughout Christian history, one especially cherished benefit often towers above the rest in a particular spiritual tradition. Some community captivated by the moral vision of Christ, for example, might argue that an axiomatic relation exists between the pattern of discipleship promoted by its spirituality and the synoptic portrait of Jesus. A second tradition might want to postulate an indissoluble connection between Christ and the sacramental worship and

moral witness of his mystical body, whilst a third could argue for
an axiomatic correlation between Christ and justification. The
procedure of the early Barth effectively excluded the virtues of
Christ apprehended by other confessional traditions whilst simultaneously claiming an exclusivist axiomatic validity for his own
highly selective interpretation of Reformation doctrine. The
legitimacy of the first Christological tradition was disputed
because it turned faith into a human work. It was further argued
that historical criticism of the New Testament resulted in only a
tentative picture of Jesus which was, moreover, always liable to
revision at some future date. These facts were taken to imply that
there was no reliable information about Jesus capable of inspiring
people to discipleship. The Christ of *Nachfolge*, furthermore,
offered no firm foundation for faith, deprived the individual of any
certitude of salvation, and made religious belief dependent upon
historical science. The Christ which interested Barth by contrast
was not the 'outer' Christ of external history, but the efficacious
'inner Christ', massively present to believers in their contemporary
faith experience. Criticisms such as these were directed not only
against romantic, confessional, secular, or 'unscientific' reconstructions of Jesus, but also against the scholarship and moral
earnestness of an Albert Schweitzer. The second confessional
stance fared no better, for its 'metaphysical Christ' too turned faith
into a work—this time into a cognitive work—by making faith
dependent upon intellectual assent to highly questionable 'truths'.
The moral dignity of the individual was grievously compromised
by the 'external authority' of hierarchical institutions, clerics, and
doctrinal formulations which themselves were nothing more than
questionable amalgams of outmoded metaphysics and quasi-legal
stipulations. Since the benefits of Barth's Christ were immediately
bestowed upon the individual by God, the notion that they could
be mediated through tradition, history, or social structures, was
believed to deprive believers of his actuality and this was a capital
offence according to Barth. The authority of his Christ was an
inner authority, to which the religious individual gladly submitted
without any compromise to moral autonomy because its validity
was individual or experiential and not general and juridical. The
ecclesiastical Christ of Roman Catholics seemed therefore to
'pervert' the gospel. That the strength of Christianity might lie in
the sheer diversity of spiritualities that have been, and will

continue to be, attracted and captivated by Christ was a possibility never entertained by Barth's earliest writings nor, for that matter, by his latest.

Before leaving this consideration of how Barth and Herrmann hoped to restore the authority of more or less traditional doctrinal language, there are two subsidiary points of some importance. First, the way theological language was deemed to function made it utterly subordinate to a particular religious experience. The problem with this approach to theological language, which Barth acutely felt later in his career, was the lack of any necessary connection between revelatory experience and its conceptualization in *Glaubensgedanken*. Whereas it might have been possible to justify such traditional doctrinal language on the sociological ground that it predisposes individuals to have Christian experiences, the immediacy attributed to faith in Barth's earliest writings excluded all mediations—whether social, historical, linguistic, or literary. A later Barth attempted to overcome his earlier experiential justification of doctrinal language by postulating a necessary link between given revelation and theological language. This was achieved through the analogy of faith on the one hand and the doctrine about the threefold form of the Word of God on the other. Even to this day the scientific character of theology is sometimes felt to depend upon a special 'inner logic' whereby given revelation is of necessity bound to a particular set of theological formulations.

The second point concerns the nature of tradition. Whereas religions have often regarded their sacred writings, teachings, rituals, and moral prescriptions as indispensable resources that originate in divine providence for the maintenance and propagation of faith and communal spirituality, tradition in the early Barth loses its historicity and naïvety. Its justification does not lie in either historical continuity or in divine providence; it rather enters a posteriori, after personal revelation. Paradoxically Barth was prepared to subject 'external' tradition to Enlightenment criticism by magnifying the values of liberal individualism, yet contemplated a new 'historic' *Universum* in which figures of the past were effective in contemporary experience. This new totality dawns upon the individual only after an experience of revelatory ingression. Tradition is thus no divinely inspired means to the noble end of preserving, affirming, or propagating the faith and values of Christianity in time and space; it remains completely subordinate to an individual's contemporary experience and can even become something of an impediment to true religion. Tradition therefore does not bestow meaning upon individual experience, but rather the reverse is affirmed. It is perhaps superfluous to comment that this was one more aspect of Barth's earliest theology that underwent radical revision.

It is patently evident that the donative cognitive style of Marburg theology was strongly influenced by a definite theology of faith and that this is only to be expected since philosophies and their epistemologies have usually been only ancillary aids to expounding revelation throughout the history of theology. Barth and Herrmann, however, placed much emphasis upon the passive nature of faith which was afforded priority over any active or spontaneous elements in religious belief. For Herrmann faith was primarily a matter of pure surrender to a gift bestowed by God. Barth, though anxious to affirm that active and passive traits of personality coincide in the *Universum* of Christian experience, made the genesis of Christian belief completely dependent upon 'ingression' and upon the necessity of actualization being given. Whereas Natorp and Cohen affirmed that meaning for human existence is to be created through struggle, work, and resolute application to moral tasks, Barth and Herrmann said that such meaning is always miraculously given. A position which perhaps spoke more profoundly to the modern temper was later offered by Paul Tillich. In the ecstatic moment of vision, as well as the miracle of divine revelation, there is always a demand of finite appropriation. Faith involved for him not only surrender to a miraculously given meaning for life, but costly struggle, martyrdom, or simply 'courage' to affirm this meaning from the depths of one's finitude.

The theme of the divine and its efficacy for human acculturalization has been perennial in theories, myths, and religions from Gilgamesh to Freud. Many such writings, as well as affirming the worth, joys, and moral benefits of culture have, without euphemism or evasion, proclaimed costly struggle to be necessary for a breakthrough to truth, equity, or beauty. The struggles are social, psychological, manual, and intellectual, but embracing them all is the costly, but potentially liberating, struggle with finitude. The partly divine Gilgamesh perceived his inescapable finitude when he encountered the uncivilized 'Thou' of Enkidu. The wild man for his part became aware that the goods of life, particularly those of human society and friendship, demanded courage, struggle, and fraternal co-operation. Both learned that meaning must of necessity pass through death's dark vale before returning once more to illumine the workaday world. It is perhaps indicative of the realism encountered in Barth's earliest work, as well as in the ethics of Herrmann, that hardly any reference to death is to be found. The only struggle to which these authors allude is that of spirit with nature, in which the former is inevitably victorious. Barth's brief exegesis of Plato's parable forgot to expound the last episode: the return to the cave.

B. APPEALING TO THE GIVEN

A recent generation of students was encouraged to regard philosophy as a form of therapy. By dispassionate analysis it offered the prospect of release from pseudo-problems induced by the bewitchment of language. Though I would not subscribe to this understanding of philosophy, there is a sense in which language is apt to conceal, as well as to reveal, and this is particularly evident when philosophers, theologians, or conservers of culture appeal to the given.

With reference to the philosophical and theological debates at Marburg it has been suggested that realist, in contrast to idealist, beliefs about reality suppose that there exists something prior to its being thought or known by rational agents. Cognition will consequently be more akin to discovering or exploring what is, than to either construction or conceptual generation of reality. The German language offers a variety of linguistic forms for existential statements, but when ordinary speech wishes to acknowledge the existence of something either *es ist* or *es gibt* is normally used. The presence of the verb *geben* in the second instance might easily encourage one to suppose that by affirming something to have been given (*gegeben*), its reality is simultaneously affirmed. Even more strongly, and more questionably, by asserting, insisting, or stating that something is given it is possible to be misled by language into believing one has thereby proved that 'the given' is ontologically instantiated. Any appeal to the given may therefore involve the acceptance of several philosophical and ontological suppositions, the cogency of which depends upon a common linguistic element—the verb *geben*. The appeal to a factual or given state of affairs could well involve a variety of concealed ontological and epistemological beliefs, such as there is (*a*) a giver, (*b*) someone receiving what is given, (*c*) a 'gift' or something real given, and (*d*) a transaction by which the 'gift' is presented to the recipient by the giver.[34]

The first proposition assumes that there is some extra-mental reality, whether it be a deity, a human agent, nature, or mind, which is responsible for, and ontologically prior in, the giving process. The second may invite an entire metaphysic of the recipient subject, whilst the third, the assumption that extra-mental realities exist, lies at the heart of realism and is not objectionable—provided good reasons are forthcoming to support it. The fourth presupposition might easily lead to an intricate theory of cognition to account for knowledge of the given reality.

All these assumptions and presuppositions, which could arise from believing that something has been given, are encountered in Barth's earliest theological writings. With regard to (*a*) and (*b*), he affirmed the giver to be God and the recipient to be the unrealized possibility for life. The third, the gifts, were the benefits of Christ which actualized life, awareness, and history. Finally (*d*) asserted that the whole process of giving and receiving could be termed 'revelation', which was responsible for establishing the Christian consciousness and its unique kind of faith-knowledge. From that point onwards the existence of a factual state of affairs or synthesis, in which God's revelatory effects were indissolubly related to the recipient subject, seemed indubitable. In short Barth's early realist understanding of revelation and his relationism were both intimately bound to a whole catena of metaphysical and epistemological assumptions that had been built into an appeal to the given.

Though it may well be the case that these epistemological and ontological propositions are legitimate, each proposition must be justified if it is to be given credence and it is also imperative to clarify the ontological commitments that are being adopted. The appeal of Barth and Herrmann to the givenness of revelation involved neither, principally because they believed that each proposition was self-authenticating. It has to be said in conclusion that the laudable realist intentions of Marburg theologians led from appealing to the given to the affirmation of several complex and controversial theses which were, despite denials, metaphysical as well as epistemological in character. Since they were all deemed to be self-authenticating, neither metaphysics nor reasoned justification was required.

C. REVELATORY POSITIVISM

Three formal elements were involed in Barth's appeal to the legitimacy of the 'Christian revealed, given'. In opposition to Marburg idealism there was the proposition that religious cognition is not essentially productive but receptive and the belief that some real resource (a *Lebensmacht*) was available to help find one's way through life by bestowing meaning upon it. There was, secondly, the thesis that construed the 'given' to be self-authenticating. Thirdly, there was a systematic tendency to accord reality to 'the given' alone.

The first proposition does not warrant the epithet of positivism. By arguing that something is given, whether the given in question is sense data, nature, matter, or God as a gracious resource, realism, not positivism, is being embraced. The young Barth, however, leapt from the first to the second proposition. This leap was facilitated by an amazing variety of doctrinal, confessional, and apologetic strategies. What was established as 'given' in the first step, became fundamental, beyond all doubt, and exempt from either rational criticism or reasoned justification. The third step was a slide from the second. The given, now being self-evidentially real and self-authenticating, was credited with such an overwhelming degree of reality that every other reality was utterly relativized. From the perspective of revelatory experience, anything not internally related to it was ontologically deficient. For the young Barth therefore everything 'outside' the Christian consciousness was devoid of reality and consequently merited no theological evaluation. God's actualizing power realizes the *Universum* of Christian experience alone and any relative autonomy the world, its inhabitants, and human cultures might enjoy *vis-à-vis* the Creator of that consciousness is severely curtailed, ultimately to the point of attenuation.

If there is any trace of *Offenbarungspositivismus*, it must surely be found in the leap from the first to the second and third propositions mentioned above. The first, it must be stressed, does not of necessity lead to religious or revelatory positivism. It is a realist proposition and, provided it receives justification, its adoption does not deserve the epithet of positivism. Without such realism there would probably be no theology, since religions by and large see their beliefs as witnessing to some reality. It is an urgent theological and philosophical task to investigate how, and under what conditions, religions are entitled to make claims that testify to a dimension of reality perceived to be related, yet discontinuous, with the workaday world and its contemporary cognitive map of sciences, ethics, sociologies, psychologies, politics, and aesthetics.

Barth's earliest theology, and that of Herrmann also, certainly fulfil all the criteria for revelatory positivism. Whether his later work does so is a question that transcends the scope of this book.

IV. ALTERNATIVES TO REVELATORY POSITIVISM

Revelation, according to many, has become the principle of contemporary theology. Whether revelation is construed in the positivist manner outlined in the previous section or less so, it has to be admitted that the approach to revelation adopted by much modern theology possesses an attractively elegant symmetery. An appeal to given revelation is seen to provide a promising means whereby the requirements of epistemology, ontology, and religious experience are all neatly satisfied. The unique form of cognition through which human beings enjoy knowledge of God is said to depend upon revelation and since revelation is also an act of divine self-revelation, the concept answers the ontological question of who or what is known. By axiomatically connecting both with religious practice and traditional theological conceptuality, revelation is seen additionally to be a uniquely religious category as well as the sole arbiter of what should count as theological method. It is interesting to observe the degree to which all other doctrines have increasingly become subordinate to and often derived from the doctrine of revelation. Barth and Herrmann anchored soteriology, Christology, and the doctrine of God in their doctrine of revelation. Later in the century nearly every other theme of the Christian religion—creation, eschatology, anthropology—became a subspecies of revelation. Whereas an older theology certainly regarded the manifestation of God's name as a divine revelation, it was nevertheless accounted as one, amongst many, astonishing noble deeds whereby the Creator interacts with his creation. The echoes of this older tradition, which beheld revelation as one, alongside many other instances of divine activity, are heard in Schleiermacher's *Glaubenslehre*—revelation is one form of divine causality, but there are others. To theologians influenced by Marburg theology, revelation became the only form of divine activity that could be spoken about. Perhaps the resolute exclusion of metaphysics from theology encouraged them to forget that whatever revelation might be, it has usually been presented as an act of God, and to speak about God acting upon the world or human agents is to make a statement that is at once religious, metaphysical, and Christian. It is not simply an affirmation about cognition. In all knowledge there is the question of how we know and the question of what we know. Epistemological and metaphysical questions are inextricably bound together and it is likely to be the case that no satisfactory answer can be given to one question without the other also being considered. Speaking about God, divine activity, and human or natural reality involves metaphysics and, as Hegel's *Logic* succinctly put it, 'the real question is not whether we shall apply metaphysics, but whether our metaphysics is of the right sort'.

Since the style of revelatory positivism has often proclaimed itself to be the only possible theological methodology, it is fitting to conclude by mentioning three promising trends in contemporary British theology that offer credible alternatives worth exploring. The first is a philosophical programme that attempts to secure a reasoned justification of religious belief. Theologians are truly indebted to Basil Mitchell and his students for showing that logical positivism and linguistic analysis need not throw theology into the deathly embraces of fideism. Secondly, there is the promising revival of theistic metaphysics. Though not revisionary in the Strawsonian sense, it nevertheless explores the possibility that revelation, reason, and the multidimensional facets of experience go together and invite rigorous consideration of the realities apprehended. Both Maurice Wiles and Keith Ward have opened up a fruitful avenue which the positivists dogmatically proclaimed to be a *cul-de-sac*. Finally, there is a third option which takes us back to the beginning of this century when it was an alternative to the Marburg way of doing things. Wobbermin, the long-forgotten author of *Monismus und Metaphysik*, the annoyingly pedantic Troeltsch, and, before them, Schleiermacher, each in his own way acknowledged the value of religious studies for theology. The desired *Selbständigkeit* of religion was not seen by these thinkers to lie in self-authenticating revelation, but rather in the observation that humans are religious, as well as social, political, and intellectually curious beings. These theologians were awake to the possibility that religious activity and beliefs might testify, first, to a resource which graciously assists human beings to find moral bearing in their world, secondly, to an intellectual quest which aspires to perceive purpose, value, and meaning in the environment that surrounds them, and finally, to the sheer excess of beauty in human and natural creation which, despite sombre and tragic accents, nevertheless inspires adoration, worship, and thankfulness. Such possibilities may well encourage one to consider whether something profound is offered by revelation, one form of which is affirmed in Christian belief and portrayed by its *Glaubenslehre*. These three alternatives to the style of revelatory positivism have much to commend them and are worth exploring further.

The author of this book accounts himself a religious being, but finds that revelation most convincing which offers a *Diesseits-offenbarung*. The struggle to find and create meaning in the face of the genocide, simplistic political *clichés*, and policies of mass deprivation—to name but three daemons that have infected this particular century—is no easy task. Neither is it easy to wage war against them; though this must be done for love of the world. Yet when one turns to Christology, some form of which is inevitable for any Christian theology, it is salutary and encouraging to recall the first modern theologian of liberation. The world, he realized, affirms itself automatically and needs no theology of culture to lend vigour to its affirmation.[35] Perhaps, then, an important question for Christology to consider is why the Christ proclaimed by Paul, or the Christ depicted in the Gospels, should periodically 'rise up against the modern spirit and send upon earth not peace, but a sword' and generate alternatives for his disciples to follow when the world tells them there are none. Christ may be as much a symbol of revolution as one of revelation. Is this one of his benefits for our present culture, as well as being an instance of 'divine causality'?

One is anxious to affirm truth, beauty, and goodness wherever and whenever they are encountered—even in the most ordinary, mundane, and sometimes costly struggles of everyday life. According to the poetry of Hölderlin, no less a person than the saintly Socrates perceived that even sages in the end must bow to worship beauty—however unconventional its source. Something similar might be said about truth and goodness. Yet despite the valiant attempts of patristic exegesis to turn the death and humiliation of Jesus into a thing of beauty, one wonders at its cogency. He was despised and rejected: there was no comeliness nor pleasing form. Courage, martyrdom, and moral passion certainly; but hardly beauty. Is this the realism he bequeathes his theologians?

There are no final conclusions or definitively given answers. This rather marginal footnote to Barth's theology simply observes that between ecstatic vision and protest, idealism and realism, the Kingdom of God and the values of culture, it is the destiny of theologians to labour.

NOTES

1. *Jesus: An Experiment in Christology* (Collins, 1979), 48.
2. Ibid.
3. Witness the reaction of one Barth supporter to Schillebeeckx's book: 'the results of this book are largely determined by the method and presuppositions with which the work is approached . . . Behind everything that is written in this book is the hidden God of neo-Kantian dualism'! C. Gunton in the *Scottish Journal of Theology*, Apr. 1980.
4. L. Kolakowski's *The Alienation of Reason: A History of Positivist Thought* (Doubleday, 1964), 3–9, offers a succinct summary of the general features of positivism, the most important being:

   1. The rule of phenomenalism which tolerates no real difference between essence and phenomenon and predicates validity only to inventories of what is manifested in experience.
   2. The rule of nominalism which does not admit the legitimacy of any insight formulated in general terms to have real referents other than individual concrete objects.
   3. The rule that denies cognitive worth to value judgements and normative statements, irrespective of whether those values and norms be of an aesthetic, moral, or religous nature.
   4. A belief in the essential unity of scientific method that applies

the canons and criteria for acquiring and adjudicating knowledge in natural science to all other cognitive or theoretical enterprises.

5. *Twentieth Century Religious Thought* (SCM, 1963), 95.
6. Ibid. 74 ff., 95, 97.
7. Ibid. 76; see also *Thinking about God* (SCM, 1975), 30.
8. Ibid. 318.
9. Ibid. 301 ff.
10. Ibid. 318.
11. H. R. Mackintosh in his widely read and influential book *Types of Modern Theology* (James Nisbet, 1937) once more popularized the view that there was a 'positivist temper' in Ritschl's theology and that 'apropos of history as the sphere or realm of Divine revelation . . . this positivist temper comes most plainly to the surface' (p. 172).
12. Thus R. T. Osborn's 'Positivism and Promise in the Theology of Karl Barth', *Interpretation*, 25 (1971).
13. Letter of 5 May 1944.
14. See Barth's letter to Landessuperintendent Herrenbrück (21 Dec. 1952) in R. G. Smith (ed.), *World Come of Age: A Symposium on Dietrich Bonhoeffer* (Collins, 1967), and the later letter to Bethge in *Fragments Grave and Gay* (Fontana, 1971).
15. See H. Ott's *Reality and Faith: The Theological Legacy of Dietrich Bonhoeffer* (Lutterworth, 1971), 122 ff.
16. Letter of 8 June 1944.
17. This is particularly evident in the very difficult, but none the less important *Akt und Sein*—a work which is unfortunately often neglected.
18. See P. Eicher's *Offenbarung: Prinzip Neuzeitlicher Theologie* (Kösel, 1977), 234 ff.
19. For Barth's memories about his positive father see E. Busch, *Karl Barth* (SCM, 1976), 1 ff.
20. F. Barth, *Die Hauptprobleme des Lebens Jesu* (C. Bertelsmann, 1899).
21. For this sort of 'positive' approach see C. Fabricius, *Positive Christianity in the Third Reich* (H. Pueschel, 1937).
22. See pp. 268 ff.
23. *Schleiermacher II*, 163–4.
24. Ibid. 164–5.
25. Ibid. 162.
26. Ibid. 166–7.
27. Ibid. 167.
28. Ibid. 161.
29. F. H. Bradley, *Ethical Studies*, rev. edn. (Oxford University Press, 1927), 316.
30. See Origen's celebrated letter to Gregory Thaumaturgus.
31. The notes for the work on *Religionsphilosophie* contain the following

words: 'Und ohne diese Realitätsbeziehung käme ein Kulturbewusstsein einzeln, empirisch gar nicht zustande, wie auch die
Theorie der Vernunft (Hypothese) sie nicht entbehren kann.'
32. *Romans II*, 240.
33. It is interesting to note what a later Barth had to say about the many
lights of creation and their relation to the one true light in *CD*, iv/3/
1: they are (*a*) challenged and relativized by it and then (*b*)
integrated into it (pp. 155ff.). In passing, it is fascinating to compare
Barth's earlier understanding of how revelation actualizes Christian
consciousness in culture with his account of Jesus Christ's sovereign
'self-actualization' in the same volume (pp. 40ff.). On the topic of
music, it must be noted that the early Barth valued the works of
Bach, Mozart, and Beethoven because 'at their most profound level
they are testimonies of faith or transparancies which, speaking with
Paul, "portray Christ before our eyes" ' (*GUG*, 70).
34. See J. J. Ross, *The Appeal to the Given: A Study in Epistemology* (George
Allen & Unwin, 1970), and P. M. Schlick, 'Positivismus und
Realismus', *Erkenntnis*, 3 (1932–3), 1–31.
35. See Albert Schweitzer, 'Religion in Modern Civilization', *The
Christian Century*, 21, 28 Nov. 1934.

APPENDIX I

Books in Barth's Private Library

Barth's private library, which is now at the Karl Barth Archives, contained the following works by the neo-Kantian philosophers of Marburg:

Herrmann Cohen:

Religion und Sittlichkeit. Berlin, 1907 (obtained by Barth at Marburg during the Winter semester 1908–9).
Ethik des reinen Willens. Berlin, 1904 (obtained in Geneva, June 1910).
Der Begriff der Religion im System der Philosophie. Giessen, 1915 (a gift from Barth's mother-in-law, Christmas 1917).
Kommentar zu Immanuel Kants Kritik der reinen Vernunft. Leipzig, 1910 (second edition).

Paul Natorp:

Philosophische Propädeutik. Marburg 1905 (obtained at Marburg during the Summer semester of 1909).
Religion Innerhalb der Grenzen der Humanität. Tübingen, 1908 (obtained during the Winter semester 1908–9).
Allgemeine Psychologie, Marburg, 1910 (obtained in Geneva, 1910).
Logik. Marburg, 1904.
Jemand und Ich. Stuttgart, 1906.
Die Seele des Deutschen. Jena, 1918 (a gift from Heinrich Barth, Christmas 1918).
Volkskultur und Persönlichkeitskultur. Leipzig, 1911.
Sozialpädagogik. Stuttgart, 1920 (fourth edition).

This list of works was obtained for the author by Professor Gerhard Sauter from the *Karl-Barth Archiv*.

APPENDIX II

Continuities and Discontinuities in Barth's Dialectic

The theologian who undertook the formidable task of translating Barth's *Der Römerbrief* was exasperated by many perplexing words and sentences that presented 'almost insoluble' problems of translation. Amongst the several passages which Hoskyns signalled out as being particularly elusive was 'Die Philosophen nennen diese Krisis des menschlichen Erkennens den Ursprung.' It is no surprise that Hoskyns found these words so problematical, for they allude to the transcendental ground of knowledge (*Denken*) and reality (*Sein*) which philosophy aspires to fathom, but in fact never attains. This is one important continuity between Barth's earlier and later forms of dialectic. '"God is in heaven and thou upon the earth". The relation [*die Beziehung*] of *this* God to *this* man is for me the theme of the bible and the sum total of philosophy in one. The philosophers call this crisis of human knowledge the Origin.'[1]

Throughout the second edition of *Der Römerbrief*, as well as the dialectical writings collected in *The Word of God and the Word of Man*, there are countless references to the great transcendental ground:

> Above and beyond the apparently infinite series of possibilities and visibilities in this world, like a flash of lightening there breaks forth the impossibility and invisibility of the other world, not as some separate, second other thing, but as the Truth which is now hidden, as the Origin [*Ursprung*] to which all things are related [*auf den alles bezogen ist*], as the dissolution of all relativity and, therefore, as the reality [*Wirklichkeit*] of all relative realities.[2]

An address of 1920 affirmed in a similar vein:

> the bible offers us a knowledge of God: we look to it not so much to give us knowledge about this or that particular thing, but for knowledge of the beginning and the end, the Origin [*Ursprung*] and the Limit [*Grenze*), the creative unity and the ultimate problem of all knowledge. 'In the beginning God created heaven and earth' and 'Amen. Even so, come, Lord Jesus'. Such is the meaning of the world according to the Bible. ... It is not just one meaning like others, neither can they simply coexist with it. In this interpretation of reality all others—natural science, history, aesthetics, and religion—are at once included and concluded. In the final analysis this meaning will be found to be identical with the meaning of philosophy—in so far as philosophy understands itself.[3]

Dialectic cannot itself solve riddles concerning the relations between what is human, earthly, and finite; and that which is divine, transcendent, and eternal. It can, however, point to the resolution of such riddles in God's revelation—in fact the very method of dialectic presupposes the riddles of worldly existence, ontology, and epistemology are all resolved by the original living Truth.

> The utterance of the dialectician is based upon a mighty presupposition, upon the presupposition of that living original [*ursprünglich*] truth there in the centre. His talk itself, however, does not establish this presupposition . . . on occasions when dialectical speech has seemed to succeed . . .—and to several questioners of Plato, Paul, and the Reformers it appears to have succeeded—it was not because of what the dialectician did, not because of the ambiguous statements he made . . . but because, through his ambiguous and unambiguous statements, the living truth in the centre, the Reality of God, asserted *Itself*. It created the question upon which his assertions depended and *gave* him the answer which he sought because it *was* both the right question and the right answer.[4]

This sort of dialectic is not far removed from that which presupposes an original unifying truth like the *Wahrheitsgehalt* of logic, ethics, and aesthetics which Barth's fragment of *Religionsphilosophie* identified with religion or consciousness of God. This truth is *given* by God's revelation and the individual's experience of it is incapable of being encapsulated in any conceptual system. Even the religious *Glaubensgedanken* are mere ciphers and symbols which must not be identified with the experience. In Barth's later dialectic the contraries, which the transcendental ground is said to 'include and conclude', are focused in one great antithesis, namely the diastasis between the justifying holy God and the fallenness of worldly existence.

The discontinuity is profound. Human consciousness is no longer the locus of synthesis. The synthesis lies in God alone: 'The original [*das Ursprüngliche*] is the synthesis . . . Insight into the true transcendence of the divine origin [*Ursprung*] of all things permits, indeed offers us, the opportunity of always comprehending the specific form of being and existants *as such* in God, in their connection with God.'[5] The relationship between the religious consciousness and revelation, which was previously an internal relation founded upon the ingression of a revelatory *Lebensmacht*, could no longer be deemed actual in the contents consciousness nor did it actualize the possibilities of consciousness: 'There is in us, above us, behind us, beyond us, an awareness of the meaning of life, a remembrance of the origin [*Ursprung*] of man, a kind of return to the Lord of the world; a critical "No" and a creative "Yes" in relation to all the contents of our consciousness, a turn from the old to the new aeon. Its sign and fulfillment is the cross.'[6]

Rather than thrusting consciousness into 'total actualization', the principle of Origin now provokes a cognitive crisis for human knowledge. It no longer descends from Divine Truth into consciousness to endow it with life and actualize its cultural potentials. Instead there is the impossible possibility of a new world: '"Behold I make all things new!" The affirmation of God, man, and the world given in the New Testament is based exclusively upon the possibility of a new order absolutely beyond human thought and, therefore, as a prerequisite to that order there must come a crisis which denies human thought.'[7] In the language of the revised commentary on *Romans*: 'The true God, himself removed from all objectivity, is the origin and the crisis of every objectivity. He judges the non-being of this world, including the "god" of human logic.'[8]

Unlike the earlier system of truth, there is no elevation of religion and culture to meet divine truth in a vividly present *Universum* of experience:

> Faith and revelation expressly deny there is any way from man to God and to God's grace, love, and life. Both words indicate that the only way between God and man is that which leads *from* God *to* man. . . . Religion is not the sure ground upon which human culture rests; it is the place where civilization and its partner, barbarism, are rendered fundamentally questionable.[9]

With God's sovereignty now restored over the relation between revelation and faith, the religious consciousness, though not completely disappearing, was seen to contain nothing but highly questionable projections of unredeemed aspirations and Faustian possibilities: 'The curtain is raised; the music must cease. The temple has gone: far in the distance looms the terrifying form—of the Sphinx.'[10]

NOTES

1. See Sir Edwin Hoskyn's Preface to *The Epistle to the Romans* (Oxford University Press, 1933); *Romans II*, p. xiii.
2. *Romans II*, 315–16.
3. *Gotteswort*, 70.
4. Ibid. 174.
5. Ibid. 51.
6. Ibid. 34.
7. Ibid. 89.
8. *Romans II*, 57.
9. *Gotteswort*, 154; *Romans II*, 240.
10. Friedrich Schlegel on Schleiermacher's *Reden* quoted in *Romans II*, 241.

APPENDIX III

Chapter analysis of a fragment of Religionsphilosophie

Since it was not possible to give a translation of the text of Barth's fragmentary 'Ideas and Thoughts on the Philosophy of Religion', the following chapter analysis is offered as an indication of its structure and contents.

Prolegomena

1. The Concept of *Religionsphilosophie*
2. The History of *Religionsphilosophie*
3. The Task of *Religionsphilosophie*.

A Philosophy Of Religion

1. Religion within culture as a feeling which nurtures culture teleologically
2. The feeling which nurtures culture and the individual (alternatively: religion as personal experience of the individual)
3. Religion outside culture as feeling of absolute dependence
4. Religion as constituting a symbolic system: the concept, task, and method of *Glaubenslehre*

The text covers seven typewritten pages of manuscript and two pages of footnotes.

INDEX

Lightning Source UK Ltd.
Milton Keynes UK
UKOW03n0629230514

232184UK00009B/91/A